NAPOLEON & MARIE LOUISE

Also by Alan Palmer

Napoleon in Russia

An Encyclopaedia of Napoleon's Europe

Twilight of the Habsburgs

Victory 1918

Metternich

Alexander I

Bernadotte

Napoleon & Marie Louise

The Emperor's Second Wife

Alan Palmer

St. Martin's Press
New York

www.stmartins.com

ISBN 0-312-28008-4

First published in Great Britain by Constable Publishers

First U.S. Edition: July 2001

10 9 8 7 6 5 4 3 2 1

Contents

List of Illustrations

Acknowledgements

The Bonaparte book industry has flourished for some eighteen decades and my debt to earlier authors will be clear to anyone who turns to the select bibliography. I have used some primary material printed in the late nineteenth century but strangely neglected. Marie Louise's correspondence with Napoleon was only published by Librairie Stock as late as 1955, edited by C.F. Palmstierna from the Swedish royal archives. These letters form a revealing source for the characters of Emperor and Empress. Three comparatively recent books were of outstanding interest : Irmgard Schiel's *Marie Louise* includes facsimiles of several letters from the Archduchess/Empress to her father; Angelo Solmi's *Maria Luigia* is an invaluable study of the Duchess of Parma; André Castelot's definitive *Napoleon's Son* has been admirably translated for Hamish Hamilton by Robert Baldick. I feel much beholden to these authors.

It is a pleasure once more to express my gratitude to the General Director of the Haus-, Hof- und Staatsarchiv, Vienna, for the permission I received in 1971 to use the archives. I remain deeply appreciative of the patient assistance accorded by the HHSA staff to me at that time and during my later visits.

I am again grateful to the staff of the London Library and to many friends at the Bodleian Library for their help over the past two years. In Parma I received assistance from unknown admirers of the 'good Duchess' whose portrait still adorns many public places and restaurants. My Italian is so limited that I benefited greatly from the fluent linguistic skills of Miranda Jones who charmed closed doors to open in the city and at Colorno and Piacenza. Miranda also speedily translated several printed passages for me.

Carol O'Brien, who first commissioned the book, continued to support it with a heartening enthusiasm which she conveyed to her assistants at Constable and Robinson. In preparing the maps and genealogical tables, Stephen Dew skilfully brought graphic clarity to my rough outlines. At ADS, Woodstock, I have profited from the secretarial aid and advice of Kate Hotson, Clare Jeans and Amanda Keylock. Long ago, Araminta Morris Verdin invited me to the Christie's auction to which I refer in the reference notes and kindly gave me a copy of the excellent catalogue, which has proved to be a useful source.

To all these friends and helpers who have contributed to the writing and production of this book, I shall remain forever grateful.

Preface

In the spring of 1810 Napoleon, Emperor of the French, married Archduchess Marie Louise of Austria by proxy in Vienna and at civil and religious ceremonies in Paris. He was a divorcee of forty, his bride an immature innocent of eighteen; and the wedding united the oldest and newest imperial dynasties of the continent. Contemporaries dismissed the event as a cynical act of political necessity: Napoleon sought an heir from union with the most fecund of princely families while, to recover Austria's authority in Europe, Emperor Francis offered his daughter as a ritual sacrifice to the 'Corsican scoundrel' who had defeated his armies repeatedly over the past dozen years. Historians accept the verdict of the times; all too frequently they dismiss the Austrian marriage as of little importance or general interest. They also show scant sympathy for Marie Louise herself. Napoleon's biographers in particular consistently give her a bad press. To them she lacked the mettle of her predecessor, Josephine; and, so they allege, she betrayed both her husband and her son. The judgment seems harsh. It makes no allowance for the Empress's youthfulness nor for the courage she displayed in the critical days after the fall of Paris. She is a more complex and interesting personality than her detractors allow. I have long wished to write a book about the couple who, in the mere 200 weeks that they were together, undoubtedly loved and respected each other.

But *Napoleon and Marie Louise* is not simply a vindication of this second Empress of the French. When I was in Vienna thirty years ago, dipping into the archives for a biography of Metternich, I was fascinated by the way in which a French connection repeatedly surfaced as an option of Austrian policy. With great interest I read the journal of Engelbert von Floret, senior counsellor in the Austrian embassy in Paris in the crucial years of the Empire, and I made more notes than were relevant to the work in hand. When long afterwards I came across these notes, I began to reflect on the curious dynastic pull of Paris and

Vienna from the days of his grandson-in-law, Chancellor Metternich. With a shock I realised how brief was the interval between the execution of Queen Marie Antoinette and the marriage of her great-niece to Napoleon: a mere sixteen years and five months – a slightly shorter time span than between the Falklands War and NATO action over Kosovo. Memories sustained an anti-Austrian prejudice in Paris throughout Marie Louise's years in France. There were strong feelings, too, in Vienna, where the coming of the first accredited ambassador after Marie Antoinette's execution resulted in a riot, which is commemorated by a street-name even today. Changes in the perception of 'Buonaparte' at court and in society are interesting. So, too, is the tolerant affection which the Viennese accorded Napoleon's reluctant father-in-law, Emperor Francis. I was surprised to find how much he was concerned, not simply with the tottering imperial power in Germany, but with the affairs of a divided Italy, the peninsula where – at Florence – he was born and had the good fortune to spend his boyhood. It is easy to forget that Habsburgs ruled in Italy long before Metternich decided it was no more than 'a geographical expression'. Of course, the Bonapartes are an even older Italian family, though far less exalted.

Increasing fascination with this period of history soon made me abandon my original idea of planning a book devoted solely to the French imperial couple in marriage and in enforced separation. *Napoleon and Marie Louise* is therefore the story of a political relationship in which romantic love was briefly kindled; but it is a tale set down within the context of a Europe unhinged by revolution and protracted war. For only against this background of conflict and diplomatic bargaining is it possible to comprehend the extraordinary character of the marriage bonds contracted in the spring of 1810 and assess their consequences. How well do Napoleon and Marie Louise emerge from this long-running melodrama? And who are the villains? These are questions which readers might like to judge for themselves.

Alan Palmer
Woodstock, Oxfordshire
March 2000

Note on Proper Names

So far as possible I have used the version readily familiar to English readers today.

People: I have anglicised most personal names : thus Francis for Franz, Charles for Karl, Victoria for Victoire. Difficulties, however, arise over women's names in the house of Habsburg. Every archduchess in the late seventeenth and eighteenth centuries received the first name 'Maria'. French usage changed 'Maria' to Marie and hyphenated the first and second names: thus, in France, we have Queen Marie-Antoinette and Empress Marie-Louise. With some inconsistency, I accept Marie, but reject the hyphen. Within the family the archduchesses were known by their second name: Antoinette rather than Marie Antoinette, for example. For formal and official usage I have written 'Marie Louise', but on most occasions I refer to her as 'Louise', as she was called by her father, her brothers and sisters and by Napoleon. But some combinations recur with confusing frequency. In this book the mother of the Emperors Joseph and Leopold II appears as 'Maria Theresa the Great'. The second wife of Emperor Francis and the mother of all his surviving children appears in the French form, 'Marie Thérèse', to distinguish her from the matriarch. Other possible confusions are, I hope, identified in the text. But see, also, the genealogical tables.

Places: The placenames of Napoleon's Empire are rendered in the form most commonly found in English atlases: thus Mainz for Mayence, Piacenza for Plaisance. Alternative names to German forms within the Habsburg empire include: Brünn: now Brno (Czech); Erlau: now Eger (Hungarian); Laibach: now Ljubljana (Slovene); Ofen: now Buda (Hungarian); Pressburg: now Bratislava (Slovak), formerly Pozsony (Hungarian); Raab: now Györ (Hungarian).

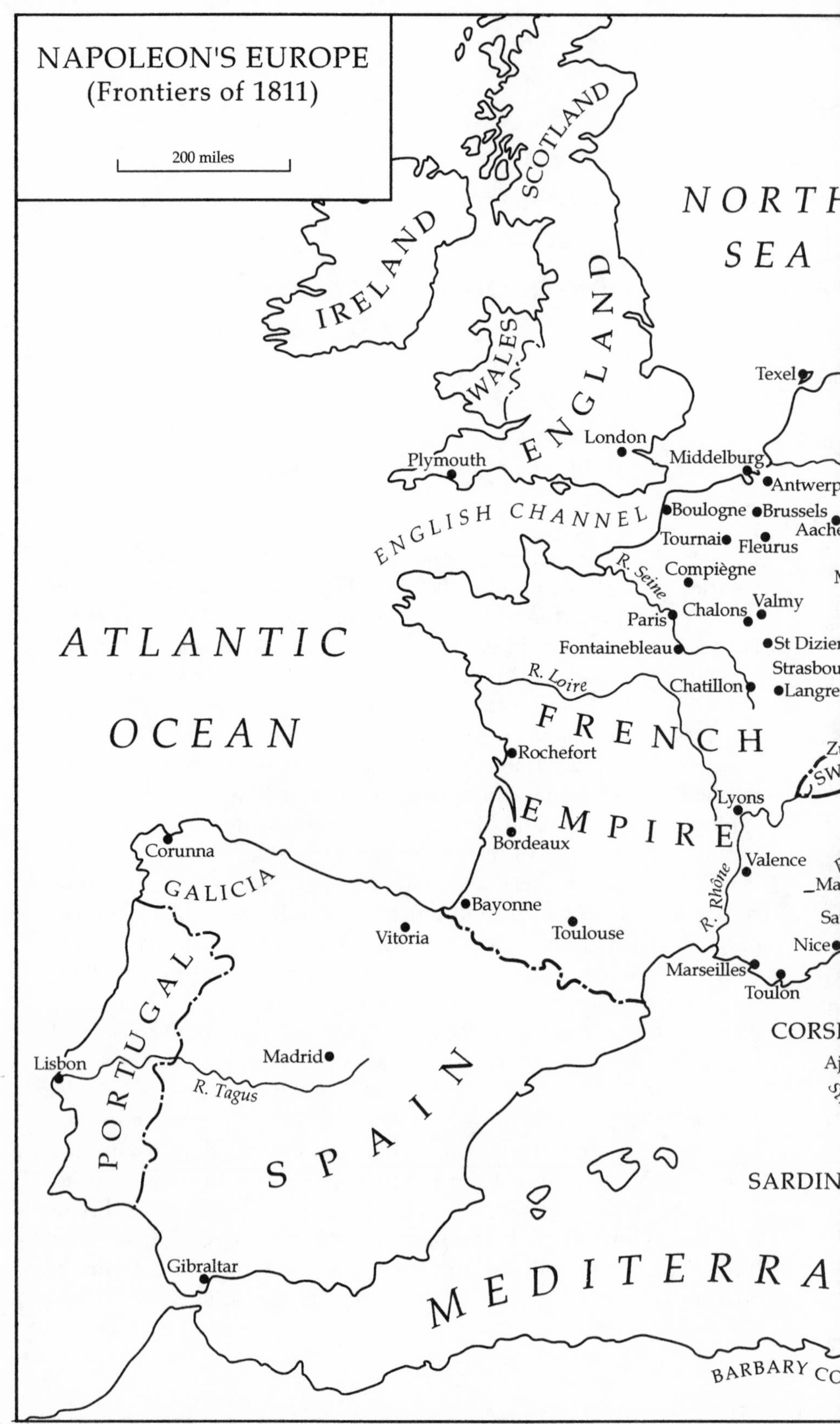

NAPOLEON'S EUROPE
(Frontiers of 1811)
200 miles
SCOTLAND
IRELAND
WALES
ENGLAND
NORTH
SEA
Texel
London
Plymouth
Middelburg
Antwerp
Boulogne
Brussels
Tournai
Fleurus
ENGLISH CHANNEL
R. Seine
Compiègne
Valmy
Paris
Chalons
ATLANTIC
OCEAN
Fontainebleau
St Dizier
R. Loire
Chatillon
Langres
FRENCH
EMPIRE
Rochefort
Lyons
Bordeaux
Corunna
GALICIA
Valence
R. Rhône
Bayonne
Vitoria
Toulouse
Nice
Marseilles
Toulon
PORTUGAL
Madrid
Lisbon
R. Tagus
SPAIN
SARDINI
Gibraltar
MEDITERRA
BARBARY CO

SWEDEN
BALTIC SEA
Copenhagen
Vitebsk
Smolensk
R. Niemen
Smorgon
Vilna
Borisov
Friedland
Danzig
Lübeck
amburg
PRUSSIA
R. Vistula
R. Beresina
RUSSIA
Berlin
WESTPHALIA
Warsaw
Leipzig
SAXONY
R. Oder
Bautzen
Erfurt
Dresden
Breslau
Frankfurt
R. Elbe
Cracow
Prague
Würzburg
Rhine
BOHEMIA
Brno
Austerlitz
Znaim
Ulm
Münich
Krems
Wagram
HUNGARY
Linz
Melk
Vienna
Braunau
BAVARIA
Leoben
Raab
Budapest
AUSTRIAN EMPIRE
TYROL
Tarvisio
LOMBARDY VENETIA
Ljubljana
Milan
Rivoli
Venice
Lodi
Mantua
ILLYRIAN PROVINCES (FRENCH)
Genoa
Parma
Modena
R. Danube
TUSCANY
Florence
ELBA
K. OF ITALY
ADRIATIC SEA
OTTOMAN EMPIRE
Corte
Cattaro
Rome
a Maddelena
Bonifacio
KINGDOM OF NAPLES
Naples
Corfu
IONIAN IS.
SICILY
SEA

MARIE LOUISE'S
EUROPE
(Frontiers of 1815)
200 miles
London
Rotterdam
Walcheren
Antwerp
Brussels
KINGDOM OF THE
NETHERLANDS
R. Scheldt
Cologne
Coblenz
Frankfurt
Mainz
R. Rhine
Cherbourg
Compiègne
Paris
Courcelles
Rambouillet
R. Seine
Orleans
R. Loire
Blois
Strasbourg
Dijon
Basle
FRANCE
Berne
Lucerne
Lausanne
SWITZERLAND
Geneva
Culoz
Aix-en-Savoie
Milan
R. Po
Piacenza
PIEDMONT
Genoa
DUCHY
OF PARMA
Livorno
R. Rhône
CORSICA
Madrid
SPAIN
MEDITERRANEAN
SEA

RUSSIA
SSIA
Berlin
R. Vistula
KINGDOM OF POLAND
SAXONY
BOHEMIA
Cracow
Lemburg
Carlsbad
Troppau
Olmütz
GALICIA
Brno
MORAVIA
Kosice
AUSTRIA
Braunau
Persenbeug
Eger
Pressburg
Vienna
Hatvan
Salzburg
Baden
Komarom
Budapest
Ischl
STYRIA
Graz
HUNGARY
EMPIRE
AUSTRIAN
VENICE
Trieste
Laibach
Temesvar
Venice
Belgrade
R. Danube
Ancona
ADRIATIC SEA
OTTOMAN
PAPAL STATES
Rome
Naples
KINGDOM OF THE TWO SICILIES
Corfu
IONIAN ISLANDS
Athens
GREECE
Palermo

NAPOLEONIC PARIS AND ITS ENVIRONS

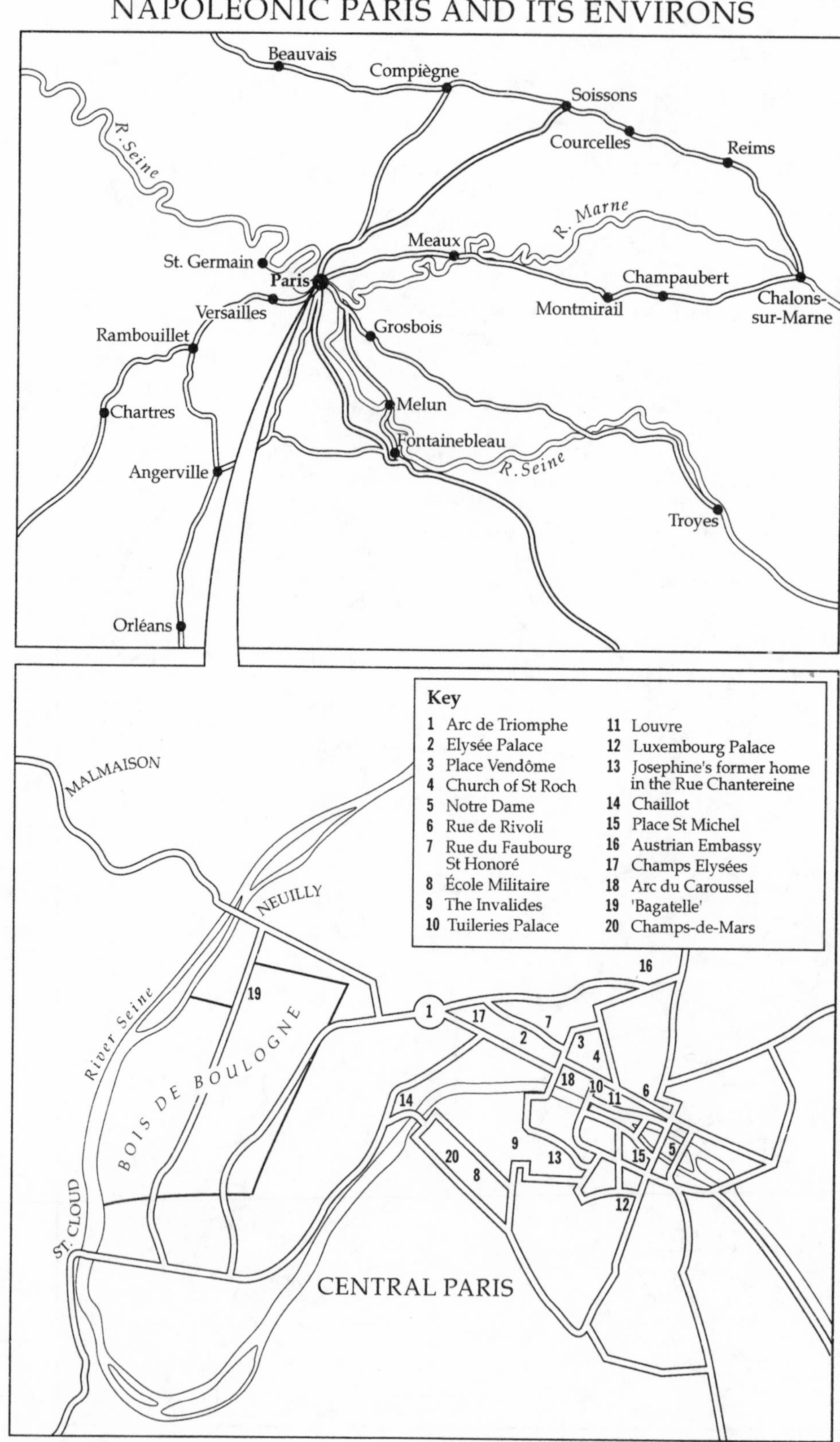

VIENNA AND ITS ENVIRONS c.1800

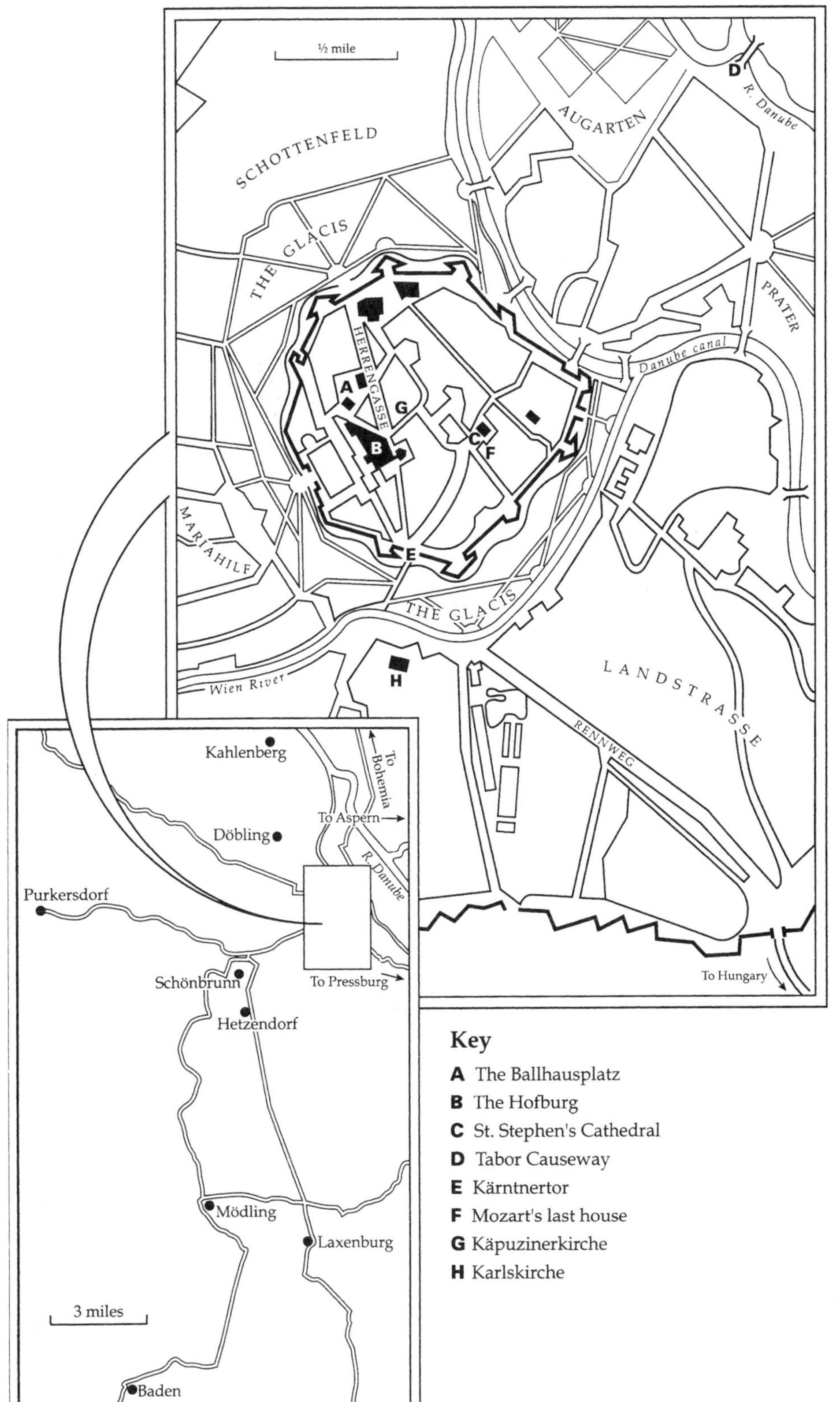

Prologue

12 December 1791

Winter came early to Vienna in 1791, with snow lying deep in the Inner City by the end of October and a blizzard sweeping down from the east on 1 November, All Saints' Day. Over the next fortnight icy fog enveloped the capital and the surrounding countryside, to be followed by the notorious *Föhn*, a wet wind from the south-west which saps the energy in any season of the year. Such sudden variations of weather were unhealthy; overheated rooms became bacterial incubators. People complained of sore throats and rheumatic pains, choking sensations and spasms. No one was prepared to give a name to the inflammatory fever which ran like an epidemic through the narrow, winding streets, but whatever its nature, there was no questioning a startling rise in the incidence of sickness during the last days of November.

One tragedy from these troubled weeks passed into history. In the small hours of Monday, 5 December, the thirty-five-year-old Wolfgang Mozart died in his apartments in the Rauhensteingasse at the peak of his musical talents and barely seven weeks after the première of *The Magic Flute* at the Theatre an der Wien. He succumbed, it would seem, to broncho-pneumonia caused by streptococcal infection. A Europe still at peace was surprised and shocked: the news reached Prague by the end of the week, Berlin soon afterwards, and London before 23 December, when *The Times* confirmed rumours circulating in the capital over the last four days.[1] But though Europe mourned one particular death that month, Mozart's fate was not unique in Vienna. A court doctor later recalled the 'great number ... labouring under the same complaint', adding that there were many cases which ended 'fatally, like that of Mozart'.[2] For many Inner City families, the year 1791 was to close with agonising days of fear and uncertainty.

There was deep concern, too, at the Hofburg, the imperial *Residenz* a quarter of a mile from Mozart's home. Within the Emperor's apartments on the first floor of the long rambling Leopold wing, his physicians had every reason to be anxious. At any time it was hard to prevent town epidemics from seeping into a palace built around quadrangles open to horsemen and carriers coming in from the city and the villages beyond the walls. But in these particular weeks the doctors needed to be especially on their guard, for Emperor Leopold II's daughter-in-law – Marie Thérèse of Bourbon-Naples, wife of his heir, the twenty-three-year old Archduke Francis – was soon expecting her first child and the mortality rate in confinements for both mothers and infants in Austria was alarmingly high. It is true that Leopold's consort, Maria Luisa of Bourbon-Spain, had successfully given birth to twelve sons and four daughters in twenty-six years of married life. But Archduke Francis had already tragically lost one wife, soon after bringing into the world a daughter who was herself to live only sixteen months. Nor was the risk of infection the doctors' only problem: Marie Thérèse and Francis were first cousins and behind the recognised risks of childbirth at such a place and time loomed uncertainties posed by consanguinity. To offset these dangers, however, the Archduchess possessed three assets: a strong physique; the will-power to seek fulfilment of a genuinely happy marriage; and all the advantages of a radiant youth, for Marie Thérèse was only nineteen years old.

In the event, all went well with the confinement. The Archduchess avoided infection and, at half past eleven at night on Monday, 12 December 1791, gave birth to a daughter. Although Francis had hoped for a son, to become second in line of succession to the imperial titles, the parents were content, thankful for a safe delivery; a grateful Marie Thérèse gave 4,000 guilders to relieve the suffering of Vienna's poor in this cruel winter.[3] On Tuesday morning the cannons fired a salute to the newborn Archduchess from the walls behind the Leopold wing and the gloom of the Inner City was lifted by welcoming peals of bells from some dozen church towers, and from the *Pummerin*, the great boomer of St Stephen's cathedral, cast from Turkish cannon captured when Vienna's Ottoman besiegers retreated just over a century previously. It was exactly a week since, in total silence, the cheapest of funeral wagons bore Mozart's corpse from the cathedral to the common grave east of the city, in the cemetery of St Marx.

Imperial infants were baptised early in Vienna. Bells rang out again at five o'clock on Tuesday afternoon when the child was held in the arms of her grandmother, Empress Maria Luisa, and Jordan holy water sprinkled on her head by Prince Archbishop Maximilian of Cologne, her great-uncle. Everyone knew what the first baptismal name would be, for throughout the eighteenth century each daughter of a Habsburg sovereign was christened Maria, as a tribute to the Holy Virgin. There followed a virtual roll-call of recent family history in feminine dog-Latin: 'Ludovica Leopoldina Franziska Theresia Josepha'. But there was no 'Antonia' to recall the great-aunt whose peril as Queen of France was so often in her family's thoughts during these months. Instead, as a final baptismal name, came Lucia, bestowed to honour the saint of the day.[4]

This impressive list was seldom (if ever) used in full. Although Versailles might no longer dictate social fashion, the European courts still favoured French as the most civilised of languages, and within the family at the Hofburg the newcomer was soon being called 'Louise'. On those rare occasions when she emerged from a nursery world, grandeur enveloped the child and she became Her Serene Highness the Archduchess Marie Louise. Among the court dignitaries and ambassadors at her baptism there was no doubt that, if she survived the illnesses of childhood, she would eventually be elevated to a higher pedestal, for Austrian Habsburgs proverbially excelled in dynastic marriage diplomacy. But in December 1791 it would have needed a remarkably gifted clairvoyant to predict Louise's future with any semblance of accuracy.

1

Habsburg and Bourbon

'Things are well with us and the carnival season is progressing cheerfully,' Archduke Francis wrote on 16 January 1792 to his brother, Charles, in Brussels. 'There are two balls a week now and soon there will be three.'[1] It was a lighthearted start to a year which would all too soon become full of portent. For what nowadays might be called Vienna's 'mystery virus' continued to strike people down indiscriminately: Francis himself was too ill to enjoy his twenty-fourth birthday celebrations on 12 February, though he recovered within a fortnight;[2] and from Christmas onwards his father, Emperor Leopold II, complained constantly of colic and general fatigue. As Leopold was a confirmed hypochondriac, few at court took their sovereign's ailments seriously. They were wrong. On Tuesday, 28 February Leopold was 'seized with a rheumatic fever accompanied by pains in the chest'.[3] Thereafter his sufferings seem almost to follow a pattern set by poor Mozart eleven weeks earlier. 'Three bloodlettings' on Wednesday were said by his physicians to 'bring relief'. But such treatment was far too drastic. The forty-four-year-old Emperor was left with little strength to resist 'horrible convulsions' which shook his body next afternoon. By four o'clock it was over. On that Thursday evening – 1 March 1792 – another letter went off to Archduke Charles. Francis broke news to his brother of 'the greatest misfortune that might fall on our family': their father, he wrote, had died from a stroke, 'without receiving the last sacrament', but in their mother's arms. That was all Francis could bring himself to say. 'In my monstrous calamity I am too frightened to write more', he explained, with the honest simplicity of shocked grief.[4]

The burden thrust so unexpectedly on Marie Louise's young father was heavy. No other European sovereign ruled so varied an accumulation of lands. They straddled middle Europe, from Trieste north-eastwards through Austria and Hungary into Polish Galicia and much of modern Romania and the Ukraine; there were Habsburg dependencies in northern Italy and smaller ones in southern Germany; and since 1714 the Habsburgs had also ruled the 'Austrian Netherlands' (Belgium). Fourteen distinct nationalities dwelt within this sprawling empire: Germans; Magyars (Hungarians); Czechs; Italians; Romanians; Flemish Netherlanders; Walloons; Slovaks; Poles; Ruthenes; Ukrainians; Slovenes; Croats; Serbs. They spoke, with varying dialects, eleven languages; and in some districts Yiddish or the gypsy Romany was in common use. Many communities possessed historic rights and assemblies, some – as in Hungary – with long, proud traditions of independence which challenged administrative decisions taken in Vienna. The Belgians, too, resented financial exactions imposed by officials 800 miles away.[5]

There was no precisely defined Habsburg Empire. By inheritance Francis became King of Hungary, King of Bohemia, Archduke of Austria and much else besides; but he was not yet 'Holy Roman Emperor of the German Nation'. That paramount title depended upon the decision of German princely electors. Almost certainly they would give him their vote, for apart from a three-year interlude before Maria Theresa married, the Habsburg hold on the imperial crown had remained unshaken for three and a half centuries. But in an age of political change, nothing could be taken for granted. When Leopold II was elected, less than two years previously, there had been signs of growing support for the leading Lutheran ruler, King Frederick William II of Prussia. It would be essential for Francis's envoys to strike territorial bargains with the German electors: in the East, the final fate of the Polish lands was still unresolved after the collapse of the elective Polish monarchy thirty years previously. And above all, in the West, the emperor-elect and the German rulers had to decide on a common policy towards the challenge of an increasingly belligerent revolutionary France.

Francis had gained administrative experience as Regent for several months while Emperor Leopold was attending to Habsburg problems in Italy. But he acceded with little knowledge of foreign affairs or understanding of diplomacy. The mysteries of Habsburg statesmanship remained the preserve of Wenzel von Kaunitz, the octogenarian Chancellor who had shaped Austrian policy abroad for four decades. Kaunitz, a member of the lesser nobility with estates in Moravia, was first given charge of foreign affairs by the great Maria Theresa in 1753, when she was a young queen of thirty-four. His outstanding achievement was to reverse the established pattern of European diplomacy: in May 1756 Austria for the first time became an ally of the traditional foe, France, and soon afterwards an enemy of (Hanoverian) Britain and of the new German kingdom, Prussia. To Maria Theresa this French connection became a 'natural alliance ... very near to my heart'. It was, she told her youngest daughter, Marie Antoinette, 'necessary to the religion of thousands of people', because it bound together the two great Catholic dynasties.[6] In this spirit she sanctioned Marie Antoinette's marriage in 1770 to the Dauphin of France, who four years later came to the throne as King Louis XVI.

The earliest manifestations of the revolution in France did not unduly disturb Kaunitz or his sovereign. Leopold II was consistently a 'peace emperor', not least because he thought wars so costly that they would threaten state bankruptcy. He refused to be drawn into France's revolutionary upheaval: he urged his sister, Queen Marie Antoinette, to take no precipitate action to restore monarchical authority; and he scorned wild-cat schemes for intervention which were put forward by the French émigré leaders who had fled to the Rhineland: Prince Condé at Worms and the Count of Artois at Coblenz.

Marie Antoinette ignored her brother's advice. His carefully balanced policy was put at risk by the royal family's attempt to escape to the frontier on 20 June 1791 and their re-capture at Varennes next day. Leopold was in Italy at the time. Fear for his sister's safety induced him to issue from Padua on 6 July an appeal to Europe's sovereigns for joint action to uphold the liberty and honour of the King of France.[7] But the Padua Appeal was not a call to arms. It was a plea for common sense, an attempt to put collective political pressure on France's revolutionary legislators. Right down to that day in late February 1792 when Leopold was 'seized with rheumatic fever' he strove for peace. Only radical extremists in Paris and ambitious counter-revolutionaries in Germany wanted the armies to march, he thought. Perhaps he was right.

In the closing months of 1791 the threat of war seemed to recede, with a compromise political settlement in Paris. On Tuesday, 14 September, Louis XVI as 'King of the French' swore to uphold a constitution which gave legislative authority to a national assembly, but affirmed that 'supreme executive power resides exclusively in the hands of the King'. There was widespread rejoicing at what many believed to be the end of the revolution. King Louis was cheered on the following Monday when he went to the Théâtre Italien and next day at the Opéra. Even as late as 28 December 1791 – a fortnight after the birth of her great-niece, Marie Louise – the Queen was publicly acclaimed there.

Gluck's *Iphigénie en Aulide* was presented that evening: '*Chantons! Célébrons notre reine!*', sang the chorus, and applause filled the house. But the radical members of the Assembly were in a grimmer mood; on 29 December they voted credits to make ready for a war against Austria. They insisted that the German princes, with the Emperor at their head, were putting armies at the disposal of the émigrés in the Rhineland.[8]

Yet however much the demagogues might clamour for 'war as a national benefit' there was widespread apathy in the capital. People were more worried at the rising price of sugar and coffee, because of a slave insurrection in Haiti; on 23 January there was some looting of grocery stores. But it was a mild month; the dramatic days of revolution were fast receding and Parisians found the theatre season especially good that year. A protracted military campaign seemed unlikely, let alone a conflict enveloping half the continent. So London thought, too. On Friday, 17 February 1792, Prime Minister Pitt assured the House of Commons: 'There never was a time in the history of this country when, from the situation of Europe, we might more reasonably expect fifteen years of peace, than we may at the present moment.'[9]

It is tempting to speculate what might have happened had Leopold recovered from the illness that struck him down after a mere 710 days on the throne: western Europe could well have enjoyed the long peace Pitt anticipated and the name Bonaparte would scarcely merit a footnote in Corsica's history. But it was not to be. On the Friday that Pitt spoke so confidently to parliament, Leopold approved yet another conciliatory message to Paris from Kaunitz. The French were warned that any invasion of the Rhineland would be resisted by the imperial armies, for the Emperor was the elected protector of the German nation, but he would not support provocative moves by the émigré leaders in Westphalia. At the same time Kaunitz concluded a military convention with Prussia which, Leopold hoped, would give Austria the opportunity to hold in check the hot-headed war party around King Frederick William in Berlin.[10]

These approaches, to Paris and Berlin, were the last moves in Leopold's patient game of wise appeasement. Within three weeks he was dead and the Habsburg hold on the reins of diplomacy suddenly relaxed. The new Emperor at once begged Kaunitz to remain Chancellor and serve him as he had his father, uncle and grandmother. Yet while Francis was ready to listen courteously to the old man's advice, he gave less and less attention to his opinions. On the day he invited Kaunitz to stay in office, Francis also appointed his former tutor Count Colloredo to head a newly created personal secretariat, with a team of younger men to assist him. There was thus, at this critical moment in Europe's affairs, a virtual change of government in Vienna.[11]

Inevitably the diplomatic initiative passed to Berlin. As early as 7 March King Frederick William II appointed his favourite general, the Duke of Brunswick, to command the combined Prussian and Austrian armies watching the frontiers of France. The appointment seemed to confirm all the warnings in the French Legislative Assembly over the menacing intentions of Germany's crowned heads and their backing for the counter-revolutionaries in exile. Six weeks later – on 20 April 1792 – the Assembly in Paris applied a taper to ignite the powder trail of war. Archduchess Marie Louise was then four months old. By the time genuine peace returned to Europe, Marie Louise was aged twenty-three and the map of the continent had been ripped apart more drastically than in any previous conflict between the Powers.

No one expected the war to last more than a few months. France seemed a ready victim. The officer corps was under strength, for many of the nobility had gone into exile. Several regiments were close to mutiny even before the war began and at least three, raised originally by mercenary enlistment in Germany, went over to the enemy within a month. There was no machinery of mobilisation. Generals who received postings were slow to leave Paris: Alexandre de Beauharnais, for example, still lingered in the capital eight weeks after being given a command near the frontier. And there were junior officers who, when called back to the colours, found excuses for service locally.[12] Among them, on leave in Corsica, was Lieutenant Bonaparte, whose artillery regiment was stationed in Valence. Napoleon thought it was his duty to remain in Ajaccio and serve as Adjutant-Colonel of the newly raised National Guard.[13] Corsica was a long way from troubled Paris, and even further from the Rhine and Moselle where the first battles were fought.

The Austrians, too, drifted into war with disconcerting casualness. Francis's immediate purpose was to consecrate his sovereignty. Preparations went ahead for three coronations that summer: with the 'Holy Crown of St Stephen' of Hungary at Pressburg (now Bratislava); with the Bohemian crown in Prague; and with the full imperial regalia at Frankfurt, the city where in 1273 the Electors first offered the throne to a Count of Habsburg. By the late eighteenth century the archaic pageantry of an imperial coronation had lost any spiritual significance it held when Catholic Europe was still undivided, but the festivities provided magnificent theatre, in which ambitious members of the lesser nobility hoped to catch the eye of their sovereign lord and win patronage for themselves or their family. Among these social climbers was Count Francis George von Metternich, who at the previous coronation had induced Leopold II to give him an official post in Brussels. Now the Count – or, more precisely, his ambitious wife Beatrice – sought to advance the career of their son, Clement, a student at Mainz university. Backstairs lobbying ensured that Clement von Metternich was given ceremonial duties on behalf of the Counts of Westphalia.[14]

Despite the coming of war and the imminence of action west of the Rhine, the German nobility burnished up their golden coaches for the journey to Frankfurt, determined – as young Metternich wrote – to give that summer's ceremonial 'a more imposing character' than ever before.[15] The Habsburg imperial title went unchallenged by the Prussian king or by any other elector; and on the second Saturday in July 1792 Francis II, robed in the traditional dalmatic, was crowned as sovereign of the German Nation, the fifty-fourth Holy Roman Emperor since Charlemagne.

The religious ceremony was followed by a grand ball, which was not so much a carnival celebration as a continuation of the coronation's ordered solemnity in secular guise. The opening processional minuet was headed by the Ceremonial Marshal to the Catholic Bench of the College of the Counts of Westphalia, Clement von Metternich, elegantly high-waisted, in pale green satin with a lace cravat. This tall, blue-eyed cavalier, his high forehead crowned with blond curly hair, cut a very different figure from the worldly-wise statesman who looks down cynically from the portraits of half a century later. No one can have failed to notice him at the coronation ball of the sovereign he was to serve as chief minister for more than a quarter of a century. He had the good fortune on that evening to escort a beautiful partner, the sixteen-year-old Princess Louise of Mecklenburg-Strelitz. She, too, left a mark on history, for she was soon to become Queen Louise of Prussia, a royal consort deservedly respected for her courage in defying Napoleon.[16]

Within fifteen weeks the tricolour flag of the French Republic would fly over Frankfurt. Yet nothing suggests there was any sense of deep concern on that July evening. The celebrants went through the ritual festivities oblivious to any sign that the city's independence was under threat and princely particularism doomed to extinction. Yet was this a deliberate pose, a gesture of contemptuous disdain? For the day chosen for Francis's crowning was 14 July, the anniversary of the fall of the Bastille. On that same morning, in Paris, Francis's aunt watched anxiously as her husband Louis took part in what became his last ceremony as a reigning monarch, the 'Festival of Federation', an assertion of national unity in the Champ de Mars. It is tempting to see in the German princes' selection of 14 July for their Emperor's coronation a defiant affirmation of monarchy resurgent. As yet there had been little more than feints and skirmishes along the frontier. Now war would begin in earnest. Three days after the coronation a top-level conference in Frankfurt agreed that the allied armies should march on Paris. On 25 July a 'manifesto', published in the Duke of Brunswick's name, threatened the citizens with exemplary punishment if they harmed their king or their queen.[17]

By late July Paris was in an ugly mood; the Festival of Federation had brought 20,000 National Guard volunteers to the capital. Many soon left for the frontier to resist the invaders; but several thousand remained in Paris, their numbers strengthened by ardent revolutionaries from Marseilles, Toulon and Brest, who were determined to destroy what they regarded as Emperor Francis's Trojan Horse within the Tuileries palace. Lieutenant Bonaparte was by now in Paris, visiting the Ministry of War almost daily to explain events in Corsica, and talk the 'Artillery Committee' into promoting him captain. Although he had helped organise the National Guard in Ajaccio, he had little sympathy for the *Fédérés* in the capital and even less for the rabble whose violence their presence encouraged. On 20 June he watched an armed mob break into the Tuileries to force Louis XVI to drink with them and wear the *bonnet rouge*, the red revolutionary cap of liberty. In this crisis 'the King showed up well,' Napoleon wrote home to his brother, Joseph. But he disapproved of the whole episode: the mob's behaviour was 'unconstitutional and sets a very dangerous precedent,' he told Joseph.[18]

For King Louis and his Queen the decisive day came seven weeks later. On 10 August an angry mob again burst into the Tuileries, convinced of royal contact with the Austrians. Before a shot was fired, the royal family escaped through the gardens to put themselves under the protection of the Legislative Assembly, virtually a form of self-imposed house arrest. But the King's abandonment of the palace could not prevent the massacre of his loyal Swiss Guards. The newly promoted Captain Bonaparte was again a witness: had Louis mounted his horse and ridden out as leader of the nation order could have been restored, Napoleon said later. But he was shocked by the fate of the Swiss Guards; their butchered corpses conveyed to him the true nature of death more graphically than on any battlefield, he would remember on St Helena.

It was a gruesome day. The Tuileries palace was looted; the wine cellar pillaged; dead bodies were mutilated, by women as well as men. In the Rue des Petits-Champs Napoleon was confronted by a hideous group carrying a head impaled on a pike: 'They insisted that I shout, "Long Live the Nation" which, needless to say, I did without a moment's hesitation,' he was to recall.[19] He found safety above a furniture shop owned by the brother of his friend, Louis Bourienne. It looked out across the gardens of carnage to the doors of the Assembly House, where Louis and Marie Antoinette, with their son and daughter, found precarious sanctuary until they were removed to the improvised prison at the Temple, three days later.

They were never to return to the Tuileries. But within eight years Captain Bonaparte was back – in residence as First Consul. 'Look,' he said to Bourienne, pointing from a window towards the old furniture shop, 'from there I watched the siege of the Tuileries, and the capture of that good Louis XVI; but *I* shall remain here.'[20] Ten years later still, he sat enthroned as Emperor in the palace, with Marie Antoinette's great-niece as Empress beside him.

2

'A Corsican Scoundrel named Buonaparte'

France did not become a Republic until six weeks after the assault on the Tuileries, but Louis XVI's authority was 'provisionally suspended' that day, while the mob was pillaging his palace. Next morning, 11 August, the 'executive council' of ministers announced that commissioners would travel to every army command to enforce a new oath of loyalty, a pledge of service to the French Nation rather than to the King. Arrest would follow any show of hesitancy or reluctance. Officers from aristocratic families were deemed suspect; they were to be suspended from all duties, pending investigation by good and blameless patriots. Such measures eased the path of Brunswick's invaders more effectively than any phantom Trojan Horse within the Tuileries. Three regiments facing the Prussian vanguard soon found themselves deprived of a commander. The Marquis de Lafayette, idol of all who had served in America, did not wait for the coming of the commissioners. He crossed the Rhine on 19 August, taking with him to internment in Berlin twenty experienced staff officers.

The stupidest inquisitorial folly came four days later. On that morning, as the Prussians were entering Longwy, the first small fortress on the frontier, Brigadier-General Louis Berthier, chief-of-staff to the Army of the North, had his commission revoked. He was not only a veteran of the siege of Yorktown but a specialist expert on the Prussian army and its tactics, which he had studied at Potsdam itself. It was enough for France's new masters that Berthier was born at Versailles into a family which supplied successive Kings Louis with officers. Not until March 1795 was he rescued from civilian non-activity by Lazare Carnot, the far-sighted Minister of War.[1] Ten years later Napoleon, recognising Berthier's skill as chief of staff, raised him to the new marshalate. In 1810 he sent him to Vienna to escort Marie Louise to Paris.

Berthier was not the only future Marshal of the Empire to serve in the Republic's early campaigns. Several distinguished themselves. Colonel Davout led infantry raids on Austrian outposts in 1792, before autumn rain turned fields into quagmires and made the Argonne forest impenetrable. Sergeant Soult, who was to receive Napoleon's coffin back from St Helena in 1840, was drilling grenadiers that autumn on the upper Rhine. Lieutenant Bernadotte was at Strasbourg, soon to become controller of traffic along the great river at Bingen. Captain Macdonald won praise for his courage at Jemappes against Austrian horsemen (who included a dashing seventeen-year-old hussar lieutenant named Neipperg). The future Marshals Brune, Jourdan, Gouvion St-Cyr, Mortier, Ney and Oudinot also answered the call to arms that summer. And it was the oldest of the Marshals-to-be, François Kellermann, who ordered the historic 'cannonade at Valmy' which on 20 September 1792 forced Brunswick to halt his advance on Paris and, ten days later, abandon the invasion of France. One in four of the generals who marched on Moscow in 1812 had tramped through the mud of Champagne with the Republic's raw recruits in these desperate weeks twenty years before.

But not Napoleon. He had come to Paris that summer primarily to explain events in Corsica and the island's interests remained uppermost in his calculations as the speed of revolution in the capital quickened during August. But he had family concerns, too. His eldest sister, fifteen-year-old Élisa, was completing her education – with, in effect, a royal scholarship – at the convent school at St Cyr, near Versailles. With the enforced closure of religious houses in mid-August she needed a protector; and Napoleon talked the departmental authorities at Versailles, not only into appointing him as her escort for the journey back to Ajaccio, but to paying their travelling expenses as well. On 1 September he fetched Élisa from the convent to his lodgings in Paris. There brother and sister remained throughout one of the bloodiest weeks in the city's history; for on 2 September the mob began the massacre of 3,000 suspects herded into the prisons. The Bonapartes set out for Marseilles on 9 September; that Sunday fifty-three prisoners were summarily executed along the road from Versailles to the capital, the route they had taken a few days previously.[2]

Napoleon was home in Ajaccio by mid-October, when the armies of the Republic began to carry the revolution across the frontier into Germany. He remained in Corsica until June 1793, welcoming the news of victories in the north and east but with his political ambitions and commitments concentrated within his native island, which had only been formally annexed by France in the year before his birth. He now set about the task of winning recognition for the Bonapartes as natural leaders of the new order in Corsica, the true agents of *la Nation*, defenders of the Republic 'one and indivisible'.

It was a considerable challenge for a young officer of twenty-three. The veteran Corsican patriot Pasquale Paoli had returned to his homeland at Christmas 1789 with support from the government in Paris. He still enjoyed great prestige in the island, whose clannish communities were scarred by vendetta wounds notoriously slow to heal.[3] To many families, the 'Buonapartes' were suspect. How Corsican were they? How French, for that matter? They were certainly of Italian origin, with a firm foothold in Tuscany, though as early as 1616 a 'Buonaparte' served in the administrative council of Ajaccio. Most of Napoleon's kinsmen were lawyers by profession, investing their earnings in vineyards. His father, Carlo, enrolled in the law faculty at Pisa but never completed his studies, returning to Ajaccio in 1764 to marry Laetizia Ramolino: Carlo was eighteen, Laetizia fourteen. The Ramolinos, too, came from Italy; they were Lombard soldiers, settlers in Corsica from the war-ravaged peninsula early in the sixteenth century. Laetizia's father, who died when she was five, maintained the military tradition as a captain in Louis XV's army, responsible for inspecting Corsica's roads and bridges, such as they were. Her eldest surviving son, Giuseppe (later King Joseph of Naples, and of Spain), studied law at Pisa none too assiduously before practising politics in Ajaccio's council chamber in the family tradition. But Napoleon, who was born in 1769 as Mass was being sung in Ajaccio cathedral on the Feast of the Assumption, early showed the strong character of the Ramolinos. The boy was self-willed and pugilistic, ready – so his mother would recall – to daub soldiers on the nursery wall with his first box of paints.[4]

This playroom militarism is not surprising. Much of Laetizia's fourth and fifth months of pregnancy had been spent dodging French bullets amid the thick undergrowth of shrubs on Corsica's hilltops or hiding from French patrols in a cave on Monte Rotondo. For in that spring of 1769 Carlo backed Paoli in support of Corsican independence. The Buonapartes, however, remained in the island when Paoli was forced into exile. They prospered under an amnesty. Carlo received a royal certificate of minor nobility, without which no son of the family could have entered the military academy at Brienne, nor a daughter the convent school at St Cyr. To true Paolists the Buonapartes were trimmers and collaborators for from 1773 until his death twelve years later Charles Marie de Bonaparte (as Carlo had become) was Royal Counsellor and Provincial Assessor in Ajaccio. In 1791–2 Carlo's sons were far from popular in their native island.[5]

Napoleon might have ensured his family's ascendancy by a victory of arms. With support from Paris, and grudging approval from Paoli, he prepared a plan to seize the Sardinian islands of Maddalena, which dominate the Strait of Bonifacio separating Sardinia from Corsica. The command of a force of 150 regulars and 450 National Guardsmen was given, not to young Bonaparte, but to Colonel Colonna-Cesari, Paoli's nephew. Napoleon was allowed to join the expedition as an artillery officer – with two cannon and a mortar; and on 24 February 1793 this battery opened fire on the principal island, La Maddalena, from the much smaller island of Santo Stefano. But the main attack on La Maddalena never took place. Discipline was poor; there was friction between the seamen, regular army officers and the National Guardsmen. The escorting corvette and most of the transports sailed off to Ajaccio, leaving Napoleon and his gunners to fend for themselves on Santo Stefano. Remarkably Napoleon succeeded in getting the force away in a small vessel before the Sardinian garrison in La Maddalena town was able to kill or capture them. But it was a near thing. Napoleon's active campaigning could well have ended in fiasco and death in obscurity on the day it began.[6]

Was that the intention of the Paolists? Perhaps so, for Paoli was by now turning away from the revolution in disgust and disappointment: he deplored the execution of Louis XVI and could see no prospect of autonomy for Corsica within the new France. The Buonapartes represented all that he abhorred and mistrusted. An assembly packed with Paolists met at Corte, in central Corsica, and denounced the Buonapartes as outlaws. Napoleon went into hiding; Laetizia and her younger children fled from Ajaccio shortly before the family home was attacked by a Paolista mob. After a vain attempt to recover Ajaccio, Napoleon was reunited with his mother and the children at Calvi and escaped to France. On 11 June 1793 they landed at Toulon. 'Traitors and enemies of the Fatherland, condemned to perpetual execration and infamy,' ran a final malediction on the Buonapartes proclaimed by the Paolists in Corte.[7]

Napoleon had finished with the island of his birth. In 1799 he unexpectedly passed five restless days in Ajaccio on his way back from Egypt, waiting for the wind to veer southwards and carry him to the French coast; and on a May morning fifteen years later he was to sight folded hills above familiar inlets from the frigate bearing him to Elba. But, after 1793, Corsica stood no higher in his reckoning than any other *département* of metropolitan France and when people spoke of him as 'the Corsican' he became angry. For the moment, however, he was prepared to benefit from his origins: it was as 'Corsican Jacobin patriots' that Christophe Saliceti, spokesman for the island in Paris, induced the Convention to vote generous compensation to the family for the loss of their house, land and vines on the island.[8] Laetizia and the children sought shelter in a succession of small villages until they could be found safe lodgings in Marseilles. Napoleon at last returned to his regiment, which was engaged in stamping out rebellious discontent along the lower Rhone.

But it was the Rhine on which he wished to serve, not the Rhone. That was where, in the gamble of action against France's historic enemies, reputations were made, and lost. Lieutenant Bernadotte, rallying panic-stricken volunteers to throw back Austrians south of Speyer and Prussians outside Mainz, saw General Custine dismissed and General Beauharnais follow him a few months later; both perished under the guillotine. Lesser names in lower ranks suffered a similar fate for military incompetence or political incorrectness. But Lieutenant Bernadotte soon became Captain Bernadotte and, a few weeks later, Colonel Bernadotte, elevated through election by the troops he inspired. Oudinot's career rose rapidly in similar fashion that summer; and ex-Sergeant Soult became a staff-captain. As yet none of these names was familiar to Captain Bonaparte. But every report in *Le Moniteur* showed clearly where an ambitious young officer needed to be. Despite the absurd frustrations at La Maddalena, Napoleon had every confidence in his command of artillery. From Avignon he sent a request to the Ministry of War for a posting to the Army of the Rhine with the rank of lieutenant-colonel. The letter reached Paris on 28 August.[9] But by then there was every reason for ensuring that a good gunnery officer who knew the Mediterranean coastline should remain in Provence.

The execution of Louis XVI on 21 January had led to war with Britain, Holland and Spain within a couple of months. In Mediterranean waters it was the British who posed the greatest challenge to the Republic, with Admiral Hood commanding the fleet based on Gibraltar. On paper, the French navy looked formidable. When the Bonapartes landed as refugees at Toulon in June there were twenty-two ships-of-the-line ready to meet any challenge from Hood. Morale, however, was low and there was a constant threat of mutiny. Within four weeks of the Bonapartes' return Toulon rose in revolt against the tyranny of the local Jacobins. By mid-August royalists in the port were in touch with Hood; they undertook to proclaim the imprisoned Dauphin 'Louis XVII', fly the white flag of the Bourbons from the citadel, dismantle all naval vessels and allow Admiral Hood to enter the harbour, provided he could land troops to protect the port from French Republican wrath. On the morning that Napoleon's request for a transfer reached Paris, a French army was approaching Toulon, intent on recovering the great port and punishing the traitors. With the army came Christophe Saliceti, sent by the ruling Convention in Paris as a political 'representative'. On 16 September Saliceti gave his friend and compatriot 'Citizen Bonaparte' command of the artillery in the fast developing siege of Toulon. Promotion followed with astonishing speed: Napoleon leapt from captain to brigadier-general of Artillery in a mere ninety-seven days. He could hardly have done better by serving on the Rhine.[10]

The advancement was well-merited. It was Napoleon who devised ways to force the British fleet out of the inner anchorage of Toulon, thus cutting off any prospect of troops, military supplies or food coming in from the sea. From high ground to the south-west of the anchorage, red-hot shot would rain down upon Hood's ships below. Differences between senior French officers delayed full implementation of the projected attack, and it was mid-December before the French secured control of the essential heights, after fierce hand-to-hand fighting in which Napoleon received a wound in the thigh from an English bayonet thrust. But on 18 December Admiral Hood was forced to order his ships to sea. Next morning, Toulon passed once more into Republican hands.

Napoleon's military reputation was made. His plan had received backing from Carnot in person; praise for his energy, his courage and his siting of cannon was conveyed to Paris by his commanding officer, General Dugommier, and by successive 'representatives', including the skilful political manipulator, Paul Barras, and Augustin Robespierre, young brother of the most fervent of Jacobins. Barras's patronage would eventually bring Napoleon both political power and a wife, but Augustin Robespierre's might well have proved disastrous. On returning to Paris, Augustin presented to the Committee of Public Safety proposals drawn up by Brigadier-General Bonaparte for a two-pronged offensive against France's principal enemy, Austria. This earliest of Napoleonic master-plans was put before the Committee on 19 July 1794.

It was a bad moment to expect rational consideration of grand strategy. The Jacobin Terror was at its height. For six and a half weeks heads rolled under the guillotine in Paris at an average rate of twenty-nine a day. On 27 July – *9 Thermidor, An II* by the revolutionary calendar – Robespierre fell from power. On the following evening the two brothers went to the guillotine, together with twenty other prominent Jacobins. Brigadier Bonaparte was lucky to be well away from the capital. Even so, he was arrested on 9 August and imprisoned for eleven days at Antibes during the anti-Jacobin reaction.[11]

Within a fortnight of his release Napoleon submitted a revised plan to Lazare Carnot, the second of many he presented over the following eighteen months. Although differing in detail, essentially the plans were variations on a single theme: defeat Austria by convergent attacks. From the west one army would advance across Franconia into Bohemia. From the Rhine a second would strike eastwards into Bavaria and the Tyrol. South of the Alps a third would clear Lombardy and destroy Habsburg power in Italy. Napoleon hoped that it might then turn northwards to enter Austria, either by the Brenner route or into Carinthia and Styria, so as to threaten the capital. He was beginning to look upon Vienna with much of the destructive intensity Marcus Cato had once shown towards Carthage. There was no doubt in Napoleon's mind that, on land, Habsburg Austria was the Republic's implacable foe.

Militarily this was a fair assumption. Emperor Francis could muster a multi-national army of 350,000 men, allowing him to put into the field more trained troops for service than any other ruler in Europe, a third as many again as the King of Prussia, and greater than the Tsar could concentrate in the west.[12] No one rated the artillery highly, but the Austrian cavalry – 58,000 strong – had every reason to be proud of a tradition of superb horsemanship. Yet despite these assets, the Austrian contribution to the first campaigns of the war was unimpressive. During 1792–3 only a fraction of the army's strength was committed to the defence of the Austrian Netherlands. After the failure of Brunswick's invasion overall command was given to the elderly Prince Coburg (Frederick of Saxe-Coburg-Saalfeld). Although in March 1793 a victory at Neerwiden enabled Coburg to recover Brussels, the subsequent campaign lacked initiative. Every fortified town was methodically invested, and no imaginative use made of the Austrian hussars and dragoons.

Not all the fault lay with Coburg. In Vienna there was no enthusiasm for the war among military leaders or politicians. To them the unresolved contest with Prussia and Russia over the Polish lands was more important than what was happening in the west. Possession of Belgium was burdensome and had little to offer the Austrian economy. Their British ally was puzzled by such an attitude. To Pitt's ministers the Austrian Netherlands served both as a barrier to contain French expansion and as a springboard for a descent on Paris. They were relieved when, on Kaunitz's death in June 1794, Emperor Francis entrusted foreign affairs to Baron Johann Thugut, who genuinely hated

French republicanism and was ready to commit himself more deeply to war in the West.[13] The British sent an expeditionary force across to Holland, which later moved into Belgium, with Ostend as its base. The command was held by the young Duke of York, though he accepted Coburg as generalissimo. For Pitt it was gratifying to find in Thugut a determined partner rather than a wavering co-belligerent. Or so it seemed.

The unfolding tragedy of events in Paris strengthened this new bond. For on 16 October 1793 Marie Antoinette went to her death under the guillotine, after a perfunctory trial in the Grand Chamber of the former *Parlement*. Not surprisingly, news of her execution provoked anger in the Austrian court. It was intensified when details of the humiliations she suffered in her last hours reached Vienna: Louis XVI had been taken to the scaffold in a closed carriage, with a priest beside him to read the psalms for the dying; Marie Antoinette, her hands tied behind her white shawl, was made to sit in a tumbril facing backwards, so that the crowd could mock her misfortune. So slowly did the cart lurch its way across the cobbles that the radical deputy and artist, Jean-Louis David, had time to sketch *l'Autrichienne* as she passed beneath his window. Under the plain white bonnet and the newly cropped hair David's pencil lines preserve a profile as proudly self-assured as her mother looking down from the full majesty of a state portrait.[14]

The execution was an insult to the imperial house which Marie Antoinette's nephew could neither forgive nor forget. A defeat for the Austrians at Wattignies in Flanders on the same day as the execution increased Emperor Francis's sense of humiliation. Heavy rain a week later saturated the thin crust of top-soil and churned up the clay to create liquid mud; there could be no counter-offensive that winter. But Francis was losing patience with Coburg's shilly-shallying. As soon as spring came and the roads were passable once more, he was determined to travel to his headquarters, with Thugut in attendance, and enforce inter-allied collaboration. It was agreed with the British that the Austrian army would be increased to 170,000 men and supported by 40,000 allied troops, mainly German mercenaries in British pay.[15] The time was ripe to inflict condign punishment on the Jacobin regicides. Paris was said to be only ten marching days distant from headquarters at Tournai.

In late March 1794 Francis duly set out for the theatre of war. The journey westwards was hard-going. 'Forgive me for not writing you until we got to Brussels ... the roads were very bad,' he apologised on 10 April 1794 to Marie Thérèse, who was again expecting a child. 'I am now exceedingly glad that I kept you from making this trip, for the road is very uneven and miserable, so that we arrived in a completely wrecked coach.'[16] By 16 April he had reached Le Cateau, where he took the salute as 160,000 Austrian and allied troops paraded before him. But still Coburg would not bring the war to the boil; there must be no march on Paris until every regiment was supported by wagons carrying nine days of full rations, he argued. On 24 April the French seized the initiative, gained some success around Menin and Courtrai, but were checked by the British. Both sides thereupon reverted to inactivity.[17]

Two and a half weeks later another letter to Marie Thérèse hinted at pending excitement: 'God grant you the best of health and a successful confinement and we shall give the French a thorough beating,' Francis wrote.[18] The confinement ended on 8 June with the birth of a delicate daughter who, sadly, lived for only nine months. The 'thorough beating' remained a pious resolve for a distant future. Instead, another French attack, this time on the British at Tourcoing, captured nineteen of twenty-four guns and narrowly missed bagging the Duke of York, too. Not a single Austrian was to be seen that day, a British major grumbled; allied cohesion, hurriedly glued together, was becoming unstuck at the very moment the French were preparing a summer offensive. On the day of the skirmish at Tourcoing, General Jourdan was marching northwards with more than 70,000 men, the nucleus of the famous Army of Sambre-et-Meuse, the earliest élite army of the Republic.

Francis had left the southern Netherlands by then. Although as a junior officer he had shown courage in the field against the Turks, the Emperor knew he was not a natural military commander. After seeing for himself the problems of fighting in Flanders, Francis was prepared to leave military decisions to his brother, the Archduke Charles, who was the outstanding soldier in the Habsburg family. Even though Charles's rhythm of conducting a war was uneven – he would slip at times into an epileptic trance – his chief of staff, General Karl Mack von Lieberich, was a methodical professional whose grasp of detail had impressed the British on a visit to London. The Charles-Mack combination gave Francis confidence. He no longer wished to march on Paris. The two gifted generals should be able to hold the line of the Sambre and its tributaries until the fire of revolution consumed those who fed its flames.

In Belgium Francis discovered a precept of government which was long to elude Napoleon: a huge empire cannot be ruled effectively for any length of time from field headquarters in a distant battle front. There were problems over the future of Poland, and in particular the fate of Cracow, a city the Austrians regarded as well within their sphere of influence. Moreover, while he was in Belgium, Francis learnt of the first rumblings of discontent at home: the war, and the taxes accompanying it, were unpopular; police reports from Vienna spoke of Jacobin sentiments expressed in high places.[19] There was, too, a personal reason why Francis wished to leave campaigning to Charles and the professionals. By temperament he was an intensely family man, who hated long separation from Marie Thérèse and her children: family news was exchanged in letters which passed almost daily between husband and wife. When she was annoyed with 'the people who attend our children' she let him know her grievances, and he replied with the best advice he could offer from eight hundred miles away. He was, so he wrote from headquarters in Tournai on 23 May, distressed at 'news that our daughter has acquired such bad habits and is beginning to be naughty. Keep her much in your company and do everything you can to better her.'[20]

Poor Marie Louise! The nature of her naughtiness and bad habits is not revealed; can they have merited fatherly censure at the age of two years and six months? But the suggestion of bringing Louise more frequently into her mother's company was sound. Habsburg children spent much of their time in the care of an *aja*, or governess of the nursery; and ever since her birth the Archduchess had been the responsibility of Countess Maria Anna von Wrbna, a member of the aristocratic Auersberg family before her marriage to a court chamberlain. Now Louise was taken away from the Countess. Briefly the family relationship became affectionately less remote, until an *aja* of less impeccable nobility was appointed. Louise was eight years old before an *aja* could be found who was acceptable to Marie Thérèse and loved by her charge.

Graver problems followed Francis back to Vienna. On 18 June General Jourdan turned the whole force of his army against the Austrians. The opposing armies clashed eight days later at Fleurus, a village eight miles north-east of Charleroi where the plain is so suited to cavalry manoeuvre that it had already twice served as a battlefield – in 1622 and 1690 – and in June 1815 it was to be fought over yet again. 'Fifteen hours of the most desperate fighting I ever saw in my life,' Soult was to recall many years later; for, as a colonel rallying his infantry on that Thursday, he had no less than five horses killed under him.[21] Colonel Bernadotte, too, would remember Fleurus; he was promoted Brigadier-General on the battlefield for checking four squadrons of Dutch cavalry as they came to help their ally. Throughout the long summer day Coburg's predominantly Austrian force beat off wave after wave of attacks. Towards dusk Archduke Charles proposed to send the cavalry forward, screened by a small wood, so as to cut the French lines and open up the route to Charleroi. But Coburg was too conventionally minded to sanction an attack late in the day: he would bide his time. Meanwhile he ordered his troops back to a defensive ridge above the next village along the Brussels road. The ridge was called Mont St Jean and the village, Waterloo.

So heavy were the French losses at Fleurus that Coburg and Archduke Charles saw the battle at first as a mere setback to Austrian arms rather than a defeat. But Paris rightly celebrated. The Sambre-et-Meuse had given the Republic its first decisive victory. There would be no serious threat to the frontiers of metropolitan France for another eighteen years. For, though Coburg's troops retired in good order, allied cohesion was shattered by recrimination at the council table over the failure of national contingents to support each other. The British fell back on Antwerp; the Dutch headed north across the Scheldt; the Austrians turned towards the Rhine. There was little to keep the French from absorbing the Austrian Netherlands and fanning out across the old frontiers. Brussels fell on 8 July; Aachen eleven weeks later. By 6 October the Sambre-et-Meuse army was across the Rhine at Cologne. Nothing now seemed able to check the armies of the Republic, not even a harsh winter. Amsterdam was occupied on 19 January 1795. Four days later French cavalry galloped across a frozen Zuyder Zee to capture the Dutch fleet, as icebound in the Texel as in the Arctic.

For Emperor Francis the past twelve months of campaigning had proved a disillusioning experience. By January 1795 there was a strong peace party among his advisers in Vienna. Even Archduke Charles favoured the conclusion of a treaty with France, to be followed by total re-organisation of the army and its methods of going to war. Francis was not unsympathetic to his brother's ideas, especially after Prussia concluded a separate peace in early April. Yet, in the end, he decided to stay in the war, bolstered by a treaty in which the British guaranteed a £4.6 million loan provided that the Austrians kept 170,000 men in the field against France. In the autumn Archduke Charles launched a counter-offensive which by Christmas 1975 recovered Mannheim, Frankfurt and much of the left bank of the central Rhine.

Yet there was little fighting in Europe that year. Instead, the British – and, more hesitantly, their Austrian ally – backed an 'underground war' of encouraging royalist resistance in the French provinces and conspiracies in Paris itself. Most dramatically, on 4–5 October 1795 (*12–13 Vendémiaire, An IV*), royalist agitators, incongruously supported by extremists of the Left, roused the Paris mob for a march on the Convention (the assembly) in protest at the electoral arrangements for the councils proposed under the latest constitutional improvisation, the Directory. The maintenance of order was entrusted by the Committee of Public Safety to Paul Barras, who presided over sittings of the Convention. Barras sought the backing of Brigadier-General Bonaparte, who had been desk-bound for three months in the Committee's Topographical Department, studying the terrain of northern Italy. Although there were at least four other generals propping up the Convention in these critical days, Napoleon became effective commander in the streets.

Without artillery Napoleon knew he could achieve little. He therefore ordered Major Murat, whom he now met for the first time, to ride out to Neuilly, six miles away, with his squadron of cavalry and seize forty cannon in the artillery park at the Place des Sablons. Steady October rain and a high wind delayed the expected march on central Paris by the would-be rebels, giving Napoleon all morning to site the guns. Not that he needed the time: key points in the approaches to the Convention hall at the Tuileries were soon carefully covered. In mid-afternoon the ill-disciplined mob, supported by National Guardsmen, advanced up the Rue St Honoré and the Rue St Roch to be met with salvoes of grapeshot at point-blank range. Over 200 *citoyens* fell dead in the few minutes of gunfire; probably another 400 were wounded. Some were hunted down later inside St Roch church. The prospect of a royalist insurrection perished with them.[22]

In the Convention next day 'Citizen Bonaparte' was praised for having saved the Republic. *Le Moniteur*, the semi-official gazette, made the name familiar to the public for the first time. Within three weeks he was a full general and Commander-in-Chief of the Army of the Interior. One of many Austrian agents in France dutifully sought information about the unknown who was credited with dashing royalist hopes. In the new year the agent sent a report to his paymaster in Berne, Jacques Mallet du Pan, with the additional news that the General was likely to become commander of the French army in Italy. Mallet, who was Thugut's chief foreign intelligence gatherer, was sufficiently interested to write directly to Emperor Francis: the rising hope of the wretched schemers in Paris was identified as 'a Corsican scoundrel named Buonaparte, the right arm of Barras.'[23]

It was the first time Francis encountered the name of his future son-in-law, and it is unlikely he took note of it. Very soon the Austrian court had to acknowledge that 'Buonaparte' possessed accomplishments rare among scoundrels washed in by the revolutionary tide. He remained, however, 'the Corsican', civilised society's vandal outsider, almost a 'corsaire'. For the young Marie Louise this creature of whom her elders spoke so disparagingly was conjured up by the Devil – to whom, so she convinced herself, he bore a lamentable likeness.

3

Italy and Beyond

As Commander-in-Chief of the Army of the Interior, Napoleon was also Governor of Paris. He moved into headquarters at the corner of the Rue des Capucines and the Place des Piques (ci-devant Place Vendôme); a private box at the Opéra was his, and so, too, was a splendid carriage. He controlled police throughout the city; secret agents brought news of all who mattered, and many who did not. Daily he would report to France's new leaders, the collective executive of the Directory – though apart from Carnot and Barras, whom he knew already, he thought little of them. If necessary, the Governor could call on 40,000 troops to cow the politically restless. But why should he? So long as 'General Vendémiaire' remained in the capital he was certain there would not again be any occasion to rush cannon in from the suburbs to protect the nation's legislators.

No general in the field possessed such trappings of authority. Napoleon enjoyed the novelty to the full. In July he had been content to take lunch each day at the Café Cuisinier in the Place St-Michel with Andoche Junot, the sergeant who became a personal friend and whom he brought with him to the capital as a lieutenant and aide-de-camp; sometimes they were joined by Captain Marmont, another Toulon veteran. By December the General's habits had changed: he would host luncheon parties at headquarters for some twenty men and women. Back in the late summer and autumn, Barras used to take him along to the political salons; he saw and heard Mme Tallien, Mme de Staël, Mme de Beauharnais, Mme Récamier but made little impression on them; a slim and untidy shadowy figure, slight and insignificant behind the imposing hulk of Barras. A few months later, however, it became impolitic to ignore the Governor of Paris. Perhaps wryly, though with much satisfaction, Napoleon found that when he visited the salons, he was received with alert interest.[1]

So in very different circumstances had he been, less than two years previously, when he captivated Eugènie Clary, the younger of two daughters of a wealthy silk merchant in Marseilles. His brother Joseph had struck up a friendship with the family, and Napoleon visited their home frequently in the early summer of 1794, already locally famous for his achievements at Toulon. In August of that year Joseph married the elder Clary daughter, Julie, and by the following spring Napoleon was giving serious thought to an engagement with Desirée (as he re-named Eugènie). On St Helena he spoke sentimentally of Desirée, who was by then the Crown Princess of Sweden, as 'my first love'; but in 1795 she was only eighteen, unsophisticated and unsure of herself. From Paris in June he let Joseph know that he would send Desirée his portrait, 'if she still wants it'.[2] But the romance was over, though a mutual sense of personal attachment lingered on throughout both their lives. By *Vendémiaire* Napoleon was looking for an older partner than Desirée.

By modern standards Napoleon's views on the status of women were abysmally unenlightened and occasionally misogynous. A General who was rapidly climbing ambition's ladder needed a wife, he believed; she should be someone who could grace ceremonial occasions with natural dignity and a fine dress sense; someone who, caught in the reflected glory of his victories, would prolong through reminiscence their shared sense of exultation and perpetuate their triumphant name by bearing him a family. Physically he looked for small hands and small feet (as were his own); and he always welcomed a sympathetic listener. If she was also a woman of passion and character, so much the better, provided she remained loyal and faithful to her vows. He had no intention of taming a shrew; on the other hand, to a son of Laetizia, any challenge of temperament came as a natural stimulant to the emotions. There was, he felt, much to be said in favour of the happily resilient widow who acted as Barras's official hostess. Two days after he was appointed Governor of Paris, she sent him a note from her newly leased house in the Rue Chantereine. Writing as a 'deserted friend ... affectionately attached to you,' she added her first invitation: 'Come tomorrow to lunch with me.'[3] He came.

'Citoyenne the widow Beauharnais' – her supple Creole figure elegantly displayed by the fashionable brevity of costume – was six years older than he but, by a carefully acquired gentle charm, she concealed the slipping away of time (as, too, did an arithmetical failure in subtracting calendar dates when completing official registers).[4] Other invitations followed the first; and the more he visited Rue Chantereine, the more Rose de Beauharnais's ways and talk attracted Napoleon. Even her voice was caressing, words flowing slowly as if selected with sincerity, their rhythm enhanced by a Caribbean inflexion. She made, he thought, good conversation – especially 'when,' as he later recalled, 'I was sitting next to her at table, she began to pay me all manner of compliments on my military qualities.'[5] He may well have believed that she possessed a small fortune, as did so many Creoles from the sugar plantations; and he was certainly impressed that marriage had raised her to *vicomtesse*, accepted into one of the noble families of the old France. Yet such calculations were of secondary importance, perhaps forming no more than conversational asides remembered by those whom he believed to be his friends. The plain fact was that, by the coming of the year 1796, he had to acknowledge to himself that he was falling in love with the widowed Creole. On one change only he insisted. Just as Eugènie Clary was transformed into Desirée, so Rose de Beauharnais became Josephine.

Early in their acquaintance he met her fourteen-year-old son, Eugène, and admired his devotion to the memory of his soldier father. At a banquet given by Barras in the Luxembourg Palace on the third anniversary of the King's execution, Napoleon sat next to the twelve-year-old daughter, Hortense, and appears to have thought more highly of her manners than she did of his. Where, he wondered next time they met, was Hortense at school? At St Germain under Mme Campan, she who had been Lady of the Chamber to Queen Marie Antoinette? Then he must see to it that his sister, Caroline, was entered there at once. The youngest of the Bonaparte girls was thirteen months older than Josephine's daughter: 'I counted on finding a real friend in Caroline Bonaparte', Hortense reflected years later in her memoirs. Sadly she did not.[6]

But that was in the future. As the icy January days gave way to a frozen February General Bonaparte became restless; even social adulation began to pall. His mind conjured up broader vistas than the Place des Piques could offer: if Barras could not induce his fellow Directors to make Napoleon Minister of War, then he could surely find for him an army to lead against the Austrians?[7] Along the Rhine the opposing belligerents had observed an armistice since New Year's Eve; but no moratorium ruled out action in Italy. The only obstacle was General Scherer, down in Nice, who rejected every plan put forward by Napoleon for thrashing the Austrians south of the Alps and knocking Francis's ally, Victor Amadeus III of Sardinia-Piedmont, out of the war. In exasperation Scherer sent off his resignation on 4 February;

four weeks later Napoleon was nominated as his successor in command of the Army of Italy.

There remained one task for the Governor of Paris to complete before he set off for Nice. At seven in the evening of 6 March Josephine, accompanied by Barras, Tallien and his wife and a notary, arrived at the *mairie* of the 2nd arrondissement for her second marriage. Three hours later General Bonaparte – allegedly unable to break away from the maps he was studying – joined them. The civil ceremony, performed by an assistant registrar in the light of a single guttering candle with an under-age junior officer as the groom's sole witness, was of questionable validity – neither husband nor wife could produce a birth certificate. But this was no time to quibble; and the presence of Director Barras, wearing the triple-plumed velvet hat of France's newest rulers, stamped the ceremony with sound Republican approval. When the bridal pair had exchanged vows of conjugal fidelity, the acting registrar confidently made the ritual pronouncement, 'General Bonaparte and Madame Beauharnais the law unites you.'[8]

Yet what the law united, the exigencies of war soon put asunder. After two nights in the Rue Chantereine and a visit by mother and stepfather to Hortense at school in St Germain, Napoleon set out on the nine-day carriage journey to Marseilles. By the end of March he was conferring with Berthier and his staff officers at headquarters in Nice and able to see for himself the quality of the troops under his command. They did not impress him. The Army of Italy had been kept short of clothing and equipment. On paper he had more than 60,000 troops; but, after deducting from this total the sick and those needed for communications work and support behind the lines, he would be fortunate to put 37,000 fighting men into the field. Most alarmingly, the army had only sixty pieces of field artillery. So far as the Directors were concerned, Italy had always been a sideshow and would, they assumed, remain one; for drama you looked across the Rhine into the Franconian plain rather than across the Maritime Alps into the plains of Lombardy. Carnot expected Bonaparte to force Vienna's ally, Sardinia-Piedmont, out of the war and to tie down sizeable Austrian forces which would otherwise have engaged Jourdan around Mainz or Moreau's Rhine-et-Moselle army farther south. But Napoleon, true to the plans he had drawn up so often over the previous eighteen months, believed in launching convergent assaults against the Austrian enemy both north and south of the Alps, though he would ensure that northern Italy became the main theatre of operations. Yet, as instructions which he had himself drafted made clear, he did not intend to remain south of the Alpine divide. With Piedmont overrun and the fortress towns of Lombardy in French hands, he would cross into the Tyrol and make contact with the Army of the Rhine. Together the two armies would advance eastwards and 'dictate a glorious peace ... in the heart of the hereditary lands of the house of Austria'.[9] Even in these earliest weeks, with headquarters still on the coast of the Mediterranean, Napoleon saw Vienna as his ultimate objective.

The campaign of 1796 became a pedestal of the Napoleonic legend, that dangerously seductive folklore which Bonaparte shaped by his bulletins and completed with fabricated reminiscence dictated on St Helena. The reality of the advance was different: it provided far fewer moments of romantic heroism; and more than once there was a risk of disaster, offset by Austrian lethargy and a resigned defeatism in Turin, the Piedmontese capital. Yet, leaving aside contentious myths, there remains no doubt that the summer's fighting changed the pace and character of the war and ensured that Bonaparte was respected as a general throughout Europe. On 12 April he gained his first victory, driving a wedge between the Austrians and Piedmontese at Montenotte, on high ground twelve miles inland from his headquarters at Savona. Five days later Masséna defeated the allies at Dego, though Napoleon had to rescue him from an Austrian counter-attack. Highly coloured reports of these successes made welcome news in Paris and dramatic reading in the French press. London took note. On 29 April 1796 Bonaparte for the first time merited an informative paragraph in *The Times*. Within five weeks his achievements were the subject of a leading article.[10]

Sardinia-Piedmont withdrew from the war on 28 April; by the Armistice of Cherasco the Sardinians renounced claims on Savoy and Nice, and granted the French control of the Alpine passes and the right to garrison three fortified towns in Piedmont; more importantly, the armistice allowed Napoleon free passage across the Po, so as to carry the war against Austria into the Lombard plain. 'Soldiers, you have won six victories in five days, taken twenty-one colours, fifty-five pieces of cannon, several fortresses, conquered the richest region in Piedmont, captured 15,000 prisoners and killed and wounded 10,000 of the enemy ...' ran their army commander's morale-boosting bulletin.[11]

To the surprise of the Austrians, the Army of Italy did not pause to consolidate its gains. Ahead lay Milan, a Habsburg possession since 1714 and the residence of the Viceroy, Archduke Ferdinand, an uncle of Emperor Francis. The city was entered by Masséna on 14 May, after a needlessly costly assault on the bridge over the river Adda at Lodi. Next day the Milanese welcomed Napoleon as their liberator. Astride a white stallion and almost hidden beneath the tricolour plume in his hat, he made his way to the Serbelloni Palace and the planting of a Tree of Liberty. 'Our only quarrel is with the tyrants who enslaved you,' he declared.[12] They could be certain that Habsburg rule in Milan was at an end. 'Liberation' did not, however, prevent the imposition of a heavy tax, levied to pay the Army of Italy, nor did it prevent looting, both on the customary small scale by the soldiery and by the removal to Paris of art treasures. Within a month there were risings in Milan, Pavia and several smaller towns and villages. All were ruthlessly suppressed.

More was won by the French than Milan. The rulers of Parma and of Naples, both closely related by marriage to Emperor Francis, hastily concluded armistices in anticipation of a final peace settlement later in the year. Bologna, Ferrara and Ravenna accepted a truce. Three Venetian fortresses – Peschiera, Verona and Legnano – were occupied, even though the Venetian Republic was, technically, a neutral power. At the end of June Napoleon himself occupied the Tuscan port of Livorno (Leghorn), cutting British trade with central Italy. On 1 July he was in Florence, dining as a guest of the Grand Duke of Tuscany, Emperor Francis's brother Ferdinand – the first social meeting of a Habsburg with a Bonaparte. The war, of course, continued. But only in Mantua, the Lombard fortress set among the lakes and marshes formed by the river Mincio, did an Austrian army continue to resist a French blockade and siege. On 21 June Napoleon had told the Directors, 'All Italy is French.'[13] There was a certain anticipatory licence about the boast, but politically it was a more justifiable claim than many he made over the next eighteen years.

In Vienna there was widespread dismay, 'Since the beginning of this disastrous war, Austria has never been in such a critical situation,' Thugut wrote to the ambassador in St Petersburg in the third week of May. 'Austria may not only lose its possessions in Lombardy but see the enemy march even more into the Tyrol and carry its devastation to the heart of His Majesty's German provinces.'[14] Emperor Francis responded to the danger by ordering Field Marshal Wurmser to abandon plans to invade Alsace and turn southwards with 25,000 men. Wurmser, who had reached the rank of general four years before Napoleon was born, showed more enterprise than most seventy-two-year-old commanders. He relieved Mantua in late July but, in seeking to mount a general counter-offensive, was defeated at Castiglione and Bassano and forced to fall back on Mantua, where he remained besieged for five wintry months. The first attempt to re-assert Habsburg control over Italy had failed miserably.

The British were certain that Austria would soon seek terms from the French, and were surprised when Thugut declined an offer to send an envoy to join Lord Malmesbury in peace talks at Lille in the autumn.

Emperor Francis's authority seemed to be tottering in Germany as well as in Italy. For, while Bonaparte was completing his string of victories, Jourdan and Moreau thrust eastwards across Germany, pinning the Austrians back to the borders of the Habsburg heartland. The rulers of the south German states almost fell over themselves in a rush to make peace. The city of Regensburg, where an assembly of delegates had preserved the vestigial unity of the 'Holy Roman Empire of the German Nation', emptied speedily. Emperor Francis, ever a realist, perceived that his German imperial title was a hollow sham, as he long suspected. In mid-August an Austrian diplomat wrote to Thugut from Munich suggesting that Austria should either impose authoritative direction on the Holy Roman Empire or abandon it for all time. Ten years later remembrance of this summer of disillusionment contributed to Francis's decision to renounce his elected title and consign the ancient Reich to history.[15]

Yet Francis and Thugut were both obstinate and optimistic. The Emperor had entrusted command in Germany to his brother Charles, and the Archduke insisted that in allowing Jourdan and Moreau to penetrate Germany he was undertaking a deceptive strategic retreat. With the departure of Wurmser's army for Italy, Charles was left with less than 90,000 fighting troops, too few to take on the combined strength of the two French armies; but once the invading armies were deep in Germany and distant from each other, the Archduke would fall on each separately and defeat them. The strategy was effective. On 24 August Charles took Jourdan by surprise in Bavaria at Amberg, to the east of Nuremberg, and began a relentless pursuit of the vaunted Army of Sambre-et-Meuse which forced the French back across the Rhine within five weeks. News of Jourdan's defeat left Moreau hurrying to put the great river between his army and the resurgent Austrians before Charles could bring it, too, to battle. There was elation in Vienna.

On the other hand, in Paris the five-man Directory recognised that the Republic needed peace. Four years campaigning had brought France close to bankruptcy, with only the exactions imposed on pillaged Italy bringing money into the coffers. Several French agents put out secret peace feelers to Vienna in the late autumn of 1796. Thugut, however, was unimpressed by their character or credentials; he thought that if this was the best the Directory could manage, the government in Paris must be close to total collapse. So, too, Pitt believed when Malmesbury's visit to Lille proved fruitless. But in late January 1797 both London and Vienna were startled out of their complacency by news that the Army of Italy had gained another victory, between Lake Garda and the river Adige: for on 14–15 January Napoleon halted General

Alvintzi's main thrust southwards from Trent at Rivoli. Fourteen thousand men – half of Alvintzi's army – were killed, wounded or captured. In no other Napoleonic battle would there be such a high proportion of enemy losses. The victory at Rivoli sealed the fate of Mantua, which finally surrendered to the French three weeks later. There no longer seemed any danger of an Austrian counter-offensive in Italy.[16]

It is fitting that Rivoli should be the earliest Napoleonic battle commemorated by a prestigious Parisian thoroughfare, for the victory marks off a significant divide in the future Emperor's career. Over the previous seven months he had emerged as an innovative general of great merit and determination, too independently minded to conform to the agreed policies of the Directory. When not at field headquarters he enjoyed viceregal splendour in Milan with, from mid-July 1796, a not always faithful Josephine beside him. He appropriated to himself the management of political affairs and diplomacy throughout the Italian peninsula, promising 'independence' to the Italian people; in November 1796 he created a Cispadane Republic (Modena, Bologna, Ferrara and the Romagna); a month later a Lombard Republic was proclaimed in Milan (north of the Alps from Lake Lugano and the Valtelline Pass to the west bank of the Adige). Each republic had a Directory-style constitution, imposed by General Bonaparte. Had he failed to stem Alvintzi's advance at Rivoli, he would have lost control of both satrapies and might well have been summoned back to Paris, with an uncertain fate ahead of him.

The establishment of the two republics alarmed the Directors; their general enjoyed far too much independence. They sent General Henri Clarke, a diplomat and personal friend of Carnot, to Milan in early December. He was to report back on Bonaparte's political standing and, at the insistence of the Foreign Minister, Charles Delacroix, he was to raise the possibility of a peace settlement which would restore to the Austrians their Italian possessions in return for the cession to France of Belgium and the left bank of the Rhine. Napoleon had never shown the slightest regard for Delacroix and, as Clarke soon perceived, refused to treat Italy as a bargaining counter for the Rhine frontier. Victory at Rivoli put a stop to all this nonsense. So great was the enthusiasm aroused in Paris by this latest rebuff to Austria that the Directory – never a smooth-running political machine – dared not deny General Bonaparte his needs, nor challenge the assumptions on which he based his general strategy. Henceforth Italy would be the main theatre of war and Napoleon the arbiter of Austria's fate.

'Send me 10,000 men from the Rhine ... and you may expect millions, victories and a good peace,' Napoleon wrote to Carnot soon after Clarke arrived in Milan.[17] Carnot was sympathetic, even before Rivoli; it was gratifying to have found a general who promised 'millions' of francs as a 'war contribution' and not simply territorial gains. Moreover, the much harassed Carnot saw an opportunity to ease another vexatious problem. At Coblenz General Bernadotte's fiery Gascon temper had been ruffled by criticism of his handling of troops in the retreat across Germany. To Carnot there seemed much to be said for sending Bernadotte, with veterans from the Sambre-et-Meuse, southwards to strengthen Bonaparte's forces along the borders of Venetia. The Army of Italy was Bonaparte's own creation, with traditions and loyalties of its own. If it was not to become a Praetorian Guard, dangerous to the stability of the Republic, it was essential for the army to receive a leavening of 'outsiders' under a leader of character with a fine military reputation. Subsequently a division from the Rhine-et-Moselle was also placed under Bernadotte's command, giving him 20,000 experienced troops.

During February 1797, often in heavy snowstorms, the thirty-six-year-old Gascon general led the reinforcements in perfect discipline over the Mont Cenis Pass to Turin and on to Milan. To Kellermann, the veteran hero of Valmy, Bernadotte wrote that he was eager 'to champion the glory of the Army of Italy', adding that he was sure 'the young general' would 'not prove ungrateful'.[18] The self-satisfied tone of the letter was ominous: at twenty-eight a 'young general' who ruled as a virtual pre-consul was no man to patronize. Berthier's staff found the newcomers arrogant, but Napoleon was glad to have his army built up to a strength of 80,000 men. If he was to head for Vienna, he needed powerful forces to protect his left flank against an Austrian diversionary attack across the Brenner Pass from the Tyrol and to safeguard his right flank in the Romagna should the remaining Italian states risk a second round of war.

By now Vienna, too, recognised the vital importance of northern Italy. In February Emperor Francis ordered Archduke Charles to leave the Rhine and assume command in Italy. 'Take with you whom you want, transfer generals and other officers from the army of the Rhine and vice versa,' Francis told his brother, with that airy imprecision which his minsters and military commanders so often found dangerously exasperating.[19] The Archduke knew that much was expected from him and was unhappy at the prospect. He did not reach Udine until 2 March. It was clear the French would attack once the snow lifted from the lower passes. Charles had less than a fortnight to become familiar with the line of Austrian fortified positions along the Tagliamento, a river made treacherous by melting snow which had caused flooding, so that it was difficult for a stranger, new to the terrain, to identify fordable crossings.

Yet when on the afternoon of 16 March Napoleon unexpectedly took the offensive, Bernadotte was able to find a ford soon after French cannon opened up on the Austrian positions. He 'waded through numerous branches of the river under the most murderous fire', noted one of Napoleon's aides-de-camp;[20] his division followed their Gascon Major-General and by their surprise assault broke the Austrian position. Archduke Charles found his men falling back on the next river barrier, the Isonzo. Four days later he wrote to his brother at the Hofburg, 'Neither pleas, nor rewards, nor threats were of any use in trying to halt this rabble in full flight.'[21] Soon the Archduke heard reports of French columns advancing up every mountain valley towards Carinthia, and threatening the Tyrol, too. He lacked guns and he lacked cavalry. It was impossible to engage the enemy in a set battle, only in piecemeal encounters. By 24 March Charles was urging Francis to make peace. 'If this army is defeated, there is no salvation,' he bluntly told the Emperor.[22] By the time the courier brought the Archduke's letter to Vienna, three divisions of the Army of Italy and their general-in-chief, had entered Klagenfurt, the chief city of Carinthia, some 200 miles from the capital. By Napoleon's reckoning, this meant that Vienna was eight marching days away.

Marie Louise retained a blurred memory of those alarming April days, although she was only five years old at the time and later events in 1805 were to stand out more vividly in her mind. Her father was calmly confident, but Francis was puzzled by the initial reaction in the capital, and slightly contemptuous: 'You would not believe the chaos there is here and in the rear of the army, but we are doing everything we can to maintain order,' he replied to Archduke Charles on 2 April. 'We are putting Vienna into a state of defence, though the people are not only reluctant but positively unwilling; we need time to get things right, for the largest concentration of magazines in the whole monarchy is here.'[23]

Next morning a courier brought an unexpected message from the Archduke: he had received a letter from General Bonaparte urging Charles to conclude an armistice 'in the interests of humanity'. For twenty-four hours there were urgent talks in Vienna: Thugut, who had sent reliable agents to organize resistance in the Tyrol, wanted to play for time and thought the French approach a sign that Napoleon feared for his own communications; Empress Marie Thérèse sought an end to the war as a whole and pressed her husband to seek a general peace settlement which would safeguard his possessions and also the position of her mother, Queen Maria Carolina of Naples; Emperor

Francis wanted peace with dignity. He authorised his brother to send two experienced officers to negotiate. But in no circumstances should Charles conduct peace talks himself: though their brother Ferdinand had entertained the French general-in-chief at Florence in their childhood palace, territorial bargaining over maps on tables between a Habsburg archduke and a 'Corsican usurper' was out of the question. The imperial house must not be humiliated.[24]

While awaiting a response from Vienna, Napoleon continued his advance, though on 7 April a five-day truce was accepted. By 10 April he was at Bruck-an-der-Mur, well inside Styria and halfway between Klagenfurt and Vienna. In the capital the townsfolk were by now in a more courageous mood; the Rector of the university encouraged his students to form volunteer battalions, rallying behind the banner carried by their predecessors during Vienna's Turkish siege; a Commerce Battalion was raised and, after a few days training, marched off for fully two miles beside the Wien river before deciding to go home for the night and await further developments. The volunteers were sensible realists; and, as they suspected, there was by now scant prospect of their valour being put to the test. For Napoleon had abandoned the idea of dictating peace in the Habsburg capital. He wanted a settlement on his own terms, before the Directory could send General Clarke back to the Army of Italy with plenipotential authority. Some French patrols reached the summit of the Semmering Pass where, through field telescopes, their officers believed they could see the tapering spire of St Stephen's cathedral, seventy-five miles away, with a cluster of lesser towers and roofs around it. It was the closest they came to the city, for Semmering was the limit of the French advance. At Leoben, on 18 April, 'Peace Preliminaries' were signed. At once the invading army began to pull out of Carinthia and Styria; a final peace settlement would be drawn up in Italy, not within the *Erbländer*, the dynasty's hereditary Austrian crown lands.[25]

So accustomed are we to Napoleon's re-shaping of frontiers in later years that the innovative effrontery of Leoben has passed largely without comment. Technically, the general-in-chief of the Army of Italy had no more authority to end the campaign and begin discussing peace terms without reference back to Paris than had the commanders of other armies in the field. But Bonaparte could both deliver the fruits of victory and, secretly and cynically, promise more to come. By the Leoben Preliminaries Austria recognised French possession of Belgium, Luxemburg, Savoy and Nice, surrendered Lombardy, agreed to accept the decisions of a future congress over the left bank of the Rhine, and received the mainland territories of the Venetian Republic, already under French occupation. These terms relegated the Directory's principal foreign policy objective – French dominance over both banks of the Rhine – into second place, giving priority to expansion in Italy. But the Directors approved the terms imposed by Bonaparte. This was hardly surprising. For much of the summer their work was hampered by a power struggle with the elected legislature. They were glad to counter instability at home with news of achievements in Italy.

Early in May 1797 Napoleon's troops occupied the city of Venice, ending the rule of the Doge and replacing the historic Republic of St Mark by an interim government which paid lip-service to French revolutionary ideals. Genoa, too, was occupied and transformed, becoming the Ligurian Republic; and on 9 July Napoleon presided over a final ceremony in Milan, proclaiming the creation of a Cisalpine Republic, a union of the Cispadane and Lombard republics set up in the previous winter.

In Vienna, Thugut was alarmed: clearly Bonaparte was too astute for the run-of-the mill negotiators sent to Leoben. He summoned home from St Petersburg Louis Cobenzl, Austria's ablest diplomat, in order to talk peace with Napoleon and he also decided to make a direct approach to the civilian government in France. But it was a bad moment for such an initiative. On 15 July Talleyrand became Foreign Minister, the first skilled exponent of statecraft in Paris for many years; and he was far too shrewd to intrigue against the soldier-hero of the hour.

It was late September before Ludwig Cobenzl reached northern Italy. He found that by then Napoleon was living in great state at the Villa Manin in Passeriano, the most elegant of the Doges' palaces on the Venetian mainland. Their talks continued for three weeks, until on 17 October a peace treaty was signed in a neighbouring village lower down the Tagliamento, then known as Campo Formio and now as Campoformido. The Treaty of Campo Formio confirmed many proposals already made at Leoben, notably over Belgium and the Rhine. It was agreed, however, to leave the final settlement of German affairs to a Reich congress in Rastatt, attended by the traditional German delegations but now including France as a successor state. The city of Venice, and all Venetian possessions occupied by France east of the river Adige except for Modena, would in January 1798 be handed over to Austria as compensation for the loss of Lombardy and for formal recognition of Napoleon's satellite creations, the Cisalpine and Ligurian republics. Austria acquired ex-Venetian Istria and the Dalmatian littoral, although France annexed the Ionian Islands, the strategically placed Venetian archipelago in the southern Adriatic, including Corfu. On paper, the Campo Formio settlement was generous to Austria. Privately, however, Thugut told Colloredo he thought it ignominious for their Emperor to strike territorial bargains with a revolutionary republican regime.[26] There is no evidence that Francis shared his minister's misgivings.

More interesting in retrospect than the terms of the treaty are the impressions made by the two principal negotiators upon each other. Ludwig Cobenzl was the first diplomat of long experience to meet Napoleon; his views shaped lasting prejudices at the Vienna court, for they were far from flattering. Bonaparte's moods, so Cobenzl told Thugut, were unpredictable; his behaviour was theatrical, his manners appalling; he behaved 'like a man from a hovel'.[27] Other witnesses confirm that, at their eighth meeting, an impatient Napoleon did indeed smash a porcelain coffee service in a gesture of wrath, though possibly by accident; the tale that he hurled it to the ground, with a furious, 'This is what will happen to your monarchy!' seems apocryphal. It is clear that he found the supercilious Cobenzl exasperating: the Austrian envoy was 'unaccustomed to negotiation, but always to having his own way', Napoleon wrote to Talleyrand after their second day of talks. Yet when the peace treaty was signed, and Cobenzl about to return to Vienna, Napoleon made a gesture of apologetic reconciliation; 'I'm a soldier accustomed every day to risking my life,' he emphasised. 'I'm in all the fire of my youth, and I cannot show the restraint of a trained diplomat.'[28] Cobenzl was not mollified.

Austria was, for the first time in five and a half years, at peace. France was not; and the Directory sought to turn their General's 'fire of youth' against the obstinate enemy across the Channel. News of his appointment to command the 'Army of England' reached Napoleon in Milan on 5 November, but it was another eleven days before he was ready to leave Lombardy. He spent almost a week at Rastatt, irritated by the pedantic protocol hallowed in the preliminary sessions of the Congress on German affairs. A summons to Paris for consultation over 'the many great concerns of the country' was welcome; he arrived home in the capital on 5 December and for a week was feted triumphantly before concentrating on the operational planning for an invasion of England. On the day after his return, Napoleon met Talleyrand for the first time and struck up a working partnership with the Foreign Minister. Problems unresolved in Milan constantly intruded: a pro-French insurrection in Switzerland; anti-French riots in Rome, where Joseph Bonaparte was ambassador, became so grave that Berthier was ordered to assemble a force to occupy the Holy City; and there was rivalry between the generals awaiting new assignments in Lombardy.

Bernadotte was especially troublesome. Rather strangely, in the late summer, Bonaparte had sent the Gascon hero back to Paris with captured Austrian flags to present to the Directors and a letter fulsome in its praise of 'this excellent general'. To Napoleon's dismay, Bernadotte refused command of the Army of the Midi when it was offered to him in Paris and was back at Passeriano four days before Campo-Formio was signed. He returned with enhanced personal standing for, during his month in the capital, he was lionised in society and impressed several politicians, including Talleyrand: if a counter-weight were needed to Bonaparte at any future date, was Bernadotte their man, they wondered? Napoleon certainly wanted him out of the way. In December there was talk of a command for the Gascon in India, or to raise revolution in Canada or, more likely, at the head of French forces in the Ionian Islands. Yet eventually the Directors gave Bernadotte the post he most desired: on the morning of 18 January 1798 he learnt in Verona that he would be general-in-chief in Italy. But not for long. Some ten hours later a second despatch reached Bernadotte: and, to his utter consternation and dismay, he discovered that on 11 January he had been appointed ambassador of the French Republic to the imperial court in Vienna.[29]

Talleyrand sought a rapid restoration of diplomatic relations between France and Austria, two European Powers whom he consistently regarded as natural allies, in the Kaunitz-Choiseul tradition. But whom could he send to Vienna, before the revolution the most prestigious prize among the embassies? Jacobinism had decimated the ranks of aspirant ambassadors. At the start of his Paris visit, Bernadotte had been one of thirty guests dining at Talleyrand's home in the Rue Taitbout: Benjamin Constant, Thérèse Tallien, Germaine de Staël, a trio of choleric generals, two Directors and sundry companions were fascinated by the newcomer's table-talk. Talleyrand had observed the panache with which he ceremonially presented the captured regimental colours to the Republic. He was an impressive figure on horseback; his troops in Germany won respect for their discipline and for having well turned out officers, true *messieurs* rather than *citoyens*. In Parisian society Bernadotte had treated the ladies courteously, and Napoleon himself saw how easily he mingled with Austrian officers at Leoben. If Talleyrand wished to turn the General into the mould-figure of a good Republican ambassador, Napoleon had no objection. And Bernadotte's own resistance melted away when he found he would receive an immediate payment of 72,000 francs (more than £150,000 by modern reckoning), supplemented by 12,000 francs for travelling expenses, and thereafter an assured 144,000 francs a year. 'You will make arrangements to go without any delay to your destination,' Talleyrand insisted. Bernadotte took him at his word and arrived at the city gates of Vienna in a mud-spattered carriage on 8 February 1798; his coming, the British ambassador reported, was 'totally unexpected'.[30] Nobody had thought to ask Emperor Francis if the General's appointment would be acceptable to him.

Nobody, for that matter, raised with Thugut or with any Austrian delegates at Rastatt the possibility of restoring diplomatic contacts until well after Bernadotte's appointment was made public. Talleyrand's hopes of reviving the old partnership were, as yet, totally unrealistic. 'The disposition of the public mind in the capital has been, for some time, strongly pronounced against the French,' the British ambassador commented drily in a despatch to London.[31] At first Bernadotte was dependent on the kindness of the Spanish ambassador for accommodation. Once his credentials arrived from Paris – a fortnight later than Bernadotte himself – he was able, after several refusals, to find a home at a corner of the Wallnerstrasse, a few hundred yards from Thugut's Chancellery in the Ballhausplatz.

During his first fortnight in residence Bernadotte lived up to Talleyrand's expectations; Colloredo, a stickler for protocol, could find no fault with his manner when he presented his credentials to the Emperor in the Hofburg. As late as Easter Day (8 April) he was in the Burgkapelle when Empress Marie Thérèse presented her five-week-old fifth daughter at the altar; afterwards he talked at length with the Empress, giving her re-assuring news of her mother, the Queen of Naples, about whose fate at the hands of alleged Jacobins there were alarming rumours circulating in the city. But he could not break through the icy reserve of the great families. One of Marie Antoinette's brothers and two of her sisters were still living in Vienna, and her only surviving daughter, by now nineteen years old, had been found sanctuary in the Belvedere Palace. Though the Spanish ambassador remained hospitable, Bernadotte was left to ride alone in the Prater, ostracised and politically ineffectual. He seems to have decided to draw attention to his presence, specifically as the representative of the new France.

Embassies in the late eighteenth century did not display national insignia. But early in the evening of Friday, 13 April, the tricolour flag of the Republic was unfurled from the balcony of the mansion Bernadotte had leased. It was a bad evening to choose. Over that weekend the volunteers who had formed battalions when the French invaders were in Styria planned to celebrate the first anniversary of the courage they would have shown if Bonaparte had not made peace. An Austrian dynastic patriotism was coming into being, manifested at court fourteen months earlier when, on the Emperor's twenty-ninth birthday, Lorenz Leopold Haschka's *Gott erhalte Franz den Kaiser, unsern guten Kaiser Franz* was sung for the first time, to the magnificent melody of Joseph Haydn. Asking God to preserve 'our good Emperor Francis' might be less ferocious than the stirring incitement of the *Marseillaise* but the 'Austria Hymn', too, was a call to national assertiveness.[32] To see the red, white and blue banner of the revolutionary enemy billowing from a balcony in central Vienna seemed a patriotic affront.

The incensed demonstrators became violent. Two carriages were smashed; stones were thrown at windows; and a youngster climbed up to the balcony to tear down the flag, which the rioters carried to the Schottengasse where it was set alight with torches from Colloredo's personal carriage, conveniently parked there. After several hours' disturbance cuirassiers arrived to clear the narrow street between the Wallnergasse and the Herrengasse, where the rioters had gathered. Bernadotte would accept no apologies, not even when Emperor Francis sent Colloredo with a message promising a full inquiry and urging him not to let the incident endanger Austro-French relations. At midday on Sunday, 15 April, ambassador and staff were given a protective cavalry escort as, in response to Bernadotte's persistent requests, they set off for the frontier.

Talleyrand's statecraft had foundered after seven weeks. Understandably he blamed Bernadotte, whose diplomatic career ended as abruptly as it began – though not until he had spent a dreary month at Rastatt and won from the Foreign Minister two face-saving letters which were published in the official *Moniteur*.[33] Yet Tallyrand himself was at fault: he should not have chosen for such a delicate mission a fiery Gascon whom he scarcely knew; and he should not have sent him from army headquarters to an improvised embassy without careful briefing. To recover the Franco-Austrian interdependence of the Kaunitz era needed long preparation and a mutual respect which a historic dynasty was unlikely to accord to a republic. But Talleyrand did not abandon his ultimate objective as something to be achieved in the distant future. For the moment, however, talks to ease tensions which had exploded in the flag incident continued at Rastatt and in mid-summer at Seltz in Alsace, with Ludwig Cobenzl as Austria's spokesman. By then his verbal adversary at Passeriano was exuding 'the fire of [fast disappearing] youth' in Egypt.

The Friday the Thirteenth riot scarcely merits a footnote in the history of such a turbulent age. Yet it made a lasting impression on the people of Vienna, passing into city legend as a belated protest at the indignities forced upon their great Empress's youngest daughter, culminating in her execution. Even today a traveller stepping out of the modernist exit of the Herrengasse U-bahn station, in the heart of bankers' Vienna, is confronted by the name Fahnegasse ('Flag Street') on the opposite wall. There, unexpectedly, in the peace of a pedestrianised square, the mind's eye can linger briefly over the excitements of a phantom past, back in those years before a 'man from a hovel' took as his wife an archduchess from the Hofburg.

4

The Making of Empires

At Easter in 1798 the Archduchess was still only in her seventh year, old enough to be at court when her mother presented her newly born sister at the altar of the Burgkapelle, but too young to sense the tensions caused by an envoy from revolutionary France. The daughters of a Habsburg sovereign lived a secluded life, almost as isolated from reality as in a nunnery, and with no imaginative ideas allowed to stimulate their dutiful minds. Marie Louise's second governess (*aja*), Countess Josepha de Chanclos, ensured that the child's spiritual development progressed satisfactorily – though she did not make her first communion until the eve of her twelfth birthday – and she fostered Louise's innate sensitivity to the wonders of nature. At Laxenburg the Archduchess had rabbits, geese, chickens and ducks of her own to care for. However, all these creatures had to be female; for, though her mother gave birth at the rate of one child for every fourteen months of married life, her parents hoped to preserve their daughter's innocence over sexual matters at least until puberty. They may well have succeeded, and it is probable that Louise was still ignorant of the physical aspects of married life when she became a bride; statues remained fig-leafed, a legacy from Maria Theresa's prudish 'chastity commission'; and illustrations of differences between the male and female figure in any books the Archduchess might encounter were removed in advance by scissors.

So few of Marie Thérèse's babies outlived infancy that Louise was, in many ways, a lonely little girl: her eldest brother, Crown Prince Ferdinand, needed special attention, both as heir to the throne and as an epileptic; her second and third brothers, Joseph and Francis

Charles, were not born until April 1799 and December 1802 respectively; and the youngest, John Nepomuk, not until she was thirteen. Of her sisters, the first born lived only nine months, the second was physically weak and died aged three, and the remainder were too young to be companions. The Countess de Chanclos strictly observed nursery etiquette; she forbade any contact between the Archduchess and children from other families; nor was Louise allowed to converse with any of the domestic servants; always the *aja* must be an intermediary.

At the Habsburg summer palace of Schönbrunn, and to an even greater extent in the Hofburg, Louise rarely saw her parents, except on official occasions. Her father – whom she adored – was extremely conscientious: when in residence at Vienna he would spend six and a half hours each week giving audience to his subjects, receiving their petitions or listening to their grievances. Though her mother was sympathetic and understanding, frequent pregnancies made her remote, at least until Louise was fourteen. When the Emperor and Empress made the ten-mile journey out to Laxenburg, life was jollier: occasional romps in the parkland, tricks with Louise's favourite dog, Tisbé, games of hide-and-seek, and rowing on the lake with 'dear Papa' at the oars. But there was never total privacy, even at Laxenburg. One humourless busybody from Vienna was shocked to find his sovereign happily pushing the Crown Prince across the lawns in a wheelbarrow. 'An emperor might better spend his time in a more useful and proper manner,' he grumbled.[1]

Back in 1773, when Francis was four years old, the great Empress herself had selected as her grandson's future governor Count von Colloredo, who was then a thirty-seven-year-old father of six youngsters. He took up his duties as *ajo* in June 1774: at the end of the century, he was still Francis's right-hand man, and as *Kabinettsminister* the most influential figure at court, although Thugut's primacy in foreign affairs remained, as yet, unchallenged. Over the years Colloredo's strange combination of intense religiosity, casual demeanour and foppish affectation puzzled newcomers to Vienna, several of whom under-rated him (including the Metternichs, father and son). He was not simply his imperial master's voice: long association ensured that his thoughts on policy were almost invariably his master's thoughts, too. Colloredo's wife died in April 1789; he found consolation in the company of Madame de Poutet, by birth a member of a French aristocratic family and for several years the lively and intelligent widow of a colonel in a Walloon regiment. She became the second Countess von Colloredo in January 1799, and in the following October presented her sixty-three-year-old husband with a son. The Emperor and Empress admired her matriarchal qualities: they became the boy's godparents and, on Louise's eighth birthday, appointed Countess von Colloredo to succeed the Countess de Chanclos as *aja* to the Archduchess.[2]

Louise was delighted, for her new *aja* had a ten-year-old daughter, Victoire (Victoria) de Poutet, and at last the Archduchess was allowed the companionship of a playmate. Soon they were the closest of friends, with Louise wishing to share everything she possessed with Victoria. The two-year difference in age helped the Archduchess grow up. Under Countess Colloredo's tuition she began to speak French and Italian well, dipped into edifying literature, became proficient in needlework and drawing, and developed musical talents, especially as a clavichordist. An early letter to Victoria shows the pleasure she found in dancing, describing a ball where she enjoyed 'minuets, allemandes, a galopade'. Her father insisted she should be taught geography and given some idea of the background of the Holy Roman Empire. Recent history she acquired dramatically, as recounted by her *aja* from personal experience and tales of the fate of her friends. From the Countess she first learnt of the misfortunes of her great-aunt, Marie Antoinette, and the terrible deeds of the godless French Republicans. Contemporary history – virtually current affairs – filtered through to Louise in a succession of half-truths, as it still does to so many children. After threatening to ravage her father's own lands, so she understood, 'the Corsican' had gone to Egypt, where he saved himself and his armies by 'saying "I'm a Moslem and I recognise Mahomet as the great Prophet", but he came back to France, pretending to be a Catholic ... and then became First Consul'.[3]

That was not quite what happened, though it may well have seemed so, for events moved forward at a steady canter in these last years of the old century. 'The Corsican's' Egyptian misadventure gave the former allies an opportunity to regroup and, largely through British diplomatic efforts, accept Russia as a leading member of a Second Coalition. Thugut had always assumed that Campo-Formio was a formalised truce rather than a peace treaty. Emperor Francis was willing for Austrian staff officers and ancillary supply services to support the moves of a Russian expeditionary corps, commanded by Marshal Alexander Suvorov in northern Italy, while Archduke Charles successfully drove the French back in the northern cantons of Switzerland and in southern Germany. By the second week of August in 1799 the French hold on Italy had collapsed. The defeats by which Bonaparte rose to eminence seemed avenged.

But the allied success story soon came to an end. On 9 November 1799 (18 *Brumaire*) Napoleon, having arrived home from Egypt three weeks previously, carried out the coup d'etat which replaced the Directory by a Consulate which he shaped and led. Yet even before Napoleon landed in France, Masséna had surprised the Russians and Austrians with a victory close to Zurich, and before the end of the year the unpredictable Tsar Paul took Russia out of the war. There followed in May 1800 the dramatic reappearance of 'the Corsican' at the head of France's 'Army of the Reserve', 50,000 men brought unexpectedly across the snow-covered Great St Bernard Pass threatening the flank of an Austrian army which, under General Melas, was preparing to enter Provence and invade metropolitan France. On 14 June Melas engaged the French at Marengo, a village two miles south-east of the citadel of Alessandria. A combination of imaginative use of cavalry and sheer luck gave Napoleon the victory essential to consolidate his Consulate. Once again bulletins sent off to the *Moniteur* created instant legends, both over the crossing of the Alps and the way in which Marengo was fought and won in fulfilment of the First Consul's far-sighted plans. Yet it was, without doubt, a decisive victory. Melas, finding his troops demoralised, asked for an armistice, which was agreed next day; and, as after Leoben, Franco-Austrian peace talks began, continuing through the summer and into autumn, with the armistice renewed several times. Now, however, Napoleon was prepared to let others finish his work, agreeing on a final settlement with the Habsburg enemy. He was back in Paris a mere eight weeks after setting out on the campaign. New tasks demanded his attention. The great French Revolution had withered away without producing a settled constitution or a rational common code of law: Napoleon needed to prove that the Consulate would be both constructive and enduring, an orderly system of government, not the hasty improvisation of a soldier hero intent on perpetuating his political power.

It was during this Marengo summer that war's uncertainty first touched Marie Louise, though bringing fun and excitement rather than tears. In mid-August her mother's mother, Maria Carolina of Naples, arrived at Schönbrunn on a long contemplated family visit, postponed until the French tide receded from northern Italy. But she put off her coming for too many months; Marengo was fought on the day she landed at Livorno; soon the French flooded back over the plains and into Tuscany, and her cavalcade was fortunate to reach Ancona without interception by enemy patrols. By the time she arrived in Vienna it was clear there could be no return journey until a genuine peace was secured. A quarter of a century ago the Queen had been Francis's favourite aunt, just as earlier she was Marie Antoinette's favourite sister; and there had been a day in 1776 when Count Colloredo put on record his shock at finding the Queen romping on the palace floor in Florence with her nephews and nieces.[4] Now, having given birth to eighteen children in twenty-one years, her romping days were over; she was a formidable, idiosyncratic matriarch who sometimes gabbled so excitedly that her words became incomprehensible. Eight of her children died in infancy, but she brought with her from Italy one older daughter and three youngsters, including ten-year-old Prince Leopold, and their company brightened Marie Louise's nursery days. For much of her journey the Queen was escorted by the British minister to Naples, Sir William Hamilton, who, together with his wife Emma and Admiral Lord Nelson, was returning to England. Nelson was already famous across Europe for his victory at the Nile, and during three weeks at Vienna he was feted as a hero of the struggle against the common enemy; but he was also received *en famille* at Schönbrunn. It was a pleasant occasion: 'We had the noise of five fine healthy children for an hour,' Nelson observed with approval in a letter home.[5]

Maria Carolina and her children were still in Vienna when, on 6 November, Nelson and the Hamiltons landed in England. Although the French never completely severed links between the German lands and Italy, the Queen preferred to linger in her native city, and Louise became accustomed to her grandmother's presence and to the company of the young aunts and uncle. But before the end of the year these happy family gatherings were disrupted by another war scare. Napoleon, tired of fruitless negotiating but unwilling himself to leave Paris, ordered General Moreau to press forward down the Danube from Bavaria when, on 14 November, the current armistice expired.

Thugut, who was as opposed to negotiations as Napoleon and wished to resume the fighting before the coming of winter, resigned as Francis's Foreign Minister in September. He was succeeded by Ludwig Cobenzl. But, so confused was the Austrian administrative system, that Cobenzl became an absentee minister, travelling to Lunéville (in Lorraine) and even to Paris for diplomatic exchanges; the conduct of general policy in Vienna was left to the familiar combination of Thugut and Colloredo, though there was no longer close accord between them. Thugut welcomed the ending of the armistice; he much preferred a German campaign without Bonaparte to the risk of further disaster in Italy. But who should lead the Emperor's army? Archduke Charles was in poor health. Moreover he had offended Francis by an apparent show of 'insubordinate' independence earlier in the year. Surprisingly Archduke John, an inexperienced eighteen-year-old, was given command in the field, though with an undistinguished veteran general at his side to remind him what the military textbooks prescribed for every occasion. 'I could not be more calm about future events,' Thugut assured Colloredo on the day the armistice expired. Few shared his confidence; certainly not Colloredo or the Emperor.[6]

John was ordered to take the initiative and cross the river Inn, so as to cut Moreau's communications with France. On 3 December the opposing armies stumbled across each other at Hohenlinden, some thirty miles east of Munich; the young Archduke was outmanoeuvred, especially by the experienced Ney; he lost 18,000 men that day, either killed, wounded or taken prisoner. Hurriedly Francis urged Archduke Charles to come south from Prague and take over the command. But it was too late to organise effective resistance. In fifteen days Moreau's troops advanced 190 miles, and by 22 December his cavalry outriders could be seen from the great Benedictine abbey of Melk, high above the Danube fifty-five miles from Vienna. Charles insisted on an armistice, which was signed at Steyr on Christmas Day. The Emperor backed his brother, promoting him Field Marshal and giving him overall responsibility for shaping policy. Thugut was finally sent packing; 'All circles of the people are unanimously of the view that Your Excellency is holding up the conclusion of peace, and will always hold it up,' Francis bluntly told him.[7] This was a fair assessment of the public mood, as Thugut knew full well. More than once, as he stepped down from his carriage in the Ballhausplatz, onlookers had shouted abuse at him and pelted him with vegetables as he went into the Chancellery. 'The Viennese ... are drunk with joy at the mere word "peace",' he protested. 'Nobody bothers ... so long as they can run off to the ball and eat their roast chicken undisturbed.'[8]

'Peace' was the word in Paris, too; a victorious peace, of course; but, above all, a peace that would last. For that reason the defeated Austrians were once again treated generously, Talleyrand remaining true to his belief that Vienna was a natural counter-weight to St Petersburg and Berlin. Early in February 1801 peace was signed at Lunéville; the terms basically re-affirmed the Campo-Formio settlement, though adding Parma to the Cisalpine Republic and further strengthening the French hold on the Rhineland. The French formally accepted the restoration of King Ferdinand to his throne in Naples, enabling Queen Maria Carolina to return home safely. Anglo-French negotiations began in the autumn, and in March 1802 the Treaty of Amiens was concluded: London reluctantly acknowledged French hegemony in Europe; Paris, with equal reluctance, acknowledged the maritime supremacy which was allowing the British to establish their new far-flung colonial empire. The first summer of non-belligerency in ten years opened up Paris to English visitors. Yet so fragile did the peace seem to them that few ventured farther into the continent.

By now the deep hostility of the Viennese to French republicanism, so openly expressed in 1798, was fast mellowing. The drunkenness and ill-discipline of Suvorov's corps in 1799 left them disillusioned with Russia, their most powerful ally on the continent. By contrast, news reports from Paris were comfortably reassuring. The Corsican adventurer had become a champion of reconciliation: a Concordat reinstated Catholicism, though with Church subordinated to state, much as Joseph had sought for his Empire; émigrés were encouraged back to France; impeccably aristocratic names reappeared on lists of public servants. At the same time, he personally helped prepare a Civil Code which infused Roman law with the egalitarian concepts of the Rights of Man. Beethoven so admired the Consul as reformer and man of action that when, in 1803, he began work in Vienna on a third symphony – one which would impose his own personality on classical conventions – he decided to dedicate the score to Bonaparte. There remained, of course, irreconcilables; Countess Colloredo, for example, never doubted that the Corsican ogre was the Antichrist, a conviction she passed on to her young impressionable charge. But, with Napoleon consolidating his authority by becoming Consul for life, others in the Hofburg grudgingly admired their former enemy's initiative: the Habsburg lands needed a similar autocratic revolution from above, they argued.

No one was so well placed to impose change as Archduke Charles. He was popular as a soldier who did not lose battles but favoured peace, and since January 1801 he had been president of the Supreme Council of War (*Hofkriegsrat*), an executive body dating back to the early seventeenth century. Emperor Francis accepted proposals from his brother for centralising political administration and establishing responsible departmental ministers. When Sir Arthur Paget arrived as ambassador in the autumn of 1801 he reported back to London: 'The Archduke may certainly be considered at this moment as the leading man in this empire.'[9] Perhaps so; but 'at this moment' was the key phrase of Paget's assessment. For Colloredo and Cobenzl, long experienced in statecraft, found little difficulty in upstaging the leading man. He was able to play out his role as Minister of War and Marine: military administration was improved; and army training moved away from the parade-grounds to field exercises in open country; even at Laxenburg a tented 'camp of instruction' went up on the broad plain beside the road to Hungary; 'I saw companies of Grenadiers marching in the clearings ... around the old castle,' Louise wrote excitedly to her friend.[10] But Charles could not shape general policy, especially foreign relations. The Archduke favoured appeasement: he wanted a long period of peace before committing his reformed army to new campaigns. By the close of 1804, however, Colloredo, Cobenzl and (reluctantly) Francis were contemplating re-entry into the war which had resumed between Britain and France twenty months ago. The Corsican usurper's mounting ambition posed a challenge to the very existence of the Habsburg realm.

As early as February 1803 Vienna was confronted by an unexpected victory for French diplomacy. Germany's political future, left unresolved at Campo Formio, Lunéville and Rastatt, was settled by German imperial delegates assisted by French mediators. An 'Imperial Recess', first made public in Paris, swept away forty-one historic free cities and sixty-six ecclesiastical principalities; they were replaced by a buffer zone of independent states inclined towards partnership with France but not directly controlled from Paris. Prussia, Bavaria, Baden and Württemberg received territory to compensate for French gains along the Rhine.[11] Emperor Francis's share of the spoils was almost derisory: three small prince-bishoprics on the fringe of the Tyrol. Nor was this his only blow: composition of both the Electoral College of the Reich and the Imperial Diet at Regensburg was modified, giving Protestants a majority for the first time; the election of future emperors from the Habsburg dynasty, or other Catholic families, became unlikely. This rebuff to Austrian authority in Germany was complemented by continued French territorial annexations within the Italian peninsula – notably Piedmont and Elba – and, when the Anglo-French conflict was resumed, by the occupation of the Neapolitan ports of Brindisi, Taranto and Otranto. Too often after Lunéville French diplomacy seemed in Vienna to be no more than a continuation of war by other means.

Some means proved, in the long run, disastrous. In March 1804 the First Consul sent a large raiding party across the Rhine into neutral Baden to seize the Duc d'Enghien, a young Bourbon prince whom the secret police's reports linked to conspiracies seeking to kill Napoleon and throw France into chaos. Enghien was brought to Vincennes where, after a hurried court-martial, he was shot in the moat outside the fortress. Napoleon's assassination had long been an option favoured by émigré royalist conspirators, and the First Consul could – and did – maintain that by insisting on the execution he was giving a salutary warning to plotters in English pay. But the Enghien affair discredited his statecraft; the Corsican had resorted to vendetta politics on a grand scale. In St Petersburg the young Tsar Alexander I, married to a

Badenese princess, was deeply incensed: he broke off diplomatic relations and, before the autumn, his envoy in London was beginning to build up a third grand coalition against France. The Austrian court, though shocked by Enghien's judicial murder and the violation of Badenese territory, made no protest – a clear sign of Francis's commitment to appeasement and his renunciation of responsibility for shielding members of the German Reich who chose to strike bargains of their own with outsiders.[12]

On 18 May 1804, less than two months after the Enghien 'crime', the greatest constitutional innovation of all these decades of political change was heralded in Paris. A legislative decree 'entrusted the government of the republic to an emperor'; and the First Consul was proclaimed 'Emperor of the French ... a hereditary dignity'.[13] In Vienna there was indignation that the Corsican should usurp the dynastic principle at such a time; and there was, too, a certain disillusionment among those people who looked on the Consul as Enlightenment personified. Beethoven struck out the dedication of his third symphony to 'Napoleon Bonaparte'; it would enter musical history as the Eroica instead.[14] By now an aristocrat represented France at the Habsburg court, and the days of tricolour-flying ambassadors were best forgotten: Count de la Rochefoucauld assured anyone who would listen that they could be certain the coming of an empire gave 'the death blow to the Revolutionary Hydra'.[15] The assertion was not entirely convincing, for within five weeks of the decree, the guillotine removed the heads of eight 'royalist' conspirators, the most notorious being Georges Cadoudal. But Cobenzl, not yet ready to risk renewed war, was prepared to be conciliatory. With Colloredo's backing, he sought to strike a bargain: if Austria recognised his new title would Napoleon support the conversion of the German Reich into a hereditary empire under Habsburg rule? Napoleon refused. Vienna accorded him recognition, all the same.

It was left to Francis to manipulate to his advantage, for the penultimate time, the clumsy constitutional machinery of the historic Reich. In August 1804, acting with sovereign authority as Holy Roman Emperor of the German Nation, he issued a Patent granting himself permission to assume a supplementary title; his official style now became 'elected Roman Emperor, hereditary Emperor of Austria, King of Jerusalem, Hungary, etc.' (*erwähalter Römischer Kaiser, Erbkaiser von Oesterreich, König von Jerusalem, Hungarn, usw* ...). Purist pedants from German states within Napoleon's orbit doubted if Francis had any right to use his hallowed form of sovereignty to create an alternative imperial institution. No doubts troubled his conscience:

earlier Habsburgs had made certain that the 'holiness' of the Reich was rooted in pragmatism; and to Francis the Patent was simply a legal safeguard protecting hereditary lands. Carping critics closer to hand need not fear he would seek another coronation: far too expensive, and far too much fuss, for his liking. 'As usual, there is to be no ceremonial on my arrival,' was a frequent directive to members of the Household planning their emperor's official itinerary.[16]

For Francis remained very much a family man. He was deeply worried because his pregnant wife had been startled by an escaped orang-utang while walking in the gardens at Schönbrunn that spring; and his fears were sadly confirmed when, on 6 June, poor Marie Thérèse gave birth to a hideously disfigured girl. Letters from his eldest daughter out at Laxenburg brought happier news of a simple lifestyle. 'Dear Papa' was told of the 'very beautiful green, gold and blue reptile' Louise had seen, and of the 'white and grey field-mouse' that would eat out of her hand; and she begged to know when next Papa would come to see her, as she wanted to have 'the honour' (*die Ehre*) of giving him 'really lovely turnips from my garden'. Rarely can the growing of vegetables have brought a child such pleasure as in this summer of 1804 to the twelve-year-old Archduchess. 'I have in my garden French beans (the green runners are finished), peas, cucumbers, cabbages and lettuce, all of them coming on fine,' Louise's Sunday letter informed her father on 15 July. 'Later I shall grow spinach, so that when it is ripe I can serve it to my dear Papa.'[17]

In Paris on that same Sunday Emperor Napoleon and Empress Josephine were making their first carriage drive in sovereign state through the heart of the city: they went from the Tuileries over the Seine to Notre Dame to hear Pontifical High Mass with a *Te Deum*. In the afternoon the Emperor courted cheers again, up in the saddle to ride to the Invalides for a solemn oath-taking by members of the Legion of Honour. For, while Emperor Francis wished always to avoid ceremony, Napoleon had revelled in public display ever since his first victorious entry into Milan; his only concern was a fear that unsuitable robes or inappropriate ritual would make him look ridiculous. Even when in August he visited the army encamped at Boulogne, waiting to assault the Channel coast of England, Napoleon insisted on spectacular reviews. And throughout the autumn he spent much time perfecting the imperial window-dressing before giving concentrated thought to the solemnities of coronation. A commission considered insignia for the new Empire: an eagle was chosen, purposefully single-headed, unlike the Janus-bird of Habsburg heraldry which indeterminately looked both ways; the crown was to be distinctive in form, like

Charlemagne's original circlet, suggesting a golden laurel wreath bestowed on a triumphant soldier. Pre-Bourbon practices should be revived, to emphasise a link with traditions of greater antiquity than the *ancien régime*. In September, Napoleon travelled to Aachen and ordered Charlemagne's sceptre and sword to be sent to Paris. More sensationally, he insisted that the Pope, whose sovereign lands were at the mercy of his armies, should come from Rome. The pontiff was expected to anoint Emperor and Empress, to intercede for divine protection on their lives, and to bestow a blessing upon the coronation.[18]

On Sunday, 2 December 1804, Pius VII officiated at the three-hour ceremony in Notre Dame. He did not, however, reverently place the circlet on a kneeling Emperor's brow, as had Pope Leo III at Charlemagne's coronation 1,004 years back in time. Napoleon took the crown from Pope Pius's hands and, turning towards the congregation, held it aloft before lowering it slowly to encircle his head. He then crowned Josephine 'Empress of the French', as she knelt before him, with 'tears she could not repress' falling 'on her clasped hands'.[19]

Tears of pride? Tears of remorse? Tears of relief? All three, perhaps. For while for Napoleon the coronation was a day of exultant splendour, to Josephine it had brought an hour of triumph. Earlier in the year worry over her future fate made her lose weight. The proclamation of the Empire had alarmed her: she was acutely vexed by her failure to give Napoleon the son he desired; and she feared for her marital status in a hereditary Empire without an heir. The Senate assigned the Emperor a right of 'adoptive succession'; should Napoleon not adopt a successor, the line would pass to his elder brother Joseph and his male offspring if any (he and Julie only had two daughters) and then to brother Louis, who was married to Hortense de Beauharnais, with two sons. It was clear that Napoleon looked on these arrangements as unsatisfactory and likely to feed jealously and intrigue. Ought he to end his marriage to Josephine, find a suitable bride, and hope for a male heir? A divorce seemed likely at times that year: husband and wife knew each was unfaithful to the other; and many at court overheard angry outbursts from the private apartments. Yet, though never 'blindly in love', Napoleon was fond of Josephine and of his stepchildren. In their public behaviour and bearing they showed a patient dignity in striking contrast to the jealous petulance with which his sisters scaled the ladder of snobbery. By the beginning of November he was resolved that Josephine 'has a right to share my grandeur';[20] Pius VII was on his way from Rome to crown them both, he told her. It was Josephine who, on the eve of the coronation, confessed to the Pope that, because of the revolutionary upheaval, their marriage was only a civil union. His Holiness insisted that such irregularity must be corrected at once. And on that Saturday evening, secretly within the Tuileries, they were canonically married by Cardinal Fesch, Napoleon's mother's half-brother.[21] Papal misgivings were satisfied and Josephine, as she believed, secure from divorce, with a wedding certificate signed by the Cardinal. Unlike the earlier ceremony at the *mairie* of the 2nd arrondissement, there were on this occasion no witnesses. That omission cast no shadow over the next day's solemnities. It was to matter five years later.

5

1805, Milan to Austerlitz

Austrian envoys who had witnessed the two imperial coronations at Frankfurt scoffed at much of the improvised ceremonial in Notre Dame, especially the crowning of an Empress. Napoleon's sisters, ordered by their brother to be train-bearers in Josephine's procession, provided scope for ridicule: 'One sister sulked, another held smelling salts under her nose and a third let the mantle drop; and this made things worse because it then had to be picked up.'[1] The scornful reporting was however a sign, not only of misogynous indignation, but of apprehension at the scale of Napoleon's vaulting ambition. For 'the Corsican', having travelled to Aachen in September and stood reverently before Charlemagne's tomb, was engaged in 'correcting' a myth fundamental to a thousand years of Europe's history. His subjects and France's neighbours, too, were reminded that Charles the Great did not create an empire specifically 'of the German Nation'. Though Aachen became his final choice for a capital city, as sovereign ruler of the Franks, Charlemagne was in a sense the first 'Emperor of the French'. For most of his reign his word was law, not only along both banks of the river Rhine, but south of the Alps as well.

In the early summer of 1805 this Lombard connection provided a welcome Carolingian precedent for a further display of neo-imperial pageantry. Napoleon's second coronation, as *Rex totius Italiae* ('King of all Italy') in Milan cathedral on 26 May was intended to sanctify the conquests made by Republican armies in the previous decade. The 'Iron Crown', worn by Charlemagne and even earlier by the Lombard kings whom the Franks defeated, was fetched from Monza, where it had been revered as a sacred relic for almost 800 years. Coronation ritual closely followed the pattern prescribed for Notre Dame six months previously. On this occasion, however, there would be no crowning of a queen, and Napoleon felt no need to insist on the Pope's presence: he was content for Cardinal Caprara, Archbishop of Milan and papal legate, to officiate and bestow a blessing on the new order south of the Alps. But, once again, Napoleon crowned himself. 'God gives it to me; woe to him who touches it,' the new King proclaimed in Italian as he placed the Iron Crown of Lombardy on his head.[2] Beside Napoleon stood his stepson, Eugène de Beauharnais, who a few days later was to become Viceroy of Italy.

Napoleon's actions puzzled Cobenzl and Colloredo. There was no doubt that a union of France and Italy ran counter to assurances which had been incorporated in the Treaty of Lunéville. They found Napoleon's claim that the coronation safeguarded Italy's separate identity disingenuous. What purpose lay behind all this pageantry and bombast? Did he simply wish to consolidate his gains, giving Eugène an opportunity to impose an orderly system of stable government on northern Italy? Or was the satrapy to serve as a springboard for further advances, eastwards and southwards, securing for France a commercial dominance over the eastern Mediterranean and the trade routes of 'the Orient'? That seemed a likely policy when in early June the Ligurian Republic became part of the French Empire and gave Paris direct control over Genoa's merchant fleet. The Austrians were puzzled, too, by one of Napoleon's first actions after his arrival in Italy: on 5 May he revisited Marengo and inspected more than 30,000 troops drawn up on the old battlefield. This was a larger force than the army which brought him victory there four years previously, and it was not simply a reunion of veterans. Was the troop concentration a genuine threat or merely a warning of his continued strength in the peninsula? It seemed unlikely Napoleon would embark on a new campaign in the familiar theatre of war. His crack regiments were still 600 miles away, encamped on the cliffs and downland behind Ambleteuse and Wimereux and ready to invade England if Admiral Villeneuve could bring a fleet up Channel to protect their crossing. By early August 1805 Napoleon was with his troops again at Boulogne, as in the previous summer. On the first Sunday of the month he inspected 112,000 infantrymen drawn up in a single line along the shore south of Cape Gris-Nez; among them was a specifically Italian division.

In Vienna a war party, increasingly impatient with the appeasers, was eager to strike at this moment when French resources were concentrated so heavily in the west. Archduke Charles still sought at least one more year of non-belligerency before committing his reformed army to battle. But such caution was unpopular. In favour was General Mack, the Lutheran ex-ranker who had served as Charles's chief of staff in 1794 and was now Quartermaster General. Mack too backed army reform but, unlike the Archduke, was always willing to expound a forward-looking and opportunist grand strategy to Francis's councillors in the capital. Cobenzl was impressed 'What a difference one man can make in affairs when he is capable and understands his business,' he noted admiringly.[3] The Foreign Minister strengthened Austria's links with the Russians and, through them, with Pitt in London, the paymaster of any new coalition. Ambitious projects were floated at council tables in Vienna itself and out at Hetzendorf, the imperial hunting lodge two miles beyond Schönbrunn. There was talk of a grand alliance of Sweden, Russia, Prussia, Austria, Great Britain and Naples which would encircle and destroy the French Empire.

Emperor Francis was slow to accept the inevitability of a fresh conflict in central and southern Europe. During Napoleon's protracted coronation festivities at Milan, he had visited the garrison cities of Bohemia, largely as a matter of routine. There was, as yet, little thought of war in the imperial household. 'God be praised that you arrived safely and well in Prague,' wrote his 'loving wife and friend' Marie Thérèse from Vienna on 2 June. 'Full of confidence in your goodness, I pray you have a dress made for me in Prague according to your own taste, and also a cap or hat, just to see what the style may be. I send you my measurement so that it may fit.' And she added, 'All the children kiss your hands.'[4] But the mood changed in the second half of July after the arrival of General Wintzingerode in the capital from St Petersburg, bringing news of the Tsar's war plans and of his pending visit to Berlin, where he was confident of adding Prussia's military strength to their joint cause. Countess Colloredo assured Marie Louise that soon the allied armies in Germany would outnumber the French by three to one. The Archduchess was by now old enough to be excited at the prospect of a war in which she never doubted that her father and her uncles would be victorious. In August she sat proudly facing 'dear Papa' in an open carriage as he acknowledged the cheers of patriotic onlookers along the route into the city from Schönbrunn.[5] The broad-sheets had made it known that, in the coming campaign, their Emperor was expecting to assume supreme command in the field.

This report over-simplified complex arrangements. Apart from four days in Bavaria at the end of September, Emperor Francis was content to exercise supreme command from Vienna where he was prepared to await the Russian commander-in-chief, Tsar Alexander, whom he would then accompany to field headquarters. Meanwhile Francis appointed his cousin, Archduke Ferdinand d'Este, as nominal head of the army in Germany, with Mack in attendance as his personal representative. Archduke Charles was sent to command in northern Italy (where Napoleon had entrusted the Army of Italy to Marshal Masséna) and Archduke John to the Tyrol. Napoleon would take sixty-nine days to bring his army 500 miles from the Channel to the upper Danube in Bavaria, Mack confidently predicted; he told a council of war that the Russians would be there to support their Austrian ally in sixty-four days; a cautious Emperor thought it safe to order a pre-emptive invasion of Bavaria.[6]

War came on 8 September, when Archduke Ferdinand and Mack crossed the river Inn at Braunau and marched on Munich. The Bavarians, who were technically required to support the Holy Roman Emperor but had secretly struck their own bargain with Napoleon, offered little opposition. Within four days General Mack was riding into the Bavarian capital well satisfied. But the satisfaction was short-lived. The estimates on which Mack had based his plans proved hopelessly wrong. The main body of the *Grande Armée* – as Napoleon's superbly trained troops were justifiably called for the first time – slipped away from Boulogne on 27–28 August, strict censorship keeping the army's departure and subsequent movements secret over the next month. As late as 23 September Napoleon was known to be in Paris, present at a meeting of the Senate. What was *not* known was that at four o'clock next morning his carriage set out from St Cloud for Strasbourg and the war zone in Germany. To Mack's consternation, on 7 October he discovered that Napoleon and his *Grande Armée* were facing him on the upper Danube, less than six weeks after leaving the Channel coast rather than the ten weeks he had anticipated.[7] And as yet there was no sign of the advance guard of 38,000 Russians whom General Kutuzov was reportedly bringing westwards to Bavaria. It was to be 20 October before Kutuzov at last crossed the river Inn, more than 150 miles away and a full ten days behind schedule.

They were ten vital days. For on 20 October General Mack, out-manoeuvred and cut off in Ulm, surrendered personally to Napoleon; no less than 23,500 men and eighty guns passed into French hands next morning, the worst disaster to Austrian arms in more than a century. Archduke Ferdinand, with a small cavalry force, had escaped encirclement and fell back towards Bohemia, where there was a substantial army in reserve. Archduke Charles was in Italy, far to the south, and able at the end of the month to hold off three days of desperate attacks by Masséna at Caldiero. But after Ulm only Kutuzov and his weary and bedraggled Russian corps, together with 18,000

Austrians from various formations, were in any position to check the French advance down the Danube. Napoleon sent the wretched Mack to Vienna under parole to inform Francis and his councillors of the capitulation; a brief letter urged Francis to make peace speedily and save the Danube valley from the ravages of war.[8] Talleyrand, who slowly followed the *Grande Armée* eastwards, favoured the imposition of punitive territorial losses and the creation of a German buffer zone of enlarged French client states (Bavaria, Württemberg, Baden). But above all, he sought a 'reversal of alliances', a fresh alignment by which Austria would look eastwards down the Danube in an anti-Russian partnership with France. Napoleon, however, ruled out any long-term commitment against Russia: he would be content to see the Tsar's armies back behind the frontier and out of *his* Europe. He was ready to talk peace with the Austrians, but meanwhile Marshal Lannes' infantry and Marshal Murat's cavalry were to search for the elusive Kutuzov in a rolling, wooded countryside where already, in this first week of November, the valleys were under a foot of snow. On 5 November they caught Kutuzov at Amstetten, ninety miles west of Vienna, but the old fox slipped away downstream to Krems, where there was a bridge to defend over the Danube. Ominously Krems was only forty miles from Vienna.[9]

'You can have no idea of the consternation which prevails here,' Sir Arthur Paget, Britain's ambassador, wrote home to his mother on Sunday, 3 November. 'I don't know which is most feared, the arrival of the Russians, or their retreat, or that of the French. Everybody who possesses or can hire a horse is moving off.'[10] On Monday morning Emperor Francis summoned a council of war. Three decisions were taken: General Gyulai, a Hungarian count who was present at the council, would set out for Napoleon's headquarters with a conciliatory message from the Emperor; the capital was to be evacuated, with its garrison crossing the Danube; and, once established in open land on the edge of Marchfeld, the troops would link up with Kutuzov's force and deny the invaders entry to the city.[11]

In what seemed an exciting adventure, Marie Louise and the eldest children were hustled out of Vienna on that same day, 4 November. With their personal attendants, they headed east to Hungary in a succession of 'berlins', heavy carriages drawn by six-horse teams; they would not see their parents again until the new year. By Thursday night – when Louise was in Buda – Francis, Marie Thérèse and the youngest children had left Vienna, crossing the Danube and its water meadows and taking the road to Moravia. Few people realised that the imperial family had gone; it was no time to stop and stand and stare at passing carriages. 'There is a considerable degree of discontent here, which has not diminished by the departure of the Emperor having taken place without any notice of it having been given to the Public,' Sir Arthur Paget wrote to his mother on 8 November, as he prepared to set out northwards himself.[12]

On that Friday, some 110 miles away in Linz, Napoleon too was writing a letter, one for Count Gyulai to take back to his imperial master, wherever his court might be. It was a mischievous reply, urging Francis to break with Russia – for whom 'this is a war of make-believe' (*une guerre de fantaisie*) – and 'conclude an armistice immediately'; 'all possible differences between us could be settled by our ministers in five minutes'; indeed, Francis was assured, 'it is a matter of genuine preference and deliberate choice on my part to contribute to the happiness of your subjects and yourself, so long as this is consistent with my duty towards my own peoples' welfare'.[13] Francis, to whom Gyulai reported at Znaim on the following Sunday, was not tempted by Napoleon's fair words: to propose an immediate armistice was a sign of weakness, it was thought, a wish to pull back before the Austrians were joined by the main Russian army, and possibly by the Prussians, too. Gyulai was ordered to return to Napoleon and keep him talking, while Tsar Alexander was on his way southwards to Olmütz from wooing the Prussians in Berlin: final peace must be dictated by the allies from a position of overwhelming strength.

By Wednesday morning (13 November) Count Gyulai was once more at French headquarters, by now in the abbey at St Polten. But there was no time for prolonged parleying. For Napoleon was soon on the move eastwards: a courier brought news that Murat's cavalry patrols were at the outskirts of Vienna, only thirty-eight miles from St Polten. Napoleon's carriage had covered some thirty of these miles and it was already dark when, in the village of Purkersdorf, he learnt that the Austrian capital was in French hands, with the vital Tabor causeway and bridge across the Danube intact.[14] Later he was to hear how Murat and Lannes tricked the Szekler Hussar pickets guarding the wooden bridge into believing an armistice had been agreed and it would be wrong to fire the straw and gunpowder fuses already in position. Purkersdorf is only five miles from Schönbrunn, and that night Napoleon was able to sleep in the finest of Habsburg palaces. He allowed himself a moment of triumph next morning; in full dress uniform and with his generals riding on horseback behind him, the Emperor of the French became the first foreign ruler to occupy Vienna in 300 years. It was just ten weeks since he had turned his back on the English Channel.

There was some cheering as the military procession came through the Kärtnertor into the heart of the city. Most Viennese seemed to welcome the invaders, probably because the irreconcilable émigrés and hardened Francophobes had hurried away to Hungary or Moravia – and at least the newcomers were not Russian.[15] Social life continued with little change: the Theater an der Wien presented the première of *Fidelio* on 20 November, as planned, with Beethoven himself conducting the orchestra. It was exactly a week since Murat deceived the guards on the Danube bridge, and French officers had bought many of the seats; but the theme of the opera was out of keeping with the mood of the hour and it was poorly received, closing after performances on the Thursday and Friday evenings.[16] Napoleon, though a lover of opera, was not present: he had spent only three nights at Schönbrunn and was by then in Brno, the capital of Moravia. Although gratified by his reception in Vienna, he could not afford to linger there, with a formidable army gathering less than a hundred miles to his north and Archduke Charles's troops ten marching days away to the south. For the moment, the best consequence of entering his enemy's capital was narrowly material. At Braunau and at Linz the French had already captured many guns and much ammunition but these gains were small in comparison with the yield from the Vienna arsenal: there the *Grande Armée* was replenished by a haul of 2,000 cannon and no less than 100,000 muskets.[17]

During one of Gyulai's visits to French headquarters – probably at Linz – the Count remarked to a court chamberlain that he could not understand why the Emperor of the French did not divorce his Empress and marry the daughter of his own imperial master, as the Habsburg women were so fecund. The chamberlain, Théodore de Thiard, says that he passed Guylai's observation on to Napoleon: 'That would never do,' came the prompt reply. 'Archduchesses have always been disastrous for France. The name "Austrian" has always been distasteful and Marie Antoinette did nothing to dispel the antipathy. The memory of her is too recent.'[18] At first glance the whole conversation, as recorded in Thiard's memoirs, seems improbable: on the day she was hurried out of the Hofburg and into the coach for Hungary, Marie Louise was still five weeks short of her fourteenth birthday. Yet this matter of age adds verisimilitude to the episode; for poor Marie Antoinette had been only fourteen and a half when she left Austria for Versailles, as Gyulai may well have remembered. The difference between the situations of great-aunt and niece is that, while Antoinette was groomed by her mother for marriage to an heir-apparent, Louise remained a child in looks and thoughts and deeds. The experience of the ensuing weeks was to bring Louise to the borders of maturity, but not across them.

The imperial children's evacuation from Vienna had started with a slow journey of 150 miles along muddy roads on which rain or sleet fell hour after hour. A night at one of the smaller Esterhazy estates was followed by several days in the palace at Buda. But when police reports suggested French agents were formenting rebellion in Hungary, it was decided to send the children northwards into Galicia. Travel became even harder, with snow blocking the roads on the high ground around Miskolcz: overnight stops were made at wayside taverns ill-suited for 'families of distinction' at any time, least of all in an extremely cold winter. Louise, a dutiful letter-writer, reported regularly to her mother: one evening there was an insect hunt in an infested bedroom, with Louse claiming that she had swatted the largest bug of all, whom she dubbed 'Napoleon'. Writing on 21 November from Kosice – she knew the town as Kaschau, the Hungarians as Kassa – Louise reflected how angry the Almighty must be when, looking down from Heaven, he saw the French 'in our rooms at Schönbrunn'; she commented on 'the truly wretched fate' that has 'befallen our family', so scattered that 'my beloved parents are in Olmütz, we are in Kaschau' and 'a third group is gathered in Buda'. Already she had travelled 300 miles from Vienna. Soon the children were on their way again, over even worse roads, to Lemberg (Lvov), 125 miles to the north.[19]

The discomforts of travel were heightened for the children by disputes among their acting guardians. From the first days of the journey there was friction between Countess Colloredo and Baron Stefaneo, who was the *ajo* of the heir-apparent, the twelve-year-old Archduke Ferdinand. Count Joseph Esterhazy, who was responsible for the party's safety, supported Stefaneo. From Buda he endorsed complaints sent by the Baron to Emperor Francis – whom, it might be thought, had more pressing concerns on his mind. Yet to put aside family matters ran counter to Francis's nature. Moreover, his partiality for the Colloredos was on the wane. There had been some divergence of policy over the previous months, with the Count warmly supporting the war party at the council table. And Francis was finding his former tutor's presence at court irksome: too often he would offer unsolicited good advice. It is possible that the arrival in Olmütz on 18 November of Tsar Alexander and a young confident circle of advisers made the Polonius-like role of the ageing *Kabinettsminister* stand out more sharply. Whatever the immediate reason, on 28 November a curt message officially announced the withdrawal of Count and Countess Colloredo from the court to their estates. Effectively they were dismissed. No new *Kabinettsminister* was appointed, and there would be no *aja* for Louise. Esterhazy was given overall charge of the children during their absence from Vienna; once peace was restored, the Empress would supervise her daughter's further education under a succession of tutors. When the habitually docile Archduchess threatened rebellion over the supercession of her much loved *aja*, a stiff note from her mother called Louise to order: '*Le premier devoir d'un Enfant est l'obéissance pour ses Parents*' (A child's first duty is to obey its parents).[20] She might, however, write regularly to the Countess and to her daughter Victoria de Poutet, to whom Louise remained devoted.

The Tsar's arrival in Olmütz on 18 November came a week later than Francis anticipated. The delay was not entirely Alexander's fault: heavy snow and a treacherous thaw left many Bohemian roads impassable. But there did seem a lack of urgency about his movements; he had lingered at Weimar, where his sister, the Crown Princess of Saxe-Weimar, arranged for him to meet the literary lions of a supremely cultured court, including Goethe. Time, Alexander thought, was on the side of the allies; he was confident that Napoleon had over-reached himself. The Tsar was pleased by a diplomatic triumph he won in Berlin. King Frederick William III had agreed to a secret treaty stipulating that, if Napoleon rejected mediation, Prussia would within six weeks put an army of 180,000 men into the field, poised to strike westwards, re-open a Rhineland front and threaten France with invasion once more. To seal the pledge Queen Louise led Alexander and her husband down to the crypt at Potsdam where, facing each other across Frederick the Great's wooden coffin, the sovereigns swore an oath binding Russia and Prussia to eternal friendship. Theatrical symbolism always embellished Alexander's concept of diplomacy.[21]

Troop numbers in Moravia mattered more to Emperor Francis than solemn oaths. Kutuzov was already on hand, his weary men supported by the Russian Second Army, newly arrived from Galicia and in good shape. They were joined on 24 November by the crack Russian Imperial Guard. By then there were around Olmütz more than 50,000 Russians and at least 35,000 Austrians. Somewhere to the south, wheeling back north-eastwards through modern Slovenia into Hungary, were the undefeated combined armies of Archdukes Charles and John, 80,000 strong. Intelligence reports suggested that Napoleon had no more than 40,000 troops with him at Brno. It seemed as if every advantage lay with the allies. Only one commander wished to stand on the defensive. Kutuzov was ready to fall back to the Carpathians, tempting Napoleon to stretch lines of communication and supply deeper and deeper across central Europe until they snapped. But Alexander had no patience with the wily old fox. 'The young men around the Emperor referred to him as General Dawdler,' an émigré in the Tsar's service recalled many years later.[22]

To Francis's surprise, Alexander looked to the Austrian chief of staff, General Franz von Weyrother, for strategic guidance. Though Weyrother was reputedly an expert geographer, no one in the Austrian army rated his abilities highly. Nor did two of the ablest Russian generals, Prince Bagration and Miloradovich; for they had met Colonel Weyrother six years back, in Suvorov's campaign, where a route the Colonel confidently marked for them on a map ended abruptly in a precipitous wall of mountain.[23] But in 1805 Weyrother could claim one outstanding advantage: only twelve months previously he had conducted manoeuvres between Brno, the chief city of Moravia, and Olmütz, forty miles to the north-east. He knew, it seemed, every river, lake and fold of hills in the region where the *Grande Armée* awaited destruction. Alexander took the Austrian general at his word. Even Francis, who was by nature far more sceptical than the Tsar, allowed himself to be impressed.

Napoleon had not fought a battle for five and a half years; he spent ten days reconnoitring the countryside around Brno, seeking the right terrain for what he knew must be a decisive engagement.[24] He found his arena to the south-east of the city, in open fields which stretched for five miles along the Pratzen plateau and down to a valley whose ponds and marshes lay coated with deceptively thin ice. The village of Telnitz was in the west while, three miles back from the main valley, stood a cluster of houses around the Kaunitz family château at Austerlitz (now known as Slavkov), some fifteen miles to the east of Brno. Never before had Napoleon planned a battle so meticulously: he personally sited the artillery, as in his early days as a junior officer; but, as a commander of vast experience, he also used every trick of strategy to ensure that the allies attacked where and when he wished. Renewed parleying enabled him to delay action until Davout's III Corps completed their forced march from Vienna, eight-five miles to the south, and brought another 6,000 infantry to cover Telnitz. Napoleon rightly read Weyrother's mind and planned to encourage him to make an outflanking movement by pulling the III Corps back from high ground. He would then order Soult's cavalry to fight their way through the weakened centre and take the allies in the rear.

Remarkably the Russo-Austrian army did precisely as Napoleon intended. Its commanders even chose to fight the battle on 2 December, the first anniversary of his coronation in Paris; nature, too, obliged by concealing Soult's corps under a heavy mist until eight in the morning, when the sun broke through, as it did twelve months before, when the imperial carriage arrived at Notre Dame; Napoleon was always elated by such omens. Although the 'Battle of the Three Emperors' continued until late afternoon, the outcome was never in doubt once the allied centre was breached, as early as half past nine. The Russo-Austrian vanguard was left encircled and isolated as Soult's horsemen fanned out north and south. A desperate and costly cavalry charge led by the Tsar's brother, Grand Duke Constantine, was a brave gesture, but it caused confusion in the Austrian ranks, as the Russian Imperial Guard cut across their line of retreat. Among the allies only Prince Bagration, on the northern sector, withdrew his troops in good order. The Russians, who sustained seventy-three per cent of the battle casualties on that day, were bitterly critical of their Austrian ally. 'I saw the wretched Weyrother wandering from place to place bravely risking his life in an effort to redeem the disaster of which he was one of the chief causes,' recalled the Tsar's Polish confidant and mentor, Prince Czartoryski, in his memoirs many years later.[25]

Emperor Francis watched the unfolding battle in dismay, never asserting himself nor seeking to influence Tsar Alexander, whom he accepted as supreme allied commander. Austrian hussars and an infantry regiment of Szeklers (Magyar-speakers from Transylvania) had suffered heavily in the first assault on French positions around Telnitz. Prince John of Liechtenstein, in command of the Austrian cavalry, ensured that his horsemen fought gallantly in the later stages of the battle but – in the Weyrother tradition – he had misread the map in the morning, ineffectually concentrating the heavy cavalry three miles south of the position assigned to them. As darkness fell – and snow, too – Francis headed southwards to find shelter for the night at Czeitsch, some ten miles away, on the edge of Prince Liechtenstein's vast domain. He had left Marie Thérèse in the episcopal palace at Olmütz; and before heading away from Austerlitz he scribbled a hasty message to her: 'A battle was fought today which did not turn out well,' he wrote, with characteristic understatement. 'I pray you consequently to withdraw from Olmütz to Teschen with everything that belongs to us. I am well.'[26]

Napoleon, too, found time to write home: 'I have defeated the Russian and Austrian armies,' he told Josephine. 'I am a little tired; I have slept out in the open air for eight days and as many nights. Tomorrow I shall rest at the château of the Princes of Kaunitz, where I can be sure of sleeping for two or three hours. The army of the Russians is not only beaten, but destroyed. I embrace you.'[27] The night after the battle he again slept rough, on straw and wrapped in a great coat. Around him, snow-covered on the battlefield and its surrounding slopes, lay some 1,300 French corpses; and at least ten times as many enemy dead.

In the morning Napoleon – as he told his brother Joseph – 'put on a clean shirt for the first time in a week' and confidently awaited a peace envoy.[28] It was Prince Liechtenstein who rode up from Czeitsch with a message from Francis: the 'Emperor of Germany' (as Napoleon called him) did not, as he anticipated, simply seek an armistice; the Prince brought a request from him for a personal interview. It was agreed that the two rulers should discuss affairs next day, somewhere along the border between Moravia and Hungary.

Before Liechtenstein had set out from Czeitsch, Francis and Alexander met for a brief – and, in every sense, icily cold – conversation. All Austro-Russian collaboration was at end; the battle cost the combined armies a third of their effective fighting strength – either killed, wounded or taken prisoner; and the Russians, who were always short of artillery, had lost in a single day 133 guns, more than half their total strength. Pride, however, made the Tsar unwilling to sue for peace, and he still had hopes of help from Prussia: he would break off the campaign and take Russia's armies back through Hungary and into his own empire. Francis, on the other hand, was a realist; he never thought much of the Potsdam oath and had no faith in Prussian promises. After Ulm, the occupation of his capital, and now the disaster at Austerlitz, he saw no sense in continuing the war: the longer it lasted, the worse the peace terms a defeated Austria might expect. It would be better to meet Napoleon, hasten the preparation of a treaty, get the French out of Vienna, and gather the children together again as soon as possible at Schönbrunn or Laxenburg. For, as ever, Francis remained a family man. Regularly throughout this momentous week he received, at his own request, medical bulletins from the court physician, Dr Stift, sometimes twice a day. He was a worried father: some of the young ones had measles.[29]

The Emperor of the French rode south from 'M de Kaunitz's handsome château' early on 4 December to meet the 'Emperor of Germany' near Göding, a town sixty-five miles north-east of Vienna. There was an old castle at Göding, but Napoleon preferred somewhere hidden from prying eyes; he greeted Francis beneath a burnt-out windmill near Zavorice, a staging-post on the road to Breslau. 'Such are the palaces which Your Majesty has obliged me to inhabit for these three months,' he remarked, almost apologetically. 'Your stay in them makes you so vigorous that you have no right to be angry with me for it,' Francis replied wryly. Napoleon was accompanied by two Marshals, Soult and the one-time 'citizen ambassador', Bernadotte.

But the discussion was solely between the two sovereigns. They talked 'from two till four p.m.', so Napoleon reported to Talleyrand that evening. 'He wished to make peace on the spot. He appealed to my feelings; I defended myself, a type of warfare which, I can assure you, was not difficult. He asked for an armistice, which I conceded.'[30] Francis was philosophical over this humiliating first meeting with Austria's long-term adversary: 'With Buonaparte [*sic*] himself I was quite content, in so far as I could be with a victor who has a large portion of my monarchy in his hands,' Francis told Marie Thérèse.[31] He was left in no doubt that this time, unlike Campo Formio and Lunéville, the terms of peace would prove hard to bear. Yet if he let the armistice lapse and lost a new campaign, Francis feared they would be even harsher, possibly including the total dissolution of the Habsburg Empire. But he was prepared to await the coming of his brothers Charles and John before finally committing himself to peace.

Napoleon was convinced the fighting was over. He returned to the Kaunitz comforts of Austerlitz for three nights, told his officers 'we are going home', and instructed Talleyrand to settle matters with the other German states before finally imposing terms on Austria. Treaties with Württemberg and Bavaria raised their status to kingdoms; in return for military alliances 'within a German confederation' they were promised territorial gains, largely at Austria's expense. Baden received similar treatment, though as a grand duchy rather than a kingdom. After returning to Schönbrunn, Napoleon concluded an alliance with an envoy from Berlin, originally sent by Frederick William before the battle to secure peace through mediation. In return for frontier adjustments around Cleves, Neuchâtel and Ansbach and a complete break with 'England', Prussia was given a coveted prize, the French-occupied electorate of Hanover. Ironically, this treaty with Prussia was signed on 15 December, the day by which the King had assured Alexander at Potsdam that his army would be in the field fighting the common enemy. The Tsar learnt of Prussia's change of front as his carriage crossed the Polish plains heading for St Petersburg – where, as yet, people knew nothing of the terrible battle. 'Everything I have tried to do has gone disastrously against me,' Alexander remarked, as he turned Russia's back on Europe.[32]

Marie Louise heard the news of Austerlitz at Skotschau in Silesia, where Esterhazy had brought his imperial charges to give them greater protection from marauding Cossack horsemen farther to the east. She was following military events more closely than when the children first left Vienna: 'Archduke Charles and Archduke John must now be at Raab (Györ) with an army of 70,000 men,' she wrote to her mother on 10 December. 'We may trust in the good God soon to prosper our cause'; she was sure that the family would soon be reunited and their 'time of suffering' at an end.[33] One assumption was correct: Louise's uncles had, indeed, reached Györ with a powerful army. But if she believed the army would avenge Austerlitz, she was mistaken; Austria's last cohesive military force could not be squandered in a hopeless campaign. 'The Monarchy is shaken to its foundations,' Archduke Charles warned Francis on 22 December. As yet the people held their sovereign in high regard: soon, however, they would 'demand explanations for the economic ruin, the sacrifices of blood, and the ghastly consequences of this war'. Immediate peace was therefore essential, to be followed by a 'clean sweep of all the obscure quacks gathered around the Monarchy's deathbed'; younger and more energetic men were needed at the head of affairs.[34] The Archduke was aged thirty-four. Francis was impressed. As after Hohenlinden and Lunéville he was glad to turn to his brother for support. Four days later Ludwig Cobenzl, one of Charles's principal critics in the last three years, followed Colloredo to enforced retirement.

While the Austrian imperial family remained scattered in distant places of sanctuary, Napoleon was able to spend Christmas at Schönbrunn. On 26 December he rode across to Laxenburg, where he inspected an infantry division which had borne the brunt of the first allied attack at Austerlitz; it was the only visit he made to Louise's favourite childhood home. Forty miles away, at Pressburg (Bratislava), the last details were being settled of a treaty of peace, which Emperor Francis reluctantly signed early next day. Napoleon was recognised as King of Italy, the puppet kingdom receiving all the Venetian lands given to Austria in recent settlements, including Istria and Dalmatia. To Bavaria were ceded the Tyrol and Vorarlberg. The new kingdoms and grand duchy in Germany received recognition and were given Habsburg enclaves. A war indemnity of 40 million francs would be paid to France, even though Austria was close to state bankruptcy. To sweeten the bitterness of these terms, Francis gained Salzburg and Berchtesgaden. This was small consolation. By the Peace of Pressburg the Habsburgs, already virtually expelled from Italy, were given notice to quit Germany, too.[35]

The French were almost ready to set out on that homeward journey promised three weeks ago. But not quite: a proclamation in Napoleon's name thanked the people of Vienna for their restraint and good sense during the weeks of occupation; and there remained one Habsburg whom Napoleon wished to meet. On 27 December he crossed the Danube again and rode some four miles out to a secluded schloss for a long conversation with Archduke Charles.[36] They talked, it seems, of military matters, but the Archduke's political enemies maintained that Napoleon took pains to feed his dynastic ambitions, seeing in him a soldier of character, not unsympathetic to his own style of government. There is no evidence that Charles was tempted to respond to any blandishments. But the two men continued to hold each other in mutual respect over the following years.

Napoleon left Schönbrunn on the day after his meeting with the Archduke, travelling by way of Melk and Passau to see in the year 1806 at Munich. There he was joined by the Empress Josephine and, in record time, successfully carried through his first venture in dynastic diplomacy: Bavaria would be bound even more closely to imperial France by the marriage of his stepson, Viceroy Eugène, to Auguste, King Maximilian Joseph's eldest daughter, a princess of rare beauty. Munich went *en fête* for the civil ceremony on 13 January, which was also the eve of the religious wedding.[37]

In Vienna on that Monday a quieter domestic celebration was reported by the *Wiener Zeitung*.[38] Without fuss or acclamation Emperor Francis had returned to his capital; Schönbrunn housed a reunited imperial family. So, after a winter circuit of over 800 miles, Marie Louise was home again, toughened physically and mentally by ten weeks of discomfort and uncertainty. Her letters show a changed perception of Napoleon. Before the flight to Hungary, 'the Corsican' had been a distant menace, the bogeyman of other people's tales of villainy. Now his presence 'in *our* rooms' gave a personal depth to the intensity of her loathing. How terrible for 'dear Papa' to have been obliged to seek a meeting with the Ogre after Austerlitz! Yet the pious Louise remained confident that vengeance was at hand. Surely the Almighty in His wisdom must soon strike down so presumptuous a usurper?[39]

6

Almost a Kaunitz

Austerlitz was celebrated in Paris as a victory without precedent in French history. The new Caesar turned to classical Rome for inspiration: on 26 February 1806 an imperial decree ordered the erection east of the Louvre of the Arc d'Austerlitz – that delightful architectural gem, modelled on the arches of Constantine and Septimius Severus, now known as the Arc du Carrousel. Two miles to the east, astride the levelled hilltop of Chaillot, work began on an even greater Arc de Triomphe, fifty metres high and forty-five metres wide. The Senate, too, paid the Emperor a classical tribute, authorising a replacement for the statue of Louis XIV in the Place Vendôme, felled during the revolution: a Trajan-style column, surmounted by Napoleon dressed as Caesar, would be covered by spirals of battle scenes on bronze plaques made from melted down cannon captured during the campaign. Of more immediate practical value than these enduring monuments was an Industrial Exhibition of Victory, intended by Napoleon to stimulate the French economy, which was in deep recession. The exhibition was not ready to open until late September, and by then the *Grande Armée* was once more on the march, against Prussia in the first instance. News of fresh victories, at Jena and at Auerstadt, reached Paris while the 1,422 exhibitors were still basking profitably in the afterglow of last year's campaign. On this occasion, however, the rousing 'Bulletins of the Army' evoked much less enthusiasm. For the great desire throughout France in this autumn of 1806 was to celebrate a *lasting* peace. With Prussia refusing to seek an armistice and with Britain and Russia still active combatants, that prospect seemed as remote as ever.

Austria, of course, had gone out of the war by the Treaty of Pressburg and exercised little influence on events over the following two years.

In July 1806 Napoleon set up the Confederation of the Rhine, a league of sixteen German states under French protection, and including the kingdoms of Bavaria and Württemberg. Francis recognised that the new creation extinguished the Holy Roman Empire, and he was prepared to abdicate immediately as its fifty-fourth elected sovereign. But Philipp Stadion, Cobenzl's successor as Foreign Minister, feared that if the Habsburgs laid aside the imperial crown, Napoleon would claim it for the Bonapartes. Accordingly, on 6 August 1806, in his last act as ruler of the Reich, Francis II formally declared the Holy Roman Empire of the German Nation dissolved and abandoned his elected title; he remained 'Francis I, hereditary Emperor of Austria', the style he had assumed two years previously.[1] The change made no difference to the rank of his children; they remained archdukes or archduchesses. But it was a decisive break with the past. Twenty Habsburgs had ruled the old Reich: only four were to rule 'Austria'.

'It is time that Austria left me at peace and stayed at home,' Napoleon observed to Berthier, his chief of staff, early in the year. That sentiment was at first the inclination of court circles in Vienna, too. At Pressburg Emperor Francis had signed away more than 3,000,000 of his subjects and he had no intention of risking the loss of more peoples and more lands by giving reckless support to a war of revenge. He suspected that Napoleon had on hand an alternative candidate for his Austrian throne, should he suffer another defeat: his eldest brother, Ferdinand, host to General Bonaparte at Florence ten years previously, was now Grand Duke of Würzburg and, from September 1806, a loyal co-operative member of the Confederation of the Rhine. Although Stadion – a Swabian émigré, not 'Austrian' by birth – remained consistently hostile to Napoleon, Francis was inclined to follow the advice of Archduke Charles and seek an understanding with the French, perhaps even an alliance. In Paris, Talleyrand never ceased to advocate reconciliation and in the spring of 1806 he seemed to convert Napoleon to his views. Both men agreed it was essential to have an intelligent and accommodating ambassador who would represent Austria in Paris; 'Find out if there is not a Kaunitz to be sent here,' Napoleon instructed Talleyrand on 26 March.[2]

It is unlikely that the Emperor meant, literally, a man bearing the name of Kaunitz. Most probably his recent occupation of the family château at Austerlitz had reminded him of the diplomatic revolution of 1756–7, when the illustrious Chancellor converted Austria into a partner rather than a foe; and he was asking his Foreign Minister to find an ambassador in the Kaunitz tradition. But curious confusion arose. For on 28 March Englebert von Floret, the Belgian-born Austrian *chargé d'affaires*, reported to Stadion that he had discussed the ambasadorial appointment with Talleyrand: Napoleon, he said, would like to see a Liechtenstein, a Schwarzenberg or a Kaunitz in Paris.[3]

Stadion was nonplussed. The Princes Liechtenstein and Schwarzenberg were great landed magnates, soldiers with no wish to leave their estates and become cap-in-hand envoys to a self-made Emperor who had so recently humiliated their army. Count Alois von Kaunitz, a grandson of the great Chancellor, was serving as minister in Naples, but he was too young and inexperienced for Paris. Instead of these nominees, Stadion preferred a diplomat with a different surname but the closest of links to the Kaunitz family: Clement von Metternich had a creditable record as Francis's envoy to the courts of Dresden and Berlin; more cogently, he had married – at Austerlitz village church – Kaunitz's granddaughter, Eleonore. In June 1806 Napoleon agreed to accept Metternich as ambassador, though he did not reach Paris until August, a few days before Francis dissolved the old Empire. It proved a momentous appointment – not least for the young Archduchess to whom it is unlikely the ambassador had ever spoken. Over the next decade Metternich, more than any other individual, would shape Marie Louise's world and manipulate her future.

Though it was thirteen years since Metternich escorted Louise of Prussia to open the coronation ball at Frankfurt, he remained in appearance a youthful thirty-three years old: 'not lacking in wit', wrote an even younger Russian diplomat that spring, 'when he wishes, agreeable enough; good-looking, almost always in love'.[4] His father, bumbling and boring Francis George, and his mother, Beatrice, were still alive and active in the Habsburg capital. Not that Viennese society ever took such a palpably ambitious family of expatriate Rhinelanders to heart; father and son were cold-shouldered by the great families until in 1795 Beatrice's cultivation of past connections brought off the coup of Clement's marriage to Eleonore von Kaunitz. The Metternichs had lost their villages and vineyards to the French invaders, although they retained Königswart, an estate amid the pine-covered slopes of Bohemia granted to a soldier ancestor early in the Thirty Years War. Stadion, whose German possessions had suffered a similar fate, was more sympathetic to the Metternichs than his predecessors; he would have sent Clement as his own successor in the embassy at St Petersburg had not the strange request for 'a Kaunitz' come from Paris. Metternich himself was full of confidence and eager to pit his skills against the machinations of Napoleon and Talleyrand. 'I have completely outstripped all contemporaries among my colleagues,' he wrote to Eleonore, who was spending the summer in Dresden, with their three children. And to his close confidant, Friedrich von Gentz, Metternich commented on his wish to be at the centre of affairs: Napoleon, he said, was 'the only man in Europe who wills and acts'.[5]

Disillusionment speedily followed; for once the Confederation of the Rhine was established, Napoleon seemed to lose interest in Austria. He 'no longer has any regard for our armed strength', Metternich explained to Stadion on 11 August 1806, after meeting the Emperor for the first time, at St Cloud.[6] Courtesies were exchanged four days later, during the official reception for the diplomatic corps to celebrate Napoleon's thirty-seventh birthday, but twelve months passed before they met again. Napoleon left Paris on 25 September 1806, anticipating a pre-emptive strike by Prussia. He did not return to the capital until the last week of July 1807, having humiliated the Prussians at Jena (14 October 1806), narrowly avoided capture by the Russians in a blizzard at Eylau (8 February 1807) and, four months later, decisively defeated the Russians at Friedland, only sixteen miles farther east. Metternich and Stadion were not displeased at Prussia's downfall. But the consequences of Friedland were totally unexpected. For, after a fortnight of discussions with Tsar Alexander at Tilsit, Napoleon achieved a major reversal of alliances: the rulers of France and Russia made peace and prepared to divide Europe into western and eastern spheres of influence. Prussia might be eliminated; but the loser from the Tilsit alliance system was neutral Austria. Instead of supervising a diplomatic revolution, Metternich was stranded impotently in Paris while the political map of the continent was redrawn a thousand miles away.

Stadion regarded Tilsit as a catastrophe. But not so the ambassador to France; Metternich was far too conceited to admit despondency. The Franco-Russian understanding was artificial, he argued; it could not last long, 'because it depends on the life of one single human being'; the time when Alexander would fall out with Napoleon is 'much nearer than many people suppose'.[7] When the emperors disagreed, each would turn to Vienna for support. And at that moment, Austria would become the arbiter of Europe's future. It was a comforting prognosis; Stadion was glad to respect the opinions of an ambassador who basked in the reflected glory of being almost a Kaunitz.

In his letters to Vienna Metternich gave the impression that, with Napoleon and his marshals away from Paris, he reached the pinnacle of social success, receiving all the proper dignities due to an envoy of the Habsburgs. When Eleonore von Metternich became the first ambassador's wife granted a formal audience with the Empress Josephine, Metternich made certain the court in Vienna appreciated that the ceremonial was identical with the presentation of the wife of Kaunitz's ambassador forty-six years previously. He attached importance to such gestures, as he did, also, to his dress and to the careful grooming of his horses. 'Truly the grand gentleman at his most elegant', one of his mistresses, Laura Junot, recalled in later years.[8]

Inclination and political calculation made Metternich dally with amatory diplomacy. Laura Junot was little more than a capricious flirt, but Metternich treated her as a likely source of valuable information: she had known Napoleon since her childhood and was married to General Andoche Junot, now commanding the Paris garrison. Metternich also conquered Napoleon's youngest sister, Caroline Murat – an easy task for any good-looking man with social grace and ready conversation. From Caroline he was able to inform Vienna that 'the Emperor has a mistress in Warsaw' less than a month after Napoleon's first night with Marie Walewska. He does not seem to have realised that a devouring jealousy of Josephine and the Beauharnais family vitiated Caroline's character, tempting her to see in every passing quarrel of Emperor and Empress the certainty of imminent divorce. The ambassador was told of Napoleon's cold manner towards his wife after he returned from Tilsit; 'they do not even share a bedroom,' Vienna was misinformed. But of greater concern were rumours that marriage to a sister of the Tsar would follow any divorce. Remarriage to an Austrian archduchess seemed out of the question.[9]

But in this summer of 1807 such matters were of little interest to Marie Louise or to her father. Tragedy had plunged the court at Vienna into melancholy. On 6 April Marie Thérèse gave birth prematurely to her thirteenth child, a girl who lived for no more than three days. Although the Empress was only thirty-four, the frequency of these confinements – and the constant resort of her physicians to blood-letting whenever she was feverish – undermined her constitution. She died late in the evening of Sunday, 12 April; for the second time in eighteen years, Emperor Francis lost a wife in childbirth.

Marie Thérèse's death affected Francis profoundly, for husband and wife were the closest of companions. She would write to him daily when they were separated and, expecting an instant reply, was rarely disappointed, though in the dark week which followed Austerlitz, she had felt bound to chide her 'dearest, best husband': 'Today is the fourth letterless day,' she complained. 'Have you entirely forgotten me?'[10] She need not have worried: he was never to forget her. But a longing to be detached from ceremony made him appear insensible. For on the Wednesday after her death he suddenly left Vienna, taking his two eldest children with him to Buda. His brother, Archduke John, was appointed personal representative of the Emperor at the Requiem Mass and the interment of the Empress in the Capuchin crypt. Francis spent three weeks in sad reverie at the palace on Buda hill before resuming his royal duties on 6 May with a journey deeper into Hungary to open a canal at Kalocsa, linking the rivers Danube and Tisza. Unusually, Marie Louise was allowed to accompany her father, travelling eastwards with him to Arad and Temesvár in Transylvania.

Louise, though shocked and saddened by her mother's sudden death, was not grief-stricken. She had seen more of her in the previous fifteen months that in the years when the Colloredos dominated the household, and yet a curious reserve persisted; for Marie Thérèse, the fondest of wives, was the most distant of mothers, ill-at-ease with all her children and especially with an eldest daughter who so openly hero-worshipped her father. The Empress's death raised Louise's status; so long as the Emperor remained a widower, she was by right the first lady in his Empire. As the court was in mourning, her duties were not onerous, but at least she was no longer confined within a schoolroom, insulated from world affairs. Throughout the early summer, Louise scarcely left 'dear Papa's' side, particularly during his protracted Hungarian visit. Once again, as in the ten-week flight from the invading armies, her slow progress towards maturity quickened perceptibly for a few months. She still expressed herself childishly in her letters, and she was still unworldly in judgment on other people – after all, she was not yet sixteen years old – but she developed a dutiful sense of responsibility, which manifested itself in concern for her father's domestic happiness. Improbably, Louise became his go-between and even, to some extent, a matchmaker.

Francis was by nature uxorious; he found it hard to exist without a marriage partner. But his choice of a bride was limited at such a time of upheaval in Germany and Italy. For convenience, and perhaps from habit, he looked to his Habsburg kinsfolk and particularly to those who were clustered in exile around him. Maria Ludovica, the youngest daughter of his uncle, Duke Ferdinand of Modena, was a good-looking brunette, vivacious and strong-minded, a sister of Archduke Ferdinand d'Este, the General who in his first army command shook off his French pursuers after breaking out of Ulm. Their father, forced to leave Italy when the Cisalpine Republic was created, died in Vienna on the previous Christmas Eve, with a malediction against the 'Corsican usurper' on his lips. Their formidable mother – Louise's 'Aunt Beatrix' – was the d'Este heiress whose marriage would have consolidated Modena as a Habsburg family dependency had not Bonaparte's armies intervened. She wanted a good marriage for Maria Ludovica: what better than to become titular Empress of Austria and crowned Queen-consort of Hungary? Ludovica, herself ambitious and self-confident, seems to have been not in the least surprised by kindly, solicitous letters she began to receive from 'Cousin Louise' after the

Emperor's return from Hungary. A discreet meeting in Baden early in December was followed by a visit from Louise, two days after her own sixteenth birthday, with a bouquet of flowers and a huge basket in which were concealed gifts from the Emperor for Ludovica's twentieth birthday, together with a letter of affectionate greeting. Faithfully, Louise sent back to Papa a detailed account of her 'dear cousin's' delight over such a charming gesture. Three weeks later – on the evening of 6 January 1808 – Francis and Ludovica were married in the Augustinerkirche, the fourteenth-century court church outside the Hofburg: Louise, as she duly observed, lost a '*liebe cousine*' and gained a '*liebe Mama*' – just four years older than herself.[11]

Viennese society was ironically surprised at the speed with which the heart-broken Emperor of nine months ago found consolation in a new young wife. Archduke Charles deplored his brother's marriage politically, for the d'Estes were irreconcilably hostile to the French and eager for another chance to topple Napoleon. Already the Archduke had dismissed twenty-five generals, cut administrative red-tape and reduced the expense of the standing army by placing two battalions of each regiment in the reserve; in collaboration with Archduke John he was completing plans for a militia (*Landwehr*) which would augment the regular army in case of invasion. Charles wished to postpone new campaigns until he could be certain his war machine was running smoothly. Stadion, on the other hand, welcomed the mounting d'Este influence at court, for he sympathised with the so-called 'party of action'.[12]

But Stadion was cautious. Reports from Metternich suggested growing uncertainty in Paris over the conduct of affairs. Though Talleyrand had handed over the Foreign Ministry to Champagny in August 1807, he remained a close adviser to Napoleon and he continued to favour partnership with Austria. At the time of Emperor Francis's wedding, Napoleon was discussing, at first with Talleyrand and later with Metternich, ways of satisfying Austria's 'just and geographical claims' in the Danube basin, a step towards the partition of Turkey. No Austrian wished that particular issue raised at this moment – partitioning Poland had proved bad enough – but the proposal made a point of contact. Metternich urged Stadion to play for time; and once again he followed the ambassador's advice.

Two recurrent themes ran through Metternich's letters: the spread of Spanish and Portuguese resistance to French dominance of the peninsula and, less frequently, the prospect of the imperial divorce. Napoleon's contemptuous treatment of the Spanish Bourbons and his proclamation of his brother Joseph as 'King of Spain and the Indies' at Bayonne in June 1808 transformed localised uprisings into a national insurrection; the surrender of a French corps to Spanish insurgents at Baylen on 19 July convinced Archdukes John and Charles of the value of provincial militia and of encouraging a popular revolt in Germany; even such an arch-enemy of democracy as Metternich advocated government backing for a people's war. At the same time, the dethronement of the Spanish Bourbons emphasised the danger that if Austria fought and lost another war, the peace terms might put an end to Habsburg sovereignty in central Europe. Metternich was told to cultivate Talleyrand and other potential friends at court; within a few months the ex-Foreign Minister received a million francs from Austrian funds, with the promise of more to come for services rendered.

Over secrets of diplomacy Talleyrand proved gratifyingly indiscreet; in assessing palace gossip he was less reliable, despite being Napoleon's Vice-Grand Elector, the third highest dignitary of the imperial court. In March 1808 he was certain Napoleon would soon end his marriage with Josephine: the Emperor's young and demure Polish mistress had come to Paris at his bidding in late January, and he would slip away as often as possible to join Marie Walewska at her lodgings on the Quai Voltaire. But no sooner did Talleyrand confidently predict divorce than he was confounded by renewed signs of mutual love between husband and wife. Josephine joined Napoleon at Bayonne, where one morning they were seen happily running barefoot across the sands. Marie Walewska dutifully returned to Warsaw. 'Why can't that devil of a man make up his mind?' Talleyrand remarked testily.[13] The question was to puzzle others, too, over the next eighteen months.

At heart Napoleon had no wish to break with Josephine, but the vanity which made him assume imperial and royal titles impelled him to seek ways of perpetuating the dynasty. He had little confidence in any of his brothers as a successor; they lacked military skill or political insight. Hortense's four-year-old son, whom he seriously considered as an heir, died while the Emperor was at Tilsit. 'To whom am I going to leave all this?' his valet, Constant, heard him sigh on one occasion that summer. If Josephine could not satisfy his need for a son he might have to seek a younger, nubile wife. But supposing he was incapable of fathering a child? His sister Caroline Murat, always selective in her moral scruples, encouraged an experimental liaison with one of her attendant ladies, eighteen-year-old Eléonore Denuelle. In December 1806 she gave birth to a son. Yet was Eléonore made pregnant by the Emperor or by Marshal Murat? To Caroline's fury, Eléonore could never be sure. As a crude test of potency, the experiment was flawed. The only certainty about the affair was that the father was not Eléonore's husband: he was in prison for forgery.[14]

There was never any prospect of Eléonore replacing Josephine as consort. But Metternich and Stadion were worried; an imperial divorce might be followed by a union harmful to Austrian interests. For Napoleon to choose a sister of the Tsar could perpetuate the Tilsit alliance. And marriage to Marie Walewska seemed hardly less dangerous: a Polish-born Empress in Paris would ensure lasting French patronage for the Grand Duchy of Warsaw, the embryonic Polish state which Napoleon organised after Tilsit. As yet, the fledgling Grand Duchy comprised ex-Prussian lands. But Austria's share of the partitions was potentially under threat. If Napoleon found good reason to encourage Polish patriotic sentiment in his Warsaw satrapy, it would be difficult for the Austrians to retain Cracow and Galicia. All in all, the Austrians hoped there would be no imperial divorce. The Metternichs, husband and wife, made certain that they remained on good terms with Josephine.

By August 1808 the French were alarmed at the progress of Archduke Charles's army reforms and by the war talk of the d'Estes and the 'party of action' in Vienna. Napoleon berated Metternich at the birthday reception of the diplomatic corps: '*Eh bien*, is Austria arming much?' he asked; did they not know in Vienna how exposed was their country's position or sense its political isolation?[15] Six weeks later Napoleon was at Erfurt, where the thirty-six rulers of the Confederation of the Rhine were summoned to meet Tsar Alexander in congress. Although Austria was allowed to send General Baron von Vincent as an observer, Emperor Francis himself was not invited; the only Habsburg among these German princes was his eldest brother Ferdinand, present as Grand Duke of Würzburg. Napoleon was glad to let them see how little authority the former imperial dynasty possessed in the Germany of his creation.

The Erfurt Congress was a splendid occasion, with a series of banquets and balls and a succession of nine plays presented by the Comédie Française. The German states affirmed their willingness to raise armies of 63,000 men so as to safeguard Napoleon's Empire; and they gave pledges of full participation in the Continental System, the French attempt to ruin British prosperity by ensuring that all ports were closed to British commerce. So, too, did Russia – for the moment. A formal secret treaty re-affirmed the Franco-Russian alliance and guaranteed that, should Austria start another war, the Russians 'would make common cause' with the French. But Napoleon was disappointed with Alexander: the possibility of marriage to one of his sisters was raised at a private meeting; Grand Duchess Anna Pavlovna was mentioned by name, but she was only thirteen – three years younger than Marie Louise. Alexander was not forthcoming over any topic discussed. 'As stubborn as a mule,' the Emperor later complained to

Caulaincourt his ambassador in St Petersburg. Worse still, the Tsar 'wanted to treat with me as between equals'.[16]

If Napoleon believed Erfurt would steal the thunder of the war party in Vienna he miscalculated. Baron Vincent was not impressed by what he saw and heard; nor was Metternich when he assessed the appraisals he received from Talleyrand. To Napoleon the news from Spain seemed so disturbing that, after returning from Germany, he spent only ten days in Paris before heading south to restore order beyond the Pyrenees. For Vienna's Francophobes Napoleon's military embarrassment in Spain was too good an opportunity to miss. Ambassador Metternich was summoned home for consultation.

In three long memoranda Metternich argued the case for renewing the war.[17] With Napoleon heavily committed in Spain, the French could hardly find much more than 200,000 men to check advances into Germany and Italy. Many troops would be Germans, lukewarm in loyalty to their French 'Protector'. There was, Metternich asserted, little danger of effective Russian intervention: they were conducting military operations in Finland and against Turkey; and St Petersburg was habitually slow in responding to any distant crisis. Discussion in Vienna continued until Christmas. The Archdukes Charles and John conceded that in four months' time Austria would be able to put into the field some 340,000 regular troops, with a quarter of a million reservists, and the prospect of an armed revolt in the Tyrol against Napoleon's Bavarian ally. By New Year's Day in 1809, when Metternich arrived back in Paris, it seemed certain Austria would launch a war of revenge in the spring; there was no more talk of Kaunitz and his legacy of ideas. On 9 February the final decision was taken. But unfortunately for the Austrians, Napoleon returned to his capital from Spain in late January, fully aware of renewed danger in central Europe.

Even so, the form and timing of Archduke Charles's initial moves took him by surprise. On 9 April a proclamation in the Archduke's name called on Austria's armies to wage a war of liberation: 'Comrades in arms ... the eyes of all who maintain their sense of national honour focus on you,' it declared. 'Europe seeks freedom beneath your banners. Your victories will loose her bonds ... Your German brethren wait for salvation at your hands.'[18] Next day Charles crossed the river Inn, his brother John crossed the Piave in Italy, their cousin Ferdinand d'Este thrust northwards into the Grand Duchy of Warsaw, and some 12,000 troops entered the Tyrol to help Captain Andreas Hofer's revolt against Bavarian rule and French paramountcy. Fighting had been going on for three days before Napoleon was able to set out from Paris. But once again he travelled with astonishing speed. He reached the Danube around Ratisbon (Regensburg) a week after Charles's tentative invasion.

Many of these April days were spent by Marie Louise at Laxenburg but she went frequently into Vienna, where there was confident expectation of early victories. Emperor Francis left the city on the eve of war to set up imperial field headquarters at Schärding, an old fortified town on the right bank of the Inn. Like her mother in earlier campaigns, Louise wrote almost daily to him: many letters are extended weather reports; even in the third week of April it was bitterly cold, with strong winds and a heavy snowfall. But experience made Louise perceptive. She wished 'all the victories the good townsfolk celebrate had really happened' she told him wryly on Friday, 21 April: she herself remained sceptical. But soon her doubts were confounded: a courier from Schärding brought good news. Bells rang to celebrate victory, 'crowds in most of the streets were so dense that no one could get through', toasts were drunk to the Archdukes, to Emperor Francis, to the glorious army. 'It was with much joy that we heard Emperor Napoleon was there in person,' Louise wrote the following Tuesday, 'for as he has lost such a battle, he can lose his head as well.'[19]

The sober truth soon reached Vienna. There had been no triumph of Austrian arms; the battle of Eckmühl was a defeat, even though Charles was able to avoid a trap Napoleon and Davout set for his army south of the Danube. 'It seems impossible to me that this sad news is true,' ran Louise's letter on Friday, 28 April: 'I cannot believe such a calamity could befall us, but I must.' She would not despair: she assured her father, as after Austerlitz, that the strength of God will end 'Napoleon's presumption. Constantly I find myself believing a messenger has come. I rush to the door, but there is no one there.'[20]

Disappointment mounted as the pattern of events became sadly familiar. Napoleon's forces headed straight for Vienna. On 5 May Empress Maria Ludovica hurriedly left the city with her stepchildren. Louise's letters caught the drama of the next few days: twelve hours rattling along seventy-five miles of bad road to the bishop's palace at Raab (Györ); a restless night, with barking dogs, howling cats and hooting owls, in concert, and the repeated challenge of sentinels on guard duty; 'Mama' forced to sleep with twelve-year-old Leopoldina in a tiny bed which collapsed in the small hours. They were at Mass by six o'clock next morning; for Ludovica, crowned Queen of Hungary at Pressburg eight months previously, felt it her duty to be present when the bishop blessed the *Insurrectio* (the Hungarian militia) as they prepared to defend their kingdom. Next day there was heavy rain along the road to Komarom; the coach's slow weaving around muddy pot-holes 'made Mama so sick that she could hardly keep going' until Buda was reached late that evening. It is, one feels, with slightly patronising pity that Louise, hardened veteran of such journeys, lets Papa know of her young stepmother's misfortunes.[21]

At the palace on Buda hill, Louise returned to the comfort of familiar apartments. Spring came at last to brighten the twin towns beside the Danube. But news from further up the river remained bleak. On Wednesday night (10 May) Napoleon slept once more at Schönbrunn: the tricolour flag was to fly over the palace for the next five months, with the Emperor of the French formally in residence on 124 days. Vienna defied the invaders for some seventy hours; it became necessary to open fire with cannon on the centre of the city from the inner suburbs, a warning of the sustained bombardment which would follow if the capital did not surrender; one battery, on the edge of Mariahilf, opened fire from outside the home of the septuagenarian Joseph Haydn, the sudden sound of the cannonade hastening his death three weeks later. The Viennese received Napoleon sullenly, in contrast to their mood four years back. Like Marie Louise, they still had hopes of an Austrian victory: for, though Eckmühl ended Charles's plans for liberating Germany, it was not a decisive defeat. By 16 May the Archduke could concentrate 115,000 men north of the Danube, a far more powerful army than Napoleon's; and, on this occasion, every bridge across the river was destroyed before the French entered the city.

Under cover of trees and heavy undergrowth the French engineers floated nine rafts and sixty-eight pontoons to provide a crossing four miles downstream, using a group of islands as stepping-stones. Napoleon crossed the largest island, Lobau, and set up field headquarters on the north bank on the afternoon of Saturday, 20 May. Next morning the Austrians swept down on the French along a six-mile front, between the villages of Essling and Aspern. By Sunday evening they seemed poised to push the French back to the river, from sheer weight of numbers. A counter-attack, mounted by Marshal Lannes and General St Hilaire, prevented disaster, though both commanders were mortally wounded, a serious blow to Napoleon's hopes of decisive victory. The battle was fought so near central Vienna that a French regimental apothecary climbed the Gloriette in the gardens of Schönbrunn and saw 'the flashes from 400 guns and the smoke of burning houses'.[22] The fighting continued with great intensity throughout Monday. As darkness fell, Napoleon withdrew his army to Lobau island. He had suffered his first setback as a military commander. In Austrian eyes Aspern was more than a rebuff; it was a French defeat. So, too, thought the British and Spaniards. All were heartened by such a sign of fallibility.

News of Aspern reached Buda on Thursday. Empress Maria Ludovica and the younger children had left the city, travelling across the Alföld plain towards the Carpathian foothills. But Louise, Crown Prince Ferdinand and Leopoldina were still there. 'My first reaction was to thank God profoundly for granting us such a victory,' Louise wrote to her father on 26 May. 'I wish I could convey to you the delight of Ofen [Buda] yesterday ... Everybody was laughing! Wherever we went, we were welcomed with cheers and *vivats*. We saw people get together in little groups, congratulate each other and give thanks for the victory. Rumour promised more: Napoleon was cut off on Lobau and would soon sue Charles for terms, it was claimed. But Louise refused to get 'too puffed up with pride'. As she wrote to her friend Victoria de Poutet, 'I am so accustomed to disappointments that I dare not hope for too much.'[23]

The month of June brought scorching weather but no reports of peace overtures. Instead, war came to Hungary from the south-west. As in 1805, Archduke John had pulled back from Venetia and through Carinthia and Styria so as to reinforce his brother Charles east of Vienna. John was closely pursued by Eugène de Beauharnais's Army of Italy, which on 5 June crossed the border of Hungary, and soon afterwards began an advance on Raab, the town where Louise and Leopoldina had spent so uncomfortable a night a month previously. This new threat sent Louise and her brother and sister on their travels again; they were to join their stepmother at Eger, a town in northern Hungary then known as Erlau. But they had only reached Hatvan, forty miles from Buda, when, early on 16 June, the sisters were woken by their uncle, Archduke Joseph, banging heavily on their bedroom door; 'Get up at once, we must be on the road; we have lost a battle.'[24] When, with dawn breaking, their coaches trundled off northwards they learnt that they were in flight, not from the fearful Napoleon, but from his stepson, Eugène. Two days previously the Army of Italy had defeated Archduke John around a crenellated farmhouse on the heights of Szànbadhegy, east of Raab. There was no need for the panic rush to leave Hatvan: the enemy never came within seventy miles of the fugitives.

At Eger Louise found 'Mama' in poor health, and her own room in the episcopal palace 'wretchedly uncomfortable': a bed, two sofas and four chairs 'all infested with the vilest bugs', she told Victoria.[25] Although Eger is an attractive town, at the head of vine-covered valleys producing a full-bodied red wine, daily life soon became monotonous. The isolation, which guaranteed the family's safety, left too many hours to speculate on what was happening at the heart of the Empire. After three weeks of uncertainty came the news which Louise most dreaded: on 5–6 July there had been a battle at Wagram, on the Marchfeld within sight of Vienna; and the combined armies of Napoleon and Eugène had defeated Archduke Charles, forcing him to retreat on Znaim.

Wagram was a large village six miles north of Aspern-Essling, where the armies had clashed six weeks previously. Once again army engineers made effective use of pontoons, with 'Fort Napoleon' on Lobau island as a midstream base. On this occasion Berthier had prepared for the attack with meticulous staff planning, but he could not have anticipated that the opening bombardment would be accompanied by a heavy thunderstorm, soaking the armies about to go into battle. Nor did Napoleon expect the Austrians to mount such sustained counter-attacks. Only converging movements by Davout and Masséna on the second morning and a thrust at the centre by Macdonald forced Archduke Charles to pull back in mid-afternoon, shortly before the first advanced patrols from Archduke John's long-expected army came up in support; had John's troops arrived three hours earlier Wagram could have ended similarly to Aspern.

Casualties were heavy on both sides: some 40,000 in Charles's army and 32,000 among the French and their allies. By nightfall on 6 July about a quarter of the fighting force lay dead or seriously wounded in the shattered villages or amid the high corn in the surrounding fields, ripe for a harvest which would never now be gathered in. Throughout the second day Emperor Francis had watched the ebb and flow of the fighting from a distant vantage point. As sunset sharply etched the wooded ridge of the Kahlenberg, away to the west, Francis turned to a young civilian in the group beside him and gave his first comment on the lost battle: 'We shall have a lot to repair,' he observed.[26]

The recipient of this characteristic understatement was Clement von Metternich. With the coming of war, the ambassador had been forced to leave France. After passing through a strange Vienna, in which the French Foreign Minister resided in the Hofburg and he found himself briefly interned in his mother's house near Schönbrunn, he was allowed to cross into Hungary and reported to Francis at Archduke Charles's headquarters two days before the opening of the decisive battle. Much of the 'repair' work would be Metternich's personal task. His familiarity with Napoleon's ways made him a natural choice as Francis's principal adviser at this time, though he did not formally succeed Stadion as Foreign Minister until the second week in October. But the person who habitually eased for him the path of advancement was missing. Because of the perils of travelling through the battle lines Metternich had set out from Paris without his family. His wife Eleonore remained, with their three children, at the house they had leased in the Rue Grange Batelière. Even so, she had a role in the melodrama to be played out over the following months. For Eleonore's contacts in Parisian society made Kaunitz's granddaughter a chance participant in the most unlikely marriage brokerage of all time.

7

Making a Marriage

Wagram was not a second Austerlitz. Napoleon was denied complete victory, for the *Grande Armée* lost a quarter of its effective fighting strength in the two days of battle. Moreover, despite suffering even heavier casualties, the Austrian army remained a disciplined force, able to retreat in good order. Emperor Francis withdrew to Komarom, in western Hungary, eventually establishing his field headquarters twelve miles to the east in the Esterhazy mansion at Totis (now the town of Tata, with the château converted into a hospital). As Napoleon had anticipated, Archduke Charles moved northwards into Moravia. At Znaim, on 11 July, his troops were briefly engaged in heavy street-fighting with Marmont's vanguard, but the Archduke saw no point in prolonging a lost war. Next morning he concluded a ceasefire. His enemies at court, eager to make him a scapegoat, reacted swiftly to this sensible initiative, and he was deprived of his military command. Once again Prince John of Liechtenstein was left to seek a lasting armistice with the French.

Napoleon received Liechtenstein in audience at Schönbrunn ten days after Wagram. At first he demanded Francis's immediate abdication, as well as demobilisation of the militia and the reduction of the regular army to half its size. Gradually his mood mellowed; he suggested peace terms might be thrashed out in talks between his Foreign Minister, Champagny, and an Austrian delegation. Metternich became the chief Austrian envoy, appointed at the personal request of Napoleon because of his knowledge of French affairs. The talks, which did not begin until 18 August, dragged on into late September, with Metternich hoping that diversions in the Netherlands and Spain would hurry the

French into concessions. But the long awaited British landing on the island of Walcheren proved a disaster and, though Wellington won his victory at Talavera three weeks after Wagram, he was soon forced to pull back into Portugal and prepare the defensive lines of Torres Vedras, north of Lisbon. So Austria remained isolated, with few bargaining counters. There was, as yet, no sign that Tsar Alexander was prepared to break with Napoleon, as Metternich had long predicted: the Russians still hoped to receive 'compensation' from the French at Austria's expense for lands awarded to the Grand-Duchy of Warsaw.

After six weeks of negotiation both Napoleon at Schönbrunn and Francis at Totis became impatient. They were anxious to settle matters before winter set in. Metternich, who would have been prepared to go on talking indefinitely, was recalled and Liechtenstein given plentipotential powers to conclude a treaty which would accept most of Napoleon's demands but allow Francis to retain his throne. The territorial terms were severe: Francis lost the Polish lands which Austria had gained in the Third Partition and all his remaining possessions down the Dalmatian coast, together with much of Croatia and the Slovene areas of Carinthia and Carniola. Salzburg, Berchtesgaden and a segment of Upper Austria went to Bavaria. Tsar Alexander duly received a *pourboire*: Czartow and Tarnopol, districts in eastern Galicia where the people were mainly Ukrainian rather than Polish. The Austrians were also required to join the Continental System, to pay a war indemnity of 85 million francs (even though the Empire was almost bankrupt) and to reduce the size of the army to not more than 150,000 men. As if to compound Habsburg humiliation, the peace treaty was concluded, on 15 October 1809, at Schönbrunn itself and conveyed to Francis for ratification in his place of refuge at Totis.

Throughout the late summer and autumn Napoleon held court at Schönbrunn as though it were a French palace. More than twenty plays or operas were presented for him at the Habsburg's private theatre between 31 July and 15 October, as well as divertissements mounted by Fillipo Taglioini, the father of a great balletic family. Significantly there was never any suggestion that Josephine might make the journey to Vienna, as she had to Milan and Venice in earlier years and, more recently, to Bayonne. Her son, Eugène, joined him on 22 July, but he soon realised his stepfather had other diversions to hand. A week after reaching Vienna Napoleon had written to Countess Marie Walewska in Poland inviting her to join him at Schönbrunn and she set off from Warsaw before the end of May; but, with the roads blocked by rival armies, she could not complete the journey until Wagram had been fought and won. Napoleon's Belgian valet, Constant, describes how on almost every evening during late July and August, he would take a carriage to fetch Countess Walewska to the palace, for she was accommodated in a villa at Mödling, on the southern fringe of the Vienna Woods. Towards the end of September Marie discovered she was pregnant. In this instance there could be no doubt of the child's paternity. At last Napoleon could be certain that he was not impotent; he might father a lasting dynasty. Had the time now come to divorce Josephine and seek a speedy re-marriage?[1]

Not, of course, that he thought of making his Polish mistress a crowned consort. Marie Walewska's company gave him sensual satisfaction; he respected her loyalty, her courage and her resolute character; perhaps he even loved her, for so at least he assured his brother Joseph. But, as he told both Joseph and Lucien, it was essential he should conclude a matrimonial 'alliance with sovereigns'. The twenty-year-old Countess, as dutiful as ever, set off on another long, slow winter journey back to her husband's estate west of the Vistula. Fortunately the elderly Anastate Walewski's devotion to his country remained undiminished and if compliance advanced the national cause he was willing to be a patriot cuckold. After all, as Napoleon himself observed, with backing from Paris '*l'enfant de Wagram*' could well become King of Poland some day. Everyone assumed the child would be male.[2]

In his crude determination to 'marry a womb', Napoleon again perused the list of possible brides, drawn up for him two years previously: some eligible German princesses were worth considering, and he had not ruled out union with a sister of the Tsar. But, with Russia's Dowager-Empress proving so protective of her young, Napoleon was beginning to think more favourably of an Austrian connection than four years back. By now he was sure he could mould French opinion, sweeping away the traditional prejudice against an *autrichienne* which once seemed such an obstacle. After Austerlitz he had talked amicably with the Emperor Francis. Ought they again to come together, perhaps at Totis or in Pressburg? To Liechtenstein – who found Napoleon enjoying the opera from the imperial box in Schönbrunn's Schlosstheater – he made it clear that he would be pleased to meet Francis's young Empress and the eldest Archduchess, too. Liechstenstein, however, was cautious. Personally he thought a Bonaparte marriage would lift Austria's fallen prestige. But was a meeting with the Archduchess desirable? Napoleon was said to have inspected a bevy of Bavarian royalty and rejected the lot. After careful observation, might he decide against encumbering the Bonaparte profile with a Habsburg lower jaw? Moreover, though Maria Ludovica was with her husband at Totis, Louise was kept well out of the limelight; in mid-September she had shepherded the younger children back from Eger to Gödöllo and on to Buda. No effort was made to satisfy Napoleon's whim. The mere rumour that he had expressed a wish to meet the Habsburg family filled Louise with alarm. 'I assure you that to see this creature would be for me a worse torture than all the martyrdoms,' she told Victoria de Poutet.[3]

The Archduchess had no idea she was already pencilled in as a likely starter in the dynastic marriage stakes; she did not even known Napoleon was contemplating a divorce. It was Liechtenstein who first dropped her name to Champagny in September, soon afterwards writing to Metternich and to Emperor Francis on the matter. Metternich, of course, needed no prompting and there were others who, independently, saw the advantages of such a union. General Bubna, one of Francis's trusted personal representatives, floated the idea in conversations at French headquarters; and Floret's journal shows that in early October he, too, spoke of Marie Louise to Champagny.[4] There is no doubt the initiative came, well ahead of the divorce, from Austrians desperately seeking ways to induce the French to ease the penalties proposed for the peace treaty. That seemed the immediate necessity. Occasional unsubtle attempts were made to flatter Napoleon while the terms were under discussion: thus on 15 August General Bubna conveyed congratulations on his birthday from the Emperor at Totis to the incumbent of Schönbrunn.

Yet it remains hard to assess the real mood of the Austrian people towards the ruler whose army had occupied their capital twice in five years. There was a curious incident on that same birthday evening: Napoleon, with Berthier beside him, rode incognito into Vienna; they were pleased to find the city celebrating with fireworks and illuminations. That Tuesday was, of course, not only the fortieth anniversary of Napoleon's birth, it was also the Feast of the Assumption, a great day in the calendar of the Catholic Church. In earlier years the Emperor would have received congratulations from the papal nuncio: but in 1809 such a courtesy was out of the question. During the summer, relations between Napoleon and the papacy deteriorated dramatically, with French troops occupying Rome, and the remaining papal states annexed to Napoleon's Empire. On 10 June Pius VII, the sixty-seven-year-old Pontiff who had travelled to Paris to bless the imperial coronation, issued a papal bull: *Quem Memoranda* excommunicated anyone who attacked the Holy See 'whatever their honours or dignities'. Though the bull stopped short of mentioning Napoleon by name, he immediately sent (from Schönbrunn) orders that 'should the Pope preach revolt ... he must be arrested'.[5] Accordingly, early in the same morning as the battle of Wagram began, General Radet's troops seized Pius VII at the Quirinal Palace and hurried him into exile. As the Assumption was the first Catholic festival since the Pope was taken into custody, it is possible that the festivities in Vienna on 15 August were a tribute not to the Emperor of the French – as Napoleon chose to assume – but to the Pontiff defying him.

Seven weeks later, when Napoleon was about to leave Schönbrunn for Paris, he was suddenly made aware of the depth of anti-French feeling below the surface. At a military review in the palace forecourt Friedrich Staps, the eighteen-year-old son of a Lutheran pastor from Erfurt, was seen to pull a knife from his pocket and would have stabbed the Emperor had not General Rapp and a group of officers around him seized Staps. Napoleon tried to play down the incident: 'I never even noticed it myself,' he told Fouché.[6] When Staps was brought before him and assured that his life would be spared if he expressed regret, the lad refused, explaining (as Napoleon wrote) that 'he intended to assassinate me in order to rid Austria of the French'. Despite the defiance of the Spanish people, this appears to have been the earliest occasion on which the Emperor of the French realised that patriotic pride in *la Nation*, the inspiration of the earliest armies of the revolution, had become a weapon turned against their successors. 'I never saw Napoleon look so confounded,' General Rapp wrote in his memoirs.[7] Poor Staps was tried by court-martial and faced a firing squad on 16 October; a few hours earlier a pensive Napoleon set out from Vienna for the ten-day journey back to his own capital.

Josephine knew of Countess Walewska's presence at Schönbrunn soon after her arrival. But it was only while Napoleon was on his way home that she heard of his Polish mistress's pregnancy. Sadly she realised the significance of the news. When husband and wife met, at Fontainebleau on 26 October, he failed to respond to her gestures of endearment. Over the next few weeks his temper remained short; only with his sister Pauline was he able to relax. As yet he said nothing to Josephine of divorce. But he said little enough to her about anything. From cowardice, or from a sheer inability to find the right phrases, he asked Hortense to be an intermediary, gently letting her mother know the marriage was at an end. Hortense refused.[8] Still Napoleon prevaricated: when would be the best time? Ahead lay celebrations to mark yet another victorious peace; his allies among German rulers would expect suitable entertainment in the imperial capital; he needed the Empress at his side. Though the main festivities would not take place until the first week of December, King Frederick Augustus of Saxony arrived as early as 14 November. To go shooting with Frederick Augustus in the woods around Versailles and in the Bois de Boulogne relieved Napoleon's inner feelings and provided reasons for postponing the terrible scene he anticipated with Josephine. He decided to call up reinforcements: even if his stepdaughter failed him, he was sure that his stepson would prove obedient. The semaphore sent an express message to the Viceroy of Italy in Milan; Eugène was to come swiftly to Paris, 'with just three carriages and only four or five members of your personal staff'.[9] But in winter, as Napoleon had every reason to recall, there was no possibility the Viceroy could complete the journey in less than a week.

In the end he chose not to wait for Eugène. After dining tête-à-tête at the Tuileries on the last evening in November he took Josephine aside and told her that, for 'political necessity' and 'the welfare of the nation', he had decided the marriage must be dissolved: a Deed of Separation would be prepared within a fortnight. She burst into tears and Napoleon summoned the courtier in attendance, who found the Empress stretched along the carpet 'weeping and moaning'. Josephine was carried to her bedroom; Hortense then arrived, to find (as she wrote in her memoirs) her stepfather explaining to any courtier within earshot that 'Divorce has become a necessity for me.'[10]

Despite this scene, the public was not informed of what lay ahead, though subtle changes slipped into court ceremonial: thus at the *Te Deum* in Notre Dame to mark the fifth anniversary of the coronation the Empress wore her crown but did not sit beside the Emperor, either in his coach or at the cathedral. But, with support from Hortense, and after his arrival on 8 December from Eugène, Josephine acted out her role as presiding hostess of the peace celebrations with all her habitual charm and a smiling self-assurance. Whoever might follow her as second Empress would find it hard to match such natural grace and elegance.

Rather curiously, Napoleon at first believed he would still be able to call on his divorced wife for ceremonial occasions: she would stand on his right, and the second Empress on his left, he explained to Hortense and Eugène. He was puzzled by their objections and dismayed when it seemed as if both his stepchildren would retire and share with their mother the simplicity of private life. That was far from his intention. Josephine, he made clear, could be sure of a generous settlement: retention of her titles: 3 million francs a year; current debts paid off; Malmaison safeguarded as a retreat and the Élysée Palace to serve as a town residence.

Yet, despite such kind gestures, Napoleon could not spare Josephine the mortification of a ceremonial divorce. For their civil wedding six people were at the *mairie* of the 2nd arrondissement; according to Fesch, no one had witnessed the religious ceremony he conducted on the eve of the coronation; but to see the marriage dissolved and a Deed of Separation signed on the evening of 14 December, the whole court gathered in the Throne Room of the Tuileries, even Madame Mère. Napoleon was fast becoming a slave to protocol.

Josephine, with Hortense beside her, left the Tuileries for Malmaison next morning. As yet, a deeply unhappy Napoleon still looked to the past rather than to the future. He moved out of Paris and, for the first time in his reign, spent a week at the Grand Trianon, with Pauline installed close by in the Petit Trianon. The experiment was not a success. Napoleon made a hurried visit to Malmaison, and invited Josephine, Hortense and Eugène to dine at the Trianon on Christmas Day, a dismal affair, Hortense thought. Then, for Napoleon, it was back to Paris – and bride-picking once more.

Napoleon was still awaiting news from St Petersburg. Caulaincourt, his ambassador, had been ordered to raise again with the Tsar the possibility of marriage to his youngest sister, Grand Duchess Anna Pavlovna, who would be fifteen in January.[11] A matrimonial alliance with an increasingly independent Russia held out a prospect of greater political gains than defeated Austria could offer; the Russian option was backed by Murat, Fouché and several leading figures at court. But even before Christmas, the champions of a Habsburg marriage had gained the ascendancy in Paris, after considerable prompting from Vienna. On 30 November – the day Josephine collapsed in distress – Metternich told a French diplomat, Count Alexandre de Laborde, that he thought Marie Louise would satisfy Napoleon's needs, though he added that he had not yet raised the question with her father.[12] Laborde's mother was of Austrian birth and the Count was eager to promote a Franco-Austrian rapprochement. He left for Paris next day and on his arrival sought out Talleyrand, who still believed that Austria's continued existence was a necessity, guaranteeing stability within any well-ordered European system. Talleyrand, using entirely political arguments, became the main advocate of the marriage across the council table in Paris.

At the end of November Prince Schwarzenberg took up his duties as Austria's latest ambassador, with the invaluable Floret as his principal counsellor and Eleonore von Metternich on hand to ease his entry into Parisian society. But Schwarzenberg, a dignified soldier with no inclination for intrigue, was slow off the mark and inclined to send

Metternich reports of events which the Foreign Minister himself had helped to shape: as late as 21 December he gave Metternich the, hardly surprising, news that yesterday he had seen Count Laborde, who thought Marie Louise would be a suitable bride for Napoleon. The ambassador was hopelessly out of touch with events. On Christmas Day Metternich let Schwarzenberg know Emperor Francis 'will shrink from nothing that will contribute to the peace and welfare of the state'; the ambassador was given a free hand to advance the Austrian marriage project; he should not 'reject any overtures that may be made to you on that subject'. By the close of December even Josephine and Hortense were backing the Archduchess's candidature; Eleonore von Metternich was invited to Malmaison to hear their views, which she passed on by letter to her husband early in the new year.[13]

Marie Louise knew nothing of all this activity. When Emperor Francis returned to Vienna in the last week of November, his eldest daughter and the younger children remained in Hungary, for there was an influenza epidemic in the Austrian capital. Health scares continued, as so often in the closing weeks of the year, and Crown Prince Ferdinand became feverishly ill with measles.[14] Maria Ludovica was herself chronically unwell but was in Buda for Louise's eighteenth birthday. And so too over Christmas was Ludovica's eldest surviving brother, the thirty-one-year-old Archduke Francis d'Este. Vienna was full of rumour about Napoleon's matrimonial prospects, but as yet little speculative tittle-tattle reached Buda. News came from old copies of the semi-official *Wiener Zeitung* and the less constrained Frankfurt press, which Louise was in the habit of reading carefully.

On 5 January 1810 one newspaper report prompted her to act swiftly and, it would seem, decisively: 'Today I read in the newspapers of the act of separation between Napoleon and his wife,' Louise wrote to her father in Vienna. 'I must admit, dear Papa, that I am very disturbed by this news. The thought that it is not impossible that I may be counted among those from whom he will choose his future wife impels me to let you know something that I would lay in your fatherly heart.' He had, she reminded the Emperor, always told her that he would not make her marry against her will. 'Since I have been in Ofen [Buda] I have met Archduke Francis. I am certain he has all the qualities which would make me happy. I have confided in Mama [Maria Ludovica] and she shares my unbounded confidence [*uneingeschränktes Zutrauen*] and has had the kindness to suggest that I write to you about my sentiments.' Louise assured her father that she knew she could not place her future happiness in better hands than his. As 'a loving, obedient daughter' she awaited his decision.[15]

That decision seems never to have been imparted to her. It may well be that dear Papa felt Louise's letter did not ring true: was the sudden attachment to Archduke Francis concocted by the d'Estes, possibly by 'Mama' herself? The Archduke had never taken any interest in cousin Louise. The d'Estes hated 'the Corsican', whose creation of a Cisalpine republic lost them Modena. Maria Ludovica may have remembered that when, after Tilsit, there was talk of a future union between Napoleon and Grand Duchess Catherine, the Dowager Empress of Russia hastily married off her daughter to a second cousin serving in the Tsar's army. In Louise's surviving correspondence there is no other reference to marriage with the d'Este kinsman – and, significantly, not a word of any romance in letters to her closest confidante, Victoria de Poutet. Louise writes of accompanying Archduke Francis on the clavier while he sings and she mentions an improvised ballet which he devised for her amusement at the beginning of Christmas week – something to relieve the tedium of the city she now described as 'sad and dull' Buda.[16]

But, in the first weeks of the year 1810, the disturbing news from Paris came uppermost in her thoughts. She first mentioned Napoleon's divorce to Victoria de Poutet on Saturday, 6 January, adding, 'I pity the unfortunate woman on whom his choice falls; that will certainly put an end to her fine days [*ses beaux jours seront alors sûrement finis*]'.[17] By the following Wednesday she was more uneasy: her clavier teacher, Kozeluch, gossiping about the fate of Empress Josephine, 'hinted that I might replace her'. As if to reassure herself, Louise told Victoria that Kozeluch 'was badly mistaken': Napoleon would never risk being snubbed by even suggesting such a marriage, she argued, and 'Papa is much too kind to force me' to accept.[18] But she went on scanning the Frankfurt gazette day after day, hoping to read that Napoleon had found a new wife, but dutifully steeling herself to accept the sacrifice if, through the workings of Divine Providence, 'I am the one'. Eventually, despite her passive temperament, even Louise found the isolation of Buda's royal castle intolerable while, she wrote, 'all Vienna is marrying me off to the great Napoleon'.[19] On the last days of January she crossed back into Austria and, after seven momentous months apart, was reunited with her father in the Hofburg.

She sensed that by now her fate was almost settled: her father spoke ominously of duty and sacrifice. He does not seem to have realised how far Metternich had committed him by name when writing to Schwarzenberg on Christmas Day. Emperor Francis felt a deeper attachment towards his eldest daughter than towards any member of his family, including Maria Ludovica. As he insisted later in the month to Metternich, he would not force his daughter to marry Napoleon;

he was, however, convinced that she understood that once her father saw a dynastic union as the only way of restoring the prestige and influence of his Empire, her disciplined religious conscience would impel her to accept his decision. One doubt remained, however, to trouble Francis's mind: the Deed of Separation concluded on 14 December was a legal bill of divorcement and carried no ecclesiastical authority; would a new marriage be valid in the eyes of the Catholic Church? If not, Marie Louise would be joined in unholy wedlock to a bigamist.

Napoleon had foreseen this difficulty. To appeal to the Pope was useless; Pius VII was under virtual arrest in exile at Savona, and unlikely to annul the religious union upon which he had insisted five years ago. Should he marry Anna Pavlovna according to Orthodox rites, the problem would not arise. But the Russian option was becoming increasingly out of favour. As early as 22 December Cambacérès, titular Archchancellor of the Empire, informed the *Officialité Métropolitaine* – the French ecclesiastical court established by the Concordat – that the Emperor wished to marry a Catholic and sought nullification of his union to Josephine. But the court was not so compliant as the Archchancellor assumed. Cardinal Fesch submitted a written declaration that the 1804 marriage was invalid because the certificate he issued was attested by no witnesses; Talleyrand, once Bishop of Autun, stressed the canonical irregularities in the ceremony; and, after three weeks of hesitation, the *Officialité* duly declared Josephine's marriage null and void. The pronouncement was printed in the official *Moniteur* on Sunday, 14 January 1810; formal confirmation of the ruling reached the Austrian hierarchy a month later. Though Francis seems to have been satisfied, the Archbishop of Vienna thought little of the *Officialité's* impartiality.[20]

On that same Sunday Napoleon held a family council at the Tuileries: his brother-in-law King Gioaccimo of Naples (Marshal Murat) mistrusted all contact with Vienna, fearing that he might find his impromptu throne pulled out from under him; by contrast Prince Eugène de Beauharnais favoured the Austrian marriage: a Russian empress, loyal to her faith, would need Orthodox priests at the court, an obstacle to any reconciliation with 'the religion of the majority of Frenchmen'. Still Napoleon hesitated, waiting on news from St Petersburg and some positive gesture from the Austrian ambassador. A second family council gathered on 22 January; by then a despatch from Caulaincourt reported that the Tsar had told him that his sister Anna was 'not yet regular in her monthly periods'; it might be another three years before she gave birth to a child. Soon afterwards, with

Eleonore von Metternich's connivance and at her husband's bidding, a private letter from Vienna was allowed to fall into 'wrong hands'; it showed what, a few days later, Napoleon deigned to call 'the keen and dutiful attitude of Austria' towards his matrimonial intentions.[21] His mind was made up; the Tsar had prevaricated too long; he would settle for a Habsburg bride.

On 7 February, Eugène was sent to the Austrian embassy to inform Schwarzenberg that his stepfather had decided to marry the Archduchess Marie Louise. There could be no queries referred back to Vienna; no striking of bargains in protracted negotiations, Metternich's speciality. The ambassador, as his sovereign's plenipotentiary, was expected to give an immediate response, accepting the proposal. But Schwarzenberg, not anticipating any business of importance on that Wednesday, was out of Paris. At six in the evening he returned from a day's shooting to find awaiting him an anxious Viceroy of Italy in ceremonial uniform, with a marriage contract drawn up and signed by Napoleon. Schwarzenberg was a soldier: 'Do not reject any overtures' on the subject of the marriage were his orders; he obeyed them, and signed.[22]

Next morning Floret set out for Vienna with details of the marriage contract. He could not hope to complete the journey in less than ten days. But, by using visual semaphore stations to Strasbourg and fast couriers thereafter, foreign minister Champagny was able to let his ambassador, Count Otto de Molay, know of Napoleon's precipitate action within a week. Count Otto told Metternich, and he informed his Emperor. Neither man was pleased: Metternich, as Napoleon foresaw, had anticipated lengthy discussions in which he hoped to make treaty revision a condition of any marriage contract; and Francis was affronted by what he considered Napoleon's indecent haste. It was customary for a courteous emissary to convey a sovereign's request for the hand in marriage of a brother sovereign's daughter. To entrust pending Habsburg nuptials to mechanical arms waving across the fields of eastern France seemed a gross discourtesy. The cool response in Vienna may explain why, over the following weeks, Napoleon insisted that his envoys should follow the protocol laid down for Marie Antoinette's journey and reception in France forty years previously. There must be no more solecisms.

Marie Louise's fears were confirmed on 12 February when Metternich sought to explain why reasons of state made her sacrifice necessary; she was, he told the French ambassador, 'well-disposed' to the proposal. Although Francis gave his daughter twenty-four hours to consider her future, he assumed she would be dutifully submissive and he was right.[23]

Two days later ambassador Otto reported that she was asking interested questions. Were there museums in Paris which she could visit easily from the Tuileries? Was Napoleon musical? Might he allow her a private botanical garden? News of the coming marriage spread rapidly, Otto said, and the Archduchess was surprised to be cheered in the streets.[24] He did not report that, beyond the capital, there was indignation at the Corsican usurper's presumption, and especially in Hungary where Louise had stirred sentimental hearts in recent months. The Viennese, however, sensed short-term and long-term gains: ample spending during proxy wedding festivities and, above all, the certainty of no more invasions and the prospect of a lasting peace. It was wiser to sup with the Devil than to tweak his tail.

As soon as Napoleon knew that Francis would accept the marriage proposal without further negotiation he wrote, in his own hand, a suppliant letter to his future father-in-law. At the same time the letter, drafted slowly and with great care in the peace and quiet of Rambouillet, let Francis know that Alexandre Berthier, first in seniority of all the Marshals, would set out at once for Vienna as Ambassador Extraordinary.[25] Seven months previously, at Schönbrunn on his fortieth birthday, a grateful Napoleon had created his incomparable chief of staff Prince of Wagram; tact now decreed that he should, for the moment, revert to the title given him in 1806, and it was as Prince of Neuchâtel that Berthier renewed his acquaintance with Vienna.

Tact, and a long experience of adolescent women, also shaped the form of Napoleon's first letter to Marie Louise, written at Rambouillet on 23 February 1810. It is a minor epistolary gem – masterful, disarming, optimistic, gently flattering but, above all, treating Louise as a person in her own right:

> 'The brilliant qualities which make you an outstanding person have inspired us with the desire to serve and honour you. While addressing ourselves to the Emperor, your father, and begging him to entrust us with the happiness of Your Imperial Highness, may we hope that Y.I.H. will share the sentiments that prompt us to make this step? May we flatter ourselves that Y.I.H. will not be driven solely by the duty of parental obedience? Should Y.I.H. have even the least amicable feelings for us, we wish to cherish them; and we set ourselves the constant task of pleasing you in every way so that we presume that one day we shall succeed in winning Y.I.H.'s affection. That is the goal we hope to attain; and we pray that Y.I.H. will look upon it with favour.[26]

Berthier was instructed to hand the letter to the Archduchess in person 'page by page, even if that is not the done thing [*ne contrarie pas l'étiquette*] in the country where you are'. When put into operation at the Hofburg on 8 March, this shrewd tactic worked well. The spark of esteem in the letter kindled Louise's interest; old prejudices began rapidly to melt away. Francis formally recognised his daughter's betrothal and Louise gave her 'consent to union with the Emperor Napoleon'. The Archduchess was then presented with a jewel-encrusted box containing Napoleon's portrait. Berthier thought her 'fascinated' by the gift; and to her lady-in-waiting, Countess Lazanski, she seemed visibly relieved. Louise could at least see that, in looks, her husband-to-be was very different from the sinister creature depicted in so many savage caricatures.[27]

The proxy wedding was celebrated on 11 March, in the Augustinerkirche, at six o'clock in the evening, with the observance of full ceremonial, even though it was the first Sunday in Lent. On Napoleon's orders Berthier asked Archduke Charles to deputise for his former enemy at the marriage, and it was accordingly on her uncle's arm that Marie Louise was escorted back from the altar and down the long aisle of the church as the choir sang a *Te Deum* and the pealing of bells gave a signal for the cannons to fire their salvoes of salute. But Berthier, as Ambassador Extraordinary, sat at the imperial table for the subsequent banquet in the Hofburg. Every detail of his six-day mission was painstakingly noted in letters back to Paris and in a forty-page report he compiled after leaving Austria.[28] The Marshal was interested, not only in the ceremonial, but in the attitudes of individual Austrians to the marriage: he found that Archduke Charles wished to discuss purely military matters; Empress Maria Ludovica, on the other hand, 'concentrated all her small talk on the Emperor Napoleon and the habits of his private life [*dirigea tous les détails de la Conversation sur l'Empereur Napoléon et les habitudes de sa vie priveé*]'. The Empress puzzled Berthier, even though he was fully aware of the d'Este family's hatred for the Bonapartes: was she fearful for Marie Louise or envious and, to some extent, jealous? Her cold reserve broke down when, some thirty-six hours after the wedding, her stepdaughter set out on the fortnight's carriage drive to Paris. Both women were in tears, as indeed were most of the family and many onlookers, too.

Emperor Francis rode with Louise on that first morning, a leisurely thirty-eight miles to St Pölten. Father and daughter heard Mass together early on the Wednesday (14 March) before Francis turned back to Vienna, and Louise continued the journey to the frontier, with Countess Lazanski sharing the berlin with her in a long procession of nineteen carriages, split for security of armed escort into three convoys. On

Friday morning the cavalcade reached Braunau, the frontier town on the river Inn where Adolf Hitler was to be born almost eighty years later. In 1810 the latest adjustment of boundaries had placed Braunau itself in Bavaria and under French military control. The town was therefore chosen by Napoleon for the ceremonial induction of his bride as Empress of the French. Caroline Murat, Queen of Naples, was there to greet her new sister-in-law. So, too, were the ladies of the new Empress's household, headed by the Duchess of Montebello, widow of Marshal Lannes, who had died of wounds after Aspern-Essling.

The ceremonies were protracted. 'I scarcely knew what I was doing,' Louise wrote that night to her father.[29] First, the remaining members of her old household – 'my Austrian friends' – bade their former Archduchess farewell. So moving was the occasion that, as she told Francis, even Berthier 'shed tears of sympathy' for her. Neither Queen Caroline nor the Duchess of Montebello were so understanding. For, after the farewells, Louise was taken to a specially prepared rest-house where, under Caroline's supervision, she was divested of Austrian garments and became a Frenchwoman, with new perfume, new hair-style and travelling clothes in the smartest Parisian fashion. 'She took two hours re-dressing me,' Louise wrote indignantly. 'I can assure you that by now I am scented like the French ladies.' If she could not be with her father, she would sooner travel with Napoleon 'than all these women'. Though Caroline 'embraced me and seemed very friendly, I don't trust her,' Louise wrote perceptively. She was in low spirits: a golden toilet set was the latest of Napoleon's many wedding gifts, but there was no letter to greet her. It awaited her at Munich, seventy-six miles farther on. Even the best post-horses sometimes went lame.

Louise did not realise that the transformation scene at Braunau was stage-managed from afar. Her husband's precise instructions, set out originally in a directive on 26 February, were updated over the following fortnight by curt orders entrusted to fast couriers or to the semaphore. So important was the Austrian marriage to Napoleon personally and politically that for some five weeks he concentrated his mind on the reception which must be accorded his bride and on little else. Virtually all other business, civil or military, was pushed aside. In distant Portugal, Wellington heard of the dynastic marriage with alarm; it was, he feared, 'a terrible event' foreshadowing new alignments in Europe dangerous to the allied cause. He need not have worried; the marriage may even have benefited Wellington, for Napoleon's obsession with Louise distracted him from events south of the Pyrenees. While Marshal Berthier found orders awaiting him at almost every staging post – and even a sharp rebuke for having written '*l'Archduchesse*' instead of '*l'Impératrice*' – Marshals Massèna and Ney were left to devise their own means of expelling the British from the peninsula and stamping out national resistance in Spain.[30]

Napoleon continued to rely on support from Josephine's son and daughter. After informing Schwarzenberg of his stepfather's momentous decision on 7 February, Eugène had travelled back to Milan, but within six weeks he was once again in Paris, accompanied by his wife, the Vicereine Auguste, who had never previously visited her husband's homeland. Queen Hortense – who by now rarely saw her husband, Louis Bonaparte of Holland – divided her time between attendance on her mother at Malmaison and her stepfather, at first in the Tuileries and, from 21 March, at Compiègne. Louis XV and the Dauphin had received Marie Antoinette at the recently completed château in 1770; and Napoleon was therefore resolved that his family must assemble at Compiègne to welcome Antoinette's great-niece forty years later.

Hortense's memoirs vividly recall Napoleon's uneasy restlessness in these weeks of waiting. Once he asked her to teach him to waltz: but at forty it seems to have proved hard to drill feet to the steady downbeat of '*Ach du lieber Augustin*'. Two evenings of practice were enough; 'I was not meant to excel as a dancer,' he decided. Constantly he cross-questioned the aides who travelled ahead of the main party, bringing him messages from Louise and, before he left the Tuileries, a portrait which greatly pleased him – though he was heard to remark, 'Ah! That's certainly a Habsburg lip!' To one horseman Talleyrand heard him ask, 'Tell me frankly, what was your impression of the Archduchess?' 'Oh, very favourable, Sire,' came the reply. 'That doesn't tell me a thing. Come on now, how tall is she?' This was harder: but inspiration was on hand: 'Sire – she is – she is about the same height as the Queen of Holland.' 'Ah, very nice. And what colour is her hair?' 'Blonde; much the same as the Queen of Holland's.' 'Good; and her complexion?' 'Very pink and white, like that of the Queen of Holland.' 'Ha! then she resembles the Queen of Holland?' 'Not in the least, Sire,' came the final response, 'Yet I have answered every question truthfully.' Talleyrand told Hortense that after the embarrassed cavalryman had retired from the imperial presence, Napoleon complained, 'Not one of these confounded young fellows will say she is pretty. But it doesn't matter. So long as she is kind and gives me healthy sons, I will love her as though she was the most beautiful woman in the world.'[31] It was not, perhaps, the most tactful observation for the daughter of Josephine to hear.

Napoleon's impatience increased once he learned from the semaphore telegraph on Saturday, 24 March, that Louise was in France, having on that morning left Strasbourg for Lunéville. Earlier in the month he penned a note on a despatch to Berthier in which he emphasised that, 'if the Archduchess or Empress is tired, never hesitate to change the itinerary and take a few days rest, for I especially want everyone to arrive fit and well.' Now, however, poor Berthier received a sharp message chiding him for delay. He was to push on speedily, to reach Compiègne by Tuesday night.[32] But popular enthusiasm in the towns slowed the Empress's progress. And there were unexpected visitors, too: Countess Metternich and ambassador Schwarzenberg joined the party at Vitry, the last overnight halt. The Countess was on her way to Metz to greet her husband, who set out from Vienna two days after Marie Louise, on a 'special mission' to Paris.

Across the whole of northern France, Tuesday, 27 March, was a wretchedly wet day. At Compiègne all was ready to receive the Empress, with the ceremonial choreography so carefully rehearsed that everyone knew where to stand and when to come forward. By noon, however, the Emperor had decided that he could wait no longer. With a reluctant Murat beside him, he set out eastwards in a calèche, heading for Soissons and the road to Rheims.

Before daylight faded they had travelled thirty-eight miles, as far as Courcelles, a village on the river Vesle, a tributary of the Aisne. There, in heavy rain, Napoleon insisted they should step down from the calèche, much to his companion's disgust; the church porch, beyond the village graveyard, gave them some cover. They had not been waiting long before Napoleon spotted eight white horses pulling a heavy carriage. It was the berlin in which he knew that his wife and Murat's wife were travelling. Like a highwayman, he stepped out and ordered the coachman to halt at once.

The officer commanding the escort, galloped up with unsheathed sword. Fortunately, he recognised the rain-soaked figure who had dared to stop the cavalcade. Napoleon leapt into the berlin and embraced his wife. Three years later Louise, travelling along the same road, 'recognised the graveyard where the Emperor awaited me' and 'recalled the terror I felt on seeing him arrive without having been forewarned'. But, at the time, she recovered rapidly from the initial shock and had the good sense to murmur, 'Sire, your fine portrait does not flatter you.' One memoirist maintains that Queen Caroline was cast off to join her husband in the calèche, while the newly proxy-weds completed the journey together. The cavalcade hurried into Soissons, ignoring the civic welcome prepared by local worthies, but it was suddenly stopped by an urgent messenger. King Louis of Holland was waiting with a letter for Louise entrusted to him by his brother earlier that morning. He 'was astonished on opening my door to find the Emperor in my carriage', Louise wrote later in her diary.[33]

It was almost ten o'clock at night before the carriages clattered over the cobbles into the courtyard of Compiègne. A long and detailed directive, based upon precedents from Louis XV's reign, and conned again and again by Napoleon as though it were an order of battle, laid down the right place, the right dress and the right form of words for everyone summoned to greet the new Empress. For over two hours family and household had dutifully waited in full court dress at the foot of the grand staircase. But there was to be no ceremonial greeting that evening. 'We had an opportunity to kiss the newcomer, but scarcely saw her,' Hortense wrote in her memoirs. 'She seemed gentle and sweet, though a trifle embarrassed. She disappeared down a gallery where townsfolk and courtiers were gathered and was not seen again until morning.' Emperor and Empress took a brief supper together with Queen Caroline, who was then dismissed. Napoleon, assured by Cardinal Fesch that even a proxy wedding made them husband and wife, was no longer inclined to act out the charade of protocol. Soon, a whisper of shocked admiration ran through the assembled courtiers, '*Ils sont couchés* (They are in bed)'.[34]

Eight years later, amid the inevitable celibacy of life on St Helena, Napoleon recalled that night to his companions in exile: 'She liked it so much that she asked me to do it again,' he said.[35] There is no reason to doubt his word.

8

'We Suit Each Other Perfectly'

'Your Majesty's daughter has now been here for two days,' Napoleon wrote to his father-in-law from Compiègne on Thursday, 29 March. 'She fulfils all my expectations, and for the last two days I have not failed to give her, and receive from her, proofs of the tender sentiments which bind us together. We suit each other perfectly ... Tomorrow we leave for St Cloud and shall celebrate our marriage ceremony at the Tuileries on 2 April. Your Majesty should never doubt my sentiments of esteem and high regard, not least the tender affection in which I have promised to hold you.'[1]

The proxy-weds duly reached St Cloud late on Friday afternoon, to a hundred-gun salute and the Guard turned out on ceremonial parade. They made their first semi-public appearance at the court theatre next evening for a performance of *Zaire*, a play chosen by the Emperor before his wife arrived in France; it formed a curious curtain-raiser to the festivities. In the grand gallery of St Cloud, refurbished at the height of the Consulate, two thrones had been placed side by side on a dais beneath a purple canopy for the civic marriage on Sunday. Soon after midday, civil and ecclesiastical dignitaries from France and the Kingdom of Italy gathered on either side of the dais, with their ladies and all the diplomatic corps in attendance, awaiting the officers of state who led the imperial cortège to the thrones. At once some observers noticed the disparity of height between the tense, erect bride and the stockily built groom of five feet two (1.53 m) beside her: Josephine had perfected a languorous walk, slightly behind her husband, which never risked encroaching on his dignity; by contrast Marie Louise, accustomed to more conventional deportment, could not shake off her well-schooled haughtiness. The Archchancellor, Jean-Jacques de Cambacérès, the lawyer from Languedoc whom Bonaparte made Second Consul, acted as registrar, formally declaring 'in the name of the Emperor and of the Law' that the Emperor and the Archduchess were joined in matrimony. Some hundred witnesses signed the register, headed by the indomitable Laetizia Bonaparte, 'Madame Mère'. Outside, a mass of people jostled in the parkland, seeking shelter from heavy rain beneath the trees. Though eager to catch sight of the new Empress, they had to content themselves with admiring flambeaux which, in a strong east wind, fitfully threw coloured light on the cascade and fountains. It was a bitterly cold All Fool's Day; tomorrow would be better, they hoped.[2]

Next morning a hailstorm was sweeping central Paris when, at seven o'clock, the first of 8,000 guests arrived at the Tuileries. As on coronation day and at Austerlitz a pale sun broke through, promptly on cue, when the procession began to pull away from St Cloud, seven miles down the Seine. Thirty-six carriages, each drawn by teams of six horses, followed lancers, chasseurs and dragoons eastwards into the city. Most carriages were assigned to the extended family of the Emperor or to grand dignitaries of court and state and their ladies, but the special envoy from Vienna, Count Metternich, was in the procession, together with his Countess. So, too, was one Habsburg Archduke: Emperor Francis's eldest brother, Ferdinand, was present as Grand Duke of Würzburg and a sovereign prince in the Confederation of the Rhine.

Behind the carriage procession, moving at little more than walking pace, came the imperial coach, richly gilded but with glass replacing some traditional panelling so that the onlookers could see the two occupants. Marie Louise wore a heavy crown and a diamond-encrusted robe over a satin and ermine-trimmed dress. Napoleon looked like a toreador *manqué*, in a Spanish-style white satin costume with golden frills and a mantle embroidered with golden bees; on his head was a velvet cap which seems to have been designed to make him look taller, for it was covered by eight rows of diamonds beneath three swan feathers fastened by a clasp from which shone out the biggest jewel of all. By one o'clock the wedding coach had reached the Arc de Triomphe, hastily and impressively given a look of completion through clever use of wood and canvas on top of the existing foundations. For almost half an hour the procession came to a halt while the Prefect of the Seine delivered a florid speech of welcome. Then on, beneath the chestnuts of the Champs Élysées, passing a succession of six bands and a full stringed orchestra, and so across the great square where, as many Parisians could remember, the last *Autrichienne* had perished by the blade of the guillotine, a mere seventeen years ago.

By three in the afternoon bride and groom were at last in the Salon Carré of the Louvre, converted into a temporary chapel. Queen Julie of Spain, Queen Hortense of Holland, Queen Catherine of Westphalia carried the Empress's train to the altar; so, reluctantly, did Napoleon's remaining sisters, Grand Duchess Elisa of Tuscany and Princess Pauline Borghese. Queen Caroline of Naples, Vicereine Auguste of Italy and Grand Duchess Stephanie of Baden (a Beauharnais cousin adopted by Napoleon as a daughter) carried sacred regalia, between lighted tapers, ahead of the Empress. Cardinal Fesch again solemnised his nephew's marriage and for the third time in a month Louise affirmed her vows. As in the Augustinerkirche, a *Te Deum* gave thanks to the Almighty for his mercies; and guns and church bells signalled the start of festivities for the Parisians.[3]

At the end of the service, to the consternation of many guests, Napoleon seemed extremely angry. 'I shall never forget his look of fury,' Baron Lebzeltern, one of Metternich's closest associates, was to recall. Etienne-Denis Pasquier, a senior civil servant who later became Prefect of Police, saw Napoleon enter the salon, though he was not present at the service; 'When the Emperor passed before us, we were struck by the glow of triumph which filled his whole person,' Pasquier wrote in his memoirs, 'his features, serious by nature, were lit up by happiness and joy. The marriage ceremony, solemnized by Cardinal Fesch, the Grand Almoner, did not last long; but to our astonishment we saw, on the way back, that those same features which had so recently radiated contentment, were sombre and menacing. What could have happened in such a short time?'[4]

The answer was simple, but ominous. Places had been assigned in the chapel to twenty-eight cardinals, all of whom were present at the previous day's civic ceremony at St Cloud. On entering the salon, Napoleon noticed a bloc of empty seats; thirteen cardinals, their consciences troubled by the absence of any papal annulment of the marriage to Josephine, had absented themselves. Napoleon at once assumed that their refusal to attend the wedding was intended to discredit his dynasty in the eyes of Catholic Austria. Within an hour, however, he regained his composure and seemed indulgently charitable, when, at seven in the evening, he looked down from the raised table of the imperial family at the hundreds of guests enjoying the wedding banquet in the fittingly-named Salle de Spectacles of the Tuileries. All the nuptial ceremonies were oppressively formal and regulated by protocol. Yet there was, in that afternoon, one moment of significant improvisation: an elated Count Metternich raised his glass of champagne to call proleptically for a toast 'To the King of Rome'. He of all people, understood precisely what Napoleon sought. The toast was an oblique rebuttal of the absentee cardinals; it showed that the Habsburgs accepted that the first born son of the 'new Charlemagne' would carry the title borne over the centuries by heirs to the most illustrious throne of western Christendom.

By the time that the wedding banquet began, the people of Paris had been enjoying some five hours of carnival. The municipality, with backing from the Archchancellor and other officers of state, encouraged festivities through the Champs Élysées and as close to the Louvre as the Arc du Carrousel. Five improvised open-air theatres gave a choice of acrobats, wrestlers, shadow silhouettes and popular music for dancing. There was free wine and free food, with at least 3,000 sausages and a thousand legs of mutton roasted on charcoal burners. After darkness fell, onlookers from the palace and among the general populace enjoyed a grand firework display. An arcade of coloured lanterns suspended from the tree branches and a dozen garlanded triumphal arches gave an illusion of woodland glades. The people of Paris, by nature sympathetic to the châtelaine of Malmaison, were expected to glorify the French Empire in the person of Napoleon's latest conquest – a bewildered eighteen-year-old. For the moment, with Empress Josephine discreetly hustled away to Normandy, they were prepared to do so, making the most of the bread put before them, and delay judgment on the newcomer from Vienna until the imperial circus was over.[5]

Marie Louise, unaccustomed to protracted ceremonies, was totally exhausted by the two days of marriage celebration. But the ordeal was not over. On Tuesday morning she was back in the throne room of the Tuileries to receive the homage of every person of consequence in the Empire, except for the absentee cardinals, King Joseph of Spain and the military commanders assigned to securing his sovereignty in the peninsula. 'Yesterday more than fifteen hundred people were presented to me,' Louise wrote to her father on 4 April. 'I felt ill all the time, because of the diamond crown, which was so heavy that I could scarcely bear it. As a result, I *saw* absolutely nobody.'[6] Metternich sent Emperor Francis a happier report that Wednesday, commenting on the kindliness Napoleon was showing Louise and the stream of presents bestowed on her: 'In the Empress's own words, his attitude is that of a caring father rather than of an infatuated husband,' Metternich wrote.[7] Was this information really to the liking of Louise's 'dearest Papa'?

Napoleon did not entirely neglect matters of state amid the nuptial euphoria. The insulting behaviour of the cardinals rankled. Every prince of the Church resident in the capital was summoned to the Tuileries on 4 April. For two hours they waited in the antechamber of the throne room. At last an officer of the Guard appeared: on the Emperor's orders, any cardinal who had not attended the religious marriage was to be ejected from the palace forthwith. 'This expulsion of thirteen cardinals in full ceremonial dress is easier to imagine than to describe,' wrote the leading dissident, Cardinal Consalvi, in his memoirs, 'The eyes of every onlooker turned on the cardinals who were being hustled out in so public a place in front of everybody, and with such ignominy. They crossed reception rooms and the grand hall in confusion' only to find that 'their carriages had disappeared. They had to make their own way back to their apartments' through the streets of Paris.[8] Napoleon received the remaining cardinals in audience, one by one. Next day he ordered the Minister of Public Worship to banish the recalcitrants from Paris, threaten them with trial and imprisonment and forbid them to wear their scarlet robes.[9] These 'black cardinals', recognised by Pius VII but ostracised by Napoleon, remained a source of friction between the papacy and the empire throughout Marie Louise's years in France.

By the end of the week husband and wife were back at Compiègne, and it was early June before the Empress saw Paris again. During the first weeks of their marriage Napoleon taught Louise to ride and she attempted to paint a portrait of her husband in oils, but abandoned the project, either because the smell of the paint turned her stomach or because of his impatience as a sitter. The Comédie Française was in attendance, presenting a succession of classical plays, from *Phèdre*, *Britannicus* and *Le Cid* to *Tartuffe* and *Le Misanthrope*. Louise relaxed, gorged herself on creamy desserts and pastries, and found that, if she behaved kittenishly, her husband would respond with boisterous playfulness. Attendants noticed that he was soon pinching her cheeks and ears and affectionately slapping her backside. 'He is so much in love with her that he cannot hide the fact even when in public,' Metternich reported back to Vienna, adding that Louise had said to him, "'I am not in the least afraid of the Emperor but I begin to think that he is afraid of me."'[10]

After three weeks at Compiègne, they set out on an Imperial Progress into the Netherlands. For Napoleon this journey was a tour of inspection, to assess the failings of brother Louis's reign as King of Holland. For Louise it was yet another adventure, an opportunity for the first time to see the sea and board a ship: 'I set out delighted at the prospect,' she wrote in her diary. 'Never before have I travelled without sadness.'[11] Thirty-three coaches left Compiègne, for the Emperor expected his itinerant court to move in great style. Louise was pleased to have the company of her uncle Ferdinand, Grand Duke of Würzburg, who as a widower for eight years happily prolonged his wedding visit to France. Less agreeable companions were the egregious Metternich and Queen Caroline (Murat) of Naples. When they 'left us' at Cambrai, 'so much the better', Louise jotted down; but she felt disillusioned at finding herself deserted, 'very ungallantly', by Uncle Ferdinand.[12] Like Metternich, and so many other fading Lotharios, the Grand Duke was easily bewitched by the siren usurper of his aunt's throne in Naples. All three – Metternich, Ferdinand and Caroline – would still be lingering in Paris when the Progress was over.

During this journey through her father's lost provinces in Belgium and into Holland, Marie Louise entered up her journal with the engaging naivete of an innocent abroad. Her brother-in-law, King Louis, whose reign and marriage to Hortense were both in jeopardy, is never mentioned, even though their future was of deep concern to Napoleon and to Hortense's son, Viceroy Eugène, summoned north to join the Progress. By now Louise liked to think of herself as 'much travelled', but her pictorial range of experience was limited to the central Austrian provinces and to Hungary. Common features of everyday life in these flat western lands of the continent surprised her: the number of windmills, for example; and the difficulty of getting a firm footing when wishing to climb a sand dune. She is embarrassed at showing her legs while mounting the gangway of the *Charlemagne* in a steady wind and vows 'never again to go aboard a warship unless wearing trousers', a resolve broken two days later when another gangway proves 'much easier'. On 10 May, along with Queen Catherine of Westphalia, she sees for the first time 'the ocean' – the North Sea off Walcheren – 'an immense surface of water bounded only by the horizon'. But Viceroy Eugène and Marshal Bessières got poor write-ups; for they had watched with amusement as 'the strong tide swept in, faster than we could run, and wetted us up to the knees'. (Or 'soaked yesterday by seawater from head to foot' – as she wrote to her oldest friend, Victoria de Poutet.)[13]

The war rarely intrudes in Louise's narrative. She was in bed with a fever on the day that Napoleon, inspecting the forts of Flushing, directed steady cannon fire at an English frigate which ventured too close inshore. One reason for spending a week at Antwerp and another in Walcheren was to make certain the Scheldt estuary ports observed the Continental System, tolerating no illicit trade across the North Sea. But did Louise know of such problems? She notes without comment, and apparently as a matter of course, how in Antwerp the gentlemen of the household 'had been buying contraband goods all day'; and at Middelburg Napoleon's stepson took the Duchess of Montebello, her principal lady of honour, for an evening stroll 'to purchase contraband goods' while the Emperor and Empress were receiving local officials.[14]

More than once the journal complains of the Emperor's brusque manner: at Laeken he woke his wife at seven to make certain she saw the gardens; and at Breda he became so impatient that he 'treated us like grenadiers'. Yet, in reality, Napoleon showed remarkable sympathy and kindness, as Marie Louise acknowledged in later years. She was ill-prepared for the public duties thrust upon her; she admits that, when expected to receive 'some sixty ladies who are absolute strangers' each day, her personal timidity made her gauche in manner, so that, 'I usually say many foolish things.'[15] Since the Duchess of Montebello had been appointed by her husband to head the household, the Empress treated her with the confidence and affection once lavished on the governesses assigned by her father. But Louise, kept for so long in Habsburg purdah, had no small talk to share with the 'French ladies' around her, nor could she draw on effortless knowledge of the world, like so many who had moved in Josephine's orbit. Companion 'exiles' from the German courts were more understanding and sympathetic to the newcomer from Austria, even Josephine's daughter-in-law, Vicereine Auguste. Writing to her brother in Bavaria in the fourth week of May, Auguste reported that the young Empress was polite and civil, though cold in manner and without 'much sensibility'. She added, however, 'People think she is very much in love with the Emperor and he with her.'[16] This near-certainty irked sharp-eyed detractors.

Even though the ladies of court might disparage Marie Louise, scornful of that ungainly walk, the rosy complexion turning scarlet with embarrassment, those opaque blue eyes which failed to sparkle into a smile, Parisian society prolonged the nuptial celebrations into midsummer, as Napoleon wished. From Le Havre, as early as 29 May, Marie Louise told Victoria Countess Colloredo that there would be 'several fêtes' once they were back in the capital; and she singled out 'that of Princess Pauline' as 'certain to be charming'.[17] On 14 June Pauline Borghese did indeed set the fashion with her fête at Neuilly. Statuesque figures on pedestals in the parkland sprang to life as Emperor and Empress passed by, leaping down to escort them to a glade where a canvas Schönbrunn was illuminated in Marie Louise's honour: fireworks followed; and at midnight a ball. A week later General Clarke, the Minister of War, mounted his grand spectacle, a ball at which the Empress was observed at last to dance naturally, having 'shaken off her German habits'; and on midsummer's night there was yet another fête, presented by the Imperial Guard, with the scenic advantage of the École Militaire as a finer backcloth than any canvas creation.

The Austrian response, a fête given by Prince Schwarzenberg in central Paris on 1 July, was intended to surpass even Princess Pauline's ingenious contrivances. Almost 1,500 guests were invited. The ambassador commissioned Bernard, a much respected architect, to construct a wooden ballroom in the garden of his residence in the Chausée d'Antin, at the foot of Montmartre. A gallery, also of wood, linked the house with the ballroom, the roof of which was, in effect, a tarpaulin spread across a wooden frame and lined with wax-paper to give a decorative ceiling. Bracket candle lanterns hung outwards from the walls, on which there were long mirrors draped with silver and gold brocades; a massive chandelier was suspended from the roof frame. Rare hothouse flowers were clustered in bouquets fastened to tulle and gauze draperies. Bernard provided four exits and curtained windows which could be opened to admit a gentle breeze.

Even as the first quadrille ended, the weather turned stormy and a steady wind sprang up; a curtain billowed out, the brocade brushing against a candle; and the roof went up in flames like a torch, sending the chandelier crashing to the floor. Black smoke came from the gallery, cutting off the dancers from the house. There was a rush for the garden exit and for a concealed door which Viceroy Eugène had noticed leading, through service passages, to the safety of an eighteenth-century house. This was the escape route for Marie Louise who, unperturbed, had waited on the central dais until led out by the Emperor. She was sent back to St Cloud in a carriage, while Napoleon returned to direct the fire-fighters. Louise's companion, Queen Catherine of Westphalia, fainted because she feared that her husband was trapped by the flames, though he was unharmed. 'Uncle Ferdinand', Grand Duke of Würzburg, was seen carrying out Queen Caroline of Naples, who was unconscious and later suffered a miscarriage. Prince Schwarzenberg's sister-in-law was among several guests who perished in the flames; many more were badly scarred for life, including the ambassadress herself.[18]

Bernard, the unfortunate architect, was arrested; and the chief of police was dismissed, for failing to check safety precautions. Yet each of these celebrations, from the wedding weekend onwards, carried a considerable fire risk and an even greater tragedy could have happened at one of the festivities for the general citizenry. In 1770 there had been over a thousand deaths in a fire and stampede after Marie Antoinette's marriage. It seemed as if a curse lay on Austro-French dynastic weddings.

Neither King Louis of Holland nor Queen Hortense were in Paris for the succession of fêtes. On the night of the fire Hortense, having spent a few weeks with her husband in Amsterdam, was taking the

Laetizia, the formidable matriarch, "Mme Mère".

Caroline, the youngest sister, at the time of her marriage to Murat, 1800.

Elisa, the sister Napoleon fetched home from the revolutionary Terror.

Pauline Borghese posing as Venus for Canova, 1808.

Schönbrunn, 13 December 1805; beneath the Habsburg eagle, Napoleon receives a deputation from Paris to congratulate him on his triumph at Austerlitz

The future Marshal Berthier in the first Italian campaign, 1796.

Hortense, Queen of Holland, Eugene's sister.

Eugene de Beauharnais, Napoleon's stepson, Viceroy of Italy.

Victory amid the cornfields: Napoleon at Wagram, 6 July 1809.

Empress Maria Ludovica,
Francis's third wife.

'Papa François': Emperor Francis
as painted by Isabey in 1812

Archduke Charles, the finest
soldier of the dynasty.

Prince Metternich, as painted by
Thomas Lawrence, 1814–15.

The Young Empress: Marie Louise at the Tuilleries.

Emperor and Empress approach the Tuileries on the day of their marriage.
A canvas Arc de Triomphe dominates the Champs Elysee.

Napoleon poses for a portrait painted by Marie Louise (see p.105).

Dresden, May 1812. Napoleon in attendance on his personal enemy, Maria Ludovica. Emperor Francis follows, with Marie Louise on his arm.

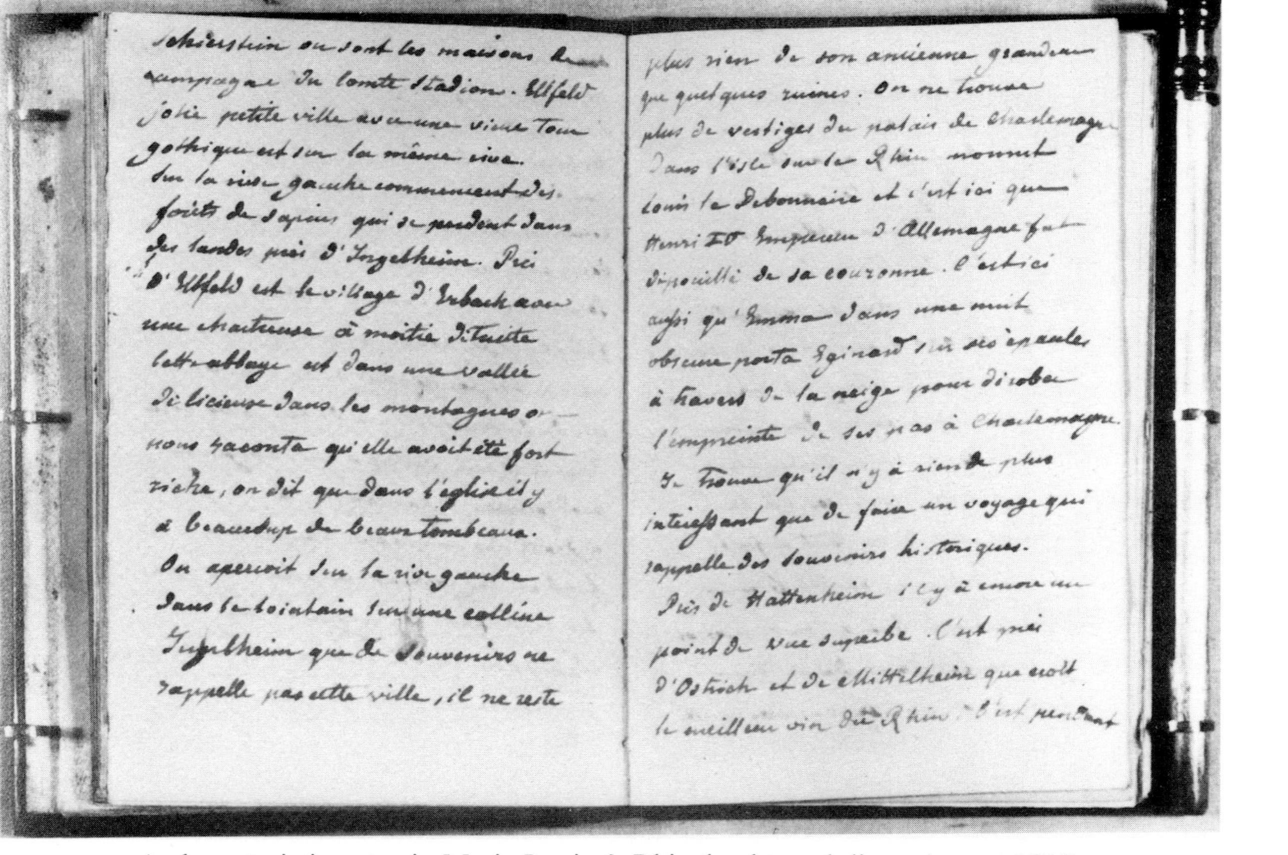

Schierstein ou sont les maisons de campagne du Comte Stadion. Elfeld jolie petite ville avec une vieille Tour gothique est sur la même rive.
Sur la rive gauche commencent des forêts de sapins qui se perdent dans des landes près d'Ingelheim. Près d'Elfeld est le village d'Erbach avec une chartreuse à moitié détruite cette abbaye est dans une vallée délicieuse dans les montagnes on nous raconta qu'elle avait été fort riche, on dit que dans l'église il y a beaucoup de beaux tombeaux.
On aperçoit sur la rive gauche dans le lointain sur une colline Ingelheim que de souvenirs ne rappelle pas cette ville, il ne reste plus rien de son ancienne grandeur que quelques ruines. On ne trouve plus de vestiges du palais de Charlemagne dans l'isle sur le Rhin nommé Louis le Debonnaire et c'est ici que Henri IV Empereur d'Allemagne fut dépouillé de sa couronne. C'est ici aussi qu'Emma dans une nuit obscure porta Eginard sur ses épaules à travers de la neige pour dérober l'empreinte de ses pas à Charlemagne.
Je trouve qu'il n'y a rien de plus intéressant que de faire un voyage qui rappelle des souvenirs historiques.
Près de Hattenheim il y a encore un point de vue superbe. C'est près d'Oestrich et de Mittelheim que croît le meilleur vin du Rhin. C'est pendant

A characteristic entry in Marie Louise's Rhineland travel diary, August 1813.
She dutifully notes down her impression of Charlemagne's ruined palace at Ingelheim (see p.145).

The King of Rome, as painted by Lawrence in Vienna.

General Count Neipperg

Count Charles de Bombelles

The domesticity of Sala Baganza, 1820. This watercolour by Marie Louise shows two pets, her parrot Margherita and her favourite lapdog, and Neipperg looking out from the open colonnades

Sala Baganza, the country residence south of the city of Parma.

Fertbauer's portrait of Emperor Francis and his family at Schönbrunn, 1826. From the left: Empress Caroline; Francis; Marie Louise; Archduchess Sophie; and Archdukes Leopold and Francis Charles (see p.219).

The Good Duchess arm-in-arm with her third husband, Bombelles, Sala Baganza (see p.230).

waters at Plombières. But nobody was sure of the whereabouts of Louis. He had suffered enough from his brother's interference with his public and private life. On the morning of 1 July he abdicated, exasperated by Napoleon's refusal to allow him to operate an independent, and specifically Dutch, diplomatic service. For several weeks, Louis disappeared, eventually surfacing at the spa of Teplitz, in Bohemia. Napoleon was at first aggrieved: his brothers seemed to think they were kings by grace of God, he grumbled; but they ruled by Family Right, not Divine Right; they remained imperial nominees. On 9 July the puppet Kingdom of Holland was incorporated in the Empire, forming part of metropolitan France.

King Louis was, however, allowed to keep his royal title. For, by that second week of July Napoleon was in a generous mood, magnanimous even towards a brother in whom he was disappointed. On the day after the fire, he had taken Louise away to the peace and quiet of Rambouillet; and there his most trusted physician, Dr Corvisart, informed him that the Empress was with child. Napoleon was overjoyed. Once again he lavished presents and tender endearments on Marie Louise, to such an extent that Corvisant became worried in case his diagnosis was premature. The Emperor was reminded that Her Imperial Majesty was in an early stage of pregnancy; the child was unlikely to be born earlier than March. Corvisart's professional caution raised him even higher in Napoleon's esteem. The Emperor never doubted Corvisart's skills. Nor did he doubt that the child would be male. For he had recently heard that on 4 May, while the Emperor and Empress were in Antwerp, Countess Walewska gave birth on her husband's estate near Warsaw to *l'enfant de Wagram* – who, as his natural father had anticipated, was a boy. With a right prediction for Marie Walewska, why should he be wrong over Marie Louise?[19]

In the previous December Napoleon boasted to the Legislative Assembly, that he had 'only to show myself beyond the Pyrenees' to force the English to 'take to the Ocean, in order to avoid shame, defeat and death'.[20] As yet, however, he gave no sign of travelling south and confirmation of the Empress's pregnancy made the Pyrenees recede even further to the back of his mind: Masséna with 130,000 men could be left to settle the Spanish Question. From July 1810 to September 1811, Napoleon and Marie Louise spent every night under the same roof, as indeed they had done since her dramatic arrival at Compiègne in late March. These were happy months for the Empress. In pregnancy she was excused attendance at those long exhausting receptions which she found so embarrassing. Only occasionally did she join her husband on visits to institutions like the Musée du Louvre and the Bibliothèque

Impériale or to assess progress on public works in and around Paris. Louise had plenty of time to paint, to receive lessons in embroidery, to enjoy her music and build up a personal library. Until late autumn she continued to ride a horse (side-saddle) and when the Emperor was hunting she would follow in a calèche. A circus gave a command performance for her in August at the Trianon, and plays were presented in one or other of the court theatres three times a week; after Mass on Sundays, there would be a concert in the afternoon or evening. For many ladies of her household, such regulated idleness seemed dull after the tempestuous uncertainties of Josephine's day; but Marie Louise was content. She wrote to Victoria from the Tuileries on New Year's Day 1811, 'You can well imagine that we are never short of amusements in a town the size of Paris, but the most satisfying moments that I pass are those when I am with the Emperor, or when I busy myself entirely on my own.'[21]

Best of all she liked the ring of palaces outside the capital. At Rambouillet in late summer the Emperor relaxed: the years rolled back, and Louise watched Napoleon seeking to cut his old friend General Duroc off from base at *balle au camp*, the form of rounders played before the revolution by French officers, men on whom the enlightenment of cricket sadly never shone.[22] The Trianon reminded Louise of Laxenburg, and in October she took carriage rides through the forest of Fontainebleau, excursions which could last as long as six hours on a golden autumn day. She could never shake off a fear of ghosts and insisted that night-lamps should burn in her bedroom. There was no question of going into residence at Versailles; to stay in the Tuileries taxed her nerves; quite apart from historical associations, she found the dark rooms and corridors claustrophobic, and the townsfolk flocked to the gardens in the hope of seeing the Empress, speculating among themselves on when the child would be born. Always she preferred to travel out from the centre of the city to St Cloud, where the air was fresher and she could enjoy greater privacy.

But from mid-November onwards, the Emperor insisted on keeping residence at the Tuileries. He needed to be in the capital for a succession of ministerial conferences as well as to observe solemnities marking the sixth anniversary of his coronation. Most of all, family pride made him determined that the confinement should come in the principal palace of the old monarchy, though in fact no Bourbon king was ever born at the Tuileries, nor indeed any sovereign for over 400 years. Once again, as before the marriage, historians and archivists diligently searched the records for precedents of protocol; detailed directives of ceremonial were issued well in advance of the confinement. Momentarily, in the new year, Louise doubted his infallibility of judgment: Habsburg wives had given birth to more archduchesses than archdukes in the past eighty years. She asked Dr Corvisart if there was any way of determining sex in advance of a birth, and was disappointed at his answer. Even Napoleon's certainty wavered: he had already consulted architects over the desirability of Chaillot as a site for the palace of 'the King of Rome'; now he made it known that should the infant be female, she would become 'the Princess of Venice'. The commandant of ceremonial artillery was ordered to be ready with a 101-gun salute for a king. Twenty-one guns would suffice for a princess.

The birth-pains began on the evening of Tuesday, 19 March, when most court dignitaries were already at the Tuileries, awaiting the arrival of their Imperial Majesties to watch a play. But the drama that night was offstage – and prolonged. The dignitaries, officers of the state and members of the family obeyed the orders they had already received: 'dressed as for Sunday Mass', they gathered outside the Empress's apartments, settling down for the night in an adjoining billiard room.[23] Dr Corvisart, with two colleagues and the accoucheur Dr Dubois, came to the Empress's bedside; so, too, did the Duchess of Montebello and the woman chosen as the child's first governess, the Countess of Montesquiou. The Emperor waited in an antechamber, hands clasped characteristically behind his back, anxiously pacing the floor.

In the small hours of the morning, Corvisart, by now the most confident of physicians, went home. At five o'clock the Emperor took some brandy and, soon after dawn, ordered his valet to have a bath prepared for him. While he was still soaking himself in the comfort of hot water, the accoucheur appeared, white-faced. The child was wrongly placed in the womb, Dubois said; the infant would have to be delivered 'by irons'; in such an operation it might become a question of having to choose between the mother's life or the child's. Napoleon's response was as resolute as in battle: 'Save the mother; it is her right; we can have another child.'[24]

Corvisart returned, and at half-past seven on Wednesday morning the doctors began the agonising operation; mercifully the Empress at last drifted into unconsciousness. The child was delivered by forceps at eight o'clock but for seven minutes gave no sign of life whatsoever. Then there came the lusty cry for which everyone was waiting. By ten minutes past eight Napoleon realised he had a son; and the mother whose survival he had insisted must be the doctors' first priority was once again conscious. Cambacérès, as official witness of state, issued a certificate of birth, confirming the boy would be known by the names

'Napoleon Francis Joseph Charles'. Beneath his signature came those of others who waited through the anxious night: Madame Mère; the Grand Duke of Würzburg; Viceroy Eugène; Napoleon's sisters, Élisa, Caroline and Pauline; Queen Hortense, Marshal Berthier – and History's perpetual prompter, Talleyrand. In her memoirs Hortense recalls that Napoleon remained shaken all day; 'My poor wife has suffered so horribly,' he murmured.[25] But, it was with pride and relief, that he ordered the ceremonial salute to be fired.

At the twenty-second boom across the city, cheering from the streets could be heard within the palace. Paris knew that the Empire had an heir, and Rome a titular king. There followed a display of more genuine rejoicing than for the wedding, eleven months back. Free wine flowed once more and, for a working day, there was sustained revelry. Gradually a simple jingle could be identified coming from the crowd, as contentedly monotonous as the chant of today's football fans:[26]

Et bon, bon, bon
C'est un garçon
Vive Napoléon

In Malmaison, only six miles from central Paris, Josephine heard the news; the distant sound of saluting guns, confirmed by an imperial equerry. Her letter of congratulation brought a reply in which a pompous fatalism never quite conceals personal jubilation: 'My son is a sturdy, healthy child. I trust he will do well. He has my chest, my mouth and my eyes. I trust he will match up to his destiny,' Napoleon wrote.[27]

Paris was not the only city to celebrate on 20 March. For the semaphore carried the news to Italy with astonishing speed: Turin knew within five hours of the birth; Milan and Bologna within six; Venice within seven. On that same morning, the Grand Duke of Würzburg sent a hurried note to his brother in Vienna; it was written with such happy confusion that, after letting Francis know he had a grandson, Ferdinand gave an assurance that 'mother and *daughter* are, thank God, as well as the circumstances permit'.[28] A hussar captain brought the letter to Vienna early on 25 April, completing a ride of almost 820 miles in 106 hours. Francis was delighted by the good news. Eventually, after carefully studying protocol, he ordered Ambassador Schwarzenberg to drive in state to St Cloud and honour the King of Rome by affixing the Grand Cordon of the Order of St Stephen to his cradle. More immediately, Francis wrote back to his daughter on 26 April. His letter told her of his happiness at becoming a grandfather, but it also showed a solicitude based upon tragic experience: Louise must rest for ten days, and take care not to tax her strength during the following six weeks.[29]

Was it by chance or from tact that neither Habsburg brother mentioned the boy's Bonaparte father in his letter? Not so Marie Louise, writing home five weeks after the baby's birth; 'Never would I believe I could be so happy,' she declared. Napoleon, she claimed, was always asking after his father-in-law and reminding her how happy he must feel at having a grandson: 'My love for my husband grows all the time, and when I remember his tenderness I can scarcely prevent myself from crying. Even had I not loved him previously, nothing can stop me from loving him now.'[30] These are hardly the sentiments of a dutiful child sacrificed to a robber bandit for reasons of state. Napoleon had assured Francis two days after meeting his daughter, 'We suit each other perfectly.' Thirteen months later Marie Louise did not simply echo his words; she amplified them.

9

The Torrent and the Sponge

Public rejoicing over the birth of an heir to the throne soon died away. For 1811 was a year of crisis, and a mood of uncertainty prevailed in Paris, dampening enthusiasm for the last of the great festive celebrations, the King of Rome's baptism in Notre Dame on 9 June. Much unease was economic in origin. A failure of banking houses in Lübeck and Amsterdam had been followed at the start of the year by the collapse of thirty-nine investment firms in the capital itself, while virtually no commercial activity was reported from Lyons, Bordeaux or Rouen. Napoleon's attempt to wage economic warfare by the gradual extension of the Continental System was facing defeat: despite new decrees in 1810 which officially tightened the blockade against English goods, there was blatant connivance of smuggling even at the highest level, as Marie Louise had so disingenuously recorded in her diary that spring.

Napoleon assumed that the closure of continental ports to British commerce would stimulate economic growth in his Empire. He was mistaken. Interference with established trade patterns deprived nascent industry of essential supplies. The German dependencies were hardest hit, though within France a shortage of cotton hampered the production and marketing of textiles. The vagaries of nature intensified the distress: Napoleon was especially concerned at the rising price of corn, after two years of wet summers and poor harvests across much of western Europe. He refused to allow the bakers of Paris to increase the cost of bread. At the same time he ordered the mobilisation of unemployed in the more restless districts of the capital to form a disciplined labour force engaged on public works. 'See to it that no situation arises where the police report that they have come across a workman for whom they cannot find a job,' he told the Minister of the Interior on 8 May

1811.[1] This ambitious instruction proved remarkably effective. From almost 22,000 unemployed in the capital that week, the figure fell to 5,750 by mid-summer.

The ruthless and efficient General Savary, who had succeeded Fouché as chief of police the previous summer, kept Napoleon well-informed of the temper of the capital and potentially dangerous regions in the provinces, too. Anxiously he studied police reports of agrarian unrest in Brittany and Normandy. In late May 1811 he took the Empress with him on a ten-day visit to Caen and Cherbourg, hoping that a show of imperial patronage would check the mounting disaffection, and also boost naval construction. At Cherbourg he had some success, but the hard-headed Normans were not satisfied with benign gestures. Ten months later demands for reasonably priced bread led to serious disturbances in and around Caen which continued for several weeks. Ominously, conscripts jointed the rioters, for the first time bringing a whiff of mutiny to taint Napoleon's army.

The burden of the Continental System fell especially heavily on Russia, for four years France's nominal ally in the war with Britain. In 1807, as part of the Tilsit settlement, Tsar Alexander agreed that, unless London accepted his mediation as a peacemaker, he would support Napoleon's measures to undermine Britain's prosperity. Canning, the Foreign Secretary, though willing to use Alexander as an intermediary, was not prepared to accept peace terms proposed from St Petersburg; and Britain fought on, alone. For some twelve months the Russian authorities made a genuine attempt to enforce the restraints of the system, but by the autumn of 1808, when the Tsar travelled to Erfurt, he was well aware of the hardship it imposed on the merchants of St Petersburg and Riga. The value of the rouble fell by sixty per cent between 1807 and 1811. The Russians lost traditional markets for hemp, grain and flax and were expected to provide outlets for French luxuries, perfumes and wines.[2]

Alexander's disenchantment with the Continental System turned to outright hostility when, in the closing weeks of 1810, Napoleon proposed to incorporate the northern coasts of Germany into metropolitan France. Among these lands was the Duchy of Oldenburg, a region on the left bank of the river Weser, where it flows into the North Sea. Dynastic associations had led successive Tsars to look upon Oldenburg as a distant Romanov fief, a link strengthened in 1809 by the marriage of Alexander's sister, Catherine, to Prince George of Oldenburg, her second cousin. The Tsar believed that at Tilsit he had safeguarded the sovereign rights of the ruling Duke. Napoleon's territorial greed therefore seemed to him a cynical betrayal of the alliance. By a decree (*ukaz*) made public on 31 December 1810 he took Russia out of the Continental System. Restraints on imports and exports by sea were lifted, though only foreign 'neutral' ships were allowed into Russian ports, not those flying British flags. At the same time, heavy duties were imposed on the wines, silks and perfumes coming from France. The decree was intended as a deliberate challenge to Napoleon's conviction he was master of Europe. It caused dismay in Paris.

Throughout the ten weeks preceding the King of Rome's birth Franco-Russian relations were under severe strain. More was at stake than questions of trade. The Polish Question returned to plague diplomacy once again. On 12 February 1811 Alexander made approaches to the Poles, offering to proclaim a Polish Kingdom, with a national government and a liberal constitution, if they would abandon the French-sponsored Grand Duchy of Warsaw and join Russia in a war against Napoleon. At the same time he offered Emperor Francis compensation in lands captured from the Turks in modern Romania if the Austrians would cede to his embryonic Polish Kingdom the remaining districts of Galicia, including Lvov. But Francis, who had been wrestling with Polish problems when his son-in-law was still an unknown 'Corsican terrorist', was uninterested in the Tsar's proposal; while Metternich was merely prepared to use it as a bargaining counter in his quest for concessions from Paris. The French, well aware of Alexander's intrigues, also noted the transference of Russian troops and guns from Moldavia to the Vistula. Briefly, in late February 1811, Napoleon feared a surprise attack on the Grand Duchy of Warsaw: a contingency plan was drawn up providing for the westward retreat of Prince Poniatowski's Polish army to defensive positions along the Oder, where Davout would mount a holding operation until reinforced by Napoleon himself and, so the Emperor hoped, by an Austrian corps on his right flank.

Yet, though Davout and Poniatowski kept their armies on the alert until early May, the war scare receded with the coming of spring and the exchange of conciliatory personal messages between Napoleon and Alexander. Neither Emperor wished to go to war, but each remained darkly suspicious of the other's motives: 'Untrustworthy, feeble and fickle,' said Napoleon of the Tsar; while Alexander wrote to his sister of the 'creature who' will only 'loosen his grip on a prize' if 'compelled by force of arms'.[3] In the second week of April Napoleon dismissed his Foreign Minister, Champagny, who favoured negotiations with Russia, and replaced him by Hugues Maret, the director of his personal cabinet office, a dutiful clerk whose ignorance made him a frequent butt for Talleyrand's caustic wit. Caulaincourt, returning to Paris after four years as ambassador in St Petersburg, urged the Emperor never to doubt Russia's ability to sustain a long war. But Napoleon would have none of it; 'one good battle will see the end of ... Alexander's fine resolutions – and his castles of sand as well,' he insisted. Caulaincourt continued to dissent.

The prolonged crisis left Marie Louise with fewer moments of relaxed domesticity than during her first summer of marriage. For much of the time she was content with music lessons from Ferdinando Paër, the ablest teacher in Paris; she became a remarkably skilled pianist, as well as a good harpist. She persisted, too, with her painting, under the tuition of Pierre-Paul Prudhon and Jean-Baptiste Isabey, who had once delighted Marie Antoinette with his painted snuff boxes. She remained shy and was often tongue-tied in the company of anyone whom she suspected of being an ardent partisan of her predecessor. Tentative efforts by her husband to arrange a meeting between the past and present Empress were firmly rejected, though Josephine would have welcomed one.

Occasionally, like any proud Corsican father, Napoleon was able to visit the nursery and admire his son; he would smile down indulgently on the wonder child in the silver-gilt cradle presented by the city of Paris and ornately designed by Prudhon. The Emperor's secretary, Méneval, describes him rushing forward to take the 'little king' in his arms, 'smother him with kisses' and hold him with an assured confidence lacking in the young mother, who was always frightened of dropping him.[4] Napoleon had chosen the Countess of Montesquiou, a member of the old aristocracy and a mother of experience, to 'shape the destinies of France'; she became, with significant prolepsis, 'Governess to the Imperial Children' even before Marie Louise went into labour, and she was with the King of Rome from the moment of his birth. At his baptism it was the Countess who carried him to the font; and it was the Countess who decided each day the hours when a wet-nurse was to meet his needs. She was so loyal to the Emperor that when Napoleon discovered how much Josephine wished to see his son, he turned naturally to her for help. The Countess let Josephine known that, on a certain afternoon, she would be at La Bagatelle, the former summer pavilion of the Duke of Artois in the Bois de Boulogne; and a 'chance encounter' enabled the fallen Empress to sit for an hour with the Countess admiring the boy whose conceptual necessity had cost her the throne.[5] Marie Louise knew nothing of the meeting. Nor indeed does she appear to have known that Marie Walewska had brought *her* son to Paris.

Not that Napoleon was blatantly disloyal to his *bonne Louise*. He was too busy for casual dalliance that summer. On days when there were no deputations to receive and no indolent ministers to assail or councillors to prod into activity, husband and wife would ride out together in the wooded upland behind St Cloud or through the forest glades beyond Rambouillet and St Germain. The Grand Trianon (*Trianon de Marbre*), with the gardens reshaped by her unfortunate great-aunt, remained the Empress's favourite small palace. Long before Marie Louise went to France she revered St Louis as her patron, keeping his festival on 25 August as her name-day, an occasion for personal rejoicing as well as holy obligation; and in 1811 it was at the Trianon that Napoleon chose to celebrate St Louis's Day for her. In the early evening several hundred guests made the sixteen-mile journey out from Paris, in the fashionable silks of summer, for a grand reception and fête. As their carriages entered the park of Versailles the fountains were playing as they had for so many days of celebration under the old regime, but behind them the massive château stood broodingly empty. Six weeks back, Napoleon had spent an afternoon with the court architect minutely inspecting the Bourbon relic, finally deciding that the Empire could not as yet breathe life into it.[6] The Trianon, barely a mile from the great palace, could better serve the imperial court as a residence, with the well-ordered gardens offering spacious grandeur for state receptions.

Yet did the guests enjoy the St Louis's Day innovation? As with most court functions, all was carefully prescribed days in advance: the reception at eight p.m.; a defile to the gardens, where the illuminated peristyle would be admired; then on to a small theatre for two light-hearted sketches, *Les Projets de Mariage* and *La Grande Famille*. Coloured lamps and flambeaux showed a path to follow northwards for a quarter of a mile to the Pavillon Français where the guests would be greeted with a cantata sung beneath the rotunda, before watching children dance around the statue of Venus and finally the country wedding scene from an opera (unspecified); and so back to the Trianon, where supper would be served at small tables. But Napoleon rarely kept to any social timetable, even one he had initialled with approval. The guests arrived that evening, as ordered, by eight o'clock to await, in cramped heat, the formal entry of their sovereigns. For an hour and a half they were left to admire the new furnishings and crystal chandeliers of the Grand Gallery, for Napoleon did not lead Marie Louise out from the private salon to begin the reception until half-past nine. It must have been well after midnight before the guests sat down to supper. There remained for most of them a long carriage drive back to the city.

Ten days previously the Emperor's birthday was, as usual, kept more formally, with an official reception in the throne room of the Tuileries.

At St Cloud in 1808 Napoleon had used the occasion to denounce Austrian preparations for war to ambassador Metternich, a dramatic scene which passed into legend and was well remembered, not least at St Petersburg. Now, in 1811, he gave a repeat performance, with the Russian ambassador, Prince Kurakin, as his victim. Every affront and every grievance over the Tsar's changes of policy was declaimed, with menacing anger mellowed by pained reproof. The forty-minute tirade left the shaken Kurakin in no doubt that his imperial master must either observe the Tilsit accord or face a war as decisive for Russia as the Wagram campaign had been for Austria. To some observers the imperial play-acting seemed so blatant that it was hard to believe he was in earnest; and he admitted in conversation with Caulaincourt that he was confident of bullying Alexander back into a nominal friendship. However, next evening (16 August) Napoleon convened a Council of State at St Cloud: it was, he said, too late in the year for a campaign in the East; but military and diplomatic preparations must begin for an invasion of Russia the following summer.[7]

Yet in the autumn Napoleon seemed once again to be looking westwards. On 19 September 1811 he arrived in Boulogne, having left a sad Marie Louise at Compiègne, their first time apart in more than 500 days. ('You cannot imagine my feelings when I pass your room and see windows and shutters closed,' she wrote to him that evening.) For four days he inspected the fleet and reviewed troops at the camps behind Wimereux and Ambleteuse, where an invasion army had twice threatened England during the past thirteen years. Now, however, Napoleon had another project in mind: the despatch of several thousand men and horses to Ireland to foment rebellion as a means of forcing the British 'to recall their troops from the Peninsula'. It was an idea he speedily abandoned. As on earlier visits to Flushing and Cherbourg, he took note of 'English cruisers' at sea and watched with satisfaction as his flotilla gave chase to isolated vessels scouting too close inshore; but he was a realist. If there was no chance of a convoy slipping out unobserved, he knew that the concentrated power of the Royal Navy would seal the fate of any transports committed to the long voyage to Irish waters. From the camp at Boulogne he travelled on to Ostend and the Scheldt estuary to re-assure himself over coastal defences. At Antwerp, on 30 September, he was re-united with the Empress, making an exhausting visit to Amsterdam, before turning inland up the Rhine.[8] Napoleon was not to see the western seaboard of the continent again until he surrendered to the British in 1815, after Waterloo.

From early December onwards Napoleon supervised detailed planning of the campaign in the East: the concentration of food supplies; the route to be followed by troops moved across Europe from Spain to the Vistula and Italy to Pomerania; the shoeing of some 6,000 horses and their movement, in wagons, to the Polish plain. Six days before Christmas he asked his librarian to supply 'good books with the best information about the topography of Russia, especially Lithuania, and covering marshes, rivers, woods, roads, etc.'. The librarian was also to find the 'the most detailed account in French' of Charles XII of Sweden's campaigns in Poland and Russia in the first years of the eighteenth century.[9]

Planning intensified with the turn of the year – and yet at court these weeks were outwardly as carefree as any in the last three decades. There were fine stagings of plays and of *Didon*, a new opera by the Empress's music teacher, Paër, and so many balls that it seemed as if she had brought with her from Vienna the carnival spirit of the pre-Lenten *Fasching*. Laura Junot describes a masked ball for 1,500 guests at the Tuileries in the first week of February which recalled the glories of Louis XIV, with one of Berthier's aides-de-camp as the Sun, presiding over a quadrille of the Seasons. Five days later, on Shrovetide or Mardi-Gras, there was a second masked ball in the palace, with Marie Louise in a folk costume tribute to Normandy – though had she seen many peasants around Caen in dresses sparkling with spangled gold and silver? There is an ominous echo of Marie Antoinette's lost gaiety in a letter sent by Louise for her sister's fifteenth birthday: 'Here in Paris we are having a wonderful time,' she told Leopoldina. 'In Vienna you cannot have the slightest idea what fun it is for us all.'[10]

There were graver messages passing between Paris and Vienna in these months. Napoleon, who was highly suspicious of Metternich in the days when he was ambassador in Paris, had come to trust him during the six months he spent at the French court after the marriage. And, indeed, in the winter of 1811–12 the Austrian Foreign Minister consistently backed Napoleon. He insisted to Francis that the only way his Empire could recover its lost status as a Great Power was to back France up to the hilt in a war with Russia: Alexander, he argued, 'did not have the remotest prospect of success; loyal compliance would bring revision of the humiliating Schönbrunn Treaty and also a French subsidy, to enable Austria to clamber back from the edge of bankruptcy. In February, however, Metternich was alarmed by news that France had concluded an alliance with Prussia which virtually deprived King Frederick William III of any power to decide the fate or disposition of 20,000 officers and soldiery in his army. Hurriedly the Austrians determined to strike a better bargain.

Napoleon expected his father-in-law to put three times as many troops into the field as the Prussians. But Francis did not have enough trained men, nor sufficient horses and guns, to mobilise such a force. Moreover Austria simply could not finance such an undertaking. The French were offered an 'auxiliary corps' of 30,000, with the troops remaining under Austrian command. Foreign Minister Maret gave an assurance of adequate territorial compensation when it came to redrawing the frontiers, though as most of the lands under discussion were in the hands of French client states there was a certain vagueness over the final terms. But Metternich urged Francis to accept the proposal before the French became impatient and on 14 March 1812 the Franco-Austrian alliance became a formal reality.[11]

By then Napoleon's thoughts were mainly on soldierly affairs. He was in the saddle most mornings, conscious of putting on weight after two years of comfortable living. It would not, he thought, be a long campaign but he knew it would prove physically taxing. An emissary set off for a meeting with Alexander in Vilna, though with little hope of reaching a settlement, for neither side was ready to compromise, especially over Poland. Yet before resorting to war, Napoleon wished to stage a public demonstration of his authority over Europe, a warning to the Tsar of the armed might massed against him. King Frederick Augustus of Saxony was invited to host a gathering of sovereigns in his capital. Dresden would outshine Erfurt, that earlier festival of Empire, now discreetly forgotten. Francis had not been invited to Erfurt. He was to come to Dresden, with his Empress, to see for himself the honours heaped upon his daughter. And so indeed was every sovereign ruler in Germany and the French dependencies.

Napoleon and Marie Louise left St Cloud early on Saturday, 9 May, reaching the Royal Palace beside the Elbe on the following Saturday evening. Musicians, actors, actresses, singers, specialist cooks and floral designers also made journeys eastward across Germany that spring. They were preceded by convoys of wagons transporting tapestries, furniture and wines; even porcelain was carried to Dresden, no doubt to assert the primacy of Sèvres over Meissen. For, though Frederick Augustus may have provided the rococco setting for Napoleon's grand gala, all the stage properties were to be French; the King became in effect a guest in his own capital. The unique nature of the occasion was early impressed on Marie Louise. Francis and Maria Ludovica were not expected until Monday, 18 April, and she wished to ride out to greet them as their carriage rolled along the last dusty miles down from Loschwitz. But Napoleon would not allow it, remaining adamant even when Louise burst into tears: as Empress of the French she was the First Lady of Europe, with precedence over other royalty, even her father and stepmother.

'The happiest two weeks of my life,' said Napoleon reminiscently on St Helena. For almost a fortnight he was the cynosure of Europe, presiding over banquets, leading a royal hunt through the forest of Moritzburg, greeted in the court theatre by a figure on the stage representing the Sun and carrying the inscription, 'Less great and less fair than He'. When, on the second Sunday, he arrived for High Mass at the cathedral he was received with ceremonies unprecedented in Dresden. On that Sunday afternoon he rode slowly through the streets, up to the heights above the river, escorted by Saxon cavalry in their white uniforms and black breastplates; no one could fail to see and hail the Emperor, for he was mounted on a magnificent grey, caparisoned in gold and crimson. Popular adulation fed his overweening solipsism, his assumption that everyone in his past and present existed only in relation to himself and the status he enjoyed. It was at Dresden that, over dinner one evening, he surprised the Emperor of Austria by referring to King Louis XVI, with condescending sympathy, as 'my poor uncle'.[12]

For Francis, who loathed all ceremonial occasions, the days at Dresden were wretchedly tedious. He could see that his daughter was devoted to her husband; improbably, Metternich's political matchmaking had become a union of love. But he could not like the man. 'My son-in-law is a frightful snob,' he commented. Yet there was one moment when Francis almost succumbed to flattery. Napoleon had proposed that the Archduke Charles should lead the Austrian Corps against the Russians, partly because he admired the Archduke's generalship but also because a corps commander of imperial rank would strengthen Austrian commitment to the common cause. When Charles refused, Napoleon pressed the Emperor himself to take personal command in the field, with ex-ambassador Prince Schwarzenberg as chief-of-staff. Francis was tempted by the proposal; to share the laurels of victory in a short campaign against an ex-ally whose soldiers were feared and hated by his subjects would lift his prestige at home. It needed devious political arguments from Metternich and personal reproaches from Maria Ludovica to dissuade Francis. Napoleon had to be satisfied with Schwarzenberg as commandant of the auxiliary corps – 'fat Schwarzenberg', as Louise called him in her journal.[13]

Both Francis and Maria Ludovica were present when, soon after dawn on Friday, 29 May, Napoleon set off from Dresden to join the great army assembling in Poland. They witnessed Louise's tearful farewell, the grief with which she watched the green-upholstered berlin pull away, with Berthier beside the Emperor in the seat that had been hers on the journey out from St Cloud. Before dusk that day the first letter reached her, a hurried note of reassurance brought by a Saxon cavalry officer from Reichenbach, some forty miles along the route. Four more letters followed over the weekend; three from Louise reached her husband in Posen (Poznan). From there, on the Monday evening (1 June) came an affectionate reply: 'You know I love you and how irritated I am not to be seeing you two or three times a day. But I think I shall be doing so again in three months time.'[14]

Louise lingered disconsolately in Dresden for six days after Napoleon's departure, before following her parents back across the frontier to a reunion with her brothers and sisters in Prague. Uncle Ferdinand of Würzburg accompanied his niece, making certain that when she crossed into Bohemia she was received with full imperial honours. That was not to the liking of Maria Ludovica, who had grown increasingly jealous of her stepdaughter. To her intense chagrin, she now had to see in Prague how the Empress of the French was feted in her own right as consort of the supreme ruler on the continent. Surprisingly, Marie Louise fulfilled the role with faultless confidence. In a city where German remained the principal spoken language and where the ladies of her household came as foreign visitors, she showed none of the shyness which so frequently inhibited her conduct at receptions within France. She benefitted, too, from not having Napoleon beside her: he warmly approved of the visit and gave her detailed written instructions on how she should conduct herself; but there was no risk that she would find one day's behaviour criticised before embarking on the next; her Grand Chamberlain, Count Montesquiou (husband of the King of Rome's governess) possessed the necessary tact and experience of court to safeguard her from ceremonial solecisms.[15]

Gifts were distributed with great generosity: gowns and jewellery for Maria Ludovica, who accepted them gracelessly; a touch of Parisian fashion to brighten life for Leopoldina; toys and confectionary for the younger ones. On 12 June, from Marienburg in East Prussia, Napoleon sent a long letter detailing the bounties which etiquette prescribed for members of her household and for Austrian dignitaries who were her hosts.[16] At the same time Napoleon sought amends for a harsh act committed on his orders by his sister Caroline in 1810 when she was escorting the bride to France. At Munich Caroline had insisted that Louise's remaining Austrian companion, Countess Lazansky, should be sent back to Vienna. Now, in Napoleon's letter, the Countess was singled out by name – or almost by name, as it was misspelt – as a person who should receive a present 'worth 50,000 livres' and 'diamonds of the same value'.

Louise was still in Prague when, in the small hours of 23 June, Napoleon crossed the river Niemen upstream from Kaunas (Kovno) and, without a declaration of war, invaded the Russian Empire. More than 160,000 men were massed along a thirty-mile stretch of the river, ready to march on Vilna and, if Alexander did not sue for peace, eastwards along the 'Big One', as Catherine the Great's highway to Smolensk and Moscow was called. This initial assault force was only a fraction of the *Grande Armée de la Russie*, more than 600,000 men, spread in an arc from the Baltic coast to Austrian Galicia and with little more than half the troops drawn from metropolitan France. Supporting them were some 200,000 animals – horses and oxen – of whom 80,000 were the finest cavalry mounts. Somewhere ahead of them in the limitless undulating Russian plain was an enemy army reckoned on paper of comparable size, though effectively cut down to 420,000 troops. Never before in history had two such great armies faced each other along an extended battle front.[17]

There was nothing at fault in the initial planning of this extraordinary campaign. New transport battalions were raised so as to keep moving eastwards the 1,200 wagons which were to supply and re-victual a succession of army depots, for on this occasion Napoleon knew that the terrain would not allow his army to live off the land, as in those distant years in northern Italy. The general strategy bore a familiar hallmark: it would be 1805 again on a huge scale, with the ablest Russian general, Bagration, drawn into a trap near Grodno by an enveloping movement, like the one which overwhelmed Mack at Ulm, while Napoleon with the main army would use the Big One as an arterial line of advance similar to the river Danube seven years back.

At first all seemed satisfactory. From Kaunas Marie Louise was assured that her husband's health was good, though the heat was overpowering; and, as he was about to leave the city for Vilna on 26 June, a further letter let her know that the first army bulletin was on its way to her; 'My affairs are going well; I am in good health, and I think of you' – three phrases which were to recur many times over the next four months. The letter and the first bulletin reached Louise while she was still in Bohemia, at Eger (Cheb); and she was able to discuss it with her father before saying farewell to him at the frontier on 6 July. Bonaparte-Habsburg relations had never seemed so good; it was clearly only a matter of time before 'fat Schwarzenberg' gave both dynasties a victory to celebrate.

By 8 July, when Louise began enjoying a week at Würzburg as the honoured guest of Uncle Ferdinand, matters in Russia were becoming serious, though no word of his problems crept into Napoleon's letters. A fortnight after crossing the Niemen, he remained at Vilna, impatiently waiting for news that his youngest brother, King Jerome of Westphalia, commanding the Third Army, had drawn Bagration towards Grodno, with Davout and Schwarzenberg ready to complete the encirclement. But the task was beyond King Jerome's amateur generalship and was made no easier by a bitter quarrel with his ablest corps commander, Vandamme. Davout, entering Minsk that day, had to report that Bagration seemed to have slipped away. Murat's patrols along the Big One brought no better news: Barclay de Tolly, commanding the Russian First Army, could not be brought to battle. At Vilna Napoleon busied himself with creating an 'active service' alternative capital for his Empire: accredited diplomats followed Foreign Minister Maret to the distant city; even the US minister, Joel Barlow, made the 1,400-mile journey eastwards.

Cannon fire was heard in Paris on Saturday evening, 18 July: a salute to the Empress, returning to St Cloud after eight weeks of absence. But for the Emperor, lodging with Carmelites along the ill-defined borderland separating historic Poland from ancient Muscovy, the only sounds were of horsemen and carriages, and a tolling bell which sought to preserve the conventual horarium. 'My health is good. I suppose you are at St Cloud. My affairs progress very well,' he wrote at noon next day. 'I shall go to Mass. It is Sunday.'[18]

A skirmish at Ostrovno on the following Saturday between Murat's cavalry and Russian hussars raised expectations: the main Russian army was at Vitebsk, ten miles away. There were further skirmishes over the next two days, graphically written up in the tenth bulletin of the *Grande Armée*, with particular praise given to a regiment largely recruited from Paris. The Emperor was confident of winning a great victory on Tuesday. But with the first light of dawn a horseman brought news from Murat's advance patrols. They had crossed the plateau at the approaches to Vitebsk – and all was quiet. Overnight the Russians had slipped away towards Smolensk. A Russian soldier found asleep under a bush was the sole prisoner taken that day. No words of frustration are in the note despatched to Marie Louise from inside Vitebsk at two o'clock on the Tuesday afternoon: 'My affairs go well. My health is fine. It is very hot. I much love you. Kiss my son.' But a few hours later, in the cool of evening, his chamberlain found Napoleon slumped in an armchair, hat still on his head, pale and pensive, and brooding over the battle he had not fought.[19]

For some days it seemed he might call a halt to the campaign, as his leading generals wished. But he was convinced that Tsar Alexander, who was still with his armies, would commit them to battle once the weather cooled; he never doubted he would win any such encounter. After sixteen days of rest and re-assessment, the strange advance was resumed, across a countryside left desolate by the retreating Russians. Many miles to the south, Schwarzenberg loyally obeyed every order from Napoleon's headquarters, waging a largely independent war of manoeuvre against the Russian Third Army around the Pripet Marshes. No victories puffed Austrian pride, as Francis may have anticipated; but no burden of casualties threatened public acceptance of the policy of compliance; and that was as Metternich intended.

On her husband's orders, Marie Louise deputised for him during the birthday celebrations in Paris that summer. Briefly Napoleon hoped that, as Austerlitz was won on the anniversary of his coronation, so decisive victory in Russia would come on the anniversary of his birth, with a battle outside Smolensk. On the previous afternoon there had been a skirmish at Krasnoe and prisoners disclosed that the First Army (Barclay) was massing north of the Dnieper while the Second Army (Bagation) was south of the river. But the Russians preferred to pull back behind the heavily fortified stone ramparts of the historic city, 230 miles west of Moscow. French artillery bombarded Smolensk for thirteen hours, leaving the city in flames. Even so, bitter fighting continued throughout 17 August along the breached ramparts before the Russians pulled away along the road to Moscow. More than 10,000 men of the *Grande Armée* – many of them Germans and Italians – were killed in the assault on Smolensk. The Russians suffered even heavier casualties before Napoleon established his headquarters in the Governor's palace, a stone building which escaped the fire. He was optimistic: the Tsar was no longer commander-in-chief in the field and therefore could not witness the plight of his armies; but Napoleon thought that the loss and destruction of one of Russia's holiest places would bring the long-awaited plea for an armistice. Once again he paused and waited in a captured city.

Letters from Paris took thirteen days to reach Smolensk. On 22 August Napoleon received a birthday present from his wife: a miniature of their son astride a sheep painted not, as he assumed by Isabey, but by Aimée Thibault. He was delighted with the gift, which remained with him on St Helena. A larger portrait, a canvas by François Gérard, was on its way eastwards in the carriage of the Palace Chamberlain, Baron de Bausset, who was delayed by the poor condition of the roads. All news of the 'little king' was welcome: his physical growth, voracious appetite, alleged naughtiness. For the moment, Napoleon had nothing to send in return to Louise for her name-day, except a sentimental reminiscence of 'last year's walk beneath the beautiful illuminations of Trianon'; but by then he was writing to her from Dorogobuzh, with the spoils of Moscow almost within reach and, as he said a few days later, the determination 'to hurry up and finish this business in order to see you and let you judge for yourself the emotions with which you inspire me'.[20] No doubt the fine sentiment was true, although the habitual 'My health is good' was not. For the strain of the campaign was taxing Napoleon's strength. Throughout the next eleven, decisive days he suffered from acute dysuria.

By now he knew that Kutuzov, the wily old fox he had chased down the Danube before Austerlitz, was Russia's commander-in-chief. A stand must be made in defence of Moscow, and Kutuzov chose to give battle on a shoulder of high ground, broken by ravines, some seventy miles west of the city, around a village called Borodino. There was murderous fighting on the afternoon of Saturday, 5 September, as Murat's advance guard struggled to eject the Russians from a fortified hilltop west of Kutuzov's main position. On Sunday the opposing sides prepared for what each recognised would be a great battle next day. At midday through their telescopes Napoleon's staff watched Russian soldiers revere the ikon of the Holy Virgin of Smolensk, which a guard battalion had escorted from the burning city. That afternoon Bausset at last completed his journey and presented Napoleon with Gérard's canvas of the King of Rome; and in the evening the Emperor placed the portrait outside his tent for officers of the Guard to admire. A note scribbled that night told Louise (twice) that he felt very tired but that 'the masterpiece' was much 'appreciated'. 'It is as beautiful as you,' he remembered to add, with affectionate gallantry.[21]

Within a few hours, soon after dawn on 7 September, he watched more than 500 of his guns open up on a four-mile front and soon saw his stepson, Viceroy Eugène, capture Borodino village. The 'most terrible of all my battles', as Napoleon recalled in exile, continued until mid-afternoon, with waves of horsemen, from heavy cavalry to lightly-mounted Cossacks, bearing down on the opposing infantry while cannon turned on each improvised defensive position. Casualties in the *Grande Armée* rose to one in four of committed combatants and among the Russians to more than one in three. Strategically the battle was inconclusive: Kutuzov withdrew from his prepared fortifications, but he kept the army in good order and took up new positions on a ridge a thousand yards to the east. 'I defeated the Russians yesterday,' Napoleon told Louise in a note from the battlefield on Tuesday morning. Kutuzov, too, found time for a letter to his wife that day: he assured her of his good health: 'I have not been beaten,' he insisted, 'and I defeated Bonaparte.'[22]

There was no second day of fighting to resolve the issue, as at Wagram. 'Bonaparte' was left master of the battlefield, which was covered in fog for much of Tuesday and Wednesday. The cloud cover enabled Kutuzov to pull back towards Moscow. The retreat continued, a dozen miles a day, the long columns protected from pursuing cavalry by a Cossack rearguard. At Fili, less than five miles from the Kremlin, Kutuzov summoned a war council early on the following Sunday afternoon (13 October). Should Holy Moscow – the 'Third Rome' to devout Orthodox believers – be defended or, despite patriotic sentiment, should it be abandoned to its fate? Kutuzov listened to conflicting arguments from his generals: two pressed for an immediate attack on the invader; four urged retreat. Kutuzov's strategic thinking ruled out set-piece battles: the vastness of Russia was Tsardom's greatest asset. The army had fallen back 500 miles from the Niemen, weakening the structure of the French Empire with every league the *Grande Armée* lengthened the distance from Paris. A foreigner could not hope to rule Europe from the Kremlin. 'Napoleon is a torrent which as yet we are unable to stem. Moscow will be the sponge that will suck him dry,' Kutuzov declared, with characteristic imagery.[23] Before midnight the first Russian troops passed through an almost deserted city, for most Muscovites had already trailed off to towns and villages away from the invader.

The first waters of the torrent lapped Moscow's walls at midday on Monday. More prosaically, Murat arrived at the city barrier and negotiated a truce with the last Russian soldiers, to allow them to complete their withdrawal before Napoleon made his entry on Tuesday, 15 September, mounted on his grey, Emir. 'Here I am then at last in Moscow, in the palace of the Tsars, in the Kremlin,' he declared to those around him, as if in disbelief. He prepared to go into residence, ordering the King of Rome's portrait to be hung on a wall of the Tsar's inner apartments. Almost immediately he wrote to Marie Louise; but the letter may well have been burnt before it could reach a courier, for we know of it only from a later reference.

He was relieved to be in a palatial city again, both for his own sake and for his men. The *Grande Armée* had suffered terrible losses during the eighty-two days since crossing the Niemen, not only at Borodino and Smolensk and in the smaller skirmishes but from the heat and from the harsh conditions imposed by the enemy's scorched earth policy. Barely one third of the original invaders reached Moscow, where their low morale was lifted by the prospect of 'abundance and good winter quarters'. From the belfry tower of Ivan Veliki Napoleon looked out on the city with contentment. A thin spiral of smoke rose from the ashes of a fire in one of the market quarters which his troops had extinguished. It did not worry him. The prospect was better than at Smolensk. He admired the fine and empty houses of the nobility, 'furnished', he told Louise later, 'in French fashion with unbelievable luxury'.[24] That night he retired early to bed certain that now that he held Moscow in his hands, Alexander would wish to talk peace.

At four o'clock on Wednesday morning Napoleon was woken with news that high winds were carrying flames from several fires towards the Kremlin walls. At first he refused to leave, despite warnings from his staff that the fire might spread to the arsenal and cause a disastrous explosion. Eventually Berthier, who was constantly at his side during these troubled days, pointed out that he risked being cut off from the troops defending the city: what would happen if the Russians, having fired central Moscow, launched a surprise counter-attack? Reluctantly, Napoleon agreed to be escorted through the burning streets to the safety of the Petrovsky Palace, two miles to the north of the walls. Even so he was back at the Kremlin within forty-eight hours, long before heavy rain quenched the last embers of the fire; the Tsar's apartments were untouched by the flames and the Kremlin, as the historic heart of Holy Russia, remained a talisman of victory for his whole campaign.

Yet, as Napoleon rode through the smouldering ruins of the city, 'with fragments of walls or half demolished pillars' as 'the only vestiges to mark the site of streets', the magnitude of the disaster impressed him.[25] His letters to the Empress still rang with confidence and two Russians of some social standing were found and sent off independently along the St Petersburg road with messages of goodwill for his 'dear brother' sovereign in the Winter Palace. But his personal staff increasingly noticed moments of doubt, 'restlessness and irritation'. The immediate future was far from clear. For he had begun to realise that, whatever their Tsar might think or do or say, the Russian people were ready to continue waging war in ways he never envisaged.

10

'Write to Papa François'

News of Napoleon's entry into Moscow and of the Great Fire which swept the city did not reach Paris until the middle of the first week in October. The Empress had assumed he was already at the Kremlin when she wrote to him on 12 September though, of course, she had not then heard of the battle of Borodino. In writing to her friend, Victoria (now Countess of Crenneville) she emphasised how miserable she felt at Napoleon's prolonged absence and her concern for his safety; 'I am endlessly tormenting myself and constantly uneasy,' she declared. 'For a day to pass without a letter from him is enough to throw me into the depths of depression, and when one does come, it brings me only an hour or two of relief.' To her formidable mother-in-law Louise gave the customary family assurance, 'My health is good'; but for Victoria there was a chronicle of migraines, stomach pains and rheumatism. She complained, too, of the unsympathetic response of Dr Corvisart, who refused to take her illness seriously. Was she bored? Napoleon certainly expected little from her. He insisted that she went to the theatre for a play or opera on Thursdays and that she was seen publicly keeping her religious observance on Sundays, duly receiving diplomats and officers of state after Mass. But she had no power of Regency; she seemed content to spend much of her time at St Cloud, 'where the air agrees with me' and she could take long walks gossiping with the Duchess de Montebello. To the pleasures of music and painting she now added, as occasional relaxation, all the excitement of a game of billiards.[1]

In his letters Napoleon made two repeated requests: 'Kiss your son three or four times for me,' was easy for Louise to fulfil; 'Write frequently to your father,' was not. For it was by no means clear to her what Napoleon wished her to say. Early in the campaign she wrote of the devotion she felt towards her husband, of how deeply she pined for him now that he was away from her. That was what Francis expected to read; he had received similar messages from Marie Thérèse in earlier years. But his son-in-law was counting on a more positive correspondence, one which would mingle political counsel with filial affection, so as to offset the influence of Maria Ludovica and the anti-French faction at the Habsburg court.

It was the future of Schwarzenberg's auxiliary corps that first put this daughter-father correspondence to the test. In July Napoleon had been well satisfied by his ally's actions against the Russian Third Army west of the Pripet Marshes. But by mid-September he was beginning to doubt the intensity of Austrian commitment to the common cause. From guarded comments in a letter from Schwarzenberg to Berthier, Napoleon deduced that the authorities in Vienna were keeping the Austrian contingent on a tight rein. 'Advise your father to reinforce Schwarzenberg's corps,' Louise was urged on 6 October, 'so that it may be a credit to him.' Dutifully, though with evident embarrassment, the Empress did as she was told, prefacing the request with an oblique *Man sagt* ('One says ...'). But she lacked a sense of urgency: the letter to her father from St Cloud is dated '4 November'; it was answered, negatively, from Baden on 5 December; Francis emphasised that the size of Schwarzenberg's corps met all treaty obligations, at a time of such menacing portent for 'my Monarchy'.[2]

By that first week in December, sixty days after Napoleon's initial plea, this refusal from Francis had little military importance. Independently, he had already sent reinforcements to Schwarzenberg, whose troops were inflicting a severe mauling on the Russians near Volkovisk on the very day that the Empress's letter reached Vienna. But the episode should have given Napoleon a double warning: it showed that Marie Louise was of little value as a transmitter of military intelligence and that her father was unlikely to heed family sentiment when shaping strategic policy. Neither lesson did he learn.

Throughout the autumn and early winter of this critical year Napoleon remained curiously imperceptive to the changed political conditions around him. Though he believed the war against the Tsar's armies won when Moscow fell, he could find no peace terms to define, nor could he decide on his next move. By despatching two Moscow citizens northwards with generalised messages of goodwill for the Tsar, he was putting the ball in the other court; and Alexander declined to serve it back to him. Napoleon remained puzzled at the Tsar's lack of response. After two and a half weeks in Moscow, Napoleon proposed sending Caulaincourt, the most respected of his ex-ambassadors, to St Petersburg to charm Alexander into setting down *his* ideas on a lasting peace. When Caulaincourt demurred, Napoleon ordered his successor as ambassador, Lauriston, to visit Russian headquarters in the field and induce Kutuzov to let the Tsar know of his wish to end for all time the conflict between two 'great and generous nations'. Kutuzov interpreted the Lauriston mission as a sign of French discomfiture. He was willing to wait upon events. But he forwarded Napoleon's message to the Winter Palace. 'Peace?' Alexander exclaimed on reading it, 'But we have still not made war. My campaign is only just beginning.' No reply was sent back to Moscow. The peace mission proved as futile as Caulaincourt had feared.[3]

Briefly Napoleon considered marching on St Petersburg, but he found little support for a northwards advance from his marshals. Instead, on 19 October he set out from Moscow along the Kaluga road, seeking a southerly route to winter quarters in Poland. Five days later Eugène's Army of Italy forced two of Kutuzov's regiments back from the town of Maloyaroslavets; but the victory was won at such heavy cost that, on 26 October, Napoleon decided to abandon the southern route and head for the 'Big One' and the familiar trail through Smolensk to Vilna. On that Monday he wrote to the Empress: she might join him at winter quarters in Poland, he suggested.[4]

The retreat began in good weather: occasional sunshine by day; ominous frost at night. 'The weather stays very fine,' Napoleon wrote from east of Viasma on Tuesday, 3 November. 'Easy marching ... not fatiguing.' And, still concerned with the Austrian alliance, he added, 'Do please write often to your father and to Vienna. If you were to come to Poland, might your father wish to visit you there and stay for a few days?'[5] By the following morning, however, such speculative planning of a family reunion was out of the question. For, overnight, heavy clouds loomed up in the east and by the small hours there was a deep covering of snow over ruts and potholes in the road and drifting in the fields where light horsemen were on the watch for Cossack raiders. Winter had struck, with an unsuspected early intensity. At the weekend the blizzard was so severe that the Emperor was forced to abandon his carriage and trudge through the snow, with Caulaincourt and Berthier guiding him forward towards Smolensk – and four days of respite in a ruined city, short of food and fodder.

None of these privations was known in Paris for another five weeks. But once jubilation over the victory at Borodino and the occupation of Moscow died away, there was mounting uneasiness in the capital. Rumours of pending disaster began to circulate. If any of these fears reached the Empress, out at St Cloud, she had the good sense to take no notice of them. She could not, however, ignore the extraordinary happening on 23 October, a Friday morning when a senior equerry hurried up to her as she was about to set off on her walk through the park. A revolution had broken out in central Paris, he claimed; she should set off at once for the military academy of St Cyr, taking the little King with her and relying on the officer cadets for loyal protection.

Marie Louise was unimpressed: speedy flight from pending doom was a familiar childhood experience which during her days in Hungary she had come to think often unnecessary; she refused to be panicked. And rightly so; for, within the hour, a second equerry rode up, insisting that she was not to worry for all was quiet again. On the previous evening General Claude de Malet, suspected of conspiracy in 1808, but deemed mentally unstable, had escaped from an asylum. Once in central Paris Malet began circulating a forged Senate pronouncement which declared that the Emperor had perished in Russia. He then called on the people of Paris to support a Republican government, of which he declared himself provisional president. Remarkably he was able to shoot and wound the commandant of the Paris garrison and rouse the Minister of Police (Savary) and the prefect of police from their beds and have them locked up. He even convinced the commandant of one of the barracks of Napoleon's death, before saner counsels at last prevailed and Malet was himself taken into custody.

For Marie Louise the whole affair continued to seem insignificant. As she later explained to her father, she refused to be alarmed 'over trouble caused by a few madcaps [*thörichte Köpfe*], for I know the loyalty and devotion felt by the people for their emperor'. Hortense, hurrying next day from Malmaison to St Cloud, was able to report to Josephine that her successor remained serenely unperturbed. Not so others in Paris. At the Ministry of War, General Clarke was so worried by the report of Napoleon's death that he swore an oath of loyalty to the King of Rome as the Emperor's successor. Cambacérès, the Archchancellor, and the extremely angry General Savary swiftly imposed order and calm in the capital. Before the end of the week Malet, and fourteen gullible dupes who assisted him, had been brought to trial and executed.[6]

News of the Malet affair first reached Napoleon on 6 November, a day of wretchedly heavy snow, when he was still forty miles east of Smolensk. He was disconcerted: for ten hours much of Paris had accepted a tale that he was dead, and the structure of imperial government had begun to totter. Had the affair been a genuine conspiracy, led by a name of repute, he might well have lost his throne. Already he was contemplating a return to the capital rather than seeking winter quarters in Poland. The Malet affair settled the matter for him. To Caulaincourt he confided that, once he had brought his army back from the frozen plains to within reach of the well-stocked Polish depots, he would head for Paris and re-assert his sovereignty.

First, however, he had to avoid a trap by which three converging Russian armies sought to destroy him along the banks of the river Berezina. At Orsha, on 20 November, 'the Emperor, for the first time, struck me as uneasy about the future', Caulaincourt later recalled:[7] Ney's corps had narrowly escaped annihilation along the road from Smolensk; Davout had lost his maps, his papers and even his marshal's baton to Russian cavalry; and Chichagov's 'Army of Moldavia' had captured Minsk, threatening the *Grande Armée* from the south. Gloomily, on that Friday morning, Napoleon ordered the destruction of all surplus baggage and the burning of official documents and private papers. Into the flames went, not only letters from Marie Louise, but Gérard's famous portrait of the King of Rome, which was hailed with such reverence on the eve of Borodino and held pride of place within the Kremlin only five weeks back.[8]

Next day Chichagov's troops raided Borisov and destroyed the bridge carrying the road from Smolensk over the Berezina. Only the ingenuity and heroism of General Eblé's pontoon builders, working under fire in blizzard conditions, enabled Napoleon and 50,000 of his troops to cross the icy, frozen river and, on 29 November, continue the retreat towards Vilna. Six nights later, at Smorgon, some fifty miles short of Vilna, Napoleon handed over command of what remained of the *Grande Armée* to Murat.

With Caulaincourt as sole companion, the Emperor set out on a thirteen-day journey by carriage and sledge through Warsaw, Dresden, Erfurt and Mainz to Paris. Shortly before midnight on 18 December Marie Louise, back in residence at the Tuileries when St Cloud became unbearably cold, was startled by a commotion in the antechamber to her bedroom. But it was not a second Malet on the loose. From out of the night came endearments in a familiar voice. The husband whom she believed more than a thousand miles away stood beside her once more.[9]

Three days previously Colonel Anatole de Montesquiou, eldest son of the 'little King's' governess, had arrived with news of the Berezina. The French people learnt how the Emperor defeated 'the combined Russian armies' gathered on the banks of the river; and the Colonel brought eight captured standards with him as tokens of victory. But on the morning of 17 December *Le Moniteur* published the famous twenty-ninth bulletin, dictated by Napoleon at Molodechno fifteen days earlier, which revealed the heavy losses of the retreat, put blame on the severity of the weather, and praised the bravest of the troops who 'saw in the various ordeals a challenge to win new glory'.

The Emperor knew that the report in *Le Moniteur* was bound to cause dismay. He hoped that his homecoming, together with a display of the captured flags, would steady nerves in the capital, giving an impression that the army had retired to winter quarters, ready to emerge and win a decisive victory with the coming of warmer weather. He insisted that the normal routine of court life be observed as closely as possible. After Mass on the following Sunday (20 December) he received the Senate and the Council of State, gracefully acknowledging their felicitations on his return. In the last days of the old year, and again on the first Tuesday in January, he was shooting in the woods around Versailles, as during the Christmas season a year previously. Although he presided over four sessions of the council of interior administration and two sessions of the council of finance, he also found time to accompany the Empress on a visit to the salon, to assess the latest canvasses by Isabey, Gérard and their pupils. These activities – ceremonial, administrative, recreational – were, with his encouragement, reported by the newspapers. His allies and his enemies would know that, for the Emperor, it remained 'business as usual'.

At Christmas and the New Year the public seemed reassured. But over the next two months so many families received bad news, or no news at all, that it became impossible to conceal the magnitude of the disaster. When the paladins of the Empire began to return from the East, prematurely aged and on extended sick leave, morale plummeted again. General Junot, the forty-one-year-old Duke of Abrantès, had been left to clear the battlefield after Borodino, later leading his Westphalian troops across the Berezina: he arrived home in January, dazed, bent low over a stick, shuffling in a shabby greatcoat. Even Marshal Berthier appeared a broken man, close to nervous collapse, when he returned to his estate at Grosbois that February. Yet the Emperor still persisted in maintaining the imperial facade. Shrove Tuesday fell on 2 March that year; from a camp near Magdeburg Viceroy Eugène, commanding the last units of the *Grande Armée*, wrote to his wife: 'For us' there had 'never been a sadder' festive day. But in Paris that evening his stepfather presided over a traditional masked ball at the Tuileries as though France was at peace. Colonel de Fezensac, a kinsman of the Montesquious, had led the 4th Regiment of the Line during the retreat; there were 3,000 men in the regiment when it crossed the Niemen but only 200 survivors when Fezensac reached the Vistula in December. Ten weeks later he found no pleasure in the ball which he dutifully attended at the Tuileries; 'I felt as if I were dancing on tombs,' he recalled in his memoirs.[10]

Such insensitivity was attributed to the influence of Marie Louise by her detractors at court; it showed an 'Austrian frivolity' reminiscent of her great-aunt's indiscretions, they scoffed. This was nonsense. The Empress was in no mood for carnival that year, as she told her friend Victoria, in a letter written two days before the masked ball: 'I do not like dancing any more,' she added.[11] More serious matters were on her mind. For, soon after his return, Napoleon had decided on an early double coronation, for the Empress and for the King of Rome: he believed a solemn service would strengthen the monarchy, bolstering it against the neo-republicanism of hotheads like Malet. At the same time, the Empress would be given powers of regency, effective in the sovereign's absence or, as she wrote to her father, 'under the saddest of circumstances': 'This sign of confidence by the Emperor flatters me,' she added.[12]

Napoleon was convinced 'Papa François' would be gratified by the decision to have his daughter and grandson crowned. He might even come to Paris in person, thus sealing the Austro-French alliance at a time when it was under strain. For, as envisaged by Napoleon, the double ceremony would match, and even outshine, the earlier coronation in Notre Dame. He was confident that the Pope would be there; for since June 1812 Pius VII had been interned in the west wing of the palace of Fontainebleau, having been brought there from Savona, where it was feared a British naval raid might 'rescue' him. By the end of the year Napoleon was ready for a revised Concordat with the Church and a public act of reconciliation. Marie Louise had visited His Holiness in the previous summer: now, in mid-January 1813, Emperor and Empress went into residence at Fontainebleau, on the ground floor of a wing adjoining the Pope's apartments.

'For the last six days we have been at Fontainebleau,' Marie Louise wrote to her father on the evening of 27 January.' 'The Emperor has settled the affairs of Christianity with the Pope ... the treaty was signed a quarter of an hour ago ... You will be happy as I am to learn the news.'[13] Next day Napoleon returned to Paris, and let the Senate know of a new Concordat which would safeguard his authority over Church appointments within France. He never doubted that, as part of a general reconciliation, the Pope would bless the double coronation. No time must be wasted. Tentatively he suggested to the privy council that the ceremony be held in Notre Dame on the first Sunday in Lent. His Austrian ally and the puppet rulers received advance notice that 7 March was a likely date; but, as yet, no formal invitations were despatched.

Francis welcomed the news of Marie Louise's advancement in status, though with more caution than his daughter anticipated. He had no intention of coming himself to Paris; as personal envoy he would send the richest landowner at his court, Prince Esterhazy. And Prince Schwarzenberg, as late commander of the auxiliary corps, would also be present to 'stand beside his commander-in-chief in order that Europe shall have no doubt of the Court of Austria's sentiments'.[14] This was what Napoleon wished to hear. Far less agreeable was another letter which included 'advice from your old father' to Louise: she should 'seek peace at home and abroad' so as to safeguard her son's future; 'My sole wish at this moment is for such a peace,' Francis wrote, 'and the opportunity to protect your husband, so far as possible, from any dangers to which he may become exposed.'[15] Was this kindly paternal advice? Or an oblique warning to his son-in-law?

Paris was denied the unique spectacle of a Bishop of Rome crowning a King of Rome on the eve of his second birthday. For there was no coronation, single or double. Nor was there a new Concordat. Under pressure from hard-line cardinals who hurried to Fontainebleau as soon as they heard a settlement had been reached, Pius VII went back on his word. More precisely he claimed, rightly, that all he had signed was an agreement on ten possible points for discussion. Without papal backing, Napoleon doubted the value of a coronation service. Instead, on 30 March 1813, Marie Louise swore an oath of fidelity to the Emperor and to the constitution at a ceremony in the Élysée Palace, during which Napoleon conferred on her the title of Regent.[16]

The proclamation was made without any propaganda trumpeting. It was an act of state, not a gala occasion. For at last Napoleon realised the urgency of the hour. Over the preceding three months he had been forced to accept a series of rebuffs to his general strategy: an unauthorised armistice with the Russians, concluded on 30 December at Tauroggen by General Yorck, took the Prussian corps operating on the left flank of the *Grande Armée* out of the conflict; King Frederick William III's diplomatic revolution in February brought Prussia into alliance with Russia and, on 17 March 1813, into a patriotic war of German liberation from France; and the Russian occupation of Warsaw on 8 February led to the collapse of Napoleon's Polish policy. There were fears over the loyalty of Saxony and Bavaria; and a new threat from Sweden, for on 23 March an open letter from Bernadotte (elected Prince Royal of Sweden in August 1810 with Napoleon's backing) warned his 'former brother in arms' of the sorrow with which he would feel bound to 'defend the rights of the people who have invited me to the succession of their throne'.[17] The powerful French-dominated combination massed against Russia nine months previously was turning into a grand coalition of France's enemies.

Yet by the spring of 1813, through long and concentrated hours of planning, Napoleon was able to raise an army of more than 200,000 troops for a campaign in Germany. He was himself aware of many deficiencies: officers so inexperienced and incompetent that 'their men laugh at them', he complained to the Minister of War, 'youngsters straight from school who have never been to St Cyr, posted to new regiments'.[18] Napoleon was certain he enjoyed numerical advantage, but he knew he could not hope to replace lost cannon until August and he remained desperately short of light cavalry. But new and lighter wagons, made according to his own specifications, promised faster movement forward than in the previous year. He envisaged a swift advance on Berlin and the relief of isolated garrisons still holding out between the Oder and the Vistula. A single Napoleonic victory would send the Russians hurrying back to their old frontier and convince waverers within the Confederation of the Rhine that so great a military genius remained invincible. And Vienna? 'From Austria there is no cause for anxiety: the most intimate relations exist between the two courts,' Napoleon assured his Archtreasurer, Charles Lebrun, a week after Marie Louise was proclaimed Regent.[19] Unconvincingly, Napoleon even let Francis know that he looked upon the Empress as his prime minister.

He left St Cloud to join the Army of the Elbe in Germany early on the morning of Thursday, 15 April, and he reached Mainz at midnight next day. By Sunday afternoon a familiar theme was creeping into his letters to the Empress. 'Write to Papa François once a week,' he asked; but on this occasion she was told 'to send him military particulars' as well as assurances of his son-in-law's personal affection. By the end of the week she was expected to warn her father against members of the Austrian court who would 'drag him into the war' against France. She was also to remind him that by now Napoleon had 'a million men under arms ... and could have as many as I choose'.[20]

By nightfall on 1 May Napoleon had reached Lützen, the small town in Saxony where, in 1632, King Gustavus Adolphus of Sweden was mortally wounded. Though there were several bloody skirmishes in the last days of April, he had not as yet been able to bring to battle the main Russo-Prussian army. Next morning, a Sunday, began uneventfully and before resuming the pursuit towards Leipzig, Napoleon was able to send off a letter to Marie Louise, in which for the first time he complained of her stepmother's implacable Francophobia. Unexpectedly, shortly before midday, he heard the sound of heavy cannonfire five miles to the south, around the village of Kaja: Yorck, Blücher and the main Prussian Guard had surprised Ney and the III Corps, with Marmont's IV Corps in support. The Emperor himself rallied the troops in the early afternoon, and before dusk successive attacks by the Old Guard and the Young Guard forced the enemy back on Dresden, which the French entered five days later. It was, so Marmont wrote in his memoirs, 'probably the day in his career when Napoleon ran the greatest personal risk on a field of battle';[21] and Paris duly celebrated another of the Emperor's victories. But in earlier years, cavalry would have exploited the evening's tactical gains and turned a repulse into a rout. Some 180,000 horses perished during the Russian campaign. It proved impossible to find and train replacements for them or their riders.

At Dresden Napoleon was little more than thirty miles from the borders of Bohemia, where Francis had begun to assemble an army of 64,000 men; and he remained deeply worried at the threat of Austrian intervention. Even before he reached the city he wrote to Marie Louise complaining, not simply of the firebrands around her father in Vienna, but of Francis's personal attitude. He ordered her to send for Floret, who was once again in charge of Austrian affairs in Paris. As Regent, she was to ask Floret to send a warning to Emperor Francis of the disasters that would follow any rupture of relations with France, for Napoleon had a million men under arms, and she was to tell Floret, 'the French will be in Vienna before September.' Marie Louise was also to write directly to her father, urging him 'not to forfeit the friendship of a man who is deeply attached to him'.[22] Dutifully the Regent did as she was told. At the same time Napoleon ordered King Maximilian Joseph of Bavaria, Viceroy Eugène in Italy and Murat as King of Naples to raise armies which could be seen to threaten Austria. 'By this means I shall attain an ascendancy over Austria, enabling me to menace her and not her me,' he explained on 12 May to the Viceroy.[23]

'People are trying to mislead Papa François,' Napoleon told Marie Louise two days later, 'Metternik [*sic*] is a mere intriguer.'[24] This conviction that Francis was under pressure from within his family was justified; but Napoleon underrated the subtlety of Metternich's policy, and he did not realise the depth of the Emperor's dependence on his minister. The 'repairing' which he had seen as necessary after Wagram was still not 'done'; and nobody other than Metternich possessed the craftsmanship to complete the task.

Francis's confidence in his Foreign Minister was well illustrated by an episode in March, about which Napoleon received only confused information. For when Metternich let his sovereign know how, a few weeks earlier, his agents had discovered that Archduke John was involved in a conspiracy to incite a people's uprising against the French in southern Germany and the Illyrian provinces, Francis at once placed his brother under house arrest in Vienna. There must be no hankering for a war of revenge, that disastrous folly of four years back. For Austrian policy, as now defined by Metternich and accepted by the Emperor, sought to acquire diplomatic strength and recover imperial status in central Europe through observance of a strict neutrality. An Austrian army might be seen assembling between Teschen and Prague, but it was to remain well behind the frontier. At the right moment, Metternich wished Francis to dictate a peace settlement under threat of armed intervention, on one side or the other; but not yet. In this spring and summer of 1813 he did not want a *total* victory for either Napoleon or his Russo-Prussian opponents. Lasting French hegemony would condemn the truncated Habsburg Empire to extinction. On the other hand, Russia remained a great threat to any Habsburg re-assertion of authority across eastern Europe; and a restored and independent Prussian Kingdom threatened to bring back the rivalries of Francis's earliest years on the throne by renewing the struggle for supremacy in both Germany and Poland. When General Count Bubna reached Dresden late on 16 May with instructions from Metternich, he came to mediate a durable peace which would, in effect, keep in being the French Empire and the Rhine Confederation while making Austria trustee for a buffer zone across Germany.

On that Sunday night Napoleon and Bubna talked until two in the morning. They met again for three hours on Monday afternoon, discussing a letter from Francis which assured his son-in-law of his personal concern for his welfare but also set down the conditions of peace which a benevolently neutral Austria would strive to attain. They were not to Napoleon's liking. Metternich required the surrender of French enclaves on the right bank of the Rhine, the revision of existing frontiers in Italy and with Bavaria, a new partition of Poland, and an opportunity to share with France in protecting and upholding the Confederation of the Rhine. With the victory at Lutzen to boost his prestige, Napoleon scoffed at such concessions: a settlement of this character, he wrote to Francis, would make him 'the laughing-stock of the English'. Once again he urged Francis to recognise family ties of affection and not align himself with the enemies of France.[25] On Tuesday afternoon Napoleon set out from Dresden, heading eastwards across the Elbe, and on Thursday (20 May) he engaged the main Russo-Prussian army under Wittgenstein outside Bautzen, in fortified woodland on the right bank of the river Spree.

Bautzen – or Wurschen, as the French called the battle – was a two-day clash of arms. Briefly it held promise of becoming another Austerlitz; even Tsar Alexander was there again, confounding commanders in the field by well-intentioned interventions. Soult broke through the centre of the enemy line, as on that distant December morning, while Ney and Oudinot prepared to complete an enveloping movement from the south. But Ney moved far too slowly and, hampered again by lack of light horsemen, could not prevent Wittgenstein and the Tsar pulling back towards Silesia. Both armies lost some 20,000 men over the two days. Tactically Bautzen was a French victory, but Napoleon insisted it should not be celebrated, like Lutzen, by the Regent attending a service of thanksgiving at Notre Dame. He was depressed: his commanders had been unable to exploit their breakthrough; and he had also suffered a deep personal loss. On 22 May, General Duroc, Grand Marshal of the Palace and Duke of Friuli, was mortally wounded by a Russian cannon-ball as he rode behind him at Reichenbach (Dzierzoniow). Duroc, with whom he played *balle au camp* at Rambouillet three summers back, was a friend and companion in arms from the siege of Toulon. Napoleon mourned his fate, simply and sincerely, in two successive letters to the Empress: 'You know how fond I was of the Duke of Friuli.'[26]

A rumour that it was the Emperor himself who had been killed on that day spread as far as Dresden. Caulaincourt and Berthier were alarmed. In pursuing the enemy into Silesia, Napoleon ran a risk of overstretching the reins of government, as in Russia seven months previously. They urged him to accept an Austrian proposal for an armistice, both to counter summer exhaustion in his army and to attend to pressing problems elsewhere in the Empire. On 1 June Napoleon occupied Breslau, now the Polish city of Wroclaw. It was the farthest east his armies ever reached after the previous winter of disaster. Next day he accepted a thirty-six hour suspension of hostilities and at Plaeswitz on 4 June it was agreed there should be an armistice, operative until at least 20 July, while negotiations continued for a settled peace on the continent.

Napoleon told Viceroy Eugène that, during the armistice, he would 'take up residence near Dresden': it would be a good centre from which to keep in touch 'with my states of Italy and France', he explained.[27] The semaphore telegraph now reached Mainz, whence couriers could carry news to Dresden in about twenty hours of hard riding. Close contact with events in Paris was essential, for Napoleon had never intended Marie Louise to exercise any real power. The Regent was, almost literally, the figurehead of the state: she might preside over the Senate, but neither decide the agenda nor propose any law on her own initiative. Her mind was held by her husband to be 'too young' for defilement by the reading of police reports; and ministers were ordered not to raise any matters 'that might worry her'. Cambacérès, the sixty-year-old Archchancellor of the Empire, remained effective head of the administration, telling the Regent exactly what was to be said or done. His homosexuality made him as safe an intimate adviser as any eunuch, and Marie Louise trusted him. One day in early June she even received him while still in bed, as she casually wrote to her husband. But such a lapse of propriety brought a stern rebuke posthaste back from Saxony: 'Under no circumstances or on any pretext are you to receive anyone while you are in bed,' Napoleon decreed. 'It is improper conduct until over the age of thirty.'[28]

The familiar pleas to write to Papa François dropped out of the correspondence from Dresden. There was no need for them, as Napoleon remained in touch directly with the Austrians, receiving Bubna within a few hours of his return to the city. Francis himself was close at hand, having left Vienna for Bohemia in the last week of May. He went into residence at Gitschin, a castle only eighty miles south-east of Dresden, where Metternich joined him a few days later. Although Napoleon continued to believe in Francis's personal goodwill, he was convinced of Metternich's duplicity and, as he told Eugène, highly doubtful if any good would come out of the proposed peace talks. The lost opportunities of this summer of 1813 all sprang from Napoleon's consistent failure to understand that Metternich still genuinely hankered after a neo-Kaunitz partnership. He wished to keep a French Empire in being, as a counterweight to Russia and a restored Prussia.

The presence at Tsar Alexander's headquarters of Metternich's Francophobe predecessor, Stadion, reinforced Napoleon's fears. In mid-June the Tsar crossed into Bohemia to spend several days at Opotschna, one of the Colloredo family's estates; and Metternich met Alexander there for two days of discussion. They were not easy talks: the Tsar wanted nothing short of total victory over the French; he mistrusted Metternich as the Habsburg-Bonaparte marriage broker. So concerned was Napoleon over this encounter that when Metternich arrived back at Gitschin he found awaiting him an invitation to cross into Saxony for further talks. 'My evil star calls me to Dresden,' he informed Stadion cryptically.[29]

He was received by Napoleon in the Marcolini Palace outside Dresden on Saturday, 26 June, at a quarter to twelve in the morning. They were still talking at half past eight in the evening. No one else was present. In later years, Metternich dramatised the occasion: his memoirs describe how Napoleon angrily threw his hat into the corner of the room as his visitor calmly prophesied disaster unless France accepted a compromise peace. That, said Napoleon, would be tantamount to losing four battles: the Empire could hardly survive such a fall in prestige; 'My reign will not outlast the day when I have ceased to be strong and therefore to be feared,' he is supposed to have admitted. A report prepared that weekend by Metternich for Emperor Francis describes a more reasonable discussion. But for Napoleon, too, it was a storm-tossed encounter. To

Caulaincourt he insisted that he had won a series of arguments with his visitor; 'Thirteen times I threw the gauntlet down and thirteen times he picked it up again, but the last time it stayed in my hands,' he declared. To Marie Louise he merely complained of a long and exhausting conversation. Metternich was a poor adviser for 'Papa François', he observed in his next letter home.[30]

It is clear nothing was settled that Saturday. But Metternich stayed in Dresden four more nights: long enough for a courier to reach Schwarzenberg and return with news that he needed three weeks to complete mobilisation; long enough, too, for Metternich to discover in talks with Maret, Caulaincourt and Berthier how narrow was the gap between their views on peace and his own. As he was about to leave for Gitschin early on Wednesday morning he was summoned again to the Marcolini Palace where Napoleon walked with him along the gravelled paths of the garden, putting forward constructive proposals for a peace conference. After an hour, they adjourned to the study, where Maret drafted a declaration for them to sign: Napoleon accepted Austria's armed mediation in principle, though without preconditions; a peace congress would meet at Prague on 10 July; and the armistice was extended to 10 August, in the hope that the talks would rule out the need for any further military action.

This Dresden Note ran counter to proposals agreed between the Tsar and Metternich at Opotschna. They stipulated that Napoleon must accept certain general terms for a new settlement before any peace congress opened; and, while Metternich was at Dresden, Stadion committed Austria to a secret alliance based upon the Opotschna terms. Not surprisingly, the Russians and Prussians were, at first, angry at what they regarded as Metternich's double-dealing. The Austrians, however, were in a strong position, for if Russia and Prussia sought to renew the fighting, they needed Schwarzenberg's army. And Emperor Francis was well-satisfied with his Foreign Minister's initiative. He still hoped not to be at war with his favourite daughter. Even so, he recognised that the prospects for peace were poor. Somehow some concessions had to be won from his son-in-law if the Prague conference was to succeed – and as yet Napoleon remained undefeated in battle.

Marie Louise knew little of such affairs. For her husband, true to his commitment to shield the Empress from 'worry', continued to minimise the risk of conflict with Austria. A distraction delighted her: on Tuesday, 20 July, she received a letter written by him in Dresden on the previous Friday: she was to set out on 22 July for Mainz, and he would join her for a week of relaxation. The letter gave detailed instructions for the journey: twelve carriages, to travel in groups of three; a suite of eighteen officers and ladies in waiting, with fifty-one servants. All was to be ready within forty-eight hours, although in the end the departure was postponed by a day, until the Friday morning, 23 July. Before setting out Louise received one of the kindest notes her husband ever sent her: she must never feel upset if he at times corrected her, Napoleon explained, for he was training her for the future; 'Nothing that you could do would make me angry, for you are too good and perfect for that'.[31] Was he showing remorse for past rebukes, or a tender concern for the strains which he knew the tide of war would soon impose on her?

Louise again kept a travel diary, a pocket book of slightly over a hundred pages, neatly entered up each day in easy-to-read, copy-book French. The naive spontaneity of earlier journals is missing: but the narrative gives a clear insight into her changing moods, the alternation of anticipatory happiness with pique at the constraints of official ceremonies. The war never intrudes – apart from a passing comment on a certain German princess who had the misfortune to be 'as fat as Prince Schwarzenberg'. At Mainz – 'Mayence' to the French – Napoleon once again surprised Louise by arriving late at night: 'He crossed all the antechambers (*salons*) where my page and my women were sleeping without anyone hearing him,' she wrote: 'I will not attempt to put on paper all the joy I experienced at seeing him; that is not for writing down; it can only be felt.'[32] They had been apart for three and a half months. Now her husband enjoyed six days' leave, like one of his officers. No son was there, of course; but Louise wrote to Madame de Montesquiou, telling her, on the Emperor's orders, that she was to buy toys up to the value of 100 Louis for 'the little king'.[33]

By 4 August Napoleon was back in Dresden. Louise, however, lingered in the Rhineland, and it was 9 August before she arrived home at St Cloud. By then it was clear the Prague Conference would accomplish nothing. Though Francis authorised Metternich to offer concessions, even dropping demands for the return of the Illyrian Provinces, Russia and Prussia would not budge. Napoleon was willing to accept the loss of Danzig, the Grand Duchy of Warsaw, and the French foothold in Dalmatia, but he would not allow his spokesman, Caulaincourt, to offer a compromise over the German lands or Italy. With the armistice about to expire, Metternich reluctantly handed Caulaincourt a virtual ultimatum on 8 August and the conference broke up soon afterwards. Four days later Austria joined the allied coalition and went to war with France.[34]

Napoleon sought to keep the news from Louise for as long as possible. He may have hoped a swift and decisive victory would bring the return of peace before she fully comprehended the challenge to old loyalties. As Regent she was to deputise for him at the opening of a new dock for the fleet at Cherbourg. He proposed to Cambacérès that she should leave St Cloud on 17 August and not be told of the spread of the war until her return. But her departure was delayed by six days, and she learnt the news before setting out for the coast. Small wonder if she seemed sullen and short-tempered towards her ladies and the officers of her escort.[35] A letter from her father eased the pain of rejection: 'Do not worry,' he wrote. 'This is quite a different war from the earlier ones we waged. I am not your husband's enemy, and never will be; and I rely on the fact that he will not be mine either.'[36] From a ruler at war with France for the fifth time since his accession such a disclaimer makes curious reading; but it gave his daughter comfort.

Soon Marie Louise was to discover that her family links would not be sundered by the clash of arms. Napoleon felt no personal hostility towards Emperor Francis: she was urged not to worry unduly over his conduct; 'He has been misled, as he has sometimes been before,' she could read in a brief note awaiting her at Cherbourg. Father and daughter continued to exchange letters throughout the campaign, with Napoleon himself ensuring safe transmission and secure confidentiality. Such thoughtfulness sprang no doubt from his sense of kinship, that Corsican bond of family affection which, with his brothers and sisters, so often played him false. But political calculation, too, lay beneath the surface kindness. For from Caulaincourt's private meetings in Prague and his own talks with Bubna in Dresden, Napoleon was aware of the suspicion and resentment with which the Austrians joined the Russo-Prussian partnership. Neither Metternich nor his sovereign wished to see Tsar Alexander as the arbiter of peace. There might come a time when writing to Papa François was the surest way to ease apart the Grand Coalition and secure a settlement acceptable to both Paris and Vienna.

11

Fickle Fortune

At Dresden, during the weeks of armistice, Napoleon learnt of the final collapse of the Bonaparte kingdom in Spain. News of the decisive battle of Vitoria – in which on 21 June Wellington defeated King Joseph and his chief of staff, the veteran Marshal Jourdan – reached Dresden on 1 July, the day following Napoleon's final interview with Metternich. Joseph himself narrowly escaped capture by two squadrons of hussars on the road to Pamplona and Jourdan lost his marshal's baton, which was sent to London as a gift for the Prince Regent. Vitoria was barely a hundred miles from Bayonne, the back gateway into France. Marshal Soult, who had so recently distinguished himself at Bautzen, was hurriedly sent from Saxony to the Pyrenees in place of Jourdan; he delayed Wellington's thrust northwards, while Marshal Suchet held on to Catalonia. Napoleon had planned to draft troops from Spain to help build up a buffer against the Russo-Prussian drive into Germany, and Jourdan had already seen four regiments of the Imperial Guard head eastwards. But the threat of the enemy advancing through Bayonne on Bordeaux or Toulouse remained so grave that Napoleon was forced to leave more than 100,000 experienced troops to protect south-western France from invasion.[1]

For the moment, however, the crucial theatre of war remained 1,100 miles from Bayonne, on either side of the 'Ore Mountains', the Erzgebirge massif which separates Saxon Lusatia from Bohemia. By the middle of August Napoleon was faced, not only by the combined Russian and Prussian invaders he had thrashed at Lützen, but by Schwarzenberg's Army of Bohemia and by the Army of the North, commanded by Bernadotte as Prince Royal of Sweden. On paper, the French were outnumbered: the allies could put 800,000 troops into the field against Napoleon's 700,000 men, many of whom were conscripts of poor fighting quality or National Guardsmen hastily called to the colours and trained as infantry of the line. 'At Wagram Napoleon complained he no longer had the soldiers of Austerlitz,' Fezensac was to recall, 'and in 1813 we certainly did not have the soldiers of Wagram.'[2]

Many senior officers shared Fezensac's doubts and deplored the failure to agree on peace terms at Prague. Yet Napoleon appeared confident. He had the advantage of interior lines of communication, whereas his enemies needed to co-ordinate a strategy based upon a great arc sprawling across central Europe from the Baltic to the Danube basin. He suspected there would be mounting discord in allied counsels. Tsar Alexander had accepted Schwarzenberg as supreme allied commander only with reluctance; Napoleon knew both men well enough to anticipate that the Tsar would seek to impose his own strategy on the Prince who was, by nature, gentlemanly and accommodating; and Blücher's Prussians mistrusted Sweden's Prince Royal. Despite the lessons of the march on Moscow, Napoleon clung to his illusion that a single French victory would prove decisive. Drive a wedge between the allied armies, as at Austerlitz, and their leaders would seek peace, he convinced himself.

To stand on the defensive ran counter to his nature. He spread out maps that had served him well in the earlier campaigns. Again he played with concepts of grand strategy, for the right banks of the rivers Elbe and Spree formed natural routes along which his troops could move to the north or the south. Uncharacteristically, he hesitated. Should he threaten Berlin, drawing the Swedes and Prussians away from the Austrians and the main Russian army in Bohemia? Or should he cross the Erzgebirge and follow the upper Elbe towards Prague, 120 miles away, while Eugène led the Army of Italy into Styria for a march on Vienna? Ominously, however, the master-planner Berthier was looking to the west. Apparently on his own initiative, he issued urgent orders to garrisons along the Rhine: they must be certain their food supplies and equipment were on a war footing.

'My affairs are beginning to look good,' Louise was assured in a letter sent on Friday, 20 August, from Zittau. On Thursday morning Napoleon had himself led a column reconnoitring the Zittau Pass through the Erzgebirge. He found no difficulty in reaching the foothills around Gabel, where his troops surprised an Austrian detachment which fell back to await reinforcement. This minor skirmish is ignored by most military historians, as Napoleon did not exploit his success, preferring to turn aside and deal with a mounting threat from Blücher in the east. Yet he thought the crossing into Bohemia merited comment in his next letter. Curiously, he singled out the Austrian commander for special mention: 'I drove out General Néperg,' he wrote, with habitual mis-spelling. He had briefly met the General after Marengo, but can he possibly have remembered him? Or did he scribble his note that Friday with a sense of premonition? For Neipperg's name belongs to a future he would not share.[3]

On 31 August, the last evening of her visit to Cherbourg, Louise received good news. The semaphore reported 'a great victory', won at Dresden only three days previously. At the insistence of Tsar Alexander, Schwarzenberg had unwisely advanced on the Saxon capital while Napoleon was in pursuit of Blücher on the Katzbach river, fifty miles east of the city. The Emperor was able to break off the pursuit and, to the amazement of the allies, reach the outskirts of Dresden late on 25 August, launching a series of counter-attacks next morning which within twenty-four hours forced the enemy back across the frontier into Bohemia. When the Empress left Cherbourg the warships were flying flags to celebrate the good news; several thousand naval gunners were serving with the artillery in Saxony. But the victory was not decisive. Over the following week, mistakes by weary and confused corps commanders prevented Napoleon exploiting his army's success. Marshals St Cyr, Macdonald, Oudinot and Ney were all out-manoeuvred, while the over-zealous General Vandamme had the misfortune to get cut off at Kulm by a Prussian corps which, by chance, fell on the rear of his column.[4]

For Napoleon, an unusually wet September became a month of hesitancy and irresolution. Several times he crossed the Erzgebirge by the lower passes, once coming within sight of allied headquarters at Teplitz. But Vandamme's fate made him cautious, and he was acutely conscious that his supply line across Germany was overstretched. He dared not press forwards towards Prague. Back in Dresden, he became puzzled, frustrated by a problem he had experienced in the Russian summer campaign; he found it impossible to bring his foes to battle. Whenever intelligence reports brought him news of enemy dispositions and he moved forward to engage Blücher or Schwarzenberg, he found that they had withdrawn ahead of him. The constant marching exhausted an army already war-weary and on short rations. Battle casualties and illness cost Napoleon nearly 70,000 troops in the first month of the new campaign, and he also lost 300 cannon, most of them when Vandamme was forced to surrender at Kulm. He knew, too, that he could no longer rely on support from his German allies, even from the Bavarians whose Electoral ruler he had raised to the dignity of kingship after Austerlitz. Frederick Augustus of Saxony, whose loyalty had wavered in the spring, remained personally true to his alliance commitments, but those officers and men in his regiments who, in 1809, fought under Bernadotte at Wagram were encouraged by their old commander to join a 'Saxon Legion' he established within the Swedish expeditionary force. 'My affairs are in fairly good shape' was the best assurance Napoleon could give Louise in his final letter of that month.[5]

Did she realise the significance of this variation in her husband's well-established formula? Probably not, for the Empress was too self-centred to sense the subtlety of such nuances of style. But she had with her at St Cloud counsellors of insight and intelligence. Baron de Méneval, who had served Napoleon as secretary through every campaign of the last ten years, was now attached to her household and, as his memoirs show, the Empress turned increasingly to him for explanation and advice. General Clarke, as Minister of War, and Cambacérès, Archchancellor and President of the Senate, were with her again, as during the Russian campaign. Talleyrand, as Vice-Grand Elector, remained a dignitary at court, still held in esteem by Berthier and Caulaincourt, who were with the Emperor, though mistrusted by the Regent's closest advisers.

Talleyrand, Clarke and Cambacérès were present at the Tuileries on 7 October when Marie Louise delivered a speech to the Senate, written for her by the Emperor eleven days previously. It was a patriotic appeal: 'our people' must never allow themselves to be vanquished by 'our enemies ... England and Russia, who have trapped Prussia and Austria within their net'. Stirring words, delivered (so Talleyrand observed) 'with a dignity, enhanced by tact and self assurance'.[6] But the well-chosen phrases had a practicable purpose. The conscripts for 1814 had been called to the colours as early as February 1813. Now, when the applause for the Regent died down, the Minister of War went through the formality of seeking senatorial approval for the call-up of 120,000 men in previously exempt categories and conscripts in the 'Class of 1815'. Some 160,000 boys, aged sixteen or seventeen, were to report for hurried training. In contrast to the cynicism of *les grognards* (the hardened veteran grousers), these fresh-faced youngsters were keen, but battle-innocent. Inevitably they became known as '*les Marie Louises*'. Yet they were not to be under-rated. Within six months one lad was to capture a Russian general, hiding in a wood.

At least they missed the suffering and disillusionment with which the year's fighting came to an end. Already in early October the sick-lists contained 50,000 names. Far worse was to follow: for in the last quarter of 1813 typhus swept across Germany, constituting 'a dreadful war ... behind the army in creeping form', as one allied doctor was to recall in his memoirs.[7] Yet to those who had so recently marched with pride in the *Grande Armée* all privation was overshadowed by the reality of defeat. It came at Leipzig, a lost contest in attrition fought out between Saturday, 16 October and Tuesday, 19 October, through rain-swept meadows, walled gardens, and lush lawns sloping down to the Elster, Pleisse and Parthe rivers. If Austerlitz was the Battle of Three Emperors, Leipzig became the Battle of the Nations. The same three rulers were there beside the Elster, together with three Kings and a Prince Royal. But the war's character had changed. A quarter of a million men who came from 'all the Russias', Prussia, Sweden, twelve nationalities in the Austrian Empire, and even a troop of the Royal Horse Artillery, converged on some 175,000 weary French and Poles. These were greater numbers than were engaged in any previous battle.

The outcome was not a foregone conclusion. Napoleon had no intention of standing on the defensive. He hoped that a particular feat of arms would tilt the balance in his favour, as in earlier encounters. It nearly did, on the Saturday morning: Murat's cavalry broke through the inner lines of Schwarzenberg's Army of Bohemia and almost captured the Tsar; but Alexander was saved by his personal escort of heavy cuirassiers who threw themselves into the mêlée, forcing the horsemen back. Thereafter Napoleon lost the initiative. For much of Sunday he was unwell, with a high fever, though he was able to receive a senior Austrian officer, captured on the previous day, and send him back to Emperor Francis in the hope of securing an armistice while Leipzig was still in French hands. There was no response, and Napoleon prepared to resume the fighting on Monday morning. By then, however, he had missed any chance of an orderly withdrawal. Swedish reinforcements dramatically increased allied firepower. Throughout the day an unremitting cannonade pounded the crowded French lines and the city itself. In the early afternoon a Württemberg cavalry brigade went over to the allies and some 2,500 Saxon troops followed their example soon afterwards. Bavaria had formally changed sides on 8 October, by a treaty with Metternich, signed at Ried. The Empire was rapidly disintegrating. Outside Italy and Belgium, only Poniatowski's Poles remained loyal to the French.

By dawn on Tuesday, 19 October, Napoleon had recognised the need to begin the long retreat to the Rhine and some horsemen and wagons were already heading westwards. Though he found one route out of Leipzig jammed by guns and their carriages he was able to cross the Elster safely at eleven in the morning. Disaster struck a couple of hours later. A corporal and four sappers, ordered to demolish the bridge when the city was finally evacuated, panicked at the approach of Russian mounted pillagers and blew the bridge with troops still making the crossing. A whole army corps was left stranded on the right bank. By this single error more than 20,000 men passed into captivity, many of them Poles and Italians. Prince Poniatowski, created a Marshal of the Empire the previous Friday, was among those drowned in the Elster. Nobody knows how many others perished in the rivers on that Tuesday afternoon.[8]

Emperor Francis heard that the French were heading westwards while he was at a tobacco-mill three miles south of the city which Napoleon had himself used as a vantage point on the previous afternoon. With victory confirmed soon afterwards, Francis took off his hat, made the sign of the cross and stood silent in prayer. Then he rode into Leipzig, the last allied ruler to enter the city. At the Marktplatz he was welcomed by the Prince Royal of Sweden, whom he had received sixteen years before in Vienna as envoy of the revolutionary Republic and last saw in deferential attendance on Napoleon after Austerlitz. But the Austrian and Prussian leaders, though divided over many issues, were agreed in doubting Bernadotte's commitment to the common cause, and Francis spent little time with him. There were proclamations for the Austrian Emperor to approve, so that his subjects might learn of what was already hailed as a decisive battle. Schwarzenberg chose Count Neipperg to carry the news of victory. He proved a speedy courier. The people of Prague were told late on Wednesday and soon after midday on Friday he galloped into Vienna, almost 200 miles farther south. As a bearer of welcome tidings, Neipperg was able to bask for several days in reflected glory.[9]

Across France the semaphore telegraph remained ominously still. No news, good or bad, reached St Cloud during the week, and alarming rumours circulated in Paris, as so often a year ago in the Russian campaign. Communications were hampered by an unusually early heavy snowfall in the Thuringian Forest, which gave the first intimation that one of western Europe's coldest winters lay ahead. At last, at the very end of October, the first reports arrived, with letters, despatches and army bulletins coming together. To Louise Napoleon gave no details of the battle: his health was 'very good', he assured her; he was falling back on Mainz as he needed to re-equip the army in winter quarters; 'the bulletins will tell you all about my affairs,' she was told.[10] It was left to Empress and subjects alike to read in *Le Moniteur* of the hard-won gains in the early stages of the battle at Leipzig; of a change in fortune; and finally of 'the disaster' of 19 October. The public was shaken by such candour in the Press. Until now, '*désastre*' was a noun applied to an enemy's plight.

Yet before Napoleon reached the Rhine on 2 November he had recovered the old confidence in his destiny. On 30 October he defeated the Bavarians and an Austrian corps at Hanau. He still had around him a fighting force of some 80,000 men; perhaps as many as 40,000 sick and wounded were seeking to catch up the main army, while isolated garrisons tied down enemy troops at Magdeburg, Dresden, Wittenberg, Torgau, Würzburg and several more distant German cities. From Mainz on 3 November he ordered sixteen enemy flags captured at Leipzig and Hanau to be sent to General Clarke, the Minister of War: they were to be paraded through the streets of Paris and presented to the Empress in the throne room of the Tuileries. About a hundred flags captured in Spain, especially six taken from 'the English' were to be included in the procession back to the Invalides. 'Unfortunately,' the imperial impressario sadly noted, '40 flags I captured at Dresden were left behind in that city.' Normally he cared little for such shows, he admitted; but 'at the present moment' a 'full parade' would 'be useful': 'Each flag must be borne by an officer on horseback.'[11]

Napoleon spent six days in Mainz, strengthening long neglected forts along the river. From his correspondence it seems he had intended to stay far longer, making the city a military headquarters and interim administrative centre, with a speedy semaphore link to Paris. But he had now been away from the capital for 200 days, almost as long as for the Russian campaign. From an accumulation of reports he soon realised that he needed to have his hand on the pulse of the nation. Late on Sunday, 7 November, he set out for Metz and Paris, where gun salutes welcomed him home to St Cloud on Tuesday evening.

He still had hopes of detaching Austria from the coalition by striking a bargain with Papa François. A separate peace would throw the allies into confusion. He was convinced that, in Metternich's new power game, Austria would need France as a counterweight to the mounting influence of Russia and Prussia and to the menace of a fundamentally democratic German nationalism. There was some truth in this assessment. By now Metternich's political authority in Austria was unassailable. Immediately after Leipzig Emperor Francis created him a Prince as a mark of gratitude and confidence. Neither Metternich nor his sovereign wished for a restoration of the Holy Roman Empire but the Prince was determined to re-assert Habsburg primacy among the German dynasties. As the French retreated, so did Metternich hurry forward to Frankfurt. He reached the old coronation city on 4

November in time to organise a ceremonial entry for Francis two days later. The grand reception carried echoes of past splendour. The German princes were reminded that they might turn more naturally to Vienna for leadership than to Berlin or Paris.[12]

Emperor Francis was, on that Saturday, no more than twenty-five miles distant from his son-in-law at Mainz. After the festivities were over, Metternich held conversations with a captured French diplomat, Baron St Aignan, whose sister was married to Caulaincourt, Napoleon's trusted adviser. The Russian and British envoys in Frankfurt, Nesselrode and Lord Aberdeen, joined in these high-level talks. Metternich then sent the Baron to Mainz with a personal letter for Caulaincourt and proposals for a peace settlement: the French could keep the 'natural frontiers', including Belgium and the left bank of the Rhine; they were also assured that any justifiable 'maritime rights' would be recognised and that, though the German states must be independent, France could expect to exercise special influence over their development.[13] These were generous terms. Metternich would have been content to see a powerful Bonapartist state survive the wars, though not a preponderant one.

It was too late for St Aignan to catch Napoleon's travelling circus of ministers at Mainz. Not until he reached Paris on 14 November was he able to present the Frankfurt Proposals. But once back in his capital, Napoleon fell victim to his own propaganda: he convinced himself that the dents in his shield of invincibility would be hammered out by new armies he would raise, enabling him, as he told Louise, to 'beat the enemy sooner than he thinks'. Instead of accepting the Frankfurt Proposals as a basis for discussion, he saw them as a sign of Austria's diplomatic weakness. The Kaunitz illusion seems to have beckoned yet again: Vienna needed Paris, he thought; armed defiance could extract better terms than these proposals. He prepared a diplomatic offensive. A courier set out for Frankfurt with a reply to Metternich, and soon afterwards Maret was replaced as Foreign Minister by the more experienced Caulaincourt. But when – on 24 November – the Austrians read the reply they were disappointed; for the note made no mention of the proposals, nor did it put forward any alternative for a basic settlement. Napoleon wanted a congress at Mannheim, and to Metternich's consternation even seemed ready to travel to this 'summit conference' himself.[14]

Next day Metternich insisted there could be no peace talks until Napoleon accepted the Frankfurt Proposals and, in particular, a commitment to withdraw behind France's natural frontiers. The Austrians went beyond conventional diplomatic exchanges: six days later they circulated a proclamation to the French people, stressing the generosity of their peace terms and blaming Napoleon for prolonging the war. The imperial father-daughter correspondence was brought into service, too. On 28 November Francis wrote to Louise from Frankfurt, with a typical blend of formality and fatherly intimacy: 'That I am convinced your husband and I can get along together and live in peace, I have shown in giving you to him as a wife; and I remind myself of it each day when I offer up prayers for peace. But that does not just depend on me. In any case, though, whatever may happen, I shall never forget that your husband has you as his wife and your son is also one of my family [*dass dein Mann dich zum Weibe hat, und dasse dein Sohn der meinige auch ist*].' He looked forward, so he told his daughter, to the day when he could embrace her son; from experience he knew what happy distraction the boy's company must afford her.[15]

The kindly sentiments were, of course, intended as much for Napoleon's consumption as for Louise. Francis's letter confirmed his son-in-law's conviction that, though Austria and France were at war with each other, family ties would still influence policy. It may have prompted him to approve a change of approach, proposed by Caulaincourt; for on 5 December Metternich heard from Paris that Napoleon was now willing to 'talk peace' on the basis of the Frankfurt Proposals. By then, however, the proposals were out of date: British envoys more astute than Lord Aberdeen had realised that they would have left control of the Scheldt estuary and the Belgian coast in French hands; in London the Foreign Secretary, Viscount Castlereagh, could never approve a settlement based on the 'natural frontiers'. The French were informed that peace talks must await the arrival of a British plenipotentiary.[16]

Napoleon welcomed the delay, militarily. All remained quiet along the Rhine after his departure; with fields deep in snow there seemed no reason why the lull should not continue well into the new year. He desperately needed time, both to organise an integrated system of defence against invasion and, he hoped, to enable Viceroy Eugène and Murat to open up his old arena of battle in northern Italy and challenge Austria along a second front. On paper, Napoleon was mobilising in metropolitan France a massive army of nearly a million men. But there were not enough regimental officers to train them, and General Clarke's mismanagement of the War Ministry had become so bumbling that army depots were short of greatcoats, shakoes, boots and even muskets. In practice, only some 120,000 of these conscripts saw active service.[17]

There were weaknesses, too, in the anti-invasion plans. Troops were to be withdrawn from Suchet's army of Catalonia to form the core of a reserve army which Augereau was assembling at Lyons, but their movement northwards proved slow. The historic fortresses behind the lower Rhine, names familiar from campaigns twenty years back, were put in good order. But little could be done further south, down the line of the Vosges to the Belfort Gap. Moreover the Emperor dared not risk the political consequences of ordering work to begin on new defences for the capital itself. In 1792 he witnessed the demoniac fury of Parisians when they thought the city threatened by Prussian and Austrian armies; and it was an experience etched deeply in memory.

Not that Napoleon ever under-valued the capital. 'If I were master of France,' he had mused in 1798, 'I would make Paris not only the loveliest city that is, or that ever was, but the loveliest that ever could be.'[18] In fifteen years he had gone far to satisfy this ambition: four new bridges, the last of them – the Pont d'Iena – only recently open to traffic; two miles of quays; the spaciousness of long, straight streets; gardens seen through iron railings, not hidden behind walls; several thousand *réverbères*, hanging oil-lamps with reflectors to light the inner roads at night; public buildings with neo-classical frontage; canals, conduits, an aqueduct and fountains to give a free water supply; triumphal monuments, arched or perpendicular; a few paved sidewalks, with more to come; and the prospect of a centre of government in the west, on the plain beyond the Invalides and around Chaillot, where work continued on foundations for the King of Rome's palace. During 1813, however, police reports began to show that the citizens who stood to benefit from such enterprises were, at best, lukewarm in their loyalty. As yet, the opposition came largely from liberal salons in the Faubourg St Germain, from the professional classes, and from a newly-enriched propertied class who felt their wealth endangered by continuance of a war that had long ceased to bring them gain. None of these groups threatened revolutionary upheaval. But there was mounting unemployment among skilled workmen in the Faubourg St Antoine, where menacing placards appeared on the walls. They were not the type of artisans who would take kindly to regimentation for work on defences. They, too, wanted peace, in the hopes of recovering lost markets within Europe, if not overseas.

In a letter from Mainz Napoleon had urged Louise to 'laugh at the alarmists in Paris'.[19] But once back in the capital he saw that the sense of impending doom cast longer shadows than he thought possible. Through the last week of November and into December he reverted to the practice followed after his return from Moscow: fears would be allayed by observing the usual routine of imperial residence in the capital, he argued. Emperor and Empress were seen at the Opéra for Paesiello's pastoral, *Nina*; they inspected the post office, the latest hangings in the Louvre Museum, the newly built bonded warehouse for wine; they lingered at the flower market on the quay; and at the theatre in the Tuileries they graced performances of Nazolini's opera, *Cléopâtre* and a tragic drama by Briffaut. On successive Tuesdays Napoleon reviewed troops drawn up for him before the Carrousel, as so often in previous years.

This time, however, the imperial window-dressing made little impression. On 19 December Napoleon sought support from the Legislative Assembly, assuring its members – and the Senate, too – that they might appoint commissions to examine any peace terms the allies should offer. Though the Senate backed their sovereign, the legislature became increasingly critical. Ten days later the deputies in effect denied the Emperor a vote of confidence: the French people would fight no more, except to defend their independence, he was told; and he was asked to approve a charter guaranteeing his subjects' political and civil liberties. His response was to dissolve the legislature: 'What are you within the Constitution? Nothing! The throne – that is the Constitution. Everything resides within the throne,' he declared haughtily to them on New Year's Day; 'I am one of those men who triumphs or dies ... France needs me more than I need France.'[20]

For Marie Louise the year 1813 ended wretchedly. Her twenty-second birthday passed virtually unobserved. So, indeed, did Christmas. The long frost depressed her. She developed a persistent cough, and occasionally she spat blood. Dutifully on 12 December she sent seasonal greetings to '*liebe Papa*', who was by then in Freiburg. Everyone, including her husband, longed for peace, she assured him, but she complained that her father had not been helpful in getting negotiations started, no doubt under pressure from 'the English'. Eight days later Francis replied: good wishes were reciprocated, and ardent hopes of peace again expressed. But Louise was reminded that he had 'solemn obligations' to his allies. 'Your country [*Dein Land*] has made trouble all around,' she was told; the sorting out of these problems would take time; all was in God's hands.[21]

Not quite all, perhaps. For two days later – and before Francis's letter reached Paris – Schwarzenberg's Army of Bohemia marched into neutral Switzerland and occupied Basle. The allied invasion of France began on New Year's Day: Blücher's Prussians – the Army of Silesia – crossed the Rhine at Mannheim, while Schwarzenberg advanced from Basle on Belfort and the Langres plateau.

Sentimentalists portray Napoleon in the first weeks of 1814 as a doting father harassed by the buffetings of fickle fortune, his sole consolation the prattle of a son two months short of his third birthday. It is, of course, an incomplete portrait, though recognisable from some memoirs. Hortense, for example, describes Napoleon watching the 'little king' at play; '"Let's go and beat *Papa François*,"' she reports her stepfather as saying, and adds, 'So often and so clearly did the child repeat this phrase that the Emperor was enchanted and shook with laughter.'[22] It is a phrase with which an insensitive husband seems to have teased Marie Louise. More than once, understandably, it reduced her to tears.

Yet Napoleon can have had few leisure hours during that January. He had not anticipated an invasion so soon, especially in such appalling frost, and it was another twelve days before he completed a general directive for the defensive campaign in the homeland.[23] The immediate task of checking the enemy advance was the responsibility of five veteran marshals: Macdonald, Marmont, Mortier, Ney and Victor. For the moment, the Emperor remained at the Tuileries, seeking to co-ordinate strategy and infuse a sense of urgency into the Ministry of War: 'I need 540 sergeants and 1080 corporals,' he noted with precision on 10 January, suggesting that Clarke might call for volunteers from among the less disabled pensioners at the Invalides.[24] Increasingly Napoleon looked to the past for inspiration. Though anxious not to encourage Jacobin excesses, he sought to rekindle the patriotism of 1792–3. Regimental bands might again thunder out the '*Marseillaise*', an anthem officially discouraged when the 'government of the Republic was entrusted to an Emperor'; and on 4 January he ordered a *levée-en-masse* to be proclaimed behind France's eastern frontier. 'If the nation gives me its backing,' he wrote to Caulaincourt on that same day, 'the enemy is marching to his doom.'[25]

This is Napoleon at his most optimistic. Bad news was soon to follow. The first reports of contact between Murat and British agents ruled out all hopes of an effective second front in Italy, though Eugène's loyalty was not in doubt. In eastern France, the marshals, unaccustomed to defence in depth, failed to stem the allied advance. By the end of the second week in January Blücher had forced Marmont and Victor back to the Meuse, while even the cautious Schwarzenberg had reached the last foothills before Langres. The Emperor ordered his horses to be sent to Ney's headquarters on the upper Marne, expecting to follow soon with his Guard escort. But eleven more days went by before he set out from Paris. The delay arose, in part, from a fading hope that Caulaincourt would negotiate an armistice pending peace talks at

Lunéville. More pressing, however, was the need to settle constitutional problems in France and to make certain that the authorities in the capital had some understanding of the general strategy he wished to pursue in the following months. For, win or lose, this campaign imposed a decisive finality on his movement as no earlier departure had done. 'If fortune betrays me,' he had already told Caulaincourt, I shall not dishonour my nation or myself by signing a shameful peace. No bonds bind me to the throne.'[26]

He had no doubt that Marie Louise should again be Regent: 'She is wiser than all my ministers,' he asserted. But she needed a military adviser, for Clarke had shown himself a broken reed. In the path of any invader following the river Marne stood Mortfontaine, Joseph Bonaparte's château, where since his return from Spain, King Joseph had spent six months unemployed – and, as many thought, unemployable. Yet for all his weaknesses, Joseph had safely brought 55,000 men with him out of Spain, and he had long experience of both politics and war. As early as 7 January Napoleon invited him to 'come and stand by the throne as a French prince ... Show your devotion to me and the King of Rome; make it clear that you favour the Regency I propose for the Empress.'[27] Joseph complied; and on 24 January it was announced – though never put in writing – that in the Emperor's absence he would be Lieutenant-General of the Empire, while retaining the title of King. He was charged particularly with organising the defence of Paris and ensuring the safety of the Empress and her son.

'All matters of sentiment are valueless and dangerous,' Napoleon had gruffly written to Joseph. But, to serve needs of state, the Emperor was willing to squeeze tears from the hardest of hearts; and on the eve of departure he staged a sentimental act of imperial theatre.[28] After Sunday Mass on 23 January Napoleon summoned some 800 officers of the National Guard of Paris to the Salon of the Marshals at the Tuileries. He then presented to them Marie Louise and their son: 'I entrust to the courage of the National Guard the Empress and the King of Rome, my wife and my child, those whom after France I hold most dear in this world. You *will* protect them, will you not? You *will* protect them?' Hortense, standing among the dignitaries behind her stepfather, recalled in her memoirs the fervour of the National Guard's acclamation, '*Vive l'Empereur*'. There was hardly a dry eye in the salon.

Hortense had been present on that wretchedly wet night, four years back, when Napoleon hustled his proxy-bride to the marriage bed at Compiègne. At Louise's invitation she was present, too, at the Tuileries on 24 January, the evening before Napoleon left to join Ney on the upper Marne. Husband and wife, though often kept apart by war, had by now shared each other's company for 980 days. Louise, always desolate when he set out for the army, seemed on this Monday night sadder than ever. 'The Empress,' Hortense writes, 'never stopped weeping ... Embracing her, the Emperor murmured, "Have confidence in me. Do you think I've forgotten my trade?"'[29] The carriage and escort were ready at midnight, but Napoleon took no notice of their presence. At last, well into the small hours, he led Louise and Hortense through the antechambers and corridor down to the door into the courtyard. Both women were by now in tears. 'When will you come back again?' Hortense heard the Empress ask pathetically. 'That, my dearest, is a secret known only to God,' he replied. They did not see him step into the carriage. Soon a familiar sound clattering the cobbles told them he was gone.

12

A Child No Longer

By now Napoleon had ceased to bask in the splendour of borrowed ceremonial. Though he retained his imperial style, he became in effect General Bonaparte once more, confidently recalling to Berthier the earliest campaign in Italy, when their partnership carried an untried army short of equipment to victory. His force of personality, and reputation as a strategist, could still make an enemy cautious and raise the spirit of his troops once they saw he was among them. 'My presence on the battlefield is worth a hundred thousand men,' he assured Hortense, before setting out from Paris. Yet at first it seemed impossible to stem the allied advance. On 29 January, at considerable cost, he forced the Prussians out of Brienne, the town where he had been a military cadet thirty years back. But, in heavy snow on 1 February, a reinforced Blücher regained the initiative at La Rothière, only three miles south-east of Brienne, and prepared to make a thrust for Paris along the Marne, while Schwarzenberg was to follow the Seine to the capital. Napoleon fell back on Troyes, where he found the populace sullenly unco-operative, eager for peace and hoarding food. During the frequent blizzards of that week the French lost nearly 4,000 men from desertion. A brigade of dragoons, newly arrived from Spain, was ready to go into action without 'unsaddling since it left Bayonne' and many of the 'Marie Louise' conscripts fought well; but among foot-slogging veterans of Dresden and Leipzig morale was low. Troyes was soon abandoned. As Napoleon told the Minister of Police, there had been 40,000 desertions since crossing the Rhine. This figure was more than four times the total French casualties at Austerlitz. The Empire was in danger of withering away.[1]

In Paris the Empress dutifully presided over meetings of the Council of Regency, listening to advice from King Joseph and Cambacérès but frequently acting independently. Each day she sent reports of her activities to Napoleon in letters which were full of family news, too: Madame Mère, worried as ever over an uncertain future, in tears on her daughter-in-law's shoulder; the King of Rome, proud to wear National Guard uniform for the first time, and wishing he could join his father. The clarity of Louise's detailed reports of government business justify her husband's confidence in her judgment and breadth of comprehension. Within a few months she matured astonishingly, as she herself recognised: 'I am growing very brave since your last success,' she wrote to him. 'I hope I no longer deserve to be called a child – that's what you liked to call me before you went away.' Obstinately she rejected repeated suggestions she should go in state to the Opéra; 'I find it inappropriate at such a time to amuse oneself with entertainment' she wrote to her husband; and he warmly agreed with her. The letters show that she understood discussions on food relief for the garrison of Santona in Spain and recognised the need to fell trees at Vincennes and the Bois de Boulogne to provide defensive palisades for the city's outer defences.[2] With an ironic twist of history it was Marie Louise who signed the recall from retirement of Lazare Carnot, once the Republic's 'organiser of victory'. On Napoleon's orders he was now entrusted with the defence of Antwerp. It might have been wiser to retain him in Paris.

By the end of the first week in February the Empress was warning Napoleon of the mood in the capital. Confirmation of earlier fears that Murat, the King of Naples, was collaborating with the Austrians and the British in the hopes of saving his throne caused dismay at court; and there was no good news from the armies along the upper Seine or the Marne. 'You have no idea of the silliness [*bêtises*] that is running through Paris,' Louise told him on 7 February.[3] But she was wrong. Napoleon, who was in constant touch with his brother Joseph and with the Archchancellor, understood well enough. From Nogent-sur-Seine on that same Monday afternoon he wrote angrily to Cambacérès; 'Why have you lost your head? ... Is all Paris going mad? ... The Minister of Police ... talks and acts like a fool.'[4] More reasonably, to Joseph he wrote of his 'conviction' that 'the Empress must not leave Paris'; the city was 'not in such danger as the alarmists make out'. Louise herself strongly opposed any panic evacuation. Napoleon assured her there was no need to be anxious for, reinforced with 'several fine divisions ... I hope to beat the enemy soon'.[5]

Victory came three days later. In their eagerness to enter Paris the allies divided their armies, and on 10 February in a surprise move northwards from the Seine, Napoleon used Marmont's cavalry to isolate and destroy a Russo-Prussian division at Champaubert, only sixty-five miles from Paris. General Olssufiev, the Russian commander, was taken prisoner. Next morning the courier who brought news of the battle to Paris presented the Russian's sword to Marie Louise as she was walking in the Bois de Boulogne, to her great satisfaction. The first reports of Champaubert reached Joseph while he was reviewing the National Guard at the Tuileries. With cannon firing a victory salute from the Invalides, the city went wild with enthusiasm as in past days of glory.

Even while Paris was celebrating Champaubert, Napoleon gained a second victory. At neighbouring Montmirail he defeated a Prussian corps under Yorck and Sacken's Russian corps: Blücher was forced to pull his Army of Silesia back across the Marne, at Château Thierry. On 14 February Napoleon struck again, putting Blücher's advance guard to flight at Vauchamps. Had not heavy mud hampered the pursuit, Blücher himself would almost certainly have been captured. The allies lost some 7,000 men, including at least 3,000 sent back as prisoners to Paris; French casualties were no more than 600.

Napoleon then headed southwards to the upper Seine, forcing some troops to march sixty miles in a day and a half, in order to remove the threat to the capital posed by Schwarzenberg's Army of Bohemia. And at Montereau on 18 February Napoleon gained his fourth victory in nine days. The Austrians began a withdrawal up the river Aube towards the Langres Plateau. For the moment it looked as if Schwarzenberg was in full retreat: the gap between the Army of Silesia and the Army of Bohemia was widening. Napoleon's defensive strategy seemed vindicated. 'Fortune is again on my side,' he told Joseph. And to Louise he wrote, 'We shall have peace in a few days time, I hope, a lasting peace, one that is worthy of me and worthy of France.'[6]

There had been talk of peace throughout the campaign. To negotiate while defending the nation from invasion made good propaganda for Napoleon and was a sure way to feed dissension among his enemies, who remained deeply suspicious of each other. Tsar Alexander, working closely with King Frederick William of Prussia, wished to continue the war and make a dramatic entry into Paris, thus asserting Russia's primacy over the continent. Metternich was determined that Austria, in accord with Britain, should be a counter-weight to the Russo-Prussian combination. He did not rule out the possibility of keeping a chastened Napoleon on a throne which no longer carried authority east of the

Rhine or south of the Alps. The dynastic bond still counted in his reckoning; and a neo-Kaunitz entente remained attractive, if Vienna called the tune.

Early in February Caulaincourt arrived in Chatillon to seek an end to the war. Napoleon wanted France's 'natural frontiers', including Belgium, Nice, Savoy and the left bank of the Rhine, his springboard conquests. But he allowed his Foreign Minister a free hand to negotiate with the allied delegates, who for the first time included Castlereagh, the British Foreign Secretary. On 7 February they rejected these 'natural frontiers': not only would France be confined within her 1791 borders, but the British were also unwilling to specify which colonies would be handed back. So grave was the military situation that two days later Caulaincourt offered to accept the old frontier in return for an immediate armistice, though he pressed for agreement on the colonial issue. But nothing could be settled speedily. The Russian delegate, on Alexander's orders, delayed the negotiations, for the Tsar was unwilling to be robbed of a victorious entry into Paris. By 18 February, when the talks resumed, Napoleon had recovered the military initiative. Now it was Schwarzenberg who, so he believed, sought an armistice. 'Providence has blessed our armies,' the Emperor told Caulaincourt on 17 February. 'Sign nothing without my consent, for I alone know the situation.'[7] After winning his victory at Montereau next day, Napoleon convinced himself he would 'be at the gates of Munich within a few weeks'.

In his elation Napoleon reverted to family diplomacy. From headquarters at Nogent he wrote on 21 February to his 'very dear father-in-law' insisting that the Russian and Prussian armies were in tatters, that the Tsar's policies were vindictive and self-centred, and that the struggle between France and Austria was as harmful 'to your interests as it is to mine'. 'A single word from Your Majesty would end the war and safeguard the happiness of Austria and of Europe,' Napoleon claimed. Three days later he returned to Troyes where, as he told Louise next morning, 'Papa François' had been staying earlier in the week: he was worried and in low spirits, Napoleon learnt, seeing little of the Russians, of whom he 'is not very fond'. Louise was to write to him again: a 'strong letter, commending to him your own interests and those of your son'; her father, Napoleon conceded, 'is a fine honourable man', so often let down by those around him; now he needs 'to help us ... to show a will of his own ... to make certain he is not simply a tool of England and Russia'.[8]

Louise did as her husband wished. Within a few hours she was writing to her father, with pleas of her own. She asked him not to force a dishonourable peace on the French people: 'Try to put yourself in my position, dear Papa,' she wrote: hard terms would prove 'such a terrible blow for me that I could not survive. My dearest Papa, think of me and of my son, I beg you.' But Francis's reply to Napoleon was given to Caulaincourt before his daughter's letter reached him. There was no question of Austria making a separate peace: France would be well advised to accept a settlement based on 'the ancient limits' of the old kingdom, he urged.[9]

Napoleon remained defiant. Schwarzenberg cautiously resumed his advance on 1 March, though Napoleon was more immediately concerned with the threat from Blücher on the river Aisne. At Chaumont, on this first day of March, Castlereagh pulled off the diplomatic triumph which successive British Foreign Secretaries had sought for many years. For a cost of £5 million in subsidies, he welded together a Grand Quadruple Alliance. By the Treaty of Chaumont, the rulers of Austria, Britain, Russia and Prussia were pledged to continue fighting until Napoleon's Empire outside France's historic frontiers was destroyed. They also agreed to maintain their partnership for twenty years after the end of the war, so as to make certain that for two decades no ruler in Paris would challenge the peace of the continent. Details of the Chaumont Treaty were not published until 9 March, the news coinciding with reports of a clash of arms around the hilltop town of Laon which seemed indecisive but was to acquire a negative significance. For next morning Blücher was taken ill but Napoleon, knowing nothing of the confusion at Prussian headquarters, prematurely broke off his attack so as to turn south and check Schwarzenberg's advance down the Seine. It was a costly strategic blunder, for the Army of Silesia was near total defeat on that day.

Throughout February the Empress had shown good sense, setting an example to a nervous court by her fine composure. She remained a romantic sentimentalist. On their son's third birthday she wrote to her husband, 'I have been thinking so much about you today; three years ago you gave me such moving proof of your love that tears come whenever I recall it; so it is an especially precious day for me.' As during the Russian campaign, she sent Napoleon a portrait of his son, on this occasion with his hands locked in prayer. The Emperor exploited her sentimentality for propaganda purposes. The engraving 'will please everybody', he declared; and on 21 February he ordered copies to be made at once, with the caption 'God save my father and France'; they must go on sale in Paris within forty-eight hours, he insisted.[10]

Louise was, however, only twenty-two. After five weeks the burden of Regency began to pall. She allowed herself to be drawn into trivial quarrels among the ladies of her household. In early March, when the Emperor was striving to keep the armies of Blücher and Schwarzenberg apart, her letters rang with such intense indignation over the attitude of the King of Rome's governess towards the Duchess of Montebello that Napoleon himself had to calm her down. Louise must 'always be kind to Madame Montesquiou because she is so good with the little King', he explained. She needed to discourage tittle-tattle among her ladies: scandalous gossip would harm 'worthy and deserving people, who are most virtuous and quite blameless'.[11]

Only a few days after showing such patient understanding Napoleon was vexed by a new problem at court. For Louise was increasingly taking her brother-in-law, Joseph, into her confidence. Together they would seek to decipher Napoleon's handwriting; soon the Empress was reading to Joseph extracts from her father's letters. Napoleon became uneasy on two counts: he suspected his brother of political intrigues and did not want him to have a channel of communication with the Austrians; and he was very conscious of Joseph's dubious reputation. Louise was warned of his 'loose ways with women'. On successive days Napoleon used the same phrase: '*Tiens-le loin de toi* (see he keeps his distance from you)'; she must never admit him to her private apartments. And he made it clear that, amid so many shifts in loyalty, he would not be astonished if Joseph, like the Murats, tried to strike a bargain with the enemy. 'He is a pygmy, puffed up with conceit,' Napoleon wrote on 14 March from Rheims, a city he had relieved from seven weeks of siege only a few hours previously.[12]

Three days later Metternich used Caulaincourt as the medium for what the Austrians regarded as a last appeal to the Emperor's common sense. Castlereagh wished to restore the Bourbons; Alexander was playing with the possibility of a new monarchy under Bernadotte; only Emperor Francis was constant. 'Austria still wishes to preserve a dynasty with which it is closely connected,' Metternich insisted: if Napoleon would cede Belgium, as Francis had ceded Tyrol five years back, he could retain the throne for himself and his son. 'Peace depends still on your master,' Caulaincourt was told. 'In a little while this will no longer be the case.'[13] But Napoleon's strategy remained ambitious: he planned to strike south-eastwards into Lorraine; as at Rheims, he would relieve French garrisons locked up in Metz, Verdun and ultimately Strasbourg, cutting allied links with the Rhine and beyond. Marshals Marmont and Mortier would protect Paris, until pressure from the rear forced the enemy to withdraw.

Marie Louise's detractors among French historians maintain that at this moment in the campaign Napoleon's infatuation with his young wife caused him to make a disastrous error. On the morning of 23 March, after spending the previous days engaging Schwarzenberg's troops along the river Aube, he wearily scribbled a hurried note to Louise: he had decided, he told her, 'to head for the Marne ... in order to push the enemy's armies farther away from Paris and draw nearer to my fortresses'. Letters to the Empress were handwritten and not in code. One sent from Moscow in October 1812 was intercepted by Cossacks and its contents made public; they revealed nothing more secret than the Emperor's fond feelings for his wife. Never, in two years of campaigning, had Napoleon informed her precisely of his strategic intentions. It is odd he should have done so now, for the risk of capture by enemy patrols was high. On this occasion the courier was indeed taken prisoner and the letter read by Blücher himself – who kindly forwarded it, a little late, to 'the Emperor of Austria's august daughter'. Thus Napoleon's casualness gave his enemies notice of his intentions, plans to ponder as they studied their maps.[14]

Yet was this apparent folly an indulgence of family confidentiality, of losing all grip on reality? Or was it a simple ruse, a means of drawing the allies away from Paris? He believed that the enemy wished to defeat him personally: the pack would follow the fox, he argued. Once established astride the middle Marne, he could either advance westwards or, by crossing the river, outflank and envelop Schwarzenberg. For four days he waited at St Dizier, studying the reaction of the allies.

The pause proved fatal. For Napoleon's reasoning was at fault, not his carelessness with the pen. He rightly read Schwarzenberg's mind: if left to themselves, the Austrians would have pursued him eastwards in full strength. But they did not. Tsar Alexander took little interest in the intercepted letter. He had been shown a message from within Paris to Nesselrode which urged the Russians, not 'to grope about like children on crutches' but 'to stride forward on stilts': provenance, imagery and handwriting all suggested that the message came from Talleyrand.[15] At a council of war outside Vitry on 25 March, the Tsar's will prevailed over Austrian caution. Only one army corps was to keep in touch with Napoleon. The two allied armies, 180,000 troops, would 'stride forward' on Paris.

Napoleon made three miscalculations: he never understood that, for Alexander, the supreme prize was the capture of France's capital, not France's Emperor; he over-rated the strength of Mortier and Marmont's troops; and, though he mistrusted Talleyrand, he failed to realise the depth of treachery among others who wished to safeguard the eminence and landed wealth they owed to his beneficence. Yet there is no doubt that militarily the allies had at last duped him. He was still inactive at St Dizier on the morning of 28 March when, a hundred miles down the Marne, the armies of Schwarzenberg and Blücher joined forces at Meaux, a half-day's carriage drive from the Tuileries.

To the best of her ability Louise had kept Napoleon updated over the mood of the Senate and the Council of Regency, and of the mounting desire to call a halt to the war. But she was not so well informed of what was happening as a month previously, perhaps because she deliberately saw less of King Joseph. 'All Paris is full of good news,' she told Napoleon on Monday, 21 March, somewhat surprisingly. 'People are talking about battles won, but especially about peace.' The immediate future did not worry her. Spring was early that year and, after taking lunch in the gardens one day that week, she mentioned in a couple of letters that, if Napoleon did not object, she might move out of the Tuileries into the less sombre Élysée Palace. The move was never made. On Sunday morning (27 March) church-goers in outlying villages beyond the heights of Montmartre thought they heard distant cannon fire and some families began to head south from the city, the first in a steady flow of refugees. Yet on that evening Louise, Hortense, Louis Molé (Minister of the Interior) and the egregious Talleyrand gathered at the Tuileries for a round of whist, as unperturbed as if the clouds of war were a thousand miles away.[16]

By Monday, however, the storm seemed about to break over their heads, though it was Wednesday before the first cannon opened up on the city's inadequate defences. Despite the courage of the National Guard, General Clarke did not believe Paris could hold out for any length of time. Late on Monday afternoon King Joseph and Cambacérès spent two hours with the Empress, urging her to leave Paris, a proposal which at first she firmly rejected. Joseph – as Louise informed Napoleon that evening – then 'read to us an extract from a letter in which you told him not to let me be captured in Paris'.[17] She agreed to order her carriages to be made ready in case she wished to leave next day but would take no final decision until she had presided over a Council of Regency, where a vote would be taken on the matter.

It was a long session, dragging on well after midnight. Clarke and Cambacérès thought the Empress and the King of Rome should leave at once: two former foreign ministers, Champagny and Talleyrand, argued that their departure would finally destroy morale in the capital; and the Minister of Police, Savary, agreed with them. Antoine Boulay – a hot-headed participant in the *Brumaire* coup of 1799 – proposed that Marie Louise should ride to the Hotel de Ville, present the King of Rome to the people of Paris, and call upon them to defend their city, their Regent and the heir to the imperial throne. Rather oddly, he cited Habsburg precedent, recalling how a similar gesture by Maria Theresa evoked a rousing 'We will die for our sovereign' from the people of Hungary. When a vote was taken, the majority were against her departure. Clarke then spoke again, almost matching Boulay in fervour: it was, he maintained, the Empress's duty 'to go to the unoccupied provinces' and rally loyal support. He called for a second vote, but his rhetoric changed no one's opinion.

The Regent was about to declare the session closed, when King Joseph intervened. As yet there had been no mention of Napoleon's wishes. Now Joseph read two letters from his brother, dated 8 February and 16 March, which emphasised his conviction that his wife and son should not be allowed to fall into enemy hands. A third vote was taken: this time – as Louise wrote to Napoleon – only Boulay, Champagny and she herself advocated remaining in Paris. Reluctantly she agreed to leave next morning for Rambouillet. 'I must tell you that I am absolutely against this idea, I am sure it will have a terrible effect on the Parisians,' she wrote. 'You told me, however, that I must follow the Archchancellor's advice and I will do so on this occasion.' But she added, with a touch of spirit, 'They've all lost their heads except me.'[18]

Momentarily on the Tuesday morning Louise's nerves snapped. Exasperated by conflicting reports as she was about to leave the Tuileries, she flung her hat on the floor, sank back into a deep armchair and sobbed: 'Oh God! Let somebody decide something, and put a stop to all this agony!' But she soon recovered. After all, flight from an approaching enemy was nothing new to her. This time she had the 'little king' beside her, rather than her sisters and brothers, and the cavalcade of ten berlins rolled along better roads than in Hungary; but there was a familiar risk of interception by Cossack marauders, as in 1805, though with an escort of 1,200 horse-guards and dragoons, she had little to fear. But Joseph sent word that he thought Rambouillet too exposed and after a night's rest, the Empress spent the next day travelling to Chartres. On that Wednesday evening the Prefect of Paris visited the Tsar at his headquarters eight miles from the Ile de la Cité and negotiated the surrender of the capital.[19]

Napoleon, too, spent Wednesday on the road, at last speeding westwards from Troyes to rally the army outside Paris. So hard did he ride over the chalky plateau that after twenty-five miles the horse went lame and he covered the next fifteen in a butcher's wicker-work cabriolet. Then, after a hurried lunch at Sens, by carriage to reach Fontainebleau by eleven at night and, with a change of horses, on to the Cour de France posthouse, barely eighteen miles from the capital. There Napoleon met General Belliard heading eastwards with news that Paris had fallen. The Emperor was deeply shocked; 'Had I come sooner, all would be saved,' he was heard to remark. After conferring with Berthier he decided to 'reform his army at the approaches to Fontainebleau', as he wrote to the Empress; but he sent Caulaincourt to the Tsar's headquarters to seek an immediate peace, in the faint hope that Paris could be spared occupation by foreign troops for the first time in four centuries.

Caulaincourt had no success. At dawn on 31 March Napoleon arrived back at Fontainebleau. A few hours later Russian cavalry clattered through the Pantin barrier into Paris; and soon after midday Tsar Alexander took the salute from an improvised stand beside the Marly horses at the end of the Champs Élysées, with the King of Prussia beside him. That night the Tsar was a guest of Talleyrand at his magnificent mansion on the corner of the Rue de Rivoli. Russian Grenadiers stood at the gates through which the Vice-Grand Elector's carriage bore him to join Marie Louise for whist four evenings ago.[20]

Emperor Francis preferred to remain at Dijon. He was unsure how to conduct himself in an occupied capital city over which, theoretically, his daughter still exercised the powers of a Regent. Neither Francis nor his Foreign Minister wished to be troubled with immediate problems of protocol; they were prepared to leave such matters, in the first instance, for Alexander and the dexterous Talleyrand to thrash out with Caulaincourt. There was always a possibility that, given an opportunity to re-group his armies, Napoleon could continue the war, either marching on Paris or striking at allied communications from Orleans. By Sunday, 3 April, he had concentrated 60,000 troops around Fontainebleau, including divisions of the Old Guard and the Young Guard, devoted to their Emperor. If the campaign was not yet at an end, Austria might need to impose a compromise settlement, possibly with a Regency on behalf of Francis's grandson. Napoleon, too, thought Austria still had a role to play. On Sunday evening he scribbled a note to the Empress: she was to write to her father, commending herself and her son to his protection: 'Make clear to your father that the time has come for him to help us,' he added.[21]

Louise was now at Blois, having reached the Loire on the previous afternoon, her fourth wedding anniversary. For the next six days – Holy Week in the Church's calendar – she was in residence at the prefecture, close to the cathedral. Though uncertain what was happening at Paris, she was by no means isolated: Fontainebleau was some ninety miles away, close enough for a courier to make the journey in seven hours, if he was not intercepted by enemy patrols or Cossack marauders. Twelve letters passed between husband and wife in the first ten days of April.

At first the Empress maintained the outward trappings of court life, creating a substitute Élysée in the prefecture. In her letters she praised the clear air; Blois, so she was told, was much healthier than Orleans, thirty miles away, her original destination. There were pleasant walks in the garden, with fine views of the Loire: 'Far off I can see the turrets of the château at Chambord,' she noted that Sunday evening. She deserved moments of tranquillity. But she was determined to fulfil her duties as Regent. Earlier in the day she presided both over a Council of Ministers and a formal dinner, with her brothers-in-law, Joseph and Jerome, and their mother at table beside her. She approved and signed a ringing proclamation: 'Frenchmen, the fortunes of war having put the capital in foreign hands, the Emperor, hastening to succour it, is at the head of his armies, so often victorious ... Remain faithful to your vows, listen to the voice of a princess entrusted to your loyal support who glories in being a Frenchwoman and sharing the destinies of the sovereign you have yourselves chosen ... The rights and person of my son are under your protection.'[22]

Fine words – but, unfortunately, never circulated beyond Blois. For next morning the Empress learnt that the rump of Senators who remained in Paris had accepted Talleyrand as head of government and voted for Napoleon's deposition. Over the following twenty-four hours more bad news filtered through; the decision of Marmont to defect, taking some 20,000 demoralised men in his VI Corps with him; and the insistence of the marshals who were with the Emperor that other army chiefs, too, were ready to seek the best possible terms from the enemy. Confirmation came that Marshal Augereau had surrendered Lyons to the Austrians; and there were reports that Toulouse was in Wellington's hands and that Bordeaux had declared for the Bourbons. Finally there arrived from Fontainebleau, not another personal letter, but a formal document informing the Empress of Napoleon's conditional abdication. On 4 April, even before learning of Marmont's defection, he had sent Ney and Caulaincourt into Paris with an offer to step down from the throne provided the Empress became Regent for his son and he was assured that the basic laws of the Empire would be maintained.

Louise wrote to her father on that same Monday, as Napoleon had suggested. She entrusted the letter to Champagny, a diplomat of whom she believed her father thought highly. Her message laid stress on the wretchedness of their present position and appealed to Francis to ensure her own safety and that of his grandson, protecting their rights against 'covetous England and Russia'.[23] For more than a week Louise had borne herself with courage, a rock of confidence amid breaking seas. But at Blois the rock was gradually worn away. A mood of lassitude doused her spirits: she mistrusted the advice of her brothers-in-law, which was often conflicting; she suspected that, like such old stalwarts as Cambacérès, they were thinking of ways to safeguard their wealth and status under a new régime. Even the Duchess of Montebello upset Louise by her mounting impatience at being away from Paris. Soon Louise became dejected and hesitant over what course to pursue. She was so convinced that Champagny had fallen into Russian hands that on Maundy Thursday she sent another courier to Dijon, with a second letter to her father. Although almost identical with Monday's letter, it now included the curious assertion that Paris would have been better defended 'had we not assumed that it was being occupied with your connivance'.[24] Her letters to Fontainebleau began to puzzle Napoleon: Monday's assured him of her 'good health'; by Wednesday she had a fever and could not leave the house; by Sunday she not only remained feverish, but was coughing blood, too. Anxiously Napoleon sent a message to Méneval, her devotedly loyal secretary, asking for news: he was beginning to suspect she had no wish to rejoin him, for there were several times when she might have risked making the journey and did not.[25]

And yet did he doubt her own words? 'All I want at this moment is to be reunited with you, if that could be done. I would have more courage, more calm, if I were sharing your fate, consoling you as much as possible for all the setbacks you have experienced, and I could try to make myself useful in some way or other,' she wrote pathetically on 7 April; and, a day later, 'I'm waiting for your orders, and I beg you to let me come.' Constantly she sought to let Napoleon feel the warmth of her affection: 'I close, then, by assuring you there's no one in the world who loves you as much as your faithful Louise,'[26] runs the last sentence in her first letter from Blois. In such perplexing times it was hard to go on deserving 'no longer to be called a child', especially as a young mother to the heir of a tottering throne. She feared that, unwittingly, her actions might betray her trust. Desperately she looked for someone to tell her what to do. Significantly on Easter Sunday, when at last she reached Orleans, Louise sent two pleas to her husband, and three to her father.[27]

By now she knew that Napoleon had been offered Elba in full sovereignty and that Tsar Alexander was prepared to insert in the proposed peace treaty a stipulation that she should receive, for herself and ultimately for their son, the Habsburg Grand Duchy of Tuscany.

But Schwarzenberg strongly objected: he was certain that Emperor Francis would not wish his daughter to settle in an Italian dependency for which Elba was an off-shore stepping-stone. Napoleon told Caulaincourt he was confident that Louise could persuade her father to accept the Tsar's proposal. So, indeed, was Louise herself. 'If I can go to see my father, I am sure, almost sure, that I can get Tuscany,' she added in a footnote to her letter on Easter morning.[28]

But time was running out. Metternich reached Paris that afternoon. Reluctantly he agreed that Napoleon might have his island, but over Tuscany he was adamant; no sea coast for Marie Louise. By nine o'clock on Tuesday – 12 April – Napoleon knew that the final draft version of the treaty gave him Elba while Louise would receive land-locked Parma, together with Piacenza and Guastalla. He learnt, too, that Francis was expected in Paris on Saturday. The news made him hesitate no longer. Louise had convinced him that she wished to share his fate. Perhaps he reasoned that to have his wife and son with him at Fontainebleau would give him one last card to play; Francis might even be induced to come in person to visit his daughter and see his grandson. At all events, whatever the reasoning, Napoleon ordered Major Cambronne to set off immediately with a troop of cavalry for Orleans and escort his wife and son home for a family reunion in Fontainebleau.[29]

From Fontainebleau to Orleans was an easy journey of fifty-four miles, down roads which the Emperor had made certain were in good condition and across level, forested country. Even so, Cambronne and the guard cavalry arrived a few hours too late. Prince Esterhazy and Prince Wenzel Liechtenstein, sent by Metternich, had reached the city that Tuesday morning with orders to escort Louise and her retinue to Rambouillet, where her father would join her. At first she refused to go, insisting that she would not leave without written permission from her husband. Ominously she was told the princes could not wait: did they suspect a rescue bid? However, before early evening, when the six-coach cavalcade set out, she found time to write to Napoleon. He was told that, against her will, she was on her way to Rambouillet.[30]

The heavily loaded berlins trundled slowly northwards, west of the route from Fontainebleau. After thirty miles they rested at Angerville. Louise was close to despair, convinced she was virtually a prisoner. She scribbled a note in pencil, dating it '12-13 April' as if unsure of the passage of time, and handed it to a Polish officer to take to Fontainebleau, thirty-five miles away:

> By now you will know that they made me leave Orleans and that orders have been given to stop me from joining you and

> even by resort to force if necessary. Be on your guard, my dearest, they are out to fool us. I am worried to death for you, but I shall take a firm line with my father. I shall say that I am absolutely set on joining you, and nobody is going to prevent me from doing that.[31]

Napoleon, too, was wretchedly unhappy that night. Caulaincourt had returned from Paris with a treaty, dated 11 April and awaiting signature. The terms re-affirmed his renunciation of the French throne, permitted him to retain the title of Emperor, accepted claims for substantial revenues for himself and the Bonaparte family, and assured him of sovereignty during his lifetime over Elba and Marie Louise over Parma and its dependencies; but they offered no guarantee that she would be able to visit him, or that he would have any rights over the upbringing of the little Napoleon. For the first time the Emperor could measure the depth of his fall: the world he so recently dominated seemed to mock him.

What happened at Fontainebleau in the small hours of 13 April remains confused.[32] The testimony of those who were present varies, although Caulaincourt's carries a ring of truth; some accounts were written by memoirists many miles away. It is clear Napoleon received a letter from Louise, though if it was the 'be on your guard' note from Angerville, the Polish officer must have been a speedy night rider. But the Emperor certainly knew that his wife and son were being escorted to Rambouillet, not brought to join him for the journey into exile. Thus by three in the morning he feared that his last ray of hope was fast fading away. At that hour he wrote a farewell letter to 'sweet Louise', affirming he loved her 'more than anything in the world'. He then dissolved a poisonous powder in a small glass of water, swallowed it, got into bed, and called for Caulaincourt, whom he told what he had done. The sachet of powder had been prepared for the Emperor by his physician during the retreat from Moscow, when he feared the treatment he might receive if captured by Russian partisans. Now, some eighteen months later, the poisonous cocktail had lost its potency. For four hours he suffered stomach pains and vomiting. By mid-morning he accepted that, as he said, he was 'condemned to live'. The treaty was signed, though it did not become effective until ratified in a week's time. Meanwhile he remained in the palace, stepping out occasionally to walk meditatively in spring sunshine by the English Garden and the Grand Canal.

Louise never knew of the tender farewell note – which is, perhaps, a pity. Her spirits were low. She reached Rambouillet at nine on

Wednesday morning to find her father was not there, nor even expected. An emissary from Metternich in Paris advised her to stay in the château because of dangers posed by Russians patrolling the neighbouring forest. She found herself confined in a familiar home, with Napoleon's 'improvements' around her, almost pristine: the entrance porch, completed by Jean Trepsat before her visit in 1810; a bathroom, with neo-Pompeian decorative tiling; white and grey panelling in the oratory at the end of the imperial apartments. The place was full of memories. Not that she was under house arrest there: letters continued to pass freely between husband and wife. Each clung to the hope of a speedy reunion once Francis arrived to ease his daughter's problems. Only on the previous Friday he had written to her of the gratitude he felt towards 'your husband ... for having given such happiness' to her. Although Caulaincourt might warn his master not to place his trust in the house of Austria, Napoleon had faith in the impact of that 'firm line' Louise would take with her father once she had greeted him.[33]

On her third morning at Rambouillet Louise was told that her father wished her to meet him at the Trianon. She refused to travel further: she was unwell and had spent a feverish night – 'always a good excuse not to go', she confessed in a note to her husband.[34] Instead, on Saturday, 16 April, Francis rode over to the château. As Louise anticipated, there was an affectionate reunion, for father and daughter had not seen each other since their parting outside Prague in the first weeks of the Russian campaign. By now Francis had been on the throne for twenty-two years; he was a conscientious ruler and a kind family man who hated war, not least because it imposed long absences from home. He genuinely sympathised with his favourite daughter. But long experience had strengthened two strands in his character: a ruthless expediency of sacrifice; and a deft skill, akin to moral cowardice, in ridding his shoulders of unpopular decisions. Louise, of all people, should have realised this, from her treatment four years back. He had arrived in Paris, reluctantly and belatedly, with a clear course of action in mind, and it did not meet his daughter's expectations: he would coax her back to her Austrian homeland for the sake of her health, with his grandson in her care. By her own showing, she was too unwell to accompany Napoleon to Elba, and a visit to Fontainebleau would be distressful for them both. Francis would allow her back to Vienna as soon as possible, while Metternich could be left to unravel the knots he had tied in 1810 with such self-congratulatory pride.

From the château where Napoleon had so carefully drafted that first flattering letter to his Archduchess, she now broke to him the news that her firm line had crumbled under the impact of 'the most terrible blow'. Writing distraughtly a mere two hours after Francis rode into Rambouillet, she said:

> He forbids me to come to you, to see you; he does not want to allow me to join you on your voyage. I told him outright that it was my duty to follow you; he only said that he did not want that; he wants me to spend two months in Austria, and then on to Parma, from where I will go to see you.

The only comfort she could offer Napoleon was to look forward to July, when she hoped she would be permitted to visit him on Elba.[35]

On 20 April the Emperor bade farewell to his faithful Old Guard from the stone horse-shoe staircase at Fontainebleau, a moment which became enshrined in legend. There followed nine days by carriage to Fréjus, and five days aboard the British frigate *Undaunted*, before he went ashore at Elba on 4 May, with gun salutes greeting the newly designed flag, broken above the quay at Porto Ferrajo. Louise and the 'Prince of Parma' – no longer King of Rome – were still at Rambouillet when he set out for Fréjus. They left, with an Austrian cavalry escort, on 23 April for a long slow journey to Vienna by way of Switzerland and the Tyrol, avoiding the bridal route of four years back. But the first stage was a gentle one, only to Marshal Berthier's château at Grosbois. There, from lawns beneath the chestnuts, a sad Empress looked out for the last time on Paris, barely eight miles away. Through the haze Louise could clearly discern Hardouin-Mansart's golden dome, serenely spanning the church of the Invalides; it was an oddly prophetic vision.

13

Apart

More than seventy Frenchmen and Frenchwomen accompanied Marie Louise through Provins and Dijon and down to Basle where, on 2 May, they crossed into Switzerland. Dr Corvisart and the Duchess of Montebello were in constant attendance, while the 'Prince of Parma' was, as ever, in the care of Madame de Montesquiou, 'Maman Quiou', as he called her. Bausset, the former chamberlain of the palace, and Méneval, the secretary whom Napoleon assigned to the Empress in 1812, were also attached to her suite: both men later dictated reliable reminiscences. Louise began the journey belligerently loyal to Napoleon in all her sympathies, angered by 'the look of triumph' in the eyes of Austrian staff officers, sad for 'poor France' who 'was losing someone deeply attached to her and who weeps over her fate'. Méneval records that in Switzerland Louise spent her first nights unable to sleep and her first days with cheeks bathed in tears. Yet not, it would seem, for long. On 8 May she was at Schaffhausen, where she received Napoleon's last letter before his embarkation for Elba. She replied at once, stressing the sorrows of separation and her failure to find joy in any activity; but she was too honest to conceal one new delight: 'I have seen much wonderful country,' she wrote, 'I have seen lakes Zurich and Constance, which are remarkably beautiful.' Even through tears her eyes thrilled to this new experience, a first revelation of Alpine scenery.[1]

The obvious route from Lake Constance into the heart of Austria was by way of Innsbruck and Salzburg. But how would the imperial cavalcade be received in the Tyrol? It was only four years since the Tyrolean hero, Andreas Hofer, had been shot on Napoleon's orders after a patriotic revolt in which Vienna failed to honour pledges of support; Hofer's execution was followed three weeks later by the proxy wedding in the

Augustinerkirche. Emperor Francis was uneasy over possible insults to the imperial house, and to his daughter in person, if she travelled through the Tyrol. Count Kinsky, in command of the cavalry escort, proposed a detour northwards to Regensburg, and then down the Danube. He was firmly over-ruled by Louise, indefatigable in her sight-seeing. 'I have decided to see the country, and I am convinced the people will do us no harm,' she insisted. They would follow the Inn valley.

Her confidence in the goodwill of the Tyrolean people was fully justified. Both in the small townships near the frontier and in Innsbruck itself she was rapturously received, to townsfolk unharnessing the horses and pulling her carriage through streets covered with a fresh fall of unseasonable snow. Banners welcomed home 'the daughter of our good Emperor'. After two days of rest in Innsbruck the cavalcade continued to Salzburg where, on 17 April, Louise wrote for the first time in many months to her old *aja*, the Countess Colloredo, and also to the Countess's daughter, Victoria. Both letters were conventionally restrained, but they show for the first time that she was looking ahead to resuming life at Schönbrunn and giving old friends the opportunity to admire 'my good-looking son'.[2]

At midday on 21 May, as the cavalcade approached Vienna, the Empress Maria Ludovica came out to meet her stepdaughter, a token of respect which Napoleon forbade his Empress to offer at Dresden when she was First Lady of Europe. At eight o'clock on that Saturday evening, four weeks after leaving Rambouillet, Louise was re-united with her brothers and sisters at Schönbrunn. Outside the palace, with Napoleon's gilded French eagles overlooking the courtyard, a crowd cheered and waved as happily as the people of Innsbruck at the sight of 'Iphigenia returning alive from the embrace of the Minotaur', as Méneval recorded with gentle irony.[3] But one of many secret agents who mingled with the well-wishers reported back to Hager, the city's police chief, that the popular attraction was 'the little prince', with his courtesy and good looks.

Emperor Francis was not expected back in his capital for three weeks, even though he had remained ill at ease in Paris and politely declined an invitation from the Prince Regent to join the Tsar and the King of Prussia in victory celebrations across the Channel. In her father's absence Louise tried to keep her suite together, forming a miniature French court in the west wing of the huge palace, the apartments that were hers as Archduchess. The carriages which had made the journey from Paris retained the French imperial coat-of-arms. Though the exiles spoke now of '*le petit Monsieur*' rather than '*le Roi de Rome*', there was no doubt to whom they were referring when they spoke of 'the Emperor'. And no one could question Louise's loyalty to her husband;

his portrait was in her bedroom, his miniature in a bracelet which she would open admiringly to any Austrian who showed interest.

Yet this proud defiance was counter-productive. It was extremely unpopular with her stepmother, all the d'Este faction, and most of the Austrian ladies; and it embarrassed those exiles who were eager to feather their nests Bourbon-white in Paris. There was a steady drift homewards. Dr Corvisart was willing to insist to anyone in Vienna who would listen to him that, for the sake of her health, 'the Empress' needed to take the waters at Aix-en-Savoie; but he was not prepared to see a fashionable practice dwindle away; and on 2 June he duly set off for home. So, too, that day did the Duchess of Montebello who, though still Louise's 'dearest friend', found family demands a compelling reason to hasten back to France. Both Corvisart and the Duchess assured a sad Louise that they would join her at Aix if she made the journey; they may have thought it unlikely the Austrians would allow her to set off westwards again.

Three days after their departure Louise sent a long letter to Napoleon; it became the first to reach him since he landed on Elba. She had received no news of him since 3 May, she wrote, and was afraid her earlier letters had gone astray; he must not think she had forgotten him; she 'loved him more tenderly than ever'. His letters were, she was certain, passed to Metternich, in Paris, 'who thought it proper to leave them on his desk'. With the departure of the Duchess and Corvisart there were now 'only two people to whom I can talk of you, and I am not always able to see them'. 'Everyone who meets your son is full of admiration. People here think he much resembles you, which delights me,' she assured Napoleon. 'Your son speaks often of you ... always asking, "When shall we see Papa?"' She then outlined her immediate programme with a rare clarity of intent: she would leave Vienna on 30 June, arrive at Aix on 10 July, take the waters for six weeks and then 'go immediately to Parma'. She did not intend 'your son' to accompany her to Aix; it would be expensive and might be dangerous; Mme de Montesquiou would 'take him directly' to Parma.[4]

One sentence in the letter must particularly have surprised Napoleon, and may explain its decisiveness of tone: 'The person whom I find most sympathetic here is the Queen of Sicily,' she wrote. 'She speaks to me in good, strong terms and has immediately won my heart.' The Queen of Sicily was Louise's eccentric grandmother, Maria Carolina, now in her seventy-second year and the last survivor of the great Maria Theresa's sixteen children. She was a favourite of Louise in childhood – and of her father, Francis, too. After leaving her loutish husband in Palermo, she returned to her birthplace, determined to champion his right to recover his throne in Naples. But her health was failing and she was content to settle in one of her mother's exquisite hunting lodges, Schloss Hetzendorf, two miles south of Schönbrunn. Although the Queen remained an enemy of Napoleon, she admired his soldierly qualities, petted 'the little prince' and was indignant at Austrian attempts to keep Louise apart from a husband to whom she was so manifestly devoted. 'When one is married, it is for life,' the Queen insisted. What 'good, strong terms' she used in talking to Louise nobody knows; but Méneval records a long conversation with the Queen in which she declared emphatically that, were she in her granddaughter's place, *she* would make a rope of knotted sheets, let herself down by it from a palace window and escape in disguise.

Were those words a regretful boast by a fading romantic? Or did they conceal a purpose which good, solid Méneval chose not to perceive? For the Queen was, after all, Marie Antoinette's sister and could vividly recall the excitement of June 1791, when news reached Italy that the French royal family had escaped from Paris. Though their flight ended dismally at Varennes, thoughtful planning by outsiders brought it close to success. Was Maria Carolina testing Louise's loyal secretary with the prospect of another June flight to freedom in mind? Did she hope he would bring fugitives in disguise across the two miles of parkland behind Schönbrunn and use Hetzendorf as boarding-point for a hard-ridden carriage dash for the Tuscan coast?

In Maria Carolina's mind such fantasy was not improbable. Méneval observes that 'the daring spirit of the old Queen agreed neither with Marie Louise's character nor her sense of decorum'.[5] He was right; and he could have added that Hager's spies would have spotted knotted sheets long before his Empress slipped out of a palace window. A royal ancestress of Louise, ten generations back, was rowed to freedom from Lochleven to mount the fastest of stolen horses and rally a losing cause in western Scotland. But Louise was no Mary Stuart; she inherited too much of her father's caution to play the role of romantic heroine. A madcap adventure would put at risk her certainty of receiving Parma. As yet, she had not even heard from Napoleon in Elba. For the moment she was content to take Italian lessons, and to ride out occasionally to her beloved Laxenburg or to the Kahlenberg, with its view across Vienna to the stunted trees and bushes around the battlefields of Aspern and Wagram.

Louise travelled out of Vienna to greet her father on 15 June, the day before he was formally welcomed back to his capital. Almost at once she began to press her needs on him: in particular, the urgency with which she must get away from Austria and, for the sake of her lungs, take the waters at Aix before assuming responsibility for the governance of Parma. It was not a sensible moment to raise such matters. Francis was tired. He was also aware of diplomatic problems and dynastic complexities of which his daughter had no comprehension: for the future of both Aix-en-Savoie and Parma were sensitive issues. Aix had not fallen within France's 1792 boundaries and the Bourbon flag flew there now only thanks to Bonaparte's first Italian campaign. Francis was not yet sure who would rule where in Italy. It was a part of Europe over which he held strong opinions: he was born there; his Foreign Minister, Metternich, had never even seen the peninsula. Nor, of course, had Louise, who clearly had no idea how far and how fast her problems had fallen in political precedence over the past three months. Francis handled his daughter firmly, as at Rambouillet. She might see his pleasure at having her once more within his family circle but he emphasised that he could not recognise her as a sovereign individual. Yet despite his sternness, Francis responded swiftly and sympathetically to her immediate wish. Within forty-eight hours of returning to Vienna, he sent to Louis XVIII a letter seeking permission for his daughter to spend six weeks at Aix-en-Savoie taking a medically supervised cure.[6]

On 29 June the best of the berlins from Rambouillet were spruced up, turned about, and set off for Munich. Louise travelled with Countess Anne-Marie de Brignolle as principal companion. Bausset was her major-domo and Méneval her secretary. A personal staff of thirty men and women went with them. The 'little prince' and Maman Quiou remained at Schönbrunn. Louise had never intended to take the boy with her, but having 'been deeply touched by my father's kindness', she discussed the possibility with Francis, only to agree with him that the presence of Napoleon's son would cause disquiet (*troubler la tranquillité*). Over this question she did not fight and lose a battle of wills with her father: good sense prevailed. Doubts did arise over the title she should use on her travels. To cross King Louis's frontier as 'Empress' would show singular lack of tact; and, to her annoyance, she was not yet recognised as Duchess of Parma. With a firm hint to the autumn's peacemakers, she assumed a title taken from the summer residence of Parma's Farnese and Bourbon rulers and made the journey across Bavaria and Switzerland incognito as the Duchess of Colorno. But she did not try too hard to conceal her identity. Her French imperial arms remained on each door of the carriages.

A week before leaving Schönbrunn Louise received the first account of life on Elba. Not directly, however, from her husband; at least four intercepted letters from Napoleon were by now awaiting Prince Metternich's attention. The news came from General Bertrand, who had addressed his letter to Méneval. In a reply, Louise told Napoleon that she was glad the island was so attractive: he was to make certain there were good rooms for her in his new house 'in the country' – and a 'pretty garden', too; for she had every intention of visiting him as soon as possible.[7]

A mood of elation sustained her as the berlin rolled and swayed up the roads towards Munich, a land galleon on a moderate sea. She was free from 'the prison of Vienna'; her close companions were trusted friends, with not a police spy among them. They could travel at the pace she ordered, make stops where she wished, visit whom she chose: Eugène and his Bavarian wife, Auguste, in Munich itself; her brother-in-law, ex-King Louis, in Switzerland's Baden; and, wiping from her memory the tearful tension of Blois, she even stayed at Allaman with Joseph, who gave her a Spanish stallion for canters along the Swiss shore of Lake Geneva. She was in no hurry to reach Aix: why arrive before Dr Corvisart? Mountain scenery fascinated her: for six days the party lingered in the Chamonix valley. At last, on 17 July, they headed down the upper Rhone valley for Culoz, a small town at the foot of the Grand-Colombier and some fifteen miles from Aix. Here, not for the first time on long progresses, a surprise awaited her, though a less agreeable one than in earlier years. For outside Culoz she was greeted by a horseman wearing the white uniform of an Austrian general and accompanied by an aide-de-camp. The General was well-built, with a reddish sun-soaked face, fair curly hair fast receding, and a black kerchief over his right eye. At the request of His Imperial Majesty her father, Count Adam Albert von Neipperg had come to escort the Duchess of Colorno to the villa leased for her above Lake le Bourget and the thermal springs of Aix. These courtesies passed unappreciated. Happy days had gone again, it seemed. For the two last hours of her journey, the Duchess sulked.[8]

'Francis the Good,' though demonstratively a fond father, was too shrewd a monarch ever to have contemplated giving his daughter free rein at such a time. On his own initiative he sought ways to keep her in check. Clearly she needed a masterful major-domo, alert and courteous, someone familiar with Italy's problems. With Metternich preening himself in England, Francis turned for advice to Schwarzenberg, whose portly figure so often formed the butt of Louise's jokes with her husband while he was ambassador at Paris. He knew her weaknesses; he also knew Corvisart, whom he met again during the doctor's twelve days in Vienna. It did not take him long to propose General Count von Neipperg to Francis as adviser and minder for his daughter.

The Count's credentials were impressive. He fought as a hussar officer against the revolutionary armies in France and the Netherlands from 1792–4, when he lost his right eye to a sabre thrust in the battle of Doelen. By 1796, when only twenty-one, he became a staff-captain. Four years later he showed bravery with the cavalry at Marengo, subsequently basking in a – perhaps exaggerated – reputation as a dashing lady-killer. But he was an officer of high intelligence, appreciative of good music and an able linguist, who proved himself a patient diplomat, while ambassador at Stockholm in the months that Marshal Bernadotte was winning acceptance as Sweden's Prince Royal. Most recently he had negotiated tactfully with Viceroy Eugène, when Napoleon's Kingdom of Italy crumbled, and on 28 April he led the first Austrian troops into Milan for fourteen years. When Schwarzenberg put forward Neipperg's name, Francis did not hesitate. Two days before the Duchess of Colorno set out from Vienna, blissfully unaware of these machinations, Baron Hudelist of the Foreign Ministry wrote to Metternich to inform him that the Emperor was seconding General Neipperg from the 3rd Hussar Regiment at Pavia to guide and protect 'the Empress' (*sic*) at Aix and ensure she did not go to Elba.[9]

Neipperg did not welcome his new posting. In 1812 Francis had attached him to the suite of the Empress of the French, as a supplementary Austrian aide-de-camp during his daughter's state visit to Prague; she scarcely noticed him among so many acolytes; and he found her manner haughty. At that time he was living with Countess Teresa Ramondini whom he would marry in 1813, when her husband obliged them by dying. Meanwhile she had presented Neipperg with five children in rapid succession. In 1812 Teresa was a compact olive-skinned brunette, while the Empress was a proto-matriarchal blonde, with flushed complexion and shoulders as white as her innocence: definitely not Neipperg's type. But when he received personal orders drawn up for him by the Emperor himself, Neipperg was impressed. He was also sardonically amused; for so intent was Francis on preventing 'his much-loved daughter' from reaching Elba that the Count was authorised to stop her going there 'by any means whatsoever (*Kein Mittel unversucht lassen*)'. If his grandson's memoirs may be trusted, he remarked to Teresa, 'I'm willing to bet she will be my mistress within six months.'[10]

Neipperg reached Aix two days ahead of the Duchess of Colorno. She was to live in a villa north of the thermal springs which in earlier years had been leased by Empress Josephine and by Queen Hortense. The Count made certain that the rooms looked attractive and that the piano did not need tuning. Despite her initial hostility towards the Count, Louise soon began to admire his calm efficiency and appreciate his care and consideration. Twelve months previously Hortense's principal lady-in-waiting – a sister-in-law of Marshal Ney – had slipped off a plank walk above a waterfall and fallen to her death: Neipperg was too avuncularly protective for there to be any similar tragedy. Louise was well content: 'From my window, I have a marvellous view of Lake le Bourget and the mountains behind,' she wrote to her father. She enjoyed being petted: Corvisart was on hand for her medicinal needs; soon the

Duchess of Montebello would arrive, for those girlish tête-a-têtes on which Louise fed her emotions; to her surprise, Isabey was at Aix to gratify her artistic sensitivities; and there was good, reliable Méneval – so loyal that, though he hastened to Paris to be with his pregnant wife, he was back in Aix once the child was safely born, well before Louise had finished taking the waters. And now, unexpectedly, her father had attached to her suite a first-rate pianist, who could accompany her as she sang Mozart arias or listen attentively to her own playing. She does not seem to have realised how deeply her French friends mistrusted Neipperg: could they not see that he was by nature a Francophile? Within a week of reaching Aix, Louise's letters were full of the Count's praises: 'I thought he would please you,' her father replied drily.[11]

Napoleon was told of Neipperg's presence as early as 21 July: Louise was pleased by remarks which showed his 'admiration for your genius'.[12] But Napoleon never received this letter, nor three others which Louise wrote to him over the next five days. He was beginning to realise that the sovereignty accorded to him over Elba was a parody of state power. Politically he was an outcast, whose needs it was expedient for the peacemakers to ignore. He was, for example, given no news of his son; nor did he ever receive any portion of the pension – equivalent to £100,000 a year – which it had been agreed in Paris that Louis XVIII would pay him in return for the surrender of his personal fortune. One discourtesy, soon after he reached Elba, deeply shocked and saddened him: for he was never officially informed that, on the last Sunday of May, the Empress Josephine had died at Malmaison.

The fault was not his stepchildren's, as has often been said.[13] Two letters from Eugène are extant: the first warned his stepfather that Josephine was seriously ill; the second broke to him the news of her death. These letters, like those passing between the Emperor and his second Empress, were delayed by the wretched system of surveillance imposed by his ex-enemies in partnership with the authorities in Paris. A Genoan gazette, brought to Portoferraio by one of his valets, contained the earliest report to reach the island. It bore the stamp of authenticity; for two days Napoleon shut himself up in his villa on the hillside above the harbour, and grieved alone. Only much later was he to hear how Josephine caught pneumonia after walking on a cool evening with Tsar Alexander in her beloved rose-garden and of how the Tsar had ordered his crack guards regiments to line the route of her funeral procession. She died at noon on the Feast of Pentecost. Curiously – telepathically, perhaps – Napoleon, knowing nothing of her illness, chose that Sunday to attend the parish church in Portoferraio and hear High Mass celebrated for the first time in four months.

There is no reference to Josephine in any of Marie Louise's letters, though she read of her predecessor's death in a Swiss newspaper and was shocked by its suddenness. Louise had few illusions over the restraints imposed on correspondence to or from Elba; one letter, 'certainly opened in Vienna', took more than a month to complete the journey from the island to Aix; another (which has not survived) reached her with no attempt made to conceal cuts and excisions. By 18 August Napoleon could complain that he had not received any letter from her since she left Schönbrunn seven weeks previously. Ten days later, however, a long letter written on 10 August did arrive, together with a re-assuring medical report from Corvisart, and Louise's gift for his forty-fifth birthday – a cachette containing a lock of her hair. It was to be her last present to him.[14]

A vexed Napoleon grew impatient. To circumvent the delays and intrusion of the Austrian security service he made increasing use of personal envoys, men with reasons of their own for passing between the Italian coast and Upper Savoy, sometimes returning secretly to Elba by way of Genoa. A Polish officer was able to exchange messages with Louise on 18 August: she entrusted to him a letter, written freely but in haste, which he was to hide among his belongings (*cacher en ses trousses*). Louise warned Napoleon that she was 'surrounded here by agents and counter-agents – Austrian, French and Russian' and 'General Neipperg has told me he has in his pocket orders to intercept any letters I may write.' She was, she explained, preparing to come to Elba when she received a letter from her father ordering her back to Vienna for the Congress; it was essential she should be there in order to uphold the interests of her son; the Bourbons wished to return to Parma and would only offer her compensation in the 'Legations', the northern fringe of the Papal States. In her letter Louise emphasised that she wanted Parma and had every intention of visiting Elba; 'but I still do not know when that will be possible.'[15]

In reality she was less ready to set out for Elba than the letter suggests; but her dismay over Parma rings true. She had thought the matter settled: Bausset was on his way to the city to assess for her the relative merits of the ducal residences. But, from the tone of her father's letter, she could see Metternich's arrival back in Vienna on 19 July posed fresh problems. For, as ever, he favoured Austro-French understanding, co-operation to check Russo-Prussian primacy in Germany and Poland. So, too, for subtler reasons, did Talleyrand. While Napoleon was on the throne, Marie Louise had been the lynch-pin in such a partnership: but now she was expendable. On his way home from London, Metternich had talks with Louis XVIII and his Foreign Minister. The King, he reported, was 'seriously disconcerted' by the presence of 'the French Empress' at Aix-en-Savoie.[16] And Talleyrand, so Metternich found, had become a strong advocate of 'legitimacy', the return of traditional dynasties, including that branch of the Spanish Bourbons who had ruled in Parma. Was there a place for the Empress and her son in a 'legitimised' Italy? It would be far better to summon her back to Vienna and start again.

Francis was glad to see his brother Ferdinand, so recently Grand Duke of Würzburg, home again in Florence as Grand Duke of Tuscany. 'Legitimacy', however, posed awkward problems; and he remained by no means convinced that Metternich's views on Italy were sound. But at this moment a rash move by Napoleon seemed to justify Metternich's fears. On 23 August Captain Hurault, who was married to Marie Louise's personal reader, arrived at Aix from Elba to visit his wife. He immediately sought a meeting with the Empress and, like the Polish officer a few days previously, handed her a letter from Napoleon. This, however, was a different type of message: she must set out at once with Hurault for Genoa, where the brig *Inconstant* was waiting to take her to Elba.[17]

Louise resented the peremptory tone. His orders were, she later complained, 'thoughtless' and 'self-centred'. The chances of escaping from Aix were remote and such an escapade, whatever its outcome, would almost certainly forfeit any chance of bargaining over Parma. In this crisis, she showed admirable good sense; Hurault was sent back to his lodgings, to await her decision. Neipperg was informed, and formally requested to take her 'under his protection'. Hurault was arrested, sent under escort to Paris and soon released: for the restored monarchy was far from popular in the capital; and Talleyrand did not intend to give publicity to what sentimental Bonapartists might see as a romantic gesture. Neipperg reported the incident to Vienna next day; and Louise wrote to her father later in the week, emphasising her determination not to go to Elba. A postscript looked ahead with happy anticipation to next week's journey into Switzerland; General Neipperg was settling the details.

At this moment she turned decisively against Napoleon. The rescue bid had been hurriedly conceived, improvised rather than planned; it was as unrealistic as knotted sheets dropped from a palace window. What a contrast to the solicitude with which General Neipperg met her needs! Louise was angry and disillusioned with her husband. The cure at Aix was coming to an end; to the open disapproval of the Duchess of Montebello, she was enjoying more and more the afternoons when the General would take her out in a boat on the lake and the musical evenings they shared around the piano. She was pleased that 'dearest Papa' had agreed she should not be in Vienna when the allied sovereigns arrived for the grand opening of the Congress. A slow journey home, with a week of rest and recuperation in Switzerland, would be admirable; and this time the General would travel beside her in the leading carriage.

They left Aix-en-Savoie on 5 September. On that Monday Napoleon, too, decided on a change of residence; he would spend a fortnight at an old Spanish citadel farther down the coast. Life on Elba always mingled bathos with pathos. On 4 June, observing protocol as a sovereign prince, Napoleon paid a courtesy visit to the British guardship to honour the birthday of King George III. Imperious orders rang out, especially in the early weeks on the island: 'My Guards' must make certain there were racks for their muskets and sabres in 'My cutters', the vessels of 'My fleet' (*flotte*);[18] 'Grand Marshal Bertrand' should ensure that 'the commanding officer of engineers' regulates the assistance given by the grenadiers to gardeners, for to employ eleven grenadiers to load 'cartfuls of earth' from 'a garden the size of my hand' was excessive.[19] He was seriously concerned at the need to defend the island against raids by Barbary pirates; evidently he did not relish the prospect of finding himself carried to the shores of Tripoli and held to ransom. (Would anyone have paid?) Days and evenings hung heavily on his hands. Marie Walewska and their four-year-old Alexandre visited him for the first weekend in September, and Madame Mère was content to come up from Rome and spend a few days in Portoferraio – to her, a tiny Ajaccio. Soon his sister Pauline would come to pass the winter with him; she had already paid a brief visit in June. But he still hoped to see his wife and son again, as he told Louise in a letter written on 28 August.[20] Yet he can hardly have been surprised when the *Inconstant* arrived back from Genoa without her.

By now Louise had come to regard France as an adopted country which had chosen to reject her. When, on 7 September, the long carriage procession crossed the frontier and she left France for the last time, there was no show of emotional regret, no tearful farewells similar to the outbursts Méneval had noticed only seventeen weeks previously. His Empress was looking forwards, not back – and never again southwards to Elba.

After brief stops at Geneva and Lausanne the carriages trundled on to Berne. There General Neipperg, Louise and the Countess de Brignolle left the main party to spend nine days in the Bernese Oberland, often ascending mountain paths above the snow-line. Sad news awaited Louise on their return: her grandmother, the 'Queen of Sicily', had died in her sleep at Hetzendorf on the Thursday they passed through Lausanne. But the household was given no opportunity for prolonged mourning. An unexpected visitor arrived at the Hotel d'Angleterre, where they were staying: the 'highly original' Princess of Wales, having broken loose from her husband, the Prince Regent, was travelling across Switzerland on the first stage of a visit to Greece and the Italian lakes. It was hard to ignore Caroline of Wales. On 23 September she was invited to dine with the 'Duchess of Colorno'.

Caroline's mega-vulgarity and her scorn for tact and discretion were so overpowering that the visit was recalled in their memoirs by both Méneval and Bausset. The Princess was the daughter of that Duke of Brunswick under whose command so many young officers had marched confidently towards Paris in the first campaign of the revolutionary wars; but such distant matters held little interest for Caroline. She was, as she informed her hostess, a warm admirer of Napoleon and had every intention of visiting him on Elba. After dinner there was music: at Caroline's suggestion, she sang a duet with Louise, with Neipperg accompanying them on the piano. Her choice was surprising: *La ci darem il mano* from Mozart's *Don Giovanni*; Louise sang the soprano, zerlina, with a light clarity of diction: Caroline's deep contralto delivered the Don's words, intended for baritone/bass, with impressive resonance. It was a memorable occasion.[21] Next morning – with undue haste, perhaps – the Duchess of Colorno's carriages left for Lucerne.

Louise did not wish to arrive back in Vienna until 4 October, the Feast of St Francis of Assissi. For as long as she could remember, Papa's name-day had been a family occasion. She felt confident that if she delayed her return until then, she could count on a quiet reunion, well away from the foreign sovereigns who were expected to reach the capital in this coming week ready for the opening of the Congress. There was, accordingly, time for one final expedition before heading for Schönbrunn. On 27 September Louise and her closest companions went by boat from Lucerne eight miles across the lake to Küssnacht, at the foot of Mount Rigi. Back from the lakeside stood the single remaining tower of Rudolf of Habsburg's original castle, duly visited under Neipperg's stage-management, for it was a hallowed place of pilgrimage for any member of the dynasty.

But near Küssnacht there is another hallowed spot. What was then a lane, shaded at first by beeches, winds for a mile and a half up the lower slopes of the Rigi to William Tell's chapel, a local shrine erected where the hero's arrow is said to have struck down the oppressive Austrian governor, Gessler. Neipperg, Louise and her companions had climbed that far, and seen the chapel, when a heavy rainstorm swept down from the Rigi. There could be no question of returning down to Küssnacht. They were forced to spend the night in a *Gasthaus*, 'Zur Goldenner Sonne', a wayside inn with little space to spare. In later years Méneval told his grandson his bed had been close to the door into the Empress's bedroom; and he was sure that Neipperg and Louise were lovers that night. While still in Switzerland, Méneval wrote home to his wife, with sad resignation, 'I can no longer fool myself that she is the pure and spotless angel whom I held above reproach.' But, still loyal to his Emperor and to his Empress, Méneval remained dutifully in her service. The links with France were not yet cut.[22]

14

The Recluses of Schönbrunn

The Congress of Vienna was without precedent in the history of Austria or, indeed, of Europe. Earlier wars had ended in tedious conferences, with nominated delegates meeting, for the most part, in cities on the Rhine or its tributaries. But the aftermath of the Napoleonic wars was different. No previous conflict had changed the map of the continent so drastically: there were problems unresolved from the Baltic down to the Ionian Islands, and uncertainty over colonial possessions in the Americas, south Africa and the Indian Ocean. For the first time there was also a genuine desire among rulers and ruled for a long period of peace. The Treaty of Paris, which settled the frontiers of France at the end of May, was more concerned with future security than vengeance: Article 32 stipulated that 'all the powers engaged on either side in the present war' should send plenipotentiaries to Vienna for the Congress; and the first supplementary article affirmed the need to achieve 'a system of real and permanent Balance of Power in Europe'. By winning acceptance of Vienna as a cradle for this new form of diplomacy, Metternich successfully restored his imperial master's stature. Though Tsar Alexander had entered Paris as a conqueror, it was Emperor Francis who could welcome his brother sovereigns to Vienna as a peacemaker.

Francis did so, though grudgingly: for he hated fuss and needless expense. He suspected Congress hospitality would dig deeply into his funds. (It did: to the equivalent of £30 million sterling, by end of millennium values). But on 25 September he was waiting at the Tabor causeway above the Danube water meadows to escort the Tsar and the King of Prussia through the streets of Leopoldstadt and the Inner City to the Hofburg, where a wing of the palace had been virtually rebuilt to accommodate the monarchs and their households. In the stables were 1,400 horses, made ready each morning and afternoon for Francis's guests to ride out to the chestnut avenues of the Prater or the wooded hills south and west of the city. By the evening of 4 October, when Marie Louise arrived back at Schönbrunn, her father was host to the heads of five reigning dynasties and 216 princely families. The narrow streets became impossibly congested. Richard Bright, an English physician who happened to be in Vienna during the Congress, was told that on any one day between two and three hundred imperial carriages, placed at the service of the Emperor's guests, would be making their way across the city.[1]

Tsar Alexander assumed it would take no more than six weeks to safeguard peace and order on the continent; Castlereagh, heading the British delegation, expected to be home in Westminster before the end of November. Both estimates were wildly optimistic. Metternich was never so sanguine. He knew that the Polish Question continued to divide Russia and Austria. So, too, did the future of Saxony and its king, who had remained loyal to Napoleon unfashionably long. And he suspected, rightly, that Talleyrand's championship of 'legitimacy' would raise problems over the future of Italy. Here Metternich had particular reason to tread with care; he could not back Ferdinand IV, the legitimate King of the Two Sicilies, for he had recognised Murat as King of Naples when Napoleon's brother-in-law changed sides in January 1814. At the same time he knew that, while Francis no longer had any imperial ambitions within the German lands, he looked hopefully to the south and regarded a Habsburg-dominated peninsula as a legitimate prize for his dynasty and empire. With so many conflicting interests to resolve, Metternich was prepared to play for time; he became the master craftsman of diplomacy by attrition. It is hardly surprising that by Christmas the Congress had made little progress.

His critics, Austrian as well as foreign, thought too much time was wasted on frivolity – far too many balls, concerts, masquerades, and carrousels. Someone remarked that the only hard workers at the Congress were police spies, filing reports on whose carriage called on which lady of distinction, and the Festivals Committee, the court dignitaries who were responsible for the succession of entertainments. No one could doubt that they, at least, were busy: their social calendar for January 1815, for example, listed no less than sixteen grand fêtes; and, though (at Talleyrand's prompting) mourning was observed for the anniversary of Louis XVI's execution, next day everyone enjoyed themselves at a sleigh party in the Schönbrunn parkland. Yet behind these diversions there was a purpose: they kept the delegates together, soothed ruffled tempers, plugged punctured egos. In the last resort they ensured that the Tsar would converse with Metternich, not challenge him to a duel.

'The Empress Maria Louisa [*sic*] ... during all this period ... suffered with a dignity which did honour to her character,' Richard Bright wrote. 'She lived in quiet seclusion at the palace of Schönbrunn' and 'took no part in those festivities with which her father's court re-echoed.'[2] So indeed several of the Empress's letters affirm: thus, on the first Saturday in December, she invites her friend Victoria to 'come and see the recluses of Schönbrunn', explaining that 'I can give us that title from the way we live here, amid a world entirely taken up with fêtes and balls and which thinks only of amusing itself and rejoicing ... Festivities go on every day, so they tell me, for I am scarcely informed of them,' she added later in the letter, 'I do not regret it, I am even content that my situation keeps me from going to them.'[3] Perhaps so. Yet, on the previous Tuesday, Beethoven was joint-conductor at a gala concert of his own compositions, which included the Seventh Symphony. The Tsar and the King of Prussia were there. It must have been galling for so appreciative a lover of good music as Louise to miss such an occasion.

Yet, though the Congress festivities passed her by, she was never such a recluse as she pretended. Neipperg was still with her. While they were at Aix and in Switzerland he had assumed he would take up command of his regiment again once they returned to Vienna. But Louise was adamant: she depended on his good sense for sound advice; and he remained with her, the acceptable German in a household still predominantly French. As major-domo, he was present when she was at home to selected visitors. There were plenty of them. Eugène, hoping for a new domain now he could no longer be Viceroy of Italy, visited Louise twice in the first week after her return. On 10 October she had seven guests to dinner; they included Gentz (the secretary of the Congress), Stadion (former – and as many thought, future – Foreign Minister) and surprisingly the Duchess of Sagan, that tantalising sexual predator notorious for throwing the Tsar and Metternich into jealous rivalry. Tsar Alexander himself came to visit the recluses on the morning of 13 October. Three days later – a Sunday – Louise drove into the city, with Anne-Marie de Brignolle, Neipperg and Bausset in her carriage, which still carried the arms of the Empress of the French; they visited the Queen of Bavaria and the Imperial Riding School. Next evening Eugène again came out to Schönbrunn, where he stayed from seven o'clock until eleven; for whist, perhaps, or music?[4]

Such detailed information survives among the hundreds of notes which his agents sent to Baron von Hager, the Chief of Police and

Censorship in the capital. Hager studied and assessed these reports before forwarding any of interest to the Emperor, together with intercepted correspondence which he considered of particular significance. Each morning Francis received regular details of the activities of men and women 'under surveillance', including his eldest daughter. On many days the spies found nothing more exciting to report than the length of time Louise walked in the gardens with Neipperg or her ladies. Occasionally, however, Francis could read significant asides; thus the Countess of Colloredo, who visited Louise as early as 22 October, was reported as saying that the Empress no longer seemed interested in Napoleon, but 'was very intimate with Neipperg'. And Francis may not have heard from his daughter of all her meetings with Eugène, or the Tsar, or the King of Prussia.

The spy system was as intrusive as modern telephone-tapping. Even Hager became embarrassed: did the Emperor wish this 'delicate surveillance' of his daughter to continue, he asked on 30 November? Two days later Francis relented and approved the removal of all agents assigned to her.[5] It made little difference, however; for everyone else of importance was being trailed, and if they visited the west wing of Schönbrunn a report was duly filed. So Francis could discover that on 11 December Eugène spent at least three hours at Schönbrunn; and on the following afternoon, Louise's twenty-third birthday, her guests were 'the Emperor and Empress of Russia'. This fact, however, Francis knew already; for, as the report went on to inform him, 'The Emperor of Austria called, but did not stay for dinner.'[6]

Hager's material also provided some idea of rumours current in the capital. Frequently they came from a half-knowledge of discussions or memoranda. The most vexatious concerned the validity of Marie Louise's marriage. Pius VII's plenipotentiary at the Congress was the Papal Secretary of State, Cardinal Consalvi, the most prominent of the 'black cardinals' who had offended Napoleon by their absence from the wedding ceremony at the Tuileries. Soon after he arrived in Vienna Consalvi gave Metternich a memorandum which made it clear that Pius VII was prepared to confirm that the annulment of Napoleon's marriage to Josephine had been invalid and that the union between him and Marie Louise was therefore bigamous. Consalvi also noted that, since Josephine was dead and Napoleon a widower, there was no longer any canonical impediment to marriage between the Emperor on Elba and the Archduchess who had assumed she was his wife.[7]

Consalvi's initiative was embarrassing and unwelcome. A few months earlier, when Louise was seeking good reasons to join Napoleon, she might have exploited the ruling. But by now that desire had gone. She did not wish her French marriage called in question, not least because of the effect on the status of the King of Rome. Her father and Metternich sought to keep the papal pronouncement confidential: why raise even more issues at such a time? But Consalvi's views were widely known. Persistent rumours began to circulate, and were magnified. Soon it was being said that, since Louise was in the eyes of the Church a spinster, it was intended that she should marry King Frederick William III of Prussia, a widower for the last four years. This was nonsense, as Gentz took pains to emphasise in letters to influential figures within Germany. Frederick William, by temperament far less uxorious than Emperor Francis, was disinclined to marry again; and the Vatican was hardly likely to help a Catholic Archduchess to marry a Lutheran sovereign. Yet Louise received so many visits from the King in the seven weeks after her return from Switzerland that there seemed some substance in the rumours. And on 25 November one of Hager's agents could report that the Countess de Brignolle and Bausset were shocked when, at dinner, their Empress suddenly raised her glass to drink to the King of Prussia's good health. They did not know – and Louise saw no reason to enlighten them – that she had just received a letter from Frederick William in which he assured her of his warm support for her right to rule in Parma. The agents's report cannot have surprised his chief. For Hager and the Emperor were well aware of what was happening; the King's letter had been intercepted and was ready for Francis to peruse a day before it reached his daughter.[8]

Louise was determined that the pledges of the Treaty of Fontainebleau should be fulfilled: sovereignty over Parma, Piacenza and Guastalla for herself and her son was hers by right, she argued, and she continued to act as Duchess-designate. Bausset's exploratory journey to the Duchy in August was followed by lengthy visits to Vienna by Count San Vitale, chamberlain of the palaces at Parma, and by the acting governor of Piacenza. Both dignitaries were received at Schönbrunn, as the police agents duly noted. Louise was optimistic. 'We shall be going to Parma soon,' she told San Vitale a week before Christmas.[9] After recent meetings she felt that she could count on support from Tsar Alexander as well as from Frederick William; and Neipperg was constantly ready to argue her case, not only with other delegates to the Congress, but to Austrians exasperated by the Foreign Minister's devious conduct of affairs.

She faced, however, formidable opposition. Talleyrand – a signatory of the Fontainebleau Treaty – remained obdurate: he argued that Parma should return to Queen Maria Luisa, daughter of Charles IV of Spain and Regent for her son Ludovico II, legitimate descendant of the

Farneses and Bourbons who had ruled the Duchy through three centuries. The Spanish delegate to the Congress, Don Pedro Labrador, always responded dutifully to Talleyrand's call, while Metternich's hostility towards Marie Louise seemed almost personal in its intensity. He saw no reason why she should be given sovereign rights over any territory; and he feared that, if any inheritance was passed on to her son, it could serve as a nest of neo-Bonapartism, threatening the European order. The displaced Empress should, he argued, be content with a generous pension and titular fiefs for herself and her son in Bohemia. She would be a Habsburg Archduchess once more, and the child whom Metternich had once proleptically hailed 'King of Rome' would become a ducal Serene Highness. With such sustained opposition facing her, Louise's Christmas optimism was speedily deflated. By mid-February Talleyrand could assure Louis XVIII that all would be as France wished: the Bourbon dynasty would reign in Etruria and Parma, while Louise and her son dropped offstage, lost to public sight in Bohemia. But, as yet, no proposals were committed to paper.

Behind the deliberations and compromise of the Congress loomed uncertainty over Napoleon, 'the monster on Elba', as Consalvi was already calling him. As early as September there were suggestions he should be sent well away from Italy, preferably from Europe. Yet Napoleon himself still held hope of a family reunion. A few days after Louise arrived home in Vienna from Aix, he sought help from an old friend. Grand Duke Ferdinand, now back in Florence after eight years at Würzburg, had been present when the King of Rome was born and became his godfather. Napoleon asked 'my brother and very dear uncle' to forward letters to the Empress, as he had not heard 'from my wife since 10 August, nor from my son for six months'.[10] On 20 November Napoleon used this channel of communication to contact Louise. A letter reached Emperor Francis on 6 December. After three or four days' hesitation, he passed the message to his daughter, on the eve of her birthday. She was in no hurry to reply. Eventually, on 3 January, she wrote the first letter she had even attempted to send to Elba since the Hurault incident in late August.

The tone was friendly, but restrained. The letter gave Napoleon good news of his son: the boy spoke often of his father, he was told, and was learning Italian and German; he was treated with indulgence and kindness by his grandfather. Polite greetings were sent to Princess Pauline and Madame Mère. Louise emphasised to Napoleon how quiet was her life at Schönbrunn, 'where I scarcely see more than three or four people in the evening, we have some music or I sit in a corner by the fire and talk.' It is a letter with no flicker of passion to re-kindle recent flames. Napoleon was forty-five, Louise twenty-three, but she wrote as if each of them was at least a generation older. She hoped that 1815 would prove a happier year for Napoleon, that he would find tranquillity on his island and 'enjoy long years of happiness there to the great satisfaction of those who, like me, love you and are attached to you'. No words suggested that she might come to see him on Elba, and there was no mention of Parma, perhaps because she knew the letter would almost certainly be scrutinised by Metternich as well as by her father. The letter ended: 'Once again, in embracing you tenderly [*en t'embrassant tendrement*] I wish you a good year.' They were the last words Marie Louise ever wrote to Napoleon.[11]

The police, and Metternich himself, suspected that Napoleon was in touch with the 'French colony' in the west wing of Schönbrunn. Méneval was known to have heard from General Bertrand; Madame de Montesquiou, with her family in Paris, was highly suspect. Unidentified foreigners were said to lurk in the parkland, intent on kidnapping the prince and taking him to his father. When, shortly before Christmas, Louise went into residence at Baden, barely twelve miles away, the police became very agitated: mother and child were back in their familiar rooms at Schönbrunn within three days. In February the arrival of Count Anatole de Montesquiou to visit his mother led to tighter surveillance. As a young, enterprising officer he had marched on Moscow with the Emperor, and he made little effort to hide his sympathies.[12]

On Tuesday, 7 March, early in the morning, Metternich received a message from Genoa reporting that Napoleon had slipped away from Elba for an unknown destination. By ten o'clock he had passed the news to the allied sovereigns and convened a meeting of the principal delegates in his study at the Ballhausplatz. Talleyrand and Wellington (who replaced Castlereagh in late February) thought Napoleon would land in Italy and raise a national revolt in partnership with Murat: Metternich was certain he would cross to France, where there was widespread disillusionment with the restored Bourbon régime. He was right. At that moment Napoleon was already ashore and on his way to Grenoble, with the 5th Regiment of the Line, sent to check his advance, won over to his cause by the magnetism of his personality. Four more days elapsed before Vienna knew for certain he was in France. By then he was established in Lyons, with every hope of entering Paris inside a week.

There are two accounts of how the dramatic news reached the 'French colony' at Schönbrunn: a report submitted on 9 March by a police agent; and Méneval's recollections, recalled in his memoirs.[13] At first sight they seem contradictory: the agent says the news did not break until Wednesday; Méneval that Louise was informed on Tuesday afternoon. Yet both versions ring true. Neipperg, who was in Vienna on Tuesday morning, told her of Napoleon's flight confidentially that afternoon, while they were out riding, but they decided to keep the news from the French exiles until it broke officially. On Tuesday night Neipperg and the Montesquious, mother and son, were the Empress's guests; it was the usual 'recluses' evening, with dinner followed by music and billiards. Early next morning Anatole de Montesquiou returned with the exciting news, and at nine o'clock his mother told the Empress. She listened impassively until she heard some of the household clapping their hands with delight. She then lost her temper, rushed angrily to her bedroom and plunged into such grief that her sobbing could be heard in the antechamber. For the exiles' pleasure was in sharp contrast to her own worries. The 'escape' made renewed war a near certainty. There would be new demands and harsher treaties. Above all, she was likely to lose the claim to Parma for herself and her son. Despite her emotional collapse, she was well enough to order her carriage for midday and go at once to the Hofburg to consult her father. She was determined to make it clear she knew nothing of her husband's plans.

Inevitably Louise looked to Neipperg for support in this crisis. With his assistance she drafted a plea to her father, more astutely phrased than those letters to 'Papa François' which she had improvised at her husband's command. She wrote in French, so that her plea could circulate among leading figures of the Congress. It was a submissive declaration:

> At this moment when ... further misfortunes menace me I cannot hope for a surer asylum ... than the one I claim for myself and my son from your paternal affection. In your arms, my very dear father, I take refuge with the person who is most dear to me in this world ... We will not seek any other instruction than yours. With your habitual gentleness, you may order all our comings and our goings.[14]

After her experience of paternal care in 1810, it was perhaps rash to surrender such freedom of choice. But the appeal was well received by the foreign dignitaries and especially Alexander, for it effectively tapped the Tsar's romantic sentimentality, his inclination to aid any damsel in distress. The Congress declared 'Bonaparte' an 'outlaw': he could no longer be styled 'Emperor', for the 'crime' of wrecking Europe's tranquillity made his imperial pretensions forfeit. In theory, as an outlaw, he might be summarily executed. But despite the thunder of this solemn anathema, the sovereigns were fully prepared to give protection to the 'monster's' wife and child.

The immediate Austrian reaction to Napoleon's escape was practical and, in some respects, brutal. The French colony at Schönbrunn must be broken up. In particular, the 'little prince' was to lose all contact with the land of his birth. Accordingly, on 19 March, 'Franzl' – no Habsburg called him by his first name, 'Napoleon' – was taken away from the palace and housed in the Hofburg. 'Maman Quoi', who had been with him since the hour of his birth, was found an apartment close by, at 1177 Plankengasse. But next morning – it was the prince's fourth birthday – she was abruptly dismissed on Emperor Francis's orders and replaced by a Pole warmly recommended by Neipperg, Elisa Mitrovsky, who was shortly to marry the Marquis de Scarampi. One trusted Frenchwoman, Madame Soufflot, remained with Franzl, helping to accustom him to the shattering changes in his daily life. She even guided his hand as he traced notes of affection to be taken to the Plankengasse. Inevitably they were intercepted and got no further than Hager's desk.[15]

Anne-Marie de Brignolle, so often a convenient chaperone for her Empress, was already gravely ill and died a fortnight later. Bausset, who openly disapproved of Napoleon's return to France, was also unwell, suffering acutely from gout, and unwilling to take any further part in public affairs. The discreet Méneval – who maintains that he received no verbal instructions from the Empress after her return from Aix – was allowed to continue his ill-defined duties for several weeks, possibly protected by the Tsar, who was hoping to tempt him into Russian service. But on 7 May Méneval, too, set out for Paris where, little more than a week later, he was able to give Napoleon affectionate greetings from his son and assure him of the boy's well-being. Other news from Vienna the Emperor found less gratifying.[16]

Louise remained at Schönbrunn, at first with Neipperg by her side. Easter came early that year, on 26 March, and she spent much of the day with her son, taking him for a carriage ride in the Prater during the afternoon; it was agreed he should come each Sunday to join her at the palace. Necessity made her even more of a recluse. There were no further visits from Eugène; he was trailed by four of Hager's agents, and knew it; fortunately he could count on the protection of his father-in-law, the King of Bavaria, with whom on 7 April he left Vienna for Munich. By then, to Louise's great distress, she had been deprived of Neipperg's company. For Murat, on his own initiative, kindled a new war in Italy, calling on his Neapolitan subjects to fight for a unified Napoleonic kingdom; and Murat's army outnumbered the various Austrian garrisons in the peninsula. To meet this challenge Schwarzenberg ordered Neipperg and other generals who had fought in Italy to head southwards. On 1 April he left Vienna. Soon Louise was anxiously awaiting letters from the war zone, busying herself with penning news of her son, and of her own empty days. The activity was familiar. Only the recipient had changed.[17]

Napoleon, too, was writing to his Empress.[18] The earliest letter, from Grenoble on 7 March, has not survived but it is mentioned in his second letter, sent from Lyons on 11 March which described the enthusiasm his presence aroused in the mass of Frenchmen and Frenchwomen; 'Long Live the Empress' he heard some shout. On the evening of his son's birthday, a crowd greeted the Emperor as he was carried shoulder-high across the courtyard and into the Tuileries. Four hundred and nineteen days ago Hortense and Louise were there, weeping together, as the horses' hoofs grew fainter: now only Hortense welcomed him back. But he needed his wife and son, not only for domestic comfort, but to stress the continuity of a restored Empire. He even began to contemplate once more a joint coronation for the Empress and the King of Rome, which would be held in the open air as the climax of the *Champ de Mai*, a ceremony to proclaim a new, liberal constitution. On 28 March a third letter told the Empress that the army and the people were delirious with joy; 'I expect you in April,' he wrote. 'Be in Strasbourg with my son, between the 15th and 20th.' Hortense wrote to her brother, telling him she was prepared to go to Strasbourg to meet them.[19] Meanwhile work began on redecorating their rooms in the Tuileries. It was a fantasy hope.

None of these letters reached the Empress: nor did others which followed them over the next fortnight. The second and third were intercepted and read out to the principal figures at the Congress. On Alexander and on the Prussian minister, Humboldt, they made a deep impression: had the Powers any right to deny the French people a government they clearly sought or to prevent a loving husband from enjoying the company of his wife and son? But the strongest reaction came from Louise herself. She was horrified to discover that Napoleon wanted her back in Paris. She would not return to France at any price, she was heard to remark; and a fortnight later she was saying she would rather enter a convent.[20] Yet, even after his conversation with Méneval, Napoleon never realised the intensity of her feelings, nor Metternich's determination to keep the prince a virtual hostage. Long after the Strasbourg deadline had come and gone he deluded himself that they might suddenly cross the frontier. But there was a morning in May when Carnot, who had taken office as Minister of the Interior, arrived at the Tuileries and found the Emperor in tears before a portrait of the King of Rome.[21]

Napoleon's return to France imposed a sense of urgency on the Congress. It also destroyed much of Talleyrand's influence: he was no longer a counter-weight in the balance of power, for the King he represented became an exile without an army. 'Legitimacy' made less appeal when the champion of the Bourbons was reduced to excusing Louis XVIII and the wayward loyalties of his subjects. Some matters in which Talleyrand had shown a special interest were speedily settled. The King of Saxony, deprived of his backing, was forced to concede two-fifths of his lands to Prussia. No one cared what Talleyrand had to say over the frontiers of the Netherlands, or Prussian control of the forts above the Rhine and Moselle, or the affairs of the Swiss Confederation; nor did they heed fading French pleas for Polish independence. Most of the Grand Duchy of Warsaw became a Kingdom of Poland ruled by the Tsar of Russia, though Prussia recovered Pomerania and Austria retained Tarnopol and Galicia, while Cracow was made a Free City.

Italian affairs took longer to settle, partly because of Murat's rash gamble. But on 3 May he was defeated at Tolentino, on the eastern slopes of the Appenines, south-west of Ancona. Within three weeks Neipperg led his cavalry into Naples itself, enabling Ferdinand IV to cross from Palermo and rule for the last ten years of his life as 'King of the Two Sicilies'. Northern Italy was more perplexing than the south, for Metternich believed that the years of Napoleonic experiment stimulated an Italian national patriotism which might manifest itself as readily as had the revived feeling for Empire in France. Yet Louise's hopes were raised when on 2 April Austria formally assumed responsibility for the administration of Parma, Guastalla and Piacenza. Though this decision was primarily taken for military reasons, it seemed a rebuff for Talleyrand's Bourbon clients. The inner Council of Six, effectively the executive body of the Congress, at last discussed Parma on 27 May. Talleyrand, in a last stand for the Bourbons, argued that Napoleon's return from Elba made every commitment of the Fontainebleau Treaty null and void; and Metternich agreed with him. But to Tsar Alexander, consistently Louise's champion, the Parma proposals were a question of honour; he brushed aside his colleagues' objections. As usual, a compromise was reached; the Empress would receive the Duchies, but would not take possession of them so long as there was a military emergency. No mention was made of her son's rights. On Alexander's initiative, however, a secret agreement was concluded between the Russian, Prussian and Austrian rulers by which they undertook to back the young prince's claims in the event of his mother's death.[22]

On 9 June the 'Final Act of the Treaty of Vienna' committed to paper the Congress's decision on the future of Parma. Article 99 confirmed that 'Her Majesty the Empress Marie Louise' would possess 'in full property and sovereignty the Duchies of Parma, Placentia [Piacenza] and Guastalla', but the subsequent 'reversion of these countries' would be settled by the governments of 'Austria, Russia, France, Spain, England and Prussia' in consultation with the King of Sardinia-Piedmont.[23] Again no mention was made of the title-less boy whom common usage had long ago enobled as 'Prince of Parma'.

The ceremonial conclusion of this Final Act, a hurried gathering presided over by Metternich in the main hall at the Ballhausplatz, was an anticlimax. By then almost everyone had left Vienna for the war in the west, and Metternich was impatient to join them. 'A thousand candles seemed in a single instant to have been extinguished,' one memoirist was to recall.[24] The Duke of Wellington, with a heavy task awaiting him, had gone before the end of March. Alexander and Frederick William left to join their armies on 26 May. Next day Francis, with heavy reluctance, followed them, setting out again for the Rhine and beyond. As he left the Hofburg, a small voice was heard to ask anxiously, 'Dear Grandpapa, you are not going to do something nasty to Papa?'[25]

Francis did not have the opportunity. By the second week in June he was hearing talk of placenames from a half-forgotten past: Mons, Charleroi, Fleurus and the roads to Brussels. But he came no nearer the cockpit of Europe than Heidelberg, where Schwarzenberg established Austrian headquarters. There, on Wednesday 21 June, he heard that the last desperate throw of his 'devil of a son-in-law' had failed. On the previous Sunday evening an Anglo-Dutch army under Wellington, with decisive support from Blücher's Prussians, had at last broken the Imperial Guard on a ridge south of the village of Waterloo.

That Wednesday morning a white-faced Napoleon arrived back at the Élysée, prepared to abdicate for the second time in fifteen months. This time the form was different. In the small hours of Thursday morning he dictated to his brother Lucien a declaration which was to be given to the French people; he had, he explained, gone to war for the sake of their country's independence, but fate had gone against him. 'I am sacrificing myself to the hatred of the enemies of France,' he declared. 'My political life is at an end, and I proclaim my son,

Napoleon II, Emperor of the French.'[26] It was a fine gesture which would have possessed meaning had the King of Rome and his mother been in France. Instead, it strengthened Metternich's determination to make certain the caged eaglet's wings were permanently clipped.

News of Waterloo reached Vienna on 26 June. When Louise realised the decisive character of the allied victory, she was relieved Europe would be spared a long war. At first she gave little thought to her husband's fate. Letters to her father, by then in Paris, show that she was alarmed at rumours that the French might prefer a Regency for Napoleon II than a return to Bourbon rule. Once she learnt that Louise XVIII was safely back on his throne she wrote more freely, letting 'dearest Papa' know of her happiness that the campaign had ended so satisfactorily.[27] From Schönbrunn she travelled out to Baden to take the waters; her stepmother, who was in poor health, joined her there. Louise's thoughts remained narrowly self-centred: Parma beckoned like an idyllic vision of some golden Jerusalem. How soon could she set off for Italy? Was this the time to make certain the English and French governments agreed to those secret clauses, safeguarding her son's rights of succession? Francis was guardedly reassuring: she need have no doubt that, after she had spent some time with him in Vienna, Parma would be hers.[28]

By early August she knew that Napoleon had personally surrendered to a British naval captain and was aboard a ship-of-the-line off the English coast. At first it was said he would be interned in a Scottish castle. But he was too hot a catch to hold in Europe. Metternich personally sent the Empress a note, letting her know that he was bound for St Helena, an island in the South Atlantic, 5,000 miles from France. At last on 15 August, Napoleon's birthday, Louise felt pity for him. On that Tuesday she wrote again to 'dearest Papa':

> I hope that we shall have a lasting peace now that Emperor Napoleon will no longer be able to disturb it. I hope he will be treated with kindness and clemency [*mit Güte und Milde*] and I beg you, dearest Papa, to make certain that is so. It is the only request I feel I can make, and it is the last time that I shall busy myself with his fate. I owe him a debt of gratitude for the calm unconcern [*ruhige Indifferenz*] in which he let me pass my days instead of making me unhappy.[29]

This lukewarm homage to a deep mutual love has provoked scorn from biographers of both Louise and her husband. It stands in sad contrast to the letter she sent her father five weeks after their son was born. Yet, except when describing scenery or expressing the simplest of emotions, Louise never wrote easily. In this instance she searched for the right phrase, conscious of a guilt which she was reluctant to acknowledge. Inevitably she became pen-tied. The infelicity of many words gives the letter sincerity.

Napoleon spent his birthday aboard Admiral Sir George Cockburn's flagship, HMS *Northumberland*, sailing southwards, a hundred miles west of Corunna and eight days out from Plymouth Sound. He was particularly hearty on that Tuesday, so one ship's officer noted, walking briskly around the deck before dinner. After the meal, he talked of his invasion plans for England; then he settled down to a game of pontoon, at which it was fitting he should scoop up eighty gold 'napoléons'. Wednesday's routine followed a similar pattern, but with two differences: he was less lively and, instead of playing cards, his conversation turned to the recent past; before retiring to his cabin that night he spoke wistfully of his marriage to Louise.[30] There were to be many such days, though his second Empress never again figured in his small-talk. At forty-six Napoleon was entering a half-life of legend and reminiscence. Still ahead of him on his birthday lay eight and a half more weeks at sea. Ten years back he had fought and won the Austerlitz campaign in a shorter time.

15

Parma and St Helena

Emperor Francis was away from his capital for most of the twelve months after the Congress dispersed. When he had left Vienna in May 1815 he thought a new war lay ahead of him. Instead, he found himself again caught up in all the hustle of peacemaking. The second Treaty of Paris was not signed until 20 November: it imposed new penalties on France, among them an indemnity of 700 million francs and the occupation of seventeen fortresses for at least three years. Yet of greater significance to Austria were two other treaties: the Holy Alliance, a noble concept proposed by Alexander which committed rulers to upholding order among the nations by observing 'the precepts of Justice, Christian Charity and Peace'; and, more practically, a Quadruple Alliance by which Austria, Britain, Prussia and Russia agreed to undertake collective action should France disturb the new settlement. Article VI of this treaty proposed occasional meetings of rulers or ministers to discuss the general problems of Europe. This provision created the Congress System, the diplomatic instrument through which, for seven years, Metternich sought to consolidate Austrian mastery over central and southern Europe.

For mastery it had by now become. Austria was, in Castlereagh's words, 'the great hinge upon which the fate of Europe must ultimately depend'. The final settlement returned to Francis all lands lost since he first went to war against revolutionary France, except for Belgium, some enclaves in southern Germany and a part of western Galicia, snatched by Thugut in the third Polish partition. The Austrian Empire had also absorbed Venetia, Istria, Dalmatia and Salzburg, possessions over which no Habsburg ever ruled until they were given to Francis by Bonaparte in the years before Austerlitz. Astute diplomacy ensured that, with the change of military fortune, Francis's Empire was by 1815 half as large again as in 1812, when he had gone to Dresden as his son-in-law's discomfited guest. It remained a multi-national Empire, with much of its structure familiar from earlier years, but in some regions there were significant changes of character. Nowhere was this more apparent than in fragmented Italy, where Marie Louise – still officially an 'Empress' and addressed as 'Her Majesty' – was eager to assume sovereignty over her promised Duchy.

The new map of Italy showed the Habsburgs enjoying greater influence down the peninsula than ever before: Francis was titular-king of Lombardy-Venetia, his brother was back in Tuscany, a cousin ruled in Modena, and Parma awaited his daughter. Venetian control of the Adriatic was gone; Francis's troops, rather than the Pope's, garrisoned the Romagna; and King Ferdinand ruled in Naples, thanks to Austrian military intervention, not by grace of the Bourbons of Spain. Yet, during the peacemaking in Paris, Francis was uneasy. Although as a boy he knew the old Italy, he had not travelled south of the Alps since 1784, when he was sixteen. In those years Italian political nationalism scarcely ever manifested itself. Now he believed it contaminated every kingdom and every state, a disease compounded of French ideas and his son-in-law's improvisations. These fears determined his attitude towards his daughter's immediate plans. With Napoleon no longer on Elba, letters from Louise pressed him for permission to take her son with her to Parma, but Francis's response was dampening: there were too many agitators and revolutionaries at large; it would be best if she herself remained in Vienna until the central Duchies were 'secure'. And even then, Francis told her in September, the young prince could not accompany her; he must receive his education and training in the safety of the Hofburg, like an imperial archduke. For the moment, Louise acquiesced. She awaited the return home of a powerful ally, with every intention of resuming the argument in the new year.[1]

Meanwhile Francis decided to settle the affairs of his Italian lands by visiting them in person. After spending several months in Lombardy-Venetia he would be able to judge if they should be 'germanised', as he assumed, or allowed some autonomy, as Metternich recommended, in the belief that an Italian Chancery in Milan would prove a safety-valve. The Emperor began his visit in Venice on 1 December, and was gratified by the warmth of his welcome. The display of goodwill was not entirely disinterested, for seaborne commerce was stagnant and the Venetians were hoping, if not for imperial patronage, at least for a cut in port taxes. But, whatever the motive, the welcome ensured Francis's lasting sympathy for the city. Metternich was less enthusiastic when he reached

Venice three days later. He came ashore soaked to the skin by a wintry squall which caught his ceremonial *bucintoro* as it entered the Grand Canal. Understandably he became in later years a staunch supporter of those who wished to build a causeway across the lagoon.[2]

General Count von Neipperg, too, reported to the Emperor in Venice that week. In recent months he had added to his reputation, both as a soldier and an administrator. After helping suppress Murat's rebellion and serving for some weeks as military governor of Naples, he was ordered to France, where he held similar status in central Provence until the second Treaty of Paris was signed. In Venice he was received by Emperor Francis and had talks with Metternich but he had no intention of lingering there. By 9 December he was heading north, riding his horses hard, as when he had brought news of the Leipzig victory to the capital; the 400 miles across the Tyrol and through the Styrian Alps were covered in three days. This time he was spurred forward by a personal challenge. A mud-bespattered Neipperg reached Schönbrunn on the evening of 12 December well content. For he was in time to help Louise celebrate her twenty-fourth birthday. They had not met for thirty-six weeks: 'I need not tell you of the great pleasure I felt in seeing him again,' she wrote to the Duchess of Montebello.[3]

In two respects Neipperg's situation had changed in the last nine months. At Venice the Emperor confirmed that he would serve as Louise's chamberlain, principal minister and commander-in-chief in Parma; 'I am indeed happy to think that I shall take with me to a country completely new to me someone who is so trustworthy,' Louise told the Duchess of Montebello.[4] 'He is now staying for ever beside me,' she wrote with happy confidence; but the letter did not specifically comment on another, more personal change. When Neipperg set out on his campaign he had been a married man, still bound to a wife whose uncertain health detained her for several months at distant spas. Within three weeks of her husband's departure, the Countess succumbed to a chest infection while at Treviso. There was an interlude of respectful mourning, but it did not interrupt Neipperg's correspondence with the Empress, and it was long over before he arrived back in Vienna. Louise had no intention of seeking a divorce from Napoleon, nor did she wish to take advantage of the papal doubts over the validity of her imperial marriage, but now that Neipperg was a widower she made less attempt to conceal their relationship. In January he moved into new apartments she chose for him at Schönbrunn, remaining there until they left for Parma two months later.

'I am completely occupied with my son, who I have with me the whole day,' Louise wrote to the Duchess of Montebello early in the new year.

Four months previously she had reluctantly accepted one of Metternich's nominees as the boy's principal tutor. Count Maurice Dietrichstein-Proskau-Leslie was a retired major from one of the wealthiest families of the high nobility, much respected in the musical society of the capital for concerts he gave in recent years, often as a patron of Beethoven. He was dutiful, humourless and pompous; and at first the Empress thought little of him. But when she found that Neipperg, like Metternich, approved of Dietrichstein, she changed her opinion. It was agreed that the Prince of Parma should receive a thoroughly German education, with his French origins brain-washed away.[5]

On 24 February Louise, with Neipperg's assistance, wrote one last letter to her father seeking to persuade him to allow his grandson and tutor to go with them to Parma. She knew there was little chance of success. The unspecified 'dangers' were, by Francis' reckoning, too great. Twelve days later – on 7 March 1816 – mother and son parted, inevitably in tears. 'Except for the fact that I can count on seeing him again in a few months, I think I would die of grief,' she told Louise Montebello. She was wrong on two counts: it was midsummer 1818 before she saw her son again; and, so far from wasting away with grief at the long separation, there is little doubt that, once established in her Duchy with Neipperg beside her, she could have lived happily at Parma ever after.[6]

Yet it was six more weeks before they entered the Duchy. Trieste was reached by 13 March and four days later they arrived at Venice. There, however, bad news awaited Louise: Maria Ludovica, spending the winter with Emperor Francis at Verona, was gravely ill with what appears to have been breast cancer. Louise hurried to Verona and was with her father when, on 7 April, her twenty-nine-year-old stepmother died, leaving Francis for the third time a widower – though not for long.

At last, on 19 April 1816, Louise arrived at the border of her Duchy. It was two years, to the day, since the meeting at Rambouillet at which her father told her she was going to rule there. She crossed the Po at Casalmaggiore, where a pontoon bridge had been constructed for the occasion: it was 363 metres long – almost a quarter of a mile – and, like the river embankment, it was festively decorated. The carriages travelled on another six miles to spend the night at Colorno, the Farnese's eighteenth-century Versailles, whose name Louise had appropriated for the journey to Aix. Next morning her carriage covered the last nine miles, to enter the city through the Porta San Michele (now the Barriera della Repubblica). It was a sunny Saturday and most of Parma's 30,000 inhabitants were in the streets to greet their 'Imperial Princess, Serene Highness and August Sovereign'. Her carriage was escorted by a troop of cavalry, the horses long ago sent across from Elba by Napoleon in anticipation of an earlier arrival. Behind the enclosed berlin came eighteen open carriages of Parmesan worthies in a procession which merited more than 2,000 words of enthusiastic reporting in Tuesday's *Gazzetta di Parma*. The carriages drew up outside the Romanesque cathedral. The Cardinal-Bishop was 'indisposed' (genuinely) and it was left to the Abbot of Guastalla to receive 'Her Majesty': a *Te Deum* was duly sung, followed by Benediction, presided over by the arch-priest of the cathedral. Then there was a reception at the ducal palace, and fireworks in the evening.[7] From Verona Louise had written to Victoria de Crenneville soon after her stepmother's death to say that she was resting, in anticipation of 'day after day of wretched spectacles' once she reached Parma.[8] But she need not have worried. Though the ceremonial pattern might be familiar, the demands of court life were far lighter than in the past: Parma's delightful ducal palace, less than fifty years old, was more like St Cloud than the Tuileries or the Hofburg.

'I can truthfully say that I have never been so happy as I am now,' the 'August Sovereign' wrote three weeks after her arrival.[9] Although she missed her son's company, a stream of good news came in from Schönbrunn. She read commendable reports from Dietrichstein; and, after their father's return home, there were regular letters from her favourite sister, Leopoldina, now nineteen: her nephew was 'Papa's darling and mine too', the Archduchess wrote.[10] Louise's doubts over the wisdom of leaving her son in Vienna eased. Leopoldina, the most intelligent of Francis's six surviving children, had a good sense of fun and, unlike Dietrichstein, was not inclined to find the boy's mischievousness reprehensible. Louise was content.

Parma matched her high expectations. It was a pink and white city, a treasure house of Corregio frescoes, which seemed still to celebrate the sheer excitement of their creation. Louise liked her private rooms, with their delicately elegant light blue walls, and the sense of open spaciousness which freed her spirit as she looked out from the windows. She enjoyed rides into the countryside ('a veritable garden' was her first impression). Above all, she welcomed the discovery that, apart from an hour or so each morning going over official business with Neipperg, she was a woman of leisure. Fashionable society did not exist, and the Duchess herself could set the tone; she was happy to make herself gracious at evening receptions and give luncheon parties twice a week. Occasionally less welcome guests appeared, but more often at Colorno than in Parma itself. Caroline of Wales turned up again this summer, laughing so heartily at one of her own tales that the chair in which she was sitting collapsed beneath her; from the Princess there were more guffaws, but Her Majesty was not amused.[11] For Louise liked to affect a certain gentility. 'We play billiards, we make music and we rest a lot because the heat is intense,' ran one of her letters to Louise Montebello. She added, 'You will agree this is a delightful existence and, were I not to commit the sin of pride, I could say that I deserve it, because God knows all that I have suffered in my life.'[12]

On St Helena, 8,000 miles away, her husband also had long hours of leisure on his hands – and they hung heavily. Napoleon *existed* at Longwood House, with companions willing to share his exile, from time to time walking and riding with him between the scattered eucalyptus trees which broke the monotony of a dead volcanic vista. He *lived* with them too, but it was a life spent in a refashioned past or projected into a speculative future. For his task now was to consolidate a legend. During much of the day – and often in the small hours of hot and sleepless nights, too – he dictated his reminiscences. He was shaping Bonapartism, that creed of liberal nationalism which he had never found time to formulate in his years of pomp and glory. Together with 'my martyrdom' it would, he was convinced, ensure that one day 'my son ... will come to the throne, if he is still alive.'

He spoke little of the King of Rome but thought of him often: how could it be otherwise, with at least five portraits of him in the room at Longwood? The Empress was there with their son in her arms; 'my good Louise', idealised by Isabey's painting, as in the moments which Napoleon chose to remember. He would praise her trusting innocence, her lingering purity. She never lied, he told Gaspard Gourgaud, and he did not doubt that she was devoted to him. He knew about Neipperg, but made no comments on his relationship with Louise. She was now, so he liked to explain, as much a prisoner of state as himself; by nature she was unadventurous and easily frightened, a charming child', he recalled. Occasionally, in table-talk which Gourgaud faithfully noted down, the Emperor would compare his two wives: 'I esteemed Marie Louise far more, though perhaps I loved her less than I did Josephine, whose conduct was not exactly regular.' But Gourgaud – a thirty-four-year-old artillery officer from a good Catholic family – could carry sentimentality too far. On 15 August 1816 – Napoleon's forty-seventh birthday – Gourgaud presented him with a small bouquet 'on behalf of the King of Rome'. It was not well received. 'Bah! The King of Rome thinks no more of me than of ... pfft,' the Emperor exclaimed.[13]

In this dismissive comment, Napoleon did his son an injustice. For despite Dietrichstein's attempts to make the boy forget those early days in Paris, they still stood out sharply in his mind; and among them, inevitably, was an image of his father. Soon after Louise left for Italy Archduke Rainer, one of her younger uncles, commented on the curious effects on a child's upbringing of knowing much about his father but being prepared, at the age of five, to keep that knowledge to himself. Others in the family shared Rainer's disquiet; and Emperor Francis suggested to Dietrichstein that, on second thoughts, his grandson might after all be told about Napoleon's fate and situation, 'little by little'. A perplexed Dietrichstein turned to the boy's mother for guidance and received a reply from Parma which reads as if it were dictated by Neipperg:

> I believe you should speak truthfully to him about his father and, while never saying that he was a bad man and mentioning only his brilliant qualities, persuade him that it was inordinate ambition which led him from the finest throne in the world to the prison where he is today, so that his son never conceives the idea of imitating him.[14]

The directive was admirably clear. But it saw Napoleon reflected in a distorted mirror. It sought to conjure up a counter-legend, which could have endured only if presented by a tutor more skilled than Dietrichstein to a pupil far dimmer than the Emperor's son. 'Is that Austerlitz?' the boy asked one day with devastating innocence as he passed a battle painting on the Hofburg wall. 'I know something, but I don't say it because it's a secret,' the prince would remark from time to time, as if teasing his tutors.

Archduchess Leopoldina hoped that her sister would return to Vienna in November 1816 and judge for herself how well her son was progressing, especially with spoken German. She could then also be present at 'dear Papa's' marriage; for Francis had now chosen as a fourth wife the King of Bavaria's daughter, Caroline Augusta, who was two months younger than Louise herself. But Louise could not undertake any long journey that winter for, by the late autumn, she found that she was pregnant. Her intention was to keep out of the public eye at least until the summer. She moved away from the ducal palace and spent almost all her days at Colorno. The secret was well-kept, though in her letters Leopoldina idly speculated on whether Louise might be going to take advantage of those papal doubts over her marriage and accept Neipperg as a husband. On 1 May 1817 Louise gave birth to a girl who, through the special dispensation of Cardinal-Bishop Caseli, was baptised Albertina Maria in the chapel of the ducal palace.[15] Though of 'unknown parentage' in the baptismal register, Albertina was at once ennobled as the Countess of Montenuovo. There was, inevitably, much speculative talk within Parma, though it was almost entirely sympathetic to Louise and to Neipperg. Curiously no one carried tales northwards, so as to titillate the gossips of Vienna.

Even Metternich, who visited Parma early in September, heard nothing; and no rumours of Louise's love-child reached the exile on St Helena.

Her father's Foreign Minister was not a welcome visitor. Ostensibly Metternich came to Italy in a familiar role: Leopoldina was married by proxy in Vienna on 13 May 1817 to the Prince of Brazil, who was also heir to the throne of Portugal; and Metternich chose to escort her to Livorno, where she was to embark on a Portuguese warship for Rio de Janeiro. 'Nothing remains for me to do except weep with you and curse the word politics for causing me so much suffering,' Leopoldina had written to Louise in April. 'We unfortunate princesses are like dice whose happiness or unhappiness depends on the throw.'[16]

The simile was pathetically apt, as Louise well knew. It was bad enough that Metternich should again be playing at marriage politics with her family. But there were other reasons why Louise resented his protracted stay in Italy. He busied himself inspecting all that had been done in the last two years, reporting back to Francis on all that had not. The general political state of the peninsula alarmed him: he was concerned over the growth of secret societies hostile, not simply to Austrian rule, but to the 'restored' order in Europe as a whole. In Parma he was pleased by the efficiency of the administration and the absence of unrest, but to Louise's dismay he raised again the problem of the succession. 'No son of Napoleon could ever rule in Italy' was by now Metternich's maxim: the risk of upheaval was too great. 'Francis Charles', as the boy was called, could not be Prince of Parma; a dukedom should be found for him in the German-speaking lands of the empire, not in the peninsula.

With Neipperg's vigorous support, the Duchess fought a rearguard action for her son's rights. No decision had been taken over the alternative title when, at midsummer 1818, she at last returned to Vienna, to stay for ten weeks. Mother and son were re-united at Theresienfeld, a village not far from Wiener-Neustadt. It was a strange place for the Austrian authorities to choose, for Napoleon's sister, Caroline, lived a few miles away with her children, and Jerome Bonaparte was also close at hand, in the castle of Frohsdorf. While Dietrichstein and Francis Charles awaited the arrival of the Parma carriages, members of the French 'colony' applauded and saluted 'Napoleon II', speaking to him in his native language; one report even says that his aunt and his uncle were present. Dietrichstein hurriedly insisted that 'the Prince only spoke German'. He was rescued from further embarrassment by the arrival of Neipperg, who whisked the boy up, placing him firmly in his mother's berlin, which headed down the Vienna road at the gallop.[17] Louise always insisted on avoiding contact with the Bonapartes: already Pauline had been hurried away from the Duchy's borders when she was trailing round the minor spas of northern Italy.

The wrangling over Francis Charles's status and title came to an end during his mother's visit, though hardly to her satisfaction. On 22 July 1818 Emperor Francis created his grandson Duke of Reichstadt, a 'Serene Highness' with precedence immediately after the imperial archdukes.[18] The castle and estate of Reichstadt was a Habsburg appendage in the Bohemian palatinate which it was anticipated that Francis Charles would inherit. His titular regress was steady: from King to Prince and now to Duke, and all achieved before the age of eight. The castle of Reichstadt, like the cities of Rome and Parma, was a place he never visited. But the boy was happy enough in that July and August, spending much of the time with his mother, grandfather and young step-grandmother at Persenbeug, a yellow ochre castle on a promontory beside the Danube, some fifty miles upstream from Vienna. Visits to Baden and Laxenburg followed, until these dream-like days ended tearfully – and, as Francis Charles thought, abruptly – in the third week of September. Thereafter he did not see his mother for twenty-one months. By 1820, when she next spent the late summer in Vienna, he was a tall, fair German princeling, interested in history and geography, but no longer inclined to write or to speak French.

The Duke of Reichstadt had a half-brother by then, though he did not know it. William Albert (Guglielmo Alberto in the baptismal register) was born 9 August 1819, his existence kept as secret as Albertina's. On this occasion Louise was out of the public eye for a much shorter span of time. Neipperg had begun a public works programme and Parma's Duchess was present on 10 October for the ceremonial opening of a nineteen-arch bridge across the river Taro which improved links between the cities of Parma and Piacenza. Other works were in hand: a second bridge, this time across the Trebbia, in the north of the Duchy; extensions to the Palatine Library and the Academy of Fine Arts; and the first plans were broached for a Teatro Ducale ('Ducal Theatre'), an opera house to challenge La Scala in Milan and La Fenice in Venice, it was hoped. The Duchess gave royal patronage to every musical enterprise; fittingly, as early as 1817, she also interested herself in a maternity hospital as well as an orphanage.[19]

Neipperg deserved credit for many of these achievements, and especially for the vigour with which he saw they were completed. But on his arrival he was fortunate in finding the basic administration already functioning well, thanks to the enterprise of Count Philip Magawly, a twenty-seven-year-old Irish-born Parmesan landowner whom Francis appointed head of the provisional Regency Council in July 1814; he subsequently served as Minister of State. Magawly knew the Duchy well enough to make certain that the officials in the three districts (Piacenza, Guastalla and Parma itself) worked effectively together.[20] With Neipperg, he ensured that in 1820 a just civil code was promulgated – based, of course, on the Napoleonic model. Though Magawly later fell from favour, the Duchess warmly approved of all that was being done. 'I am much attached to this country, which I can say is changing to its own advantage day by day,' she wrote a trifle smugly to Victoria de Crenneville in April 1820; 'I have many means of doing good, much with which to busy myself, a pleasant and peaceful existence.'[21]

A few weeks later, far away in the South Atlantic, Napoleon's health began to fail. He complained of sudden sickening pains in his right side, which became more acute in the last quarter of the year, as the weather turned hotter. His sister Elisa Bacciochi died, at the Villa Vincentina outside Trieste, in the first week of August from 'a putrescent and bilious fever', but it was not until Christmas that the news reached St Helena. It threw Napoleon into deep depression: 'Elisa has shown us the way,' he sighed. 'My turn cannot be far off.' He went out of doors less and less: a last carriage drive on 17 March was followed by constant vomiting. Soon he could not stand without support. By late April he was convinced that he was dying of stomach cancer, like his father. Perhaps so; later theories, based on scientific testing of hair samples, suggest he may have died from arsenic poisoning, either absorbed accidentally from wallpaper or administered slowly by a companion in the pay of the Bourbons. For whatever reason, he remained virtually bed-ridden for eight weeks. In his last hours Bertrand heard him mention the King of Rome, though the final word which anyone caught on his lips was a faint 'Josephine'. At 5.41 on 5 May 1821 the St Helena garrison, as usual, observed the evening ritual of sunset. A single, distant boom of cannon echoed over Longwood House, not inappropriately. Sunset fell for Emperor Napoleon eight minutes later.[22]

The *Heron*, a fast frigate, sailed that night for England. London knew of Napoleon's death by nightfall on 3 July. Paris heard the following evening. At a reception at which Talleyrand was present the hostess remarked 'What an event!' 'No, it is no longer an event,' the most realistic of foreign ministers observed. 'It is only an item of news.'[23] And not, it would seem, a top story. For the report, which once would have been signalled speedily by visual telegraph, only reached Metternich by courtesy of a Rothschild courier on 13 July. Even then the man who had plotted Marie Louise's marriage a dozen years back did not feel obliged to let her know she was now a widow. That information the Duchess gathered from a paragraph in the *Gazzetta Piemontese* on 18 July. As it was unofficial she did not postpone a theatre visit that evening. Next day, though still 'in great uncertainty', she put down on paper her immediate reactions in a letter to Victoria de Crenneville:

> Although I never entertained strong sentiments of any kind for him, I cannot forget that he is the father of my son, and far from treating me badly, as most people believe, he always showed the deepest regard for me, the only thing one can wish from a political marriage. So I am very affected and, though I ought to be pleased that his miserable existence is finished in a Christian manner, I could have wished him many years of happiness and of life – so long as it would be far from me.[24]

The 'item of news' was confirmed in a message to Parma from Baron Vincent, the Austrian ambassador in Paris. Neipperg ordered the official gazette to announce on 24 July that 'because of the death of the most Serene Husband of our August Sovereign', 'Her Majesty' and her court would be in full mourning until 4 September. Second-class mourning would be observed for a further month, to be followed until 24 October by third-class mourning.[25]

On 30 July the Duchess and Neipperg attended a Requiem Mass in a small chapel attached to the ducal residence at Sala Baganza. It was, as the General reported to Metternich, essentially a private occasion. The name 'Napoleon' was not mentioned: the obsequies were for the soul of the 'husband of our Duchess'. In Rome, however, where Madame Mère and Cardinal Fesch still lived under papal protection, the Emperor who re-established the Catholic faith in France was remembered by his full baptismal names.

He had remembered Marie Louise – by name – in mid-April when he began setting in order his testamentary bequests. While he wished his son, on his sixteenth birthday, to receive his most cherished possessions – the sabre of Austerlitz, the blue cloak worn at Marengo, uniforms, boots, decorations – the wife of whom he had such 'tender memories' should receive a bracelet bound together by his hair; and, also, his heart. This bequest, he insisted, was to be preserved in spirits, placed in a silver casket, and borne to his widow in Parma. Such a macabre presentation was checked at the outset by his British gaolers. They had orders that Napoleon's body was to be buried on St Helena, a task fulfilled five days after his death, in Geranium Valley. The heart, removed for an autopsy, was placed beside the body, within four coffins.[26]

No gaolers could control the movements of Napoleon's fellow exiles. François Antomacchi, a young Corsican doctor for whose skills he had shown little regard, arrived in Parma in the second week of October. It was rumoured he had brought the Emperor's heart with him in a casket: in reality he was hoping for a steady pension. He requested an audience with the Duchess. Instead he was received by Neipperg; the Duchess, so the General explained, was so saddened by the thought of those last months in St Helena that he felt he could not allow the doctor to see her. There was never any doubt of the outcome of Antomacchi's visit. The Duchess had already written to her father expressing dismay over the first reports of Napoleon's bequest. In no circumstances did the August Sovereign wish the Most Serene Husband's heart to be conveyed to Parma. The relic might, she pointed out, make the city a pilgrim shrine for Bonapartists all over Italy. To her father and Metternich that was a telling consideration. By their reckoning Antomacchi was a dangerous man, with or without a silver casket. After a second interview with Neipperg, he was advised to make his way out of Italy, swiftly and pensionless. He is said to have died practising medicine in Cuba some fifteen years later.[27]

One heart was nearly broken by the news from St Helena. No one expected the ten-year-old Duke of Reichstadt to feel the loss of his father so deeply. The boy was informed not by his grandfather, Emperor Francis, nor even by Dietrichstein, but by the under-tutor Captain Foresti, who was surprised at his charge's long fit of sobbing. His mother, though indignant at her own treatment by Metternich, was slow to respond to her son's emotional needs. Only on 24 July, the Tuesday on which Parma officially went into mourning, was the Duchess prevailed upon to write a letter to him; and it did not reach Schönbrunn until the following Tuesday. 'I am sure that your grief was no less profound than mine, for you would be an ungrateful boy if you forgot the kindness he showed you in your infancy,' his mother wrote.[28] But the didactic moral was not to be left unpointed: he must 'seek to imitate' his father's virtues, while avoiding the errors which brought about his downfall.

As a message of consolation, these words lack parental warmth. It is hard to believe that the 'dearest Louise' of those hundreds of letters to an indulgent husband was by now so hard at heart. Were all her golden days tarnished in recollection? It seems so. On 10 August, the writing of a note to Dietrichstein kindled a spark of sympathy and showed the confusion of her sentiments. She told Dietrichstein how moved she had felt on hearing of Francis Charles's depth of sorrow when the news was broken to him. 'Death,' she explained, 'wipes out all one's unpleasant memories, as I found on this occasion. I could think only of the good he had done me, of the agony of his death, and of his last unhappy years; and I wept bitter tears for him.'[29]

16

'Viva Maria Luigia'

Marie Louise outlived Napoleon by more than twenty-six years. Never again did she move centre stage in Europe's affairs. Nor had she any wish to do so. Ideally she would have liked, not simply to wait in the wings, but to fade as imperceptibly as a wraith into the backcloth. That was her first instinct and, within a few weeks of hearing of her widowhood, she married Neipperg in the quietest of all weddings. It was celebrated secretly in the chapel of the ducal villa at Sala Baganza, in the wooded valley of the river Toro, south of the city; the Duchess's personal chaplain and confessor, János Neuchel, officiated. No public announcement was made.

The precise day of the wedding remains uncertain. Monsignor Neuchel registered the date as 7 August; eight years later Marie Louise herself told Metternich the marriage was in September. Neuchel's pen may well have slipped a month. On 15 August, that hallowed anniversary in the Napoleonic calendar, Louise gave birth to her second daughter. A '7 August' register entry ensured her legitimacy. But sadly the dating was of little consequence, for the child's health was frail. She died before the end of the year.[1]

Apart from this personal tragedy, the private life of the newly married couple continued almost unchanged in its cultural serenity. 'Each week Madame the Archduchess gives a concert, a ball and a dinner,' Neipperg told a friend at the start of a carnival season. 'We have an excellent opera.'[2] Madame the Archduchess was also building up a fine personal library, sumptuous volumes bound in red morocco and gilt stamped with the imperial crowned monogram 'ML': elegant editions of traditional classics; fashionable books of travel, especially illustrated 'voyages'; worthy fiction, mainly late eighteenth-century; and, beginning as early as 1822, 'political and military' lives of Napoleon.[3] She took up painting again, too, completing some light water-colours of the city and Austrian 'holiday' scenes (now to be seen in the Museo Lombardi at Parma). Musical evenings continued, though it was not until 1825 that a Johann Schanz pianoforte arrived from Vienna, to become a cherished possession. Meanwhile, on at least one occasion, counter-accusations over the correct tempo of a duet led to exchanges which in their intensity took the Duchess by surprise.[4]

A fratch of this nature was rare. For the most part, Neipperg was extraordinarily patient and sympathetic. The contentment of a shared existence flowed blissfully on, year by year. Only in two respects was there any deviation from the normal pattern of happy family life. Though Louise might refer to Albertina as 'my poor darling' and William as 'chubby little Patapouf',[5] the children did not call their parents 'Mamma' and 'Papa'; austerely they remained 'the Signora' and 'the Signor'. And, though the two Montenuovos might play occasionally with their half-brother Gustaf von Neipperg, they never met that other half-brother in Vienna – who, until April 1829, knew nothing of them or, indeed, of his mother's second marriage.

Politically, however, life was far less secure than the Duchess liked to assume. Throughout the peninsula there was resentment at the way in which Austrian arms bolstered restored autocracy and, even more, over the taxes imposed on the Italian people to pay for Austrian 'protection'. Secret police reports kept Vienna well informed about the Carbonari and other conspiratorial societies, but failed to detect dissidence at higher levels. In February 1820 a mutinous cavalry squadron outside Naples forced a terrified King Ferdinand to grant a liberal constitution, similar to one proclaimed in Spain eight years back and reaffirmed more recently by liberal insurgents in Madrid. From Naples the unrest spread in the following year to the kingdom of Sardinia, whose frontier in Piedmont bordered both Lombardy-Venetia and Parma. Austrian troops restored order in Naples and kept the peace further north, sometimes brutally, especially in Modena. Neipperg shared Metternich's concern. Subversives were thrown into prison, among them young members of much respected aristocratic families. But Neipperg wisely mitigated the severity of the sentences; the Duchess granted a general amnesty four years later.

Gradually the revolutionary embers were stamped out in Italy. Metternich, however, played on the bogey of revived Jacobinism to alert his allies to a danger which, he claimed, threatened Europe as a whole. The Congress System lumbered into action, bringing Russia, Prussia and Austria into partnership, with an increasingly isolationist

Britain trailing hesitantly behind. At the Congresses of Troppau and Laibach, Metternich achieved such personal success that in May 1821 Emperor Francis appointed him Chancellor, an office hitherto held in Austria only by Kaunitz. Summit diplomacy, where social agreeability mingled with hard-bargaining, suited Metternich's talents. To ensure collaboration against all trouble-makers, in the Iberian and the Italian peninsulas, yet another Congress was convened, to open in October 1822 at Verona. Apart from the Pope, every ruler in Italy was expected to attend. Despite her antipathy for such affairs, the Duchess of Parma could no longer stay quietly off-stage.[6]

At first she enjoyed herself at Verona, even if stage-manager Metternich was tediously omnipresent. She was glad to spend plenty of time with her father and her young stepmother, who became, and remained, her close confidante. Political questions she left to Neipperg. Nobody, however, bothered very much about Italy: it was agreed that, with the return of controlled sobriety to political life, the Austrian military presence could be gradually reduced. The main topic was Spain, a matter of little concern to Neipperg or to his consort. They were able to enjoy a magnificent banquet in the Roman arena and attend performances of Rossini's operas which were conducted by the maestro himself, with Angelica Catalini as principal soprano. Louise was petted by Tsar Alexander and escorted on occasions by Frederick William of Prussia. Of admirers from her days as a 'recluse' only Italy's one-time Viceroy, Eugène, was missing: he was now a Bavarian prince, the Duke of Leuchtenberg, and – at forty-one – his health was failing rapidly. On 18 November the Duke of Wellington, whom she never met while at Schönbrunn, entertained the Duchess of Parma to dinner. The Duke, knowing her interests, provided musical entertainment: when the hospitality was reciprocated a few evenings later, the Duchess felt she should apologise for not serving his favourite dish, roast mutton. She offered no music, either, on this occasion. But they happily sat down to play écarté and the cards fell in Louise's favour. She had the satisfaction of defeating the victor of Waterloo – who settled his debts in gold 'napoléons' (for the abhorrent baptismal name might still be used for coinage). No less gratifying to her as a mother was recent news of Reichstadt, to whom the Duke was presented at Vienna in September: 'a fine lad, educated like the archdukes', Wellington thought, 'very civil to me'.[7]

Like Metternich's small-talk, the Congress went on too long. By early December, after eight weeks at Verona, Louise could complain to Victoria de Crenneville that she was 'bored to death' with 'this congress which, thank Heavens, is drawing to a close'.[8] She was looking ahead to the coming year, 1823, and an early visit to Vienna. 'Poor health' – in reality, a miscarriage – forced her to postpone the trip, and it was early June before she was re-united with Reichstadt at Baden.

For Francis Charles the following weeks were especially happy. Although expected to continue lessons each morning, in the afternoons he enjoyed long excursions with his mother, sometimes ending with an elaborate picnic. Neipperg – 'the General' as they all called him – was there, too. His presence increased the boy's pleasure, for he admired the sabre-scarred soldier who attended his mother so protectively. Together they celebrated her name-day at Persenbeug on 25 August. The half day holiday soon passed. A week later the twelve-year-old looked across to the Danube with tears of loneliness on his cheeks while his mother and the General hurried back southwards, returning – though Francis Charles did not know it – to Albertina and William in Parma.[9]

On St Helena Napoleon had recalled 'my good Louise's honesty', contrasting her straightforward frankness with Josephine's calculated half-truths. She was a different woman now, expert at plausible explanations and skilled in devious concealment. One lapse in conduct, for which Napoleon once reprimanded her, had grown into a daily habit. For two hours each morning she would deal with affairs of state in her bedroom receiving there, not only Neipperg, but also her secretary Count Scarampi, whose wife was a prominent member of her household. Not until eleven o'clock would she get dressed, ready to immerse herself in the demands of ducal domesticity. They were rarely taxing: a light luncheon at midday; an hour or so of embroidery or painting; the afternoon carriage ride; a few pages read to her in French or even by her in English; a little music in the evening; dinner at nine; billiards or backgammon or chess; some conversation, perhaps; and so to bed before midnight. At least once a week during the season there would be a visit to the theatre; and the Duchess and the General often welcomed guests to dinner, provided they were not members of the Bonaparte family. Lamartine, who came one evening in 1823, commented on the warmth of the Duchess's hospitality. He also noted that she spoke of 'that earlier epoch' in her life as 'though it were a prehistoric age, something that did not touch her or the present day. The Empress and Marie Louise are two beings absolutely separate from each other.'[10]

This comfortable, bonnet-and-shawl existence was in keeping with the prevailing mood in Vienna, remembered now as 'Biedermeier', though the term was invented derisively by a later generation. It was an unadventurous fashion, dependent on a smug acquiescence in the stability ordained by Metternich. The Duchess made her next journey home in May 1826, at the height of Biedermeier influence. During her four months in Vienna that summer, Leopold Fertbauer was commissioned to paint 'Emperor Francis and his Family'. He produced a masterpiece of tranquil domesticity. No need now for imperial uniform, as when twenty years previously an unknown artist depicted Francis, Marie Thérèse and six children grouped in front of a classical column. Fertbauer's canvas shows Francis with his fourth wife, Caroline Augusta, two of his sons, Marie Louise, and his newest daughter-in-law, the twenty-one-year-old Archduchess Sophie, Caroline's stepsister; they relax in a garden arbour, wearing bourgeois 'Sunday best' clothes, with Caroline and Louise in similar broad-brimmed light straw hats. At the centre of the painting is the Duke of Reichstadt, as yet Francis's only grandson on this side of the Atlantic. He is astonishingly tall for his age and stands proudly erect, with hands resting on his mother's parasol. Perhaps deliberately, Fertbauer emphasises a facial resemblance between Reichstadt and Sophie's husband, the (confusingly named) Archduke Francis Charles. But no artistic concealment destroys the character of those young features: Fertbauer's brush caught the lines of a Bonaparte chin, not a Habsburg jaw. Inevitably, as we look at the painting, we focus on Reichstadt.[11]

So, too, over the next five years did many eyes in Vienna and Baden. He had many admirers, especially among daughters of the Hungarian nobility. Deitrichstein, though pedantic and conventional, sympathised with most of his pupil's aspirations. The prince's grandfather was always well-disposed towards him, but would never challenge Chancellor Metternich's veto on repeated requests to travel to Italy, preferably Parma. He was able to read more and more about his father, including memoirs by those who had been with him on St Helena. Reichstadt's ambition was to be, not simply a good parade-ground officer, but to command in battle – though he insisted that he could never fight against the French. Yet he had wider interests, too, as Archduchess Sophie soon perceived. The Archduchess, despairing of her husband's philistine tastes, began to choose 'Franzl' Reichstadt as her escort to the theatre soon after his sixteenth birthday. A close friendship developed between them, not a sexual relationship but the shared understanding of two intelligent 'outsiders' at the Habsburg court.[12]

Reichstadt's health began to cause concern in 1827, when to his irritation he missed the last four days of the carnival season with bronchial trouble. He suffered from a succession of colds the following summer and in the next winter was troubled by a persistent dry cough. 'Ill-health' – another miscarriage – again forced his mother to cancel a proposed visit but, by the summer of 1828, the Emperor was so alarmed at signs of his grandson's debility that he virtually ordered his daughter to make the journey up to Schönbrunn. She stayed for over eleven weeks and, as ever, her presence lifted Reichstadt's spirits. On this occasion he accepted her departure with equanimity, partly because he was older, but even more because in August his grandfather commissioned him as a cavalry captain in a Tyrolean regiment.[13] He could thus attend manoeuvres outside Vienna in September with three stars on his tunic, the rank his father held when he left Corsica.

Louise was more immediately worried by the health of 'the General'. In July 1824 they had sailed together from Genoa to Palermo and on to Naples where, on one evening, Neipperg collapsed with pains in his chest. Thereafter he appears to have suffered from chronic angina. The Emperor noticed his shortness of breath during the 1828 visit and was much concerned. It was on this occasion that Louise at last told Francis and her stepmother, in strict confidence, that Neipperg was her husband and the father of two children by her; she did not say when Albertina and William were born.[14] The Emperor was surprised to discover that he had two grandchildren, presumably under the age of six, but not shocked at the morganatic marriage. He had stayed in Parma and he was accustomed to seeing Neipperg in close attendance during his daughter's five visits to his court; he can hardly have failed to notice a special relationship between the Duchess and her chief minister; and by his reckoning wedlock was always preferable to protracted dalliance.

During the homeward journey from Vienna that autumn, Neipperg was taken gravely ill, with what was diagnosed as dropsy. He received treatment from medical specialists first in Milan and then in Turin. By late October, there was little hope of recovery. Reichstadt, who was fond of him, wrote anxiously and sympathetically to his mother on 2 December, though he expressed his concern a little strangely: he envied her the chance to do something which eased the General's pain instead of having to wait uselessly for news from couriers as they stepped down from their horses at the Hofburg. In Parma the bedside vigil continued into the new year. 'Day follows day in grief and desolation,' poor Louise wrote to her father at Christmas. The end did not come until 22 February 1829.[15]

Five months of diminishing hope imposed a severe strain on Louise, physically and mentally. Worse anguish was to follow. Neipperg was accorded a magnificent state funeral in the church of St Paul, with the bishop officiating at the Requiem. But the General had decided he could not take the secret of his marriage with him to the grave. To

Louise's consternation, he was found to have left a will, in which he not only declared that he was her husband but that Albertina and William were their children; and he asked his sovereign in Vienna to afford them his protection. Metternich, long out of sympathy with Marie Louise, insisted that the whole matter must be cleared up. Less than three weeks after Neipperg's death, he demanded an explanation from the Duchess.

'It is time for me to confess,' she replied wretchedly on 17 March. She admitted to the Chancellor that she had misled the Emperor over the two children: she gave the correct dates of their birth and acknowledged that 'my marriage to the General ... was not solemnised until September 1821.'[16] On the following day, 'with deep sorrow', she sent a similar 'confession' to her 'dear Papa'. She knew Francis would have to break the news to Reichstadt and feared that her son would scorn her for having 'forgotten' his father. She seemed entangled by the nemesis of her deception.

Yet the reaction from the Hofburg was gentler than she anticipated. Reichstadt took news of the marriage and the existence of a half-sister and a half-brother surprisingly well, though he asked no questions about them and the Emperor warned Louise that, if he later discovered their true ages, 'his most sacred feelings towards you may change unfavourably'. On 17 April Empress Caroline wrote re-assuringly, urging her to come to Vienna and see for herself how strong were her father's affections. 'He has not forgotten the immense sacrifice you made for interests of State in 1810,' Caroline added, with rare acknowledgement of a debt to the ex-Empress of the French which Chancellor Metternich chose not to remember.[17]

Even so, Louise felt unable to face her family that summer. She remained in Parma for the opening of the Ducal Theatre on 16 May, the completion of an eight-year enterprise with which Neipperg was closely associated. The authorities commissioned a new opera from Vincenzo Bellini, *Zaira*, but neither the production nor the singing met Louise's standards.[18] At midsummer she left Parma, travelling into Switzerland as 'Countess von Neipperg', with Albertina and William accompanying her. They stayed at Grand-Sacconex, a few miles north-east of Geneva and almost into France. The children did not remain long with their mother. They travelled up to neighbouring Neuchâtel with Albertina's *aja*, Marianne du Purey, a member of a wealthy and generous family in the town. Their mother was still at Grand-Sacconex when the first winter snowfalls threatened to close the mountain passes. Across the frontier the local prefect let Paris know of her presence soon after her arrival but he reported, disdainfully, that she had lost her personal standing and the visit possessed no political significance whatsoever.[19]

He was, of course, correct: Louise's concern was for her health; all she wished was to fill her lungs with the clear air from Mont Blanc across the lake, admire the silhouette of Alpine peaks and adjust herself to the curative system recommended by her new consultant, Dr Buttini. Politics were of no interest to her. On Neipperg's death she had entrusted affairs of state to his principal secretary, Baron Joseph Werklein, who came from a family of landowners in Croatia but had served the Parmesan administration for the last nine years. His wife was one of her ladies of honour, and she was perfectly content to leave all questions of finance and government to the Baron.

The Duchess was back in Parma in time to enjoy the Advent concerts and share Christmas with the Montenuovo children and Gustav Neipperg. Then she flung herself into the Carnival weeks, her spirits rising with revitalised vivacity – for, though at Geneva she had looked far older, she was in reality still no more than thirty-eight. She knew by now that, through subtle questioning and sifting truth from the gossip around him, Francis Charles had discovered that his half-sister and half-brother were born while Napoleon was still alive. There was a long silence of some weeks in his correspondence, but in the new year he began to write frequently and affectionately, with a far easier style. It was as if he felt that her human frailty strengthened his moral authority and entitled him to expect her backing for his claims to lead his own life. She responded with newly restored self-confidence.

In the third week of June 1830 mother and son were re-united at a castle outside Graz. Emperor Francis and Empress Caroline joined them and they left Styria for Baden. Much discussion in these first weeks concerned Reichstadt's future in the army. During a cold, wet spring he was again unwell, coughing so often that Dietrichstein became seriously concerned. Reichstadt thought his tutor too protective: 'my wife', he called him when writing to Archduchess Sophie; 'the old woman', in talk to his friends.[20] So far as possible, he concealed signs of illness. He was eager to begin his military career in earnest, with posting to a provincial garrison; and his grandfather was by no means unsympathetic.

It was an eventful summer. The court moved to Schönbrunn early in August for the birth of Sophie's first child: the future Emperor Francis Joseph arrived, uncharacteristically late, on 18 August; 'the loveliest infant you could hope to see', his Aunt Louise cooed; 'a strawberry ice with a topping of whipped cream', decided cousin Reichstadt, more imaginatively.[21] But the world the Archduke entered had, once again, a reddish-blue sky. For Emperor Francis learnt from Metternich on 9 August that a revolution in Paris had toppled the Bourbons in the last days of July: Louis Phillipe, Duke of Orleans, was now 'King of the French, by the Grace of God and the Will of the People'; the title was ominously familiar. 'When Paris sneezes, Europe catches cold,' Metternich was heard to remark. 'We must turn our attention without delay to Italy,' he told Francis. 'It is there the revolutionary impulse will undubitably spread.'[22]

The assessment was perceptive, but premature. Unrest in Brussels and Liège escalated into a successful movement for Belgian independence before the end of the year. There were demands for liberal constitutions in Brunswick, Saxony and Hesse-Cassel; and in November a revolt in Warsaw against Russian domination re-opened the Polish Question. There was, too, a sudden awareness of 'Napoleon II's' existence. A throne for him in Brussels, perhaps? Or even Warsaw, where many insurgents once fought under Poniatowski in the *Grande Armée*. Reichstadt himself thought only of serving Austria militarily, or of reigning in Paris, 'if I am called back by the French army', as he assured his grandfather. Briefly that seemed a possibility: the new French ambassador rashly sounded out Metternich on behalf 'of all the regiments quartered between Strasbourg and Paris'; and the Chancellor received a strange letter from Joseph Bonaparte offering to lead his nephew back to Paris. But Metternich was certain there must be no throne for Napoleon's son: why let the djinn out of the bottle?[23]

All was peaceful when the Duchess returned to Parma in October. She continued to ignore politics, both internal and external. Shortly before Christmas, Baron Werklein removed the Minister of Finance from office, but the Duchess knew nothing of the change until it was mentioned by the Duke of Modena a few days later. The incident so amused her that she told Victoria de Crenneville about it in her next letter. She wrote, too, of the Ducal Theatre ('our opera hissed, and the ballet no better') and looked ahead to the Carnival nights of 1831: 'The cure [for rheumatism] ... is giving my legs elasticity, and even though I shall be 39, I think I shall be able to waltz this winter,'she said.[24]

And waltz she did, it would seem. In January there were three balls at the ducal palace, while the Werklein's was so 'charming' that 'I stayed until one in the morning.' More than once in the evening festivities she took part in theatricals, with Madame Werklein playing beside her in one-act comedies or charades. Never during the years in Paris did Marie Louise's conduct so closely mirror the follies of Marie Antoinette as in these weeks when Metternich's prediction was coming true and anti-Austrian revolts crept rapidly northwards. On 3 February, when the red, white and green colours Napoleon had given Italy already draped the battlements of Bologna, she had to admit that 'our Carnival is not very gay'; but she had faith in Werklein and the loyalty of her subjects. 'All is quiet here, thank God,' she wrote to her father four days later.[25]

There was unrest inside the city gates on Thursday, 10 February, but it was only between six and seven on the Saturday evening that the situation became menacing. Louise could hear shouts coming from a crowd gathered in the main square. '*Viva Maria Luigia*', ('Long Live Marie Louise') rang through clearly and reassuringly, but mingled with it were demands for a constitution and death threats to Werklein, whom the liberals believed guilty of peculation and of ordering arbitrary arrests unknown in the Neipperg era. The Duchess again showed courage, as during the Malet conspiracy and on the eve of the fall of Paris. Werklein headed for Piacenza, where there was an Austrian garrison, as speedily as his horses could gallop. But Louise, 'knowing that my conscience is clear' (as she told her father), received a delegation of liberals, spoke sternly to them, agreed to examine their grievances, and decided to remain in the ducal palace. 'Let Her Majesty stay. We love her and we would make her Queen of Italy,' someone in the crowd shouted that Sunday evening. But she became alarmed over the safety of Albertina and William, and at one o'clock on Wednesday morning, hurried them away with her in a carriage under the cover of darkness. They reached the river Po at seven and the relative safety of Casalmaggiore an hour later. By Friday evening they were at Piacenza, protected by one of Francis's crack Croatian regiments.[26]

The Duchess's fortitude was much admired when news of the insurrection was received in Vienna at the end of the week. Reichstadt at once sought permission to head southwards and help restore his mother to her ducal throne. But that was out of the question; Bonapartist sentiment was far too widespread in Italy for his grandfather to allow it. Metternich ordered Colonel Wenzel von Marschall, a soldier-diplomat already serving as adviser to the Duke of Modena, to attach himself to Marie Louise's court at Piacenza. For the first time since her arrival in Parma, the Duchess had a first minister and commander-in-chief imposed on her from Vienna.

Austrian troops entered the city of Parma as early as 12 March. Marschall ordered a curfew until the agitation died down, but he wisely left the day to day administration to Baron Vincenzo Mistrali, a liberal-minded intellectual who had accompanied the ducal family to Casalmaggiore. The Duchess herself did not return until the end of the first week in August, partly because, as she told Victoria de Crenneville, she found life at Piacenza so restful that she was reluctant to leave her sanctuary. Even before the Austrians moved into Parma, she was insisting to her father that the people of the Duchy had treated her well, always showing respect for the imperial house.[27] At first she also praised Werklein's efforts in the past, but he fell rapidly in her estimation once his conduct was examined in detail and when, soon afterwards, he applied to her for a pension, he received a blunt reply: 'Refused, once and for all.'[28] By nature, however, the Duchess was not vindictive. On 29 September she issued a general amnesty. Outwardly her mood brimmed with benevolence. February's troubles were a masquerade that went wrong, she hoped.

Inwardly she knew this was nonsense. The city mansions might be illuminated for three evenings after her return and the audience in her theatre might cheer her to the roof when she attended a special cantata in her honour; but, as she confessed to Victoria, the townsfolk were sullen, 'insolent when court carriages passed by in the streets'.[29] It was different in the countryside. She chose to live out at Sala Baganza rather than the ducal palace. Possibly she exaggerated differences between urban and rural life. For Mistrali was by now effective head of the administration; he showed such good sense that tensions soon relaxed within the city.

The Duchess approved of Mistrali. On the other hand, her relations with Marschall became increasingly strained. She considered his manners brusque; he thought her way of life frivolous. He also decided that her moral conduct was deplorable. Gossip credited her with a succession of lovers, including the dark and soulful Luigi di Sanvitale, who would eventually marry Albertina. Marschall believed the gossip and unchivalrously enhanced it from personal observation. He never denied the story that, having learnt that the guard in her antechamber was occasionally summoned inside, he doubled the sentries, only to discover the antechamber empty a few nights later, with both guards rendering Her Majesty special service. The tale may be apocryphal, or much magnified, but no one could doubt she was by nature sensual. As the Duchess entered her forties, she became uneasy in her widowhood; her confidence sought the gratification of knowing that she still pleased men. There was, however, no way, sensual or social, by which she could win approbation from the conventionally minded Marschall. He even regretted that she did not place on display in her palace a portrait of her first husband.[30]

Some Napoleonic relics had come to Parma, though, mainly from Elba. Most went on to Reichstadt in Schönbrunn: among them a sword, a washstand, some pictures and, at his request, the ornate cradle presented to the King of Rome by the city of Paris. Reichstadt's dichotomous sense of loyalty, proud of the reflected sun of Austerlitz but wishing to serve an Emperor defeated that day, led to inconsistencies: he rebuffed rousing appeals for action from his hot-headed cousin, Napoleone, a daughter of his aunt Elisa;[31] but he welcomed long talks with Marshal Marmont, who fought beside his father from Toulon to the last days of alleged treason outside Paris.[32] In July 1831 past and present came visually together when, as a newly promoted Lieutenant-Colonel, he proudly led his batalion across Vienna; he wore the white and blue uniform of a Hungarian infantry regiment, decorated with the grand cordon of St Stephen, which ambassador Schwarzenberg had fastened to the King of Rome's cradle, and with the star of St George, presented to the Prince of Parma by his mother; and at his side he carried the curved sabre which his father once unsheathed at the battle of the Pyramids.

Yet though parades might merge his past and present, they showed pathetically that for Franzl Reichstadt there could be no future. He was thin; his voice of command faint; his skin unhealthily yellow. Deitrichstein wrote to the Duchess suggesting she should make the journey northwards. Louise refused to come, 'unless it is absolutely necessary': she felt that she should not be seen to be fleeing from her people while they were afflicted both by the scourge of cholera and by a series of severe earth tremors.[33] Hostile gossip, however, explained her absence by tales of sexual adventure. The French ambassador in Vienna thought she was pregnant. So did many other of her personal enemies.

Rather oddly, reports reaching Parma in this early spring of 1832 did not suggest any real deterioration in Reichstadt's physique. Metternich of all people should have recognised the symptoms; his son, Victor, had died from tuberculosis at twenty-six, barely three years ago: and yet in early May the Chancellor wrote to the Duchess telling her that the doctors realised Reichstadt was suffering from a complaint of the liver but encouraging her to 'hope for the best'.[34] At the end of the month she went to Venice and on to Trieste for a meeting with her father in the first week in June. Francis urged her to go to Vienna as soon as possible: he was himself remaining in Lombardy-Venetia and did not plan a return to the capital until the late summer or autumn. The horses were ready for Louise's departure on 11 June but, as so often on her travels, she became unwell and there was a nine-day delay before she could set out. A miscarriage, her critics maintain: it seems unlikely; for would she have been fit so soon afterwards to risk a rigorous carriage journey?[35]

Louise reached her son's bedside in Schönbrunn on 24 June. She was shocked by his weakness and assumed he had only a few days more to live, though he survived for four more weeks, a 'young and beautiful' prince 'tragically wasting away', as Archduchess Sophie wrote to her mother.[36] His sickbed was in the room on the first floor in which his father had slept after his victories at Austerlitz and Wagram. Next to it was the Lacquered Room, where Napoleon received Prince Liechtenstein to discuss the peace terms to be imposed on Emperor Francis; now, on his better days, Napoleon's son would sit there, hopefully telling his friends how in a few weeks he would go to Ischl to convalesce; then, so he said, he would spend the winter in Naples, for Metternich had at last decided it was politically safe for him to cross into Italy. Some afternoons he was able to spend on a balcony, looking out across the flower beds to the Gloriette. On 6 July, in another wing of the palace, Sophie gave birth to a second son, Maximilian, who was to become – disastrously – Emperor of Mexico. Reichstadt never saw this baby cousin but he repeatedly asked for news of Sophie, the 'angel of loving kindness', he called her. As the weather turned sultry and humid, the fight for breath left him weaker day by day. A cannon shot had echoed across St Helena as his father lay dying; for the King of Rome there were rolls of thunder. In the small hours of 22 July a storm broke over the palace. His mother was with him when he died, shortly after dawn that Sunday morning.[37]

Protocol precluded her presence at his interment, though she watched the funeral cortège leave the palace some forty hours after his death. A cavalry escort, bearing slow-burning torches, flanked the litter which carried the bronze coffin to the Hofburg chapel. On Tuesday his regiment lined the streets of the Inner City as the archducal funeral hearse, drawn by six white horses caparisoned in dark red, slowly made its way to the Kapuzinerkirche in the Neue Markt. There, with traditional Habsburg ritual, the coffin was entrusted to the Capuchin fathers and lowered into the imperial sepulchre.[38]

Louise was by that Tuesday afternoon with her father and all the imperial court at Persenbeug, deeply affected by its associations with 'the loved one' but – as letters to Albertina and Victoria de Crenneville show – also prepared to complain of headache, toothache and rheumatism. She stayed in Persenbeug for only three nights. Before leaving Austria, however, the ex-Empress of the French fulfilled one final duty: she wrote to the King of Rome's principal godmother, Madame Mère, who in her eighty-third year was still living by papal courtesy in the city of the Caesars. It was a letter of resigned mutual condolence, submitting 'our sorrows and our tears' to 'the supreme will of God'.[39]

Laetizia Bonaparte did not reply directly: her half-brother, Cardinal Fesch, sent an acknowledgement through the Austrian envoy to the Holy See. Though the Cardinal was too tactful to say so, there is no doubt that Laetizia was deeply saddened by the loss of a grandson in whose return to Paris she retained supreme confidence. The household went into mourning for the King whom Rome never saw. After the letter to Madame Mère there would be no direct contact between Marie Louise and the Bonapartes. It was a curiously fitting end to the strangest of dynastic unions.

17

The Good Duchess

Marie Louise had no wish to linger in Austria. By 8 August she was home in Parma: 'It is with you dear children that I will seek the only possible consolation still left for me,' she told her daughter.[1] As so often in her predictions, this was a half-truth. She supported Albertina and William as resolutely as possible, welcoming her daughter's marriage to Luigi di Sanvitale fourteen months later and in 1838 securing a commission for William in an Austrian cavalry regiment. But for Louise herself there remained one unforeseen twist of fortune. A year after her return from Persenbeug the censorious Marschall was replaced by Count Charles de Bombelles, a widower whom the Duchess had already met briefly on two occasions. She was delighted by the change. A letter to her father on 23 September struck a familiar note: 'I cannot thank you enough for your choice of Count de Bombelles. To have a better majordomo would be impossible from every point of view.' And on Christmas Day Victoria de Crenneville was told, 'M. de Bombelles ... is a real saint, and delightful in society.' On 17 February 1834 – 180 days after his arrival – the Duchess and her saint were secretly married. Their union was to last for thirteen and a half years, longer than either of her earlier marriages.[2]

The Count had been born in November 1785 at Versailles, but spent his boyhood with the émigrés in Coblenz. Charles and his younger brother Henry (*Heinrich*) entered Austrian service and became well established at court in Vienna. Count Henry was chosen by Archduchess Sophie as a tutor for Francis Joseph and his son 'Charly' became the Archduke's boyhood companion; Count Charles, a protégé of Metternich, undertook diplomatic missions. No one who knew him suggests that Bombelles was ever a dashing, romantic figure like Neipperg; nor did he share the General's gifts as a musical performer. To Louise he was an amiably reliable companion, who enjoyed concerts and the opera; and an honest and competent civil servant. By working in close partnership with the efficient Mistrali (until his death in May 1846) Bombelles ensured that the Duchy experienced more than a dozen years of good administration.

Louise's daily routine soon reverted to the steady pattern of the Neipperg years. Although scandalous tales still titillated prurient minds in Paris, her private life became sedate. A water-colour by Giuseppe Naudin captures a scene at Sala Baganza: her husband escorts the Duchess on a walk through the parkland: he wears a broad-brimmed top hat above a broad-shouldered frockcoat; she has bonnet, shawl and parasol and interlocks her left arm with his right; apart from a servant trailing them at a discreet distance, they are alone, two silhouettes heading across the rustic-railed causeway towards a winding path into the woodland.[3] Nothing about the picture looks specifically Italian: so might Sir Thomas and Lady Bertram have enjoyed Mansfield Park; and so, no doubt, had the Duchess's mother enjoyed Laxenburg, when Emperor Francis walked with her along a similar path to the Löwenbrücke. There was much that was reminiscent of Louise's childhood in these years of middle-aged marriage; very little recalled the borrowed splendour of her Paris days. Was it at times a wearisome way of life? From Louise's letters and the patronising commendation of visitors to the Parma court, it is hard to escape the impression that the Count was a dull and pompous bore.

On 12 February 1835 'good Emperor Franz' celebrated his sixty-seventh birthday with a court ball at the Hofburg. Within a fortnight he was confined to bed with pneumonia and on 2 March he died. Louise, who had been with him at the Danube summer palaces in the previous July, remained in Parma but she mourned him deeply. 'He was the person I cherished most in this world,' she declared to Victoria de Crenneville. 'To him I could confide all my thoughts, and he was everything to me, a father, friend and a counsellor in all the difficulties of my life.'[4] These sentiments form a fine testimony of love for a parent who, whatever his domestic virtues, used his daughter and her son as instruments of state. Yet there is little doubt that Louise was writing from the heart. Already, six days before, she had told Victoria movingly of her great sense of loss; and in this long correspondence with her closest friend she always wrote naturally, without artifice. Louise accepted in her mind that she and her father each imposed a limit on their mutual trust: if his was political, hers was marital. For though she would, as she said, confide her thoughts in him, she was still prepared to conceal from him her actions; he went to his grave not knowing of her third marriage – to which it is unlikely he would have objected.

Louise travelled to Vienna the following summer and, during her visit, prayed in sorrow beside the recent tombs in the imperial vault, where the coffins of her father and her son now lay close together. Her poor retarded brother, Ferdinand had succeeded to her father's titles, but all real power rested with Chancellor Metternich, still in office twenty-six years after he first went to the Ballhausplatz. She does not appear to have enjoyed her sojourn in the capital. Duty called her back to the Duchy, where she courageously visited stricken districts during the last weeks of a cholera epidemic which claimed more than 400 lives. It was a relief to turn again to the musical scene. After Niccolo Paganini conducted a concert for her birthday, she induced him to take charge of the court orchestra in these last years of his life. At the same time, twenty miles to the north of the city, a young Giuseppe Verdi was conducting the Philharmonic Society's concerts in Busseto, the nearest town to Roncoli, his native village. The musical prestige of Parma was growing, as the Duchess had always wished.[5]

At midsummer 1838, after a two year absence, she returned to Vienna. A long letter to Albertina on 23 July described the novelty of her first train journey. She was grudgingly impressed, but the short trip offended both her sense of smell and her musical susceptibilities; she climbed into a carriage pulled by a 'smoking machine' with a 'horrible whistle' for over six miles. After half an hour she stepped down at Wagram; it was a familiar placename.[6]

Her carriages – landaus and berlins – were more and more on the road in the following years as she sought to relieve her rheumatism and stave off the encroachment of dropsy. Sometimes she sought cures in Switzerland or at Baden (by Vienna), but she was also impressed by the saline waters of the Traun valley, where Archduchess Sophie was already giving her patronage to Ischl. The waters eased her rheumatic pains and the fine mountain air lifted her spirits. But nothing could hide the fact that Louise was ageing rapidly. Portrait artists treated her gently, though they could not honestly puff out the fallen cheeks, for she had long suffered from dental trouble. A dagurreotype, taken in her fiftieth year, is a sad likeness which craves for sympathy. At Berchtesgaden, in 1840, she met Eugène's widow, Princess Auguste of Bavaria, who thirty years ago had commented on Louise's love for the Emperor and the reciprocal devotion he showed his young wife. Now Auguste thought that 'she looked like ... a decrepit, stout old peasant', and was 'horrified'.[7]

A few months later, in the second week of December 1840, a French warship brought Napoleon's body back from St Helena to Cherbourg. The Emperor had wished his remains to 'rest on the banks of the Seine, amidst the French people whom I loved so well'; he was to come home to the chapel of the Invalides. Steam launches brought the coffin up river; and Marshal Soult, veteran of Fleurus but now France's Prime Minister and Minister of War, received the body of the man who created him Duke of Dalmatia. Cannons fired, bells rang out across Paris, and a magnificent hearse passed beneath the newly completed Arc de Triomphe amid cries of '*Vive l'Empereur*'. It was the last great Napoleonic festival and the first triumph of a legend.[8]

At Parma the ex-Empress, who had known only a canvas mock-up of the great arch, ignored King Louis Phillipe's appropriated Bonapartism. She was more interested in the marble monument for Neipperg's tomb which Lorenzo Bartolino had recently begun to carve from Carrara stone.[9] The sculptor once enjoyed the personal patronage of Napoleon and, like so many Italians of his generation, looked back on the opening decade of the century with a certain nostalgia. The neo-classical influence of Canova could be clearly seen in the monument when it was completed a year later. The Duchess, who commissioned the work after long deliberation, approved of its grandeur. The French would always remember the Emperor: she was determined the Parmesans should not forget the General.

Marie Louise passed her sunset years amid lengthening shadows of unrest. The eloquent appeals from Mazzini to 'Young Italy' to strive for unity and a republic rekindled liberal sentiment. Other patriots looked to Turin for a lead and, in 1843, the priest Vincenzo Gioberti advocated a federal Italy under papal presidency. Few Italians born after the turn of the nineteenth century believed that a settlement imposed in Vienna thirty years ago could last much longer. There was dissent even within the Duchess's family circle. For Luigi di Sanvitale – who had sympathised with the 'constitutionalists' in 1831 – was again drawn to the national cause; many years later he became a senator in the parliament of a unified Italy.

There were demonstrations at Rimini in 1845, but no sparks crossed the Appenines to ignite trouble in other cities. On 16 June 1846, however, Cardinal Mastai-Ferretti, Bishop of Imola, was elected Pope, taking the title Pius IX. Within a month he granted a political amnesty and introduced administrative changes in the papal states, pending the creation of city councils. Metternich was aghast: a 'liberal pope' was 'the one contingency for which I have not allowed', he said in a rare admission of fallibility. Pius IX was no liberal, though he remained hostile to Austrian hegemony in the peninsula. But Italian patriots believed what they wished, and raised cheers for '*Pio Nono*' in the heart of Rome. A few voices added, '*A basso Metternich*' to drive their point home.[10]

Marie Louise was in Vienna in July 1847 when reports reached the Chancellor of student demonstrations in Parma itself. Bombelles was hurriedly sent back with full powers to restore order in the streets. He did so drastically. The Duchess, already in poor health, was saddened by the news from her Duchy and anxious to return. At last, as winter began to set in, she risked the journey home. When she reached Parma on 16 November she was running a fever and fighting for breath, like her son in those last days at Schönbrunn. Again like Franzl, she rallied, and as all was now quiet in the city, on 9 December she took an afternoon drive. It was a mistake. That night the fever returned and she took to her bed for the last time. She died in the early evening of 17 December, five days after her fifty-sixth birthday.[11]

The people of Parma mourned the passing of 'the good Duchess', despite the political tension – and perhaps even more because of it, for her designated successor, Duke Charles of Lucca, was already in conflict with *his* subjects. It is not surprising that Marie Louise lay in state in the chapel of the ducal palace for six days, as people from the city and from far beyond, came to honour her. For she had been generous with her personal funds, contributing not only to the furtherance of music and the visual arts in the city but to schools, almshouses, and even the completion of vital roads and bridges. Uniquely she paid the finest architect, Niccolo Bettoli, to construct a colonnaded market of butcher's shops, the Beccherie (similar to the 'shambles' in cities like York and Chester), and above the colonnades she established an orphanage. There had been no other *buona Duchessa* in Parma's history.[12]

Although there was a Solemn Requiem in the city and her body remained in the chapel over Christmas and into the new year, there was never any doubt that the coffin would be borne back to Vienna for interment. Field Marshal Radetzky brought a squadron of hussars to serve as honour-guard for the Duchess, and her cortege was escorted from the river Po to the river Danube by no less than 150 outriders.[13] At last, on 17 January 1848, the final obesquies were completed at the Kapuzinerkirche and Marie Louise rested beside her father, her mother and her son. Within two months central Europe, and Italy too, was in revolt; and Metternich, so long the arbiter of her fate, had fled Vienna for exile.

Epilogue

12 December 1940

Throughout the remaining years of the nineteenth century, and well into the twentieth, the two coffins of mother and son lay side by side undisturbed in the second chamber of the Kapuzinerkirche vault. Already, in 1847, there were some seventy Habsburgs interred in the imperial sepulchre and every few years the Capuchin friars would admit other illustrious names to join them. In January 1868 the ill-starred Emperor Maximilian of Mexico was at his mother's insistence laid to rest beside his cousin. She herself – Archduchess Sophie – followed in May 1872. Ten months later came the burial of her half-sister, Empress Caroline, widow of the much-married Francis. Marie Louise's brother, Emperor Ferdinand, was eighty-two when he died in Prague in June 1875: he, too, was interred in the imperial vault. A third burial chamber received Crown Prince Rudolf in 1889, after the Mayerling tragedy, and nine years later his mother, Empress Elizabeth, stabbed by an Italian anarchist at Geneva. The dynasty's remaining link with the Empress of the French was cut at last, almost seventy years after her death, when the Court Chamberlain – her grandson and William's son, Prince Montenuovo – fulfilled the solemn ritual of knocking three times on the door of the vault, and the friars accepted the coffin of Emperor Francis Joseph. By then – November 1916 – Austria-Hungary and France were enemies in a terrible war; and it is unlikely that anyone paused to reflect how, with the death of 'the last monarch of the old school', there also passed away the great Napoleon's nephew by marriage.

More than once Francis Joseph had brushed aside informal requests from Napoleon III that Reichstadt's coffin should be 'translated' to

Paris and laid to rest beside the sarcophagus of his father, under the dome of the Invalides. After the break up of the Habsburg monarchy, sentimental Bonapartists tried again in 1932, but objections were raised by Pan-German parliamentarians hostile to the mounting French financial and political influence in central Europe. It was also claimed, with some justice, that responsibility for the imperial vault lay with the Church and the House of Habsburg, not the Austrian republic. But in March 1938 Austria was absorbed into a 'Greater Germany' and the Nazified foreign service in Berlin became the arbiter of such issues. There were talks at the Paris embassy between the Nazi diplomat, Otto Abetz, and the French historian, Jacques Benoist-Méchin. The talks were resumed after the fall of France when Abetz became ambassador to Marshal Pétain's '*État Français*'. Benoist-Méchin, an out-and-out collaborationist, proposed that as a gesture of goodwill Hitler should order Reichstadt's coffin to be brought to the Invalides on 15 December 1940, the centenary of the return of Napoleon's body. Hitler welcomed the idea: if Pétain came up from Vichy for the ossuarian family reunion, the Führer would join him, to give visual proof, before Napoleon's tomb, of the partnership of France and Germany in the struggle against 'England'.[1]

Late in the afternoon of Thursday, 12 December 1940 – the 149th anniversary of the birth of Marie Louise – a horse-drawn hearse waited in Vienna's Neue Markt, outside the Kapuzinerkirche. With total absence of ceremony, undertakers carried a heavy coffin up from the vaults and lifted it on to the hearse, which rattled through almost deserted streets to the Westbahnhof. Inside the station a group of Nazi Party officials kept watch as it was transferred to an empty baggage carriage to be attached to the night train for Munich. Two grey-helmeted German sentries stood guard. Long after his death, the son of the Emperor of the French and an Austrian Archduchess had become once more a talisman of Franco-Germanic collaboration.

History could not be manipulated so easily. Pétain's representatives in occupied Paris – who included his Prime Minister, Pierre Laval – were slow to inform him of what was taking place. The news did not reach Vichy until the Thursday on which the coffin was removed from the imperial vault. The Marshal was unenthusiastic. At eighty-four his perception of the Napoleonic Wars differed from Hitler's. To the fifty-one-year-old Führer the wars belonged to a legendary past, as *Mein Kampf* recalls.[2] Pétain, on the other hand, could remember from schooldays at St Omer veterans of Borodino and the Beresina, Leipzig and Waterloo. He was far from certain that in bitterly cold weather, he wished to travel to a swastika-beflagged Paris and receive from defeated France's conqueror the remains of Napoleon's son. On Friday morning, while the train carrying the coffin was crossing Bavaria, Laval hurried to Vichy to convince Pétain of the need to be at the ceremony.[3]

The Marshal, however, already thought his minister too inclined to attach France to Hitler's 'New Order'. On Friday evening Pétain abruptly dismissed Laval from office; briefly he was even held under arrest. There would be no meeting with Hitler. An official pronouncement acknowledged French gratitude to Germany, but Pétain's message was not as Abetz intended; 'Between the melancholy fate of the Duke of Reichstadt, a prisoner in his own family, and the cruel fate of France, exiled in her own country by the arbitrament of war, History will note a moving analogy,' the Marshal declared.[4]

The Germans were angry. Yet they could hardly go back on their word and return poor Reichstadt's remains to Vienna. The bronze coffin reached the Gare de l'Est before noon on Saturday, but it was not until after midnight that it was lifted on to an artillery wagon and, with a German military escort, borne across a silent Paris to reach the Invalides at one o'clock on Sunday morning. By now it was snowing. The Germans handed over the coffin to a double line of twenty Republican Guards in traditional uniform. Abetz made a short speech, emphasising the Führer's magnanimity. Admiral Darlan and General Émile Laure, a close friend of the Marshal, represented the French government. The coffin, now draped by a tricolour flag, was placed before the high altar and a Requiem Mass duly celebrated. 'Wreaths of incense rose into the air,' Napoleon II's biographer, André Chatelot, recalled many years later. 'The few of us who were there went away deeply moved.'[5] Most Parisians, approaching their first Christmas under enemy occupation, were unimpressed. 'What we want is not bones but meat,' was a rueful comment.[6]

The mood of cynical indifference did not outlast the years of privation. With the return of peace, the King of Rome's resting place in St Jerome's Chapel began to attract Napoleonists, as had the earlier tomb at Vienna. It is, of course, dwarfed by the classical majesty of the double crypt dedicated to the Emperor, and it seems inconspicuous beside the mass of red porphyry which forms the principal sarcophagus. Yet Napoleon II does not go unhonoured. More than fifty years after his 'homecoming' a spring bouquet adorned what is, presumably, his final resting-place.

Eight hundred miles away, in Vienna, visitors may see the first gift presented to him by Paris, 'the King of Rome's cradle', exhibited as a museum piece among the secular treasures of the Hofburg. But to go down into the crypt of the Kapuzinerkirche is a more moving experience. A post-war strengthening of the roof of the imperial vault left Marie Louise cut off by a supporting wall from Emperor Francis. This reconstruction has had a curious incidental effect: it emphasises the extent to which fate imposed a dispersed family upon her. For while Francis has four wives and ten of his thirteen children around him in the burial chamber, Marie Louise's coffin stands starkly alone. The husband and son whom history associates with her lie in Paris. Neipperg is in Parma's church of the Madonna della Staccata, whence Bartolini's monument was moved in 1905. Bombelles, who returned to his native France in 1851, lies buried in the village church of Grisy-sur-Seine. Albertina, who died of pleurisy in 1867, has a gracefully sculptured tomb in the conventual church of San Giovanni Evangelista, close to her father. Only William is buried in Austria, like his mother; he died in 1895 at Döbling, near Vienna, having suffered a mental breakdown in his late fifties. Sometimes the sombre austerity of Marie Louise's isolated tomb is relieved by a cluster of flowers. In a biography published in 1983, Irmgard Schiel recorded how she noticed violets there, and found with them a tribute from the pensioners' savings bank association of Parma.[7] Sixteen years later, at Easter 1999, a fading posy of violets caught this author's eye, too. At least in Parma the 'good Duchess' has not slipped from folk memory. But do flowers for their Empress ever come from the French? It seems unlikely.

SIMPLIFIED GENEALOGY OF THE HABSBURGS, 1736–1916

(The abbreviation M is for Maria or Marie: Emperors in capitals)

M.Theresa, 1717–1780, 'King' of Hungary, etc, Empress-Consort m. 1736 FRANCIS of Lorraine, 1708–1765,Emperor from 1745

JOSEPH II, 1741–1790
m. 1760 Isabella of
Parma, 1741–1763

2 daughters died
in infancy.

LEOPOLD II, 1747–1792
m. 1764 M. Luisa of Spain,1745–1792

Ferdinand, 1754–1806
Duke of Modena
m. 1771 M.Beatrice d'Este,
1750–1829

M.Caroline, 1752–1814,
m.1768, Ferdinand of Naples
& Sicily, 1751–1825

M. Thérèse*, 1778–1851
m. 1790 FRANCIS

7 sons, 10 other
daughters

M.Antoinette, 1755–1793,
m. 1770 Louis of France,1754–1793

2 sons, 2 daughters, only M. Thérèse,
surviving the Revolution

2 sons
9 daughters

FRANCIS, 1768–1835
(i) m. 1788 Elizabeth of
Württemberg, 1767–1790

Ludovica, 1790–1791

Francis d'Este, 1779–1846,
effective Duke of Modena from 1815,
m. 1812 M. Beatrice of Sardinia, 1792–1840

descendants

Ferdinand d'Este, 1781–1850,
Austrian General

M. Ludovica #, 1787–1816,
m. 1808 FRANCIS

2 sons, 4 daughters

(ii) m. 1790 M. Thérèse of
Naples*, 1772–1807
(iii) m. 1808 M. Ludovica
d'Este#,1787–1816
(iv) m. 1816 Caroline Augusta
of Bavaria, 1792–1873

Ferdinand, 1769–1824,
Grand Duke of Tuscany
(of Würzburg, 1805–1814)
m. 1790 Luisa of Sicily
1773–1802

descendants

Charles, 1771–1847, Field Marshal,
Duke of Teschen m. 1815 Henriette
of Nassau, 1797–1829

descendants

Joseph, 1776–1847, Palatine of Hungary
(i) m. 1799 Alexandra of Russia, 1783–1801
(ii) m. 1815 Hermine of Anhalt, 1797–1829

twin son and daughter

(iii) m. 1819 Dorothea of Württemberg, 1797–1855

2 sons, 2 daughters

John, 1782–1859,
m. morgantically
1823 Anna Plochl,
1804–1885

6 sons,
4 daughters

M. Louise, 1791–1847
(i) m. 1810 NAPOLEON, 1769–18212

Napoleon, King of Rome Duke of Reichstadt, 1811–1832

(ii) m. 1821 Adam Albert von Neipperg, 1775–1829

William Montenuovo,
1819–1896

A daughter died
in infancy, 1821

Albertina Montenuovo, 1817–1867
m. 1833 Luigi san Vitale 1799–1876

(iii) m. 1834, Charles Bombelles, 1785–1856

FERDINAND, 1793–1875 (Abdicated 1848)
m. 1831 Marianna of Savoy, 1803–1884

M. Leopoldina, 1797–1826 m. 1817 Pedro of
Brazil and Portugal, 1796–1834

descendants

Francis Charles, 1802–1878
m. 1824 Sophie of Bavaria, 1805–1872

FRANCIS JOSEPH, 1830–1916
m. 1854 Elizabeth of Bavaria, 1837–1898

Rudolf 1858–1889 and 3 daughters,
with descendants

Maximilian, 1832–1867,
Emp. of Mexico,
m. 1857 Charlotte of
Belgium, 1840–1927

Charles Ludwig, 1833–1896,
m.1862 M. Annuziata of Naples,
1843–1871from whom the present
Head of theHouse of Habsburg
is descended

1 other son
and a daughter

1 other son and
6 daughters

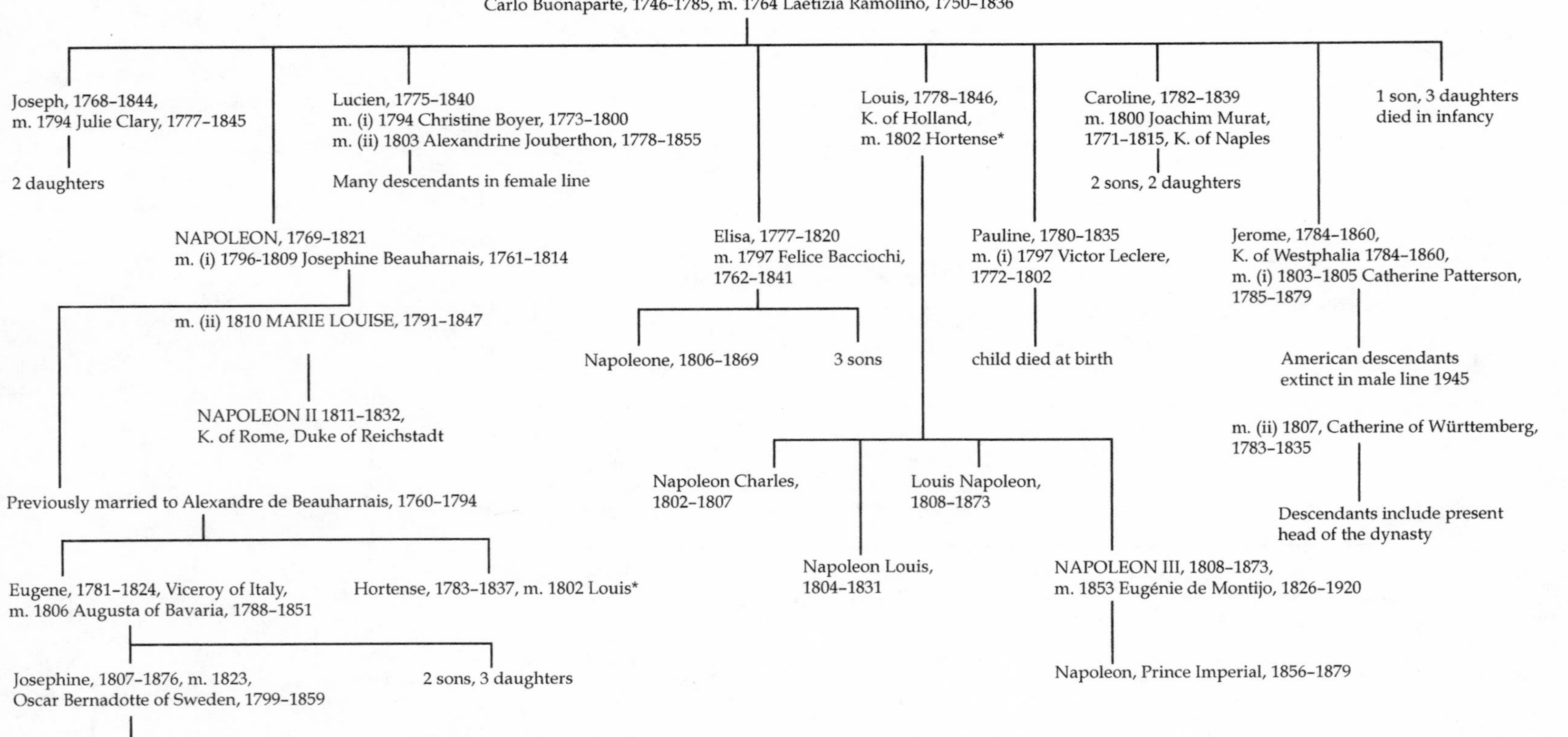
SIMPLIFIED GENEALOGY OF THE BONAPARTE DYNASTY
Carlo Buonaparte, 1746-1785, m. 1764 Laetizia Ramolino, 1750–1836
Joseph, 1768–1844,
m. 1794 Julie Clary, 1777–1845
2 daughters
Lucien, 1775–1840
m. (i) 1794 Christine Boyer, 1773–1800
m. (ii) 1803 Alexandrine Jouberthon, 1778–1855
Many descendants in female line
Louis, 1778–1846,
K. of Holland,
m. 1802 Hortense*
Caroline, 1782–1839
m. 1800 Joachim Murat,
1771–1815, K. of Naples
2 sons, 2 daughters
1 son, 3 daughters
died in infancy
NAPOLEON, 1769–1821
m. (i) 1796-1809 Josephine Beauharnais, 1761–1814
m. (ii) 1810 MARIE LOUISE, 1791–1847
NAPOLEON II 1811–1832,
K. of Rome, Duke of Reichstadt
Elisa, 1777–1820
m. 1797 Felice Bacciochi,
1762–1841
Napoleone, 1806–1869
3 sons
Pauline, 1780–1835
m. (i) 1797 Victor Leclere,
1772–1802
child died at birth
Jerome, 1784–1860,
K. of Westphalia 1784–1860,
m. (i) 1803–1805 Catherine Patterson,
1785–1879
American descendants
extinct in male line 1945
m. (ii) 1807, Catherine of Württemberg,
1783–1835
Descendants include present
head of the dynasty
Napoleon Charles,
1802–1807
Louis Napoleon,
1808–1873
Napoleon Louis,
1804–1831
NAPOLEON III, 1808–1873,
m. 1853 Eugénie de Montijo, 1826–1920
Napoleon, Prince Imperial, 1856–1879
Previously married to Alexandre de Beauharnais, 1760–1794
Eugene, 1781–1824, Viceroy of Italy,
m. 1806 Augusta of Bavaria, 1788–1851
Hortense, 1783–1837, m. 1802 Louis*
Josephine, 1807–1876, m. 1823,
Oscar Bernadotte of Sweden, 1799–1859
2 sons, 3 daughters
Descendants include present rulers of
Sweden, Norway, Denmark and Belgium

Notes

Full details of books and other cited sources will be found in the select bibliography.

Abbreviations:

Corr. Correspondence de Napoléon I, volume and document numbers
LetNap. C. de la Roncière (ed.), *Letters of Napoleon to Marie-Louise*
ML Corr. Correspondance de Marie Louise 1799–1847, Lettres Intimes
ML/PD Masson (ed.), *Private Diaries of the Empress Marie-Louise*
M-L et Nap. C.F. Palmstierna (ed.), *Marie-Louise et Napoléon, 1813–1814, Lettres Inédites*
HHSA Papers in the Haus-, Hof- und Staatsarchiv, Vienna.

Prologue: 12 December 1791, (pp. 1–3)

1 *The Times*, 23 December 1791. The fullest account of Mozart's final days and of his life and death in Vienna in 1791–2 is in H. C. Robbins Landon, *1791, Mozart's Last Year*, especially pp. 166–75.
2 Cited by Robbins Landon, p. 168.
3 *Wiener Zeitung*, 17 December 1791.
4 A. von Helfert, *Marie Louise*, p. 1.

Chapter 1: Habsburg and Bourbon, (pp. 5–12)

1 W. C. Langsam, *Francis the Good*, p. 105.
2 Langsam, p. 186.
3 Full final bulletin in translation, A. Wheatcroft, *The Habsburgs*, p. 238.
4 Langsam, p. 106; Wheatcroft, p. 239; E. Wangermann, *From Joseph II to the Jacobin Trials*, p. 107.
5 C. A. Macartney, *The Habsburg Empire*, pp. 120–33.
6 Maria Theresa to Marie Antoinette 1776: J. M. Thompson, *Lectures on Foreign History*, p. 272, citing A. von Arneth, *Maria Theresa und Marie Antoinette ... Briefwechsel*.
7 G. Lefebvre, *The French Revolution from its Origins to 1793*, pp. 210–13.
8 J. Tulard, J. Fayard and A. Fierro, *Histoire et dictionnaire de la Révolution française*, p. 340 (hereafter cited as *HRF*).
9 Looting in Paris: *HRF*, p. 340; Pitt's speech: *Parliamentary Register*, vol. 29, p. 826.
10 Langsam, p. 104; P. W. Schroeder, *The Transformation of European Politics 1763–1848*, pp. 87–90.
11 Macartney, pp. 152–3; Langsam, p. 143.
12 S. F. Scott, *The Response of the Royal Army to the French Revolution*, especially pp. 135–85.

13 F. McLynn, *Napoleon*, p. 41 includes material from recent research on this phase of Napoleon's life unavailable to earlier biographers.
14 H. Mathy, *Franz Georg von Metternich*, pp. 108–10; A. Palmer, *Metternich*, pp. 15-16.
15 R. von Metternich, *Mémoires ... laissées par le Prince de Metternich*, vol. 1, p. 13.
16 C. Wright, *Louise, Queen of Prussia*, p. 1, p. 11, p. 70.
17 A. Sorel, *L'Europe et la Révolution Française*, vol. 3, pp. 43–7.
18 Napoleon to Joseph Bonaparte, 22 June, 1792: F. Masson, *Napoléon Inconnu*, vol. 2, p. 392. J. M. Thompson, *Napoleon's Letters*, p. 40, gives an English translation.
19 J. M. Thompson, *Napoleon Bonaparte, His Rise and Fall*, p. 26, critically assessing the reminiscence recorded in Las Cases, *Mémorial de St Hélène*, vol. 5, p. 170.
20 L. Bourrienne, *Mémoires de Napoléon Bonaparte*, vol. 4, p. 200 (February 1800).

Chapter 2: 'A Corsican Scoundrel named Buonaparte', (pp. 13–24)

1 C. Raeuber, chapter on Berthier in D. Chandler, (ed.), *Napoleon's Marshals*, pp. 44–5.
2 V. Cronin, *Napoleon*, pp. 75–6; L. Garros, *Quel roman que ma vie: Itinéraire de Napoléon Bonaparte*, p. 51.
3 Corsican background: D. Carrington, *Napoleon's Parents*, especially chapter 2, which corrects several legends.
4 Larrey (ed.), *Souvenirs de Madame Mère*, cited by C. Barnett, *Bonaparte*, p. 16.
5 A. Chuquet, *La jeunesse de Napoléon*, vol. 3, pp. 124–31.
6 Chandler, *The Campaigns of Napoleon*, pp. 15–16.
7 Cronin, p. 80.
8 Chuquet, vol. 3, pp. 152–74.
9 The letter from Avignon is discussed in Garros, p. 62. See also Thompson, *Napoleon Bonaparte*, p. 30.
10 For Toulon: Chandler, pp. 20–7; Chuquet, vol. 3, pp. 180–229.
11 Garros, pp. 72–4; Thompson, *Napoleon Bonaparte*, pp. 45–6.
12 G. E. Rothenberg, *Napoleon's Great Adversaries; the Archduke Charles and the Austrian Army*, chapter 1, especially pp. 24–9; Chandler, pp. 45–6, 454, 518–20.
13 Schroeder, pp. 118–20, 130–31; K. Roider, *Baron Thugut and Austria's Response to the French Revolution*, pp. 101–26.
14 J. M. Thompson, *French Revolution*, pp. 434–6.
15 Schroeder, *The Transformation of European Politics*, p. 141.
16 Langsam, p. 160.
17 A. Bryant, *The Years of Endurance*, p. 108.
18 Francis to Marie Thérèse, 13 May 1794: Langsam, p. 160.
19 Macartney, pp. 157, 173–4; Lefebvre, pp. 182–3.
20 Langsam, p. 156.
21 N. J. de D. Soult, *Mémoires*, pp. 68–73; Rothenberg, p. 41.
22 Cronin, pp. 101–3; Napoleon to Joseph Bonaparte, 6 October 1795; *Corr.* 1, no. 72.
23 Mallet du Pan to Francis, 20 February 1796: J. Mallet du Pan, *Mémoires et Correspondance*, vol. 2, p. 13; Roider, p. 100.

Chapter 3: Italy and Beyond, (pp. 25–40)

1 E. Bruce, *Napoleon and Josephine*, pp. 145–7.
2 Napoleon to Joseph Bonaparte, 24 June 1795: *Corr.* 1, no. 42.
3 Josephine to Napoleon, 28 October 1795: Garros, p. 84; more extensively, Bruce, p. 150.
4 Cronin, p. 130; Thompson, *Napoleon Bonaparte*, p. 58.
5 Napoleon dictating to Las Cases on St Helena, cited by Bruce, p. 152.
6 Prince Napoleon, *Memoirs of Queen Hortense* (cited subsequently as *Hortense Memoirs*), vol. 1, pp. 43–6, 49.
7 Napoleon to the Executive Directory, 19 January 1796: *Corr.* 1, no. 96; Chandler, *The Campaigns of Napoleon*, p. 41.
8 Garros, p. 87; Bruce, p. 162.
9 Napoleon's draft instructions to the Army of Italy: *Corr.* 1, no. 153.
10 *The Times*, 29 April 1796, p. 3; 8 June 1796, p. 2.
11 Proclamation to the Army of Italy, 26 April 1796: *Corr.* 1, no. 234.
12 Napoleon's triumphant entry into Milan; Bruce, p. 177.
13 Napoleon to the Executive Directory from Bologna, 21 June 1796; *Corr.* 1, no. 670.
14 Thugut to L. Cobenzl, 21 May 1796, cited from HHSA, Roider, p. 207.
15 Schroeder, *The Transformation of European Politics*, pp. 187–8; Roider, pp. 208–10.
16 Chandler, *The Campaigns of Napoleon*, pp. 115–20.
17 Napoleon to Carnot from Milan, 5 December 1796: *Corr.* 2, no. 1235.
18 For the reinforcement's crossing of the Alps; A. Palmer, *Bernadotte*, pp. 37–41.
19 O. Criste, *Erzherzog Carl*, vol. 1, p. 497.
20 Palmer, *Bernadotte*, p. 44.
21 Criste, vol. 1, p. 411.
22 Criste vol. 1, pp. 510–11, as cited by Rothenberg, p. 47.
23 Roider, p. 238.
24 Napoleon to Archduke Charles, 31 March 1797: *Corr.* 2, no. 1436; Thugut to Francis, 4 April 1797: Criste vol. 1, pp. 427–8. See also Roider, pp. 238–9.
25 Roider, p. 240; Schroeder, *The Transformation of European Politics*, pp. 166–70.
26 Thugut to Colloredo, 22 October 1797: Roider, pp. 260–1. Professor Roider's detailed study of Thugut gives a good insight into the attitude of the Habsburg aristocracy to the French invaders at this time.
27 L. Cobenzl to Thugut, 14 October 1797; Roider, p. 258.
28 Cronin, pp. 173–4.
29 Palmer, *Bernadotte*, pp. 60–2.
30 Palmer, pp. 63–71 for the events in Vienna and their consequences.
31 Eden to Lord Grenville, 17 March 1798: Public Record Office, Kew, FO 7/51/18.
32 For the Austria Hymn: H. C. Robbins Landon, *Haydn, Chronicle and Works*, vol. 4, 'The Years of the Creation', pp. 241–9, 271–81.
33 There is a graphic narrative of the disturbances in a translated anonymous pamphlet, 'Eyewitness' *A Factual Account of the Riot in Vienna*, British Library 9315a7.

Chapter 4: The Making of the Empires, (pp. 41–52)

1 Langsam, p. 164.
2 Langsam, p. 165.
3 Marie Louise to Victoria de Poutet, 8 September 1803: *ML Corr.* p. 42.

4 Langsam, p. 16. The episode took place about the time of Francis's eighth birthday.
5 Letter from Nelson, 21 August 1800: F. Fraser, *Beloved Emma*, p. 266.
6 Thugut to Colloredo, 14 November 1800: Roider, p. 357.
7 Roider, pp. 359–60.
8 Macartney, p. 172.
9 Rothenberg, p. 67, citing Paget correspondence in PRO, Foreign Office 7/65.
10 Marie Louise to Victoria de Poutet, 9 October 1803: *MLCorr*. pp. 44–6.
11 Schroeder, *The Transformation of European Politics*, pp. 233–5.
12 Enghien execution: effect in France, G. Lefebvre, *Napoleon* vol. 1, pp. 181–2; effect in Russia, A. Palmer, *Alexander I*, p. 81.
13 Lefebvre, *Napoleon*, vol. 1, p. 183; Garros, p. 221.
14 T. Sipe, *Beethoven's Eroica Symphony*, chapters 1 and 3.
15 G. Mann, *Secretary of Europe*, p. 103.
16 Patent creating new title: Macartney, p. 156. F. Heer, *The Holy Roman Empire*, pp. 282–3; Francis's 'no ceremonial' directive: Langsam, p. 166.
17 These letters from Marie Louise to Francis are cited from HHSA in Irmgard Schiel, *Marie Louise* pp. 56–7.
18 Garros, p. 223 (carriage drive to Notre Dame), pp. 224–5 (reviews at Boulogne), p. 226 (Aachen); Cronin, pp. 305–6. Pope and coronation: E. E. Y. Hales, *Napoleon and the Pope*, pp. 55–73, and more extensively in his *Revolution and Papacy 1769–1846*; Lefebvre, *Napoleon*, vol. 1, pp. 184–5.
19 Bruce, pp. 363–73; *Hortense Memoirs*, vol. 1, pp. 128–36; more detailed studies, Masson, *Napoleon and his Coronation* and H. Gaubert, *Le Sacre de Napoléon I*.
20 Bruce, p. 362, citing Roederer's Journal.
21 Thompson, *Napoleon Bonaparte*, pp. 213–4.

Chapter 5: 1805, Milan to Austerlitz, (pp. 53–67)

1 Prince Clary's observations, as cited from Gaubert by Bruce, p. 371.
2 Carola Oman, *Napoleon's Viceroy*, p. 174.
3 Rothenberg, p. 85.
4 Marie Thérèse to Francis, 2 June 1805, Langsam, p. 160.
5 Helfert, pp. 13–14.
6 Rothenberg, pp. 89–90.
7 Rothenberg, p. 91; Chandler, *The Campaigns of Napoleon*, pp. 396–7.
8 On Ulm, in addition to works above, A. Horne, *How far from Austerlitz?*, pp. 116–18.
9 Chandler, *The Campaigns of Napoleon*, p. 405.
10 Sir A. Paget to Lady Paget, 3 November 1805: A. Paget and J. R. Green, *The Paget Papers*, vol. 2, p. 239.
11 Horne, pp. 122–3.
12 Paget to Paget, 8 November 1805: Paget and Green, vol. 2, pp. 241–2. For Marie Louise's response to the excitement of departure see three letters to Victoria de Poutet, of 4 and 5 November 1805: *MLCorr*. pp. 60–2.
13 Napoleon to Francis, 8 November 1805: *Corr*. 11, no. 9464.
14 Garros, p. 249; capture of Tabor bridge: Chandler, p. 407.
15 J. K. Mayr, 'Wien im Zeitalter Napoleons', *Abhandlungen zur Geschichte und Quellenkunde der Stadt Wien*, pp. 125–6; and Langsam, p. 166, citing the contemporary account, *Die Franzosen zu Wien*.
16 Earl of Harewood (ed.), *Kobbé's Complete Opera Book*, pp. 125–6.
17 Chandler, *The Campaigns of Napoleon*, p. 407.

18 A. M. T. de Thiard, *Souvenirs diplomatiques et militaires de 1804 à 1806*, pp. 173–80.
19 Helfert, p. 17; A. Mahan, *Marie-Louise*, pp. 30–1 supplements extracts from the Archduchess's letters with a map of her travels. She also wrote at least twelve letters to Victoria de Poutet: *MLCorr.* pp. 62–75.
20 Helfert, pp. 17–18.
21 N. K. Shilder, *Imperator Aleksandr I*, vol. 2, p. 132.
22 Memoirs of Langeron, cited by Shilder, vol. 2, p. 283.
23 S. Andolenko, *Histoire de l'Armée Russe*, p. 149.
24 Thiard, pp. 199–200; Horne, p. 132.
25 C. de Mazade (ed.), *Mémoires de Czartoryski*, vol. 1, p. 407.
26 Francis to Marie Thérèse, 2 December 1805: Helfert, p. 19. See also W. C. Langsam, 'An Imperial Understatement', *American Historical Review*, vol. 44 (1939), p. 852 which reproduces a photostat of the original message.
27 Napoleon to Josephine, 3 December 1805, *Corr.* 11 no. 9537.
28 Napoleon to Joseph Bonaparte, 3 December 1805, *Corr.* 11 no. 9538.
29 Langsam, *Francis the Good*, p. 159.
30 Napoleon to Talleyrand, 4 December 1805: *Corr.* 11, no. 9542; Horne, pp. 184–5.
31 Francis to Marie Thérèse, 4 December 1805, Helfert, p. 19.
32 C. de Grunwald, *Alexander I*, pp. 109–10.
33 Helfert, p. 21.
34 Criste, vol. 2, pp. 372–3; Macartney, p. 181.
35 Schroeder, *The Transformation of European Politics*, p. 284; Lefebvre, *Napoleon*, vol. 1, p. 242.
36 Criste, vol. 2, pp. 376–7.
37 Oman, pp. 203–9.
38 *Wiener Zeitung*, 13 January 1806, cited by Mahan, p. 32.
39 G. Martineau, *Marie-Louise*, p. 20.

Chapter 6: Almost a Kaunitz, (pp. 69–82)

1 H. Rössler, *Õsterreichs Kampf*, vol. 1, pp. 221–8.
2 *Corr.* 12, no. 10023.
3 M. Botzenhart, *Metternichs Pariser Botschafterzeit*, p. 8.
4 C. Nesselrode to his father, 25 April 1806: A. Nesselrode (ed.), *Lettres et papiers du Chancelier ... Nesselrode*, vol. 3, p. 132.
5 Mann, p. 127.
6 C. de Grunwald's article 'Les débuts de Metternich', *Revue de Paris* (1936), pp. 503–4.
7 Metternich to Stadion, 19 August 1807: HHSA, Dipl. Korr. Frankreich, Kart. 200, Fasc. 8.
8 L. d'Abrantès, *Mémoires*, vol. 8, p. 408.
9 Palmer, *Metternich*, p. 54.
10 Langsam, p. 159.
11 Helfert, pp. 23–6.
12 Rothenberg, p. 121.
13 Rémusat memoirs, cited by Bruce, p. 425 (with barefoot at Bayonne, p. 426). For Walewska in Paris, C. Sutherland, *Marie Walewska*, pp. 109–15.
14 Denuelle affair: Bruce, pp. 385, 400, 403; F. McLynn, pp. 317–18.
15 Botzenhart, pp. 239–41. Metternich gave three different versions of the meeting with Napoleon: see Palmer, *Metternich*, pp. 61–2 and p. 351, note 38.

16 For Erfurt: A. Vandal, *Napoléon et Alexandre I*, vol. 1, pp. 411–35; Palmer, *Alexander I*, pp. 159–62.
17 Metternich, *Mémoires*, vol. 2, pp. 240–57 prints two of the memoranda. For the third see A. Beer, *Zehn Jahre Österreischer Politik*, pp. 525–8.
18 Rothenberg, pp. 131–2; Macartney, p. 187. The proclamation was the work of Friedrich von Schlegel, a Hanoverian-born novelist and dramatist who might be regarded as The Habsburg's earliest publicist.
19 Many letters are cited by Schiel (especially pp. 57–62) from HHSA FA Sammelbände, Karton 43. Some are also in J. de Bourgoing, *Marie Louise von Österreich* and Helfert, pp. 30–51 (including the 'lose his head' letter, p. 36).
20 Marie Louise to Francis, 28 April 1809, HHSA, Schiel, p. 62; also Helfert, p. 37.
21 For these letters, Helfert, p. 39.
22 Memoirs of army apothecary de Gassicourt included in J. Lehmann and R. Bassett's delightful selection, *Vienna, a Traveller's Companion*, pp. 189–90. For Aspern-Essling: Horne, pp. 269–72; Chandler, *The Campaigns of Napoleon*, pp. 700–07; Rothenberg, pp. 147–56.
23 Marie Louise to Francis, 26 May 1809: Helfert, p. 42; Marie Louise to Victoria de Poutet, 29 May 1809: *ML Corr.* p. 85.
24 Marie Louise to Francis, 17 June 1809; Schiel, p. 397; Helfert, p. 43.
25 Marie Louise to Victoria de Poutet, 8 July 1809: *MLCorr.* p. 97.
26 Metternich, *Mémoires*, vol. 1, p. 81. For Wagram: Horne, pp. 273–8; Chandler, *The Campaigns of Napoleon*, pp. 713–30; Rothenberg, pp. 163–70.

Chapter 7: Making a Marriage, (pp. 83–99)

1 Bruce, p. 438, using the Walewski archives; Sutherland, pp. 126–35.
2 Horne, p. 288.
3 For Liechtenstein at Schönbrunn: Garros, pp. 326, 329; Marie Louise to Victoria de Poutet, 8 August 1809: *MLCorr.* p. 108; F. Masson (ed.), *ML/PD*, p. 23.
4 C. de Grunwald, 'Le Marriage de Napoléon et de Marie Louise', *Revue des Deux Mondes*, vol. 38, pp. 320–52; Grunwald, *Vie de Metternich*, pp. 81–91; E. C. Corti, *Metternich und die Frauen*, vol. 1, pp. 199–204; Bourgoing, pp. 21–3. Floret's journal for late May to mid-October 1809 is a 57-page manuscript, HHSA, Frankreich Varia, 58, Fascicle 72: 2 October entry, pp. 51–2.
5 For 15 August celebrations in Vienna: Garros, p. 327 and Marie Louise's comments in her letter to Victoria de Poutet, 27 August 1809, *MLCorr.* p. 114. For conflict with the Papacy, the clearest account is in Hales, *Napoleon and the Pope*, pp. 99–122.
6 Napoleon to Fouché, 12 October 1809: *Corresp.* 19, no. 15935. There is a detailed study of Staps and his motive: J. Tulard, *Napoléon, 12 Octobre 1809*.
7 J. Rapp, *Mémoires*, vol. 1, p. 153.
8 *Hortense Memoirs*, 1, p. 226.
9 Cited from vol. 6 of A. du Casse's collected papers of Eugène by Carola Oman, p. 283.
10 *Hortense Memoirs*, 1, p. 228; Bruce, p. 442.
11 Vandal, vol. 2, pp. 182–4. For events in St Petersburg, Palmer, *Alexander I*, pp. 185–8.
12 See Grunwald and Corti references cited Note 4, above, and Palmer, *Metternich*, p. 73.
13 Schwarzenberg to Metternich and also Floret to Metternich, 21 December 1809: HHSA Dipl. Korr. Frankreich, Karton 205, Fascicles 11 & 12. Metternich to Schwarzenberg, 31 December 1809: Grunwald article, p. 334; Eleonore

Metternich to her husband, 3 January 1810: Metternich, *Mémoires*, vol. 2, pp. 314–6.

14 Marie Louise to Victoria de Poutet, 23 December 1809: *MLCorr.* p. 133.

15 Marie Louise to Francis, 5 January 1810: facsimile in Schiel, p. 30, from HHSA.

16 Marie Louise to Victoria de Poutet, 24 December 1809: *MLCorr.* pp. 136–7.

17 Marie Louise to Victoria de Poutet, 6 January 1810: Christie's catalogue of 8 May 1985, p. 144, lot 352. This letter is not included in *MLCorr.*

18 Marie Louise to Victoria de Poutet, 10 January 1810: *MLCorr.* p. 143.

19 Marie Louise to Victoria de Poutet, 23 January 1810: *MLCorr.* p. 145.

20 Helfert, pp. 98–102, 395–6; Bruce, pp. 449–50. There is a detailed study of the annulment: L. Grégoire, *Le 'Divorce' de Napoléon et de l'impératrice Joséphine.*

21 Napoleon to Champagny, 6 February 1810: *Corr.* 20, no. 16210; Vandal, vol. 2, pp. 271–80.

22 Schwarzenberg to Metternich, 8 February 1810: Bourgoing, pp. 42–3.

23 Metternich to Otto, 15 February 1810: Grunwald article, p. 345. The twenty-four hours of reflection was only mentioned by Marie Louise to her daughter, Albertina, in the last years of her life: Bourgoing, pp. 36–7.

24 Otto to Champagny, 15 February 1810: Grunwald article, p. 346.

25 Napoleon to Francis, 23 February 1810: *Corr.* 20, no. 16287.

26 Napoleon to Marie Louise, 23 February 1810: *Corr.* 20, no. 16288. I have followed the practice of J. M. Thompson (*N's Letters*, pp. 236–7) in using the abbreviation Y.I.H.

27 Instructions to Berthier, 26 February 1810, included among more than fifty documents relating to Berthier's mission to Vienna in the Calvin Bullock Collection auctioned at Christie's, London, in 1985. Some extracts are printed in Christie's Catalogue, 8 May 1985, pp. 126–7, lot 305.

28 Report from Berthier: source as above; and *ML/PD*, pp. 36–8.

29 Marie Louise to Francis, 16 March 1810: HHSA, Helfert, p. 119.

30 Napoleon to Berthier, 20 March 1810: Christie's Catalogue, p. 126; E. Longford, *Wellington, The Years of the Sword*, p. 215.

31 *Hortense Memoirs*, vol. 1, p. 221 (embarrassed cavalryman); p. 223 (waltzing).

32 Napoleon to Berthier, 5 March 1810: in facsimile, Christie's Catalogue, p. 127 on changing the itinerary; and on 26 March (p. 126) on need to hurry.

33 *ML/PD*, pp. 50, 207.

34 *Hortense Memoirs*, vol. 1, p. 227.

35 Gourgaud, *St Helena; Journal intime*, vol. 2, pp. 275–9.

Chapter 8: 'We Suit Each Other Perfectly', (pp. 101–13)

1 Napoleon to Francis, 29 March 1810, *Corr.* 20 no. 16361.

2 Garros, p. 342; *ML/PD*, pp. 59–60.

3 *Hortense Memoirs*, vol. 2, pp. 30–2; *ML/PD*, pp. 61–4; Schiel, pp. 109–11 gives interesting extracts from the report in the *Wiener Zeitung* of 21 April 1810.

4 Pasquier, *Mémoires*, vol. 1, pp. 380–1.

5 *ML/PD*, pp. 64–8.

6 Marie Louise to Francis, 4 April, 1810, *ML/PD*, p. 68. See also Schiel, pp. 119–21.

7 Metternich to Francis, 6 April 1810: Grunwald article, p. 351.

8 E. Consalvi, *Mémoires*, vol. 1, pp. 452–60; C. S. Philips, *The Church in France, 1789–1848*, pp. 111–14.

9 Napoleon to Bigot de Préameneu, 5 April 1810: Thompson, *Napoleon's Letters*, pp. 237–8.

10 On Metternich in Paris at this time: Palmer, *Metternich*, pp. 77–9.
11 *ML/PD*, p. 71.
12 *ML/PD*, p. 76.
13 *ML/PD*, pp. 77–100 (with sea reference on p. 99); Marie Louise to Victoria de Poutet (now de Crenneville), 11 May 1810, *MLCorr*. p. 147.
14 Continental System in general, Lefebvre, vol. 2, especially pp. 255–9; Schroeder, pp. 385–8. For imperial dignitaries and contraband goods, *ML/PD*, pp. 91, 101.
15 *ML/PD*, p. 76.
16 Vicereine Auguste to her brother, Ludwig of Bavaria, 22 May 1810: Oman, p. 304.
17 Marie Louise to Countess Colloredo, 29 May, 1810., *MLCorr*. p. 148.
18 For the succession of balls: Garros, p. 346. For Metternich's report on the fire, see his *Mémoires*, vol. 1, pp. 301–7. See also: Marie Louise to Francis, 2 July 1810: Helfert, p. 151–3; *ML/PD*, pp. 104–6; Méneval, *Memoirs*, vol. 2, p. 317; A. D. C. de Lavalette, *Mémoires et Souvenirs de Comte de Lavallete*, vol. 2, p. 56; Corti, vol. 1, p. 271.
19 Bourgoing, p. 112; A. Castelot, *Napoleon's Son*, pp. 26–7.
20 Napoleon to the Legislative Assembly, 3 December 1809: *Corr.* 20, no. 16031.
21 *MLCorr*. p. 150.
22 *ML/PD*, pp. 106–7.
23 Castelot, pp. 37–8.
24 Helfert, pp. 189–91.
25 *Hortense Memoirs*, vol. 2, pp. 34–5.
26 Castelot, p. 47.
27 Napoleon to Josephine, 22 March 1811: *Corr*. 21, no. 17499.
28 Grand Duke Ferdinand to Francis, 20 March 1811: cited from HHSA, Schiel, p. 143.
29 Francis to Marie Louise, 26 March 1810: Castelot, p. 45.
30 Marie Louise to Francis, 13 April 1811: Castelot, pp. 49–50.

Chapter 9: The Torrent and the Sponge, (pp. 115–30)

1 H. Bidou, *Paris*, p. 331; Napoleon to Montalivet, 8 May 1811: *Corr*. 22, no. 17702.
2 Lefebvre, Napoleon vol. 2, p. 148; Schroeder, p. 420.
3 A. de Caulaincourt, *Mémoires*, vol. 1, p. 285; Alexander to Catherine Pavlovna, 17 July 1811: N. Mikhailovich, *Corr… . Alexandre I*, p. 51; Palmer, *Alexander I*, pp. 203–4.
4 Méneval, *Mémoires*, vol. 2, pp. 402–3.
5 *Hortense Memoirs*, vol. 2, p. 37; Mme. de Montesquiou's account: Castelot, pp. 60–1.
6 Garros, p. 357; *ML/PD*: pp. 120–1, for the St Louis's Day celebrations.
7 Vandal, vol. 3, pp. 217–8.
8 *ML/PD*, pp. 123–41.
9 Méneval ('on the Emperor's orders') to Barbier, 19 December 1811: *Corr*. 23, no. 18348.
10 Marie Louise to Leopoldina, January 1812: Masson, *Marie Louise*, p. 111.
11 Metternich, *Mémoires*, vol. 2, pp. 435–39; Palmer, *Metternich*, pp. 84–5.
12 Dresden meeting: Vandal, vol. 3, pp. 402–25; P. Fain, *Manuscrit de Mil Huit Cent Douze*, pp. 61–9: B. de Castellane, *Journal*, vol. 1, pp. 92–6; Caulaincourt, *Memoirs* (Eng. ed.), vol. 1, pp. 108–9; B. de Casse, Queen of Westphalia's memoirs article in *Revue Historique*, vol. 36, pp. 328–35.

13 Metternich, *Mémoires*, vol. 2, pp. 461–63; Palmer, *Metternich*, p. 86; *ML/PD*, p. 74.
14 Napoleon to Marie Louise, 1 June 1812, *LetNap*. p. 51.
15 Bourgoing, pp. 157–9.
16 Napoleon to Marie Louise, 12 June 1812, *LetNap*. p. 58.
17 Chandler, pp. 756–60; C. Duffy, *Borodino*, pp. 29–50.
18 *ML/PD*, p. 158; Napoleon to Marie Louise, 19 July, 1812: *LetNap*. p. 77.
19 Napoleon to Marie Louise, 28 July 1812: *LetNap*. p. 80; P. de Ségur, *History of the Expedition to Russia*, vol. 1, pp. 182–3, 213; A. de Montesquiou, *Souvenirs*, p. 213.
20 Napoleon to Marie Louise, 2 September 1812: *LetNap*. p. 94. A. Palmer, *Napoleon in Russia*, pp. 62–81, 98–105 cover the advance in more detail.
21 Napoleon to Marie Louise, 6 September 1812: *LetNap*. p. 95; L. Bausset, *Mémoires anecdotiques*, vol. 2, p. 103.
22 Duffy, pp. 95–137; chapter 7 of Palmer, *Napoleon in Russia.*
23 The 'torrent and sponge' metaphor was recorded by N. Vorontsov in a summary of the Fili council from which extracts are given in E. Tarlé, *Nashestvie Napoleona na Rossiya – 1812 god*, p. 144. See also for the council, N. Narichkine, *1812*, pp. 163–4.
24 Napoleon to Marie Louise, 18 September 1812: *LetNap*. p. 104. Entry into Moscow: Fain, vol. 2, pp. 52–4; Bausset, vol. 2, pp. 115–20; Montesquiou, pp. 223–7.
25 Fire of Moscow: chapter 9 of Palmer, cited above; D. Olivier, *L'Incendie de Moscou.*

Chapter 10: 'Write to Papa François', (pp. 131–46)

1 Marie Louise to Victoria de Crenneville, 1 October 18: *MLCorr.* pp. 160–2: *ML/PD*, pp. 159–60.
2 Napoleon to Marie Louise, 6 October 1812: *LetNap*. p. 111; exchanges between Marie Louise and her father: Bourgoing, pp. 163–4; Schiel, p. 173.
3 Caulaincourt, *Memoirs*, pp. 252–4, 268–9, 277; Fain, vol. 2, pp. 106–8; Ségur, vol. 2, pp. 70–2; B. de Castellane, *Journal*, vol. 1, pp. 170–1.
4 Napoleon to Marie Louise, 26 October 1812: *LetNap*. p. 120.
5 Napoleon to Marie Louise, 3 November 1812: *LetNap*. p. 124.
6 Caulaincourt, pp. 327–35; Fain, vol. 2, pp. 284–5; Castelot, pp. 67–70; *ML/PD*, pp. 161–2.
7 Caulaincourt, pp. 359–60.
8 Montesquiou, p. 265.
9 Palmer, *Napoleon in Russia*, p. 238, based on Caulaincourt's narrative.
10 M. de Fezensac, *Souvenirs militaires*, p. 356; Oman, p. 357.
11 Marie Louise to Victoria de Crenneville, 28 February 1813: *MLCorr.* p. 167.
12 Helfert, p. 237.
13 Schiel, p. 182.
14 Schiel, p. 183.
15 Francis to Marie Louise, 24 January 1813: Schiel, p. 183; Helfert, p. 233.
16 Garros, p. 410.
17 Open letter: F. D. Scott, 'The Propaganda Activities of Bernadotte, 1813–14', J. McKay (ed.), *Essays in the History of Modern Europe*, pp. 19–20; Palmer, *Bernadotte*, p. 192.
18 Napoleon to General Clarke, 27 April, 1813: *Corr.* 25, no. 19915.
19 Napoleon to Lebrun, 6 April 1813: *Corr.* 25 no. 19813; Bourgoing, p. 185.
20 Napoleon to Marie Louise, 24 April, 1813: *LetNap*. pp. 143–4.

21 Marmont, cited by Chandler (p. 884) in his narrative of the battle.
22 Napoleon to Marie Louise, 5 May 1813: *LetNap*. p. 23.
23 Napoleon to Viceroy Eugène, 12 May 1813: *Corr.* 25, no. 20003.
24 Napoleon to Marie Louise, 14 May 1813: *LetNap*. p. 154.
25 Napoleon to Francis, 17 May 1813: *Corr*. 25, no. 20018.
26 Napoleon to Marie Louise, 23 and 24 May 1813: *LetNap*. p. 160.
27 Napoleon to Viceroy Eugène, 2 June 1813: *Corr.* 25, no. 20071.
28 Napoleon to Marie Louise, 7 June 1813: *Corr.* 25, no. 20093.
29 Metternich to Stadion, 23 June 1813: Palmer, *Metternich*, p. 98.
30 Metternich gave three records of the conversation: the least unreliable is his report to Francis, 26 June 1813, *Mémoires*, vol. 2, pp. 461–3; increasingly dramatic are the later versions, *Mémoires*, vol. 1, pp. 147–54, 253–6. French accounts: J. Hanoteau, 'Une nouvelle relation de l'Entrevue de Napoléon et de Metternich à Dresden', *Revue de l'Histoire Diplomatique*, vol. 47, pp. 421–40; Napoleon to Marie Louise, 1 July 1813: *LetNap*. pp. 170–1.
31 Napoleon to Marie Louise, 18 July 1813: *LetNap*. pp. 178–9.
32 The small travel diary formed Lot 35 in the Calvin Bullock Collection auction at Christie's, 8 May 1985. Extracts and two facsimile pages are in the catalogue, pp. 142–3. Much of the diary is printed in Chapter 8 of *ML/PD*.
33 See letter from Napoleon to the Countess of Montesquiou, 14 August 1813, included in Thompson, *Napoleon's Letters*, p. 287. For the King of Rome's toys, Castelot, p. 78.
34 Schroeder, p. 474; H. von Srbik, *Metternich*, vol. 1, pp. 160–1.
35 *ML/PD*, pp. 210, 213.
36 Francis to Marie Louise, 11 August 1813: Castelot, p. 77.

Chapter 11: Fickle Fortune, (pp. 147–60)

1 Horne, pp. 331, 336–7; Longford, pp. 309–16.
2 Fezensac, p. 444.
3 Napoleon to Marie Louise, 20 August 1813: *LetNap*. p. 186. Napoleon's movement is not mentioned by Chandler, but see V. Esposito and J. Elting, *Military History and Atlas*, Map 133, and accompanying text.
4 Esposito and Elting, Map and text 134; Chandler, p. 912.
5 Napoleon to Marie Louise, 6 September 1813: *LetNap*. p. 143.
6 Helfert, pp. 268–9.
7 Henrik Steffens, cited by A. Brett-James, *Europe against Napoleon*, p. 247.
8 Eye-witness accounts of the disaster on the bridge: Brett-James, pp. 199–214. Chandler narrates the events of the battle, *The Campaigns of Napoleon*, pp. 925–36; Brett-James's collection of contemporary accounts makes vivid reading (pp. 112–250).
9 For Neipperg's reception in Prague and Vienna see the extracts from Gentz and Countess Thurheim in Brett-James, pp. 255–6.
10 Napoleon to Marie Louise, 25 October 1813: *LetNap*. p. 198.
11 Napoleon to General Clarke, 2 November 1813: *Corr*. 26, no. 20854.
12 An enthusiastic letter from Metternich to the Duchess of Sagan describes the occasion in Frankfurt, M. Ullrichova, *Metternich-Sagan – Briefwechsel*, pp. 81–2.
13 Srbik, vol. 1, p. 166; Schoreder, pp. 490–1.
14 Palmer, *Metternich*, p. 110.
15 Cited from HHSA, Schiel, p. 205.
16 C. K. Webster, *The Foreign Policy of Castlereagh*, vol. 1, p. 202; Palmer, *Metternich*, p. 111.

17 Chandler, pp. 249–50; Horne, pp. 343, 345.
18 Bidou, p. 306.
19 Napoleon to Marie Louise, 3 November 1813: *LetNap*. p. 200.
20 L. de Villefosse and J. Bouissounouse, *L'Opposition à Napoléon*, pp. 320–1.
21 Marie Louise to Francis, 12 December and Francis to Marie Louise, 20 December 1813: Bourgoing, p. 232; Schiel, p. 207.
22 *Hortense Memoirs*, vol. 2, p. 59.
23 Note on the Immediate Situation of France, 12 January 1814: *Corr*. 27, no. 21089.
24 Napoleon to General Clarke, 10 January 1814, *Corr.* 27, no. 21078.
25 Napoleon to Caulaincourt, 4 January 1814, *Corr*. 26, no. 21062.
26 ibid.
27 Napoleon to Joseph, 7 January 1814, L. Lecestre, *Lettres inédites*, vol. 2, no. 1123.
28 *Hortense Memoirs*, vol. 2, p. 60; Garros, p. 235.
29 *Hortense Memoirs*, vol. 2, p. 61.

Chapter 12: A Child No Longer, (pp. 161–76)

1 Dragoons: Napoleon to Augereau, 21 February 1814, *Corr.* 27, no. 21343; deserters: Napoleon to Savary, 7 February 1814, Thompson, *Napoleon's Letters*, p. 294.
2 No longer a child: Marie Louise to Napoleon, 2 February 1814, *M-L et Nap*., p. 52. The remaining instances cited in this paragraph are all from *M-L et Nap*: Madame Mère, pp. 41, 47; Carnot, p. 41; Santona, p. 43; palisades, p. 49; Opéra, p. 53.
3 Marie Louise to Napoleon, 7 February 1814, *M-L Nap*. p. 61.
4 Napoleon to Cambacérès, 7 February 1814, *Corr.* 27, no. 21197.
5 Napoleon to Marie Louise, 7 February 1814: *LetNap*. p. 209.
6 The four victories: Esposito and Elting, maps and text, 147–9; Horne, pp. 348–50; Chandler, *The Campaigns of Napoleon*, pp. 969–80. Napoleon to Marie Louise, 18 February 1814: *LetNap*. p. 223.
7 Schroeder, pp. 498–9. Napoleon to Caulaincourt, 17 February 1814: *Corr.* 27, no. 21381.
8 Napoleon to Francis, 21 February 1814: *Corr*. 27, no. 21344; Napoleon to Marie Louise, 25 February 1814: *M-L et Nap*. pp. 107–8.
9 Marie Louise to Francis, 26 February and Francis to Marie Louise, 6 March 1814: Schiel, (from HHSA), pp. 221–2.
10 Marie Louise to Napoleon, 20 February, and Napoleon to Marie Louise, 21 February 1814: *M-L et Nap*. pp. 100–1.
11 Four letters over the dispute, starting with Marie Louise to Napoleon on 28 February and ending on 3 March with his admonition to discourage tittle-tattle, are included in *M-L et Nap*. pp. 117–25.
12 Pygmy: Napoleon to Marie Louise, 14 March 1814, *M-L et Nap*., p. 153. Exchanges critical of Joseph began with a letter from Napoleon of 12 March, p. 146.
13 A. Fournier, *Der Congress von Chatillon*, pp. 194–5.
14 Napoleon to Marie Louise, 23 March 1814: *M-L et Nap*., pp. 167–8 (with facsimile); also *LetNap*., pp. 246–7, with Blücher comment; Chandler, p. 999.
15 Note to Nesselrode, forwarded to the Tsar: Shilder, vol. 3, pp. 195, 386. Feints and counter-feints of the armies can best be followed in Esposito and Elting, Maps 153 and 154.
16 Marie Louise to Napoleon, 21 March 1814: *M-L et Nap*., p. 166 ('full of good

news'); 18 and 20 March (move to Élysée), pp. 162, 165–6; Playing whist: *Hortense Memoirs*, vol. 2, pp. 81–2.

17 Marie Louise to Napoleon, 29 March 1814; *M-L et Nap*. pp. 173–5. Bernard, p. 319.
18 Marie Louise to Napoleon, later on 29 March: pp. 176–7; Méneval, vol. 3, p. 229.
19 Letters and editorial comments in *M-L et Nap*., pp. 177–85 for the journey to Chartres. On the Tsar's meeting with the Prefect of Paris: Shilder, vol. 3, pp. 203–4.
20 Chandler, pp. 999–1001; Palmer, *Alexander I*, pp. 280–1.
21 Napoleon to Marie Louise, 3 April 1814: *M-L et Nap*. p. 192.
22 Blois on 3 and 4 April: *M-L et Nap*. pp. 193–6; proclamation: Helfert, p. 298.
23 Helfert, p. 296.
24 Schiel, p. 242.
25 For the Empress's letters: *M-L et Nap*. pp. 194–210; Napoleon seeks information: p. 207; Méneval, vol. 3, pp. 269–74. See also F. Masson, *Marie-Louise*, p. 576.
26 *M-L et Nap*. pp. 197–8, 201–2; for the situation at Blois: Savary, vol. 7, pp. 165–6.
27 *M-L et Nap*. pp. 204–7; three letters to her father: Schiel, pp. 247, 408.
28 For the Tsar's attitude: Palmer, *Alexander 1*, pp. 283–91; Marie Louise's hopes for Tuscany: footnote to 10 April letter, *M-L et Nap*. p. 205.
29 For Cambronne's escort: Garros, p. 447; *M-L et Nap*. pp. 215–16; Bourgoing, p. 303.
30 Marie Louise to Napoleon, 12 April 1814: *M-L et Nap*. pp. 214–15.
31 The pencilled message is reproduced in facsimile to accompany the printed text, *M-L et Nap*. p. 216.
32 Caulaincourt, vol. 3, pp. 335–40; *M-L et Nap*. p. 217; Garros, p. 447.
33 For the days at Rambouillet: Méneval, vol. 3, pp. 270–8; *M-L et Nap*. pp. 221–6.
34 Marie Louise to Napoleon, 15 April 1814: *M-L et Nap*. p. 225. Hortense visited Rambouillet on that day and found the Empress afraid that her father would make her settle on Elba; *Hortense Memoirs*, vol. 2, pp. 81–2.
35 Marie Louise to Napoleon, 16 April 1814: *M-L et Nap*., pp. 226–7.

Chapter 13: Apart, (pp. 177–88)

1 Bourgoing: pp. 335–40; Alpine scenery: Marie Louise to Napoleon, 8 May 1814: *M-L et Nap*. pp. 250–2.
2 Marie Louise to Victoria de Crenneville and Countess Coloredo, 17 May 1815: *ML Corr.* p. 171.
3 Méneval, vol. 3, p. 274; Castelot, p. 133.
4 Marie Louise to Napoleon, 5 June 1814: *M-L et Nap*. pp. 256–9.
5 Editorial comment, *M-L et Nap*. p. 256; Méneval, pp. 276–7.
6 Francis to Louis XVIII, 18 June 1814: HHSA, Int. Korr. 78.
7 Marie Louise to Napoleon, 22 June 1814: *M-L et Nap*. pp. 260–2.
8 Méneval, p. 291.
9 Hudelist to Metternich, 27 June 1814: Bourgoing, p. 367.
10 Bourgoing, p. 369; Méneval II, *Marie Louise et la Court d'Autriche*, p. 145.
11 Méneval, *Mémoires*, vol. 3, p. 291; Bourgoing, pp. 379–81; Schiel, p. 280, citing letters from Marie Louise to her father in HHSA.
12 Marie Louise to Napoleon, 21 July 1814: *M-Let Nap*. p. 266.

13 Although Evangeline Bruce (p. 478) wrote movingly of Josephine's last days, she appears not to have known of Eugène's letters, which are printed in the appendix to *M-L et Nap.* pp. 290–1. For Napoleon on day of Josephine's death: Garros, p. 453.
14 Correspondence in *M-L et Nap*. pp. 268–71.
15 Marie Louise to Napoleon, 18 August 1814, *M-L et Nap*. pp. 273–4.
16 Metternich to Francis, 5 July 1814: Corti, vol. 1, p. 462. For the development of Metternich's views on France at this time: Palmer, *Metternich*, pp. 128–9.
17 Bourgoing, pp. 393–405 prints such details as exist on the episode.
18 George III's birthday: Garros, pp. 453–4. Elban naval and military activities: four notes included in Thompson, *Napoleon's Letters*, pp. 303–5.
19 Bourgoing, pp. 411–13; Schiel, p. 287.
20 *M-L et Nap*. p. 275.
21 F. Fraser, *The Unruly Queen*, p. 255.
22 Méneval II, *Marie Louise et ... Autriche*, pp. 157–9; Bourgoing, p. 421.

Chapter 14: The Recluses of Schönbrunn, (pp. 189–202)

1 Richard Bright's *Travels*, extract in Lehmann and Bassett, p. 122.
2 ibid., p. 191.
3 Marie Louise to Victoria de Crenneville, 3 December 1814: *ML Corr.* pp. 173–4.
4 This paragraph and the next are based on reports printed in vol. 1 of M. H. Weil, *Les Dessous du Congrès de Vienne*.
5 Hager to Francis, 30 November 1814: Weil no. 927, p. 613; reply: 2 December, no. 958, p. 630.
6 Agent to Hager, 21 December 1814: Weil, no. 1104, p. 705.
7 Schiel, pp. 302–3.
8 Agent to Hager, 29 November 1814 (reporting 25 November): Weil, no. 930, p. 614.
9 As reported to Hager, 19 December 1814: Weil, no. 1089, pp. 697–8.
10 Schiel, p. 304; editorial note, *M-L et Nap*. p. 276.
11 Marie Louise to Napoleon, 3 January 1815: *M-L et Nap*. pp. 276–8.
12 Baden reports and need for renewed surveillance, 12–26 December 1814: Weil, vol. 1, pp. 706–34, *passim*.
13 Agent to Hager, 9 March 1815: Weil, no. 1837, vol. 2, p. 303; Méneval, pp. 350–1.
14 Marie Louise to Francis, 18 March 1815: HHSA Fam. Ark, Sammelbande K. 43, partially printed in Schiel, p. 308 and more extensively in Castelot, p. 158. See also Bourgoing, pp. 461–8.
15 Castelot, pp. 160–4; Hager reports of 16, 19, 27 March 1815: Weil, nos 1910, 1937, 2037, vol. 2, pp. 351, 375–6, 392.
16 Méneval, pp. 437–43; Castelot, pp. 164, 166.
17 Schiel, pp. 315–16; Bourgoing, pp. 476–7.
18 Napoleon to Marie Louise, 11 March 1815: Bourgoing, p. 467.
19 Oman, p. 419.
20 As reported to Hager, 4 April 1815: Weil, no. 2202, vol. 2, p. 465.
21 P. Guedalla, *The Hundred Days*, p. 84 (from Carnot memoirs).
22 Bourgoing, p. 480; A. G. Haas, *Metternich, Reorganization and Nationality*, pp. 58–61.
23 Text of Article 99: M. Hurst (ed.), *Key Treaties of the Great Powers*, vol. 1, p. 85.

24 A. de la Garde Chambonas, *Anecdotal Recollections ... Vienna*, p. 241.
25 As reported (belatedly) to Hager, 2 July 1815: Weil, no. 2635, vol. 2, p. 676.
26 Thompson, *Napoleon Bonaparte*, p. 383; Castelot, p. 168.
27 Marie Louise to Francis, 7 July 1815: Shiel (from HHSA), p. 320.
28 Bourgoing, p. 500.
29 Bourgoing, p. 505.
30 Garros, p. 481, based on H. Horjane, *Napoléon à bord du Northumberland.*

Chapter 15: Parma and St Helena, (pp. 203–14)

1 Castelot, pp. 174–5; Bourgoing, p. 519.
2 Italian affairs and visits: Palmer, *Metternich*, pp. 156–8.
3 Marie Louise to Louise de Montebello, December 1815: E. Gachot, *Marie-Louise intime*, vol. 2, p. 222.
4 ibid.
5 Castelot, pp. 175–6.
6 Departure for Parma: Schiel, pp. 326–8; Castelot, p. 185.
7 A. Solmi, *Maria Luigia, Duchessa di Parma*, pp. 198–204.
8 Marie Louise to Victoria de Crenneville, 9 April 1816: *MLCorr*. p. 182.
9 Marie Louise to Louise de Montebello, 11 May 1816: Solmi, pp. 209–10.
10 Castelot, p. 190.
11 Fraser, p. 288.
12 Marie Louise to Louise de Montebello, 11 May 1816: Solmi, pp. 209–10.
13 Castelot, p. 198.
14 Castelot, p. 195.
15 Solmi, pp. 229–30.
16 Leopoldina to Marie Louise, 4 April 1817: Castelot, p. 205.
17 J. de Bourgoing, *Le Fils de Napoléon*, pp. 117–18.
18 Castelot, p. 209.
19 L. Farinelli, *Maria Luigia*, pp. 31, 33; theatre, pp. 120–1, 303–6; library, p. 146; Taro bridge, p. 162.
20 Farinelli, pp. 29, 76–7.
21 Marie Louise to Victoria de Crenneville, 20 April 1820: *MLCorr*. p. 215.
22 Garros, p. 496. For a recent assessment of the material for Napoleon's last days: McLynn, pp. 654–62; but see also G. Martineau, *Napoleon's St Helena*.
23 Duff Cooper, p. 308; Longford, *Wellington, Pillar of State*, p. 77. Both authors mention that Wellington was present at this reception.
24 Marie Louise to Victoria de Crenneville, 19 July 1821: *MLCorr*. p. 226.
25 Martineau, *Marie-Louise*, p. 262.
26 Thompson, *Napoleon Bonaparte*, pp. 402–3; Castelot, pp. 222–3.
27 Solmi, pp. 255–6; Castelot, p. 229; (fear of creating a pilgrim shrine); Bourgoing, p. 513.
28 Marie Louise to Reichstadt, 24 July 1821: Castelot, p. 227.
29 Castelot, pp. 227–9.

Chapter 16: 'Viva Maria Luigi', (pp. 215–28)

1 Solmi, p. 254; Farinelli, p. 35.
2 Neipperg to Marquis de la Maisonfort, 12 January 1827: Christie's Catalogue of May 1985, Lot 359, p. 147.
3 The catalogue cited above included more than fifty books from the library: Lot 172, p. 82, with colour illustration, p. 83.

4 Farinelli, pp. 164–7, reproduces three water-colours from the Museo Lombardi. Musical dispute: diary entry cited in Bourgoing, p. 531.
5 Solmi, p. 266.
6 Schroeder, *Metternich's Diplomacy at its Zenith*, pp. 211–36.
7 Longford, *Wellington: Pillar of State*, p. 103; P. Guedalla, *The Duke*, pp. 331–2 (though Guedalla wrongly suggests that the meeting with Reichstadt was at Verona).
8 Marie Louise to Victoria de Crenneville, 2 December 1822: *MLCorr.* pp. 234–5.
9 Castelot, pp. 237–8.
10 Lamartine, cited by P. Turnbull, *Napoleon's Second Empress*, p. 278.
11 The Fertbauer painting is reproduced, from the Historisches Museum der Stadt Wien canvas, in R. Waissenberger (ed.), *Vienna in the Biedermeier Era*, p. 181.
12 Bourgoing, *Le Fils de Napoléon*, pp. 343–5.
13 Castelot, p. 254.
14 This may be inferred from letters written in the following spring (1829) and cited below.
15 Castelot, pp. 258–9.
16 Castelot, p. 259.
17 Castelot, p. 260.
18 Marie Louise to Victoria de Crenneville, 22 April and 11 July 1829: *MLCorr.* pp. 255–7; Farinelli, pp. 120–1.
19 Switzerland: Solmi, pp. 307–10.
20 Castelot, p. 308.
21 'Loveliest infant': Marie Louise to Victoria de Crenneville: *MLCorr.* p. 271; Reichstadt and Francis Joseph: M. Stürmfeder, *Die Kindheit unseres Kaisers*, pp. 15, 16, 48.
22 Metternich to Francis, 4–5 August 1830: Metternich, *Mémoires*, vol. 5, p. 15.
23 Palmer, *Metternich*, pp. 247–8.
24 Two letters from Marie Louise to Victoria de Crenneville, *MLCorr.* waltzing, 27 November 1830, p. 275; criticising opera and ballet, 22 December 1830, p. 298.
25 Marie Louise to Victoria de Crenneville, 3 February 1831: *MLCorr.* p. 282.
26 Bourgoing, pp. 552–3; Solmi, pp. 321–33.
27 Marie Louise to Francis, 28 February 1831: Schiel (from HHSA), pp. 361–2.
28 Farinelli, p. 116.
29 Marie Louise to Victoria de Crenneville, 24 August 1831: *MLCorr.* pp. 287–9.
30 Bourgoing, pp. 569–71. Marschall's mounting criticism of Marie Louise's public policy runs through his reports to Metternich for 1831, published in P. Pedroti, *La Mission del Barone Marschall nei ducati ...*, pp. 22–167.
31 Castelot, pp. 283–6.
32 J. Bourgoing, *Le Fils de Napoléon*, gives details of what was discussed at their meetings. See also Castelot, pp. 293–6.
33 Solmi, pp. 349–50.
34 Castelot, p. 335.
35 Castelot, p. 343; Solmi for Marie Louise's letters to Albertina (especially pp. 353–4).
36 Archduchess Sophie's sorrow: A. Palmer, *The Twilight of the Habsburgs*, p. 11.
37 Bourgoing, *Le Fils de Napoléon*, pp. 360–71.
38 Castelot, pp. 361–439.
39 The letter is printed in Martineau, *Marie-Louise*, p. 284.

Chapter 17: The Good Duchess, (pp229–34)

1 Marie Louise to Albertina, 25 July 1835: Solmi, p. 365.
2 Marie Louise to Francis, 23 September 1833: Solmi, p. 371; Marie Louise to Victoria de Crenneville, 25 December 1833: *MLCorr.* pp. 308–10.
3 Farinelli, pp. 176–7.
4 Marie Louise to Victoria de Crenneville, 5 April 1835: *MLCorr.* pp. 317–9. She had already written one letter of sorrow to Victoria on 31 March.
5 Cholera epidemic: A. Pescatori, *Il Declino di Una Ducato, 1831–1859*, pp. 43–6 (a diary); Solmi, pp. 384–6. On music: S. Sadie (ed.), *New Grove Dictionary of Music and Musicians*: Paganini at Parma, vol. 14, pp. 88–9; musical life in general, vol. 14, pp. 236–7; Verdi at Buseto, vol. 19, p. 637.
6 Marie Louise to Albertina, 23 July 1838: Solmi, p. 395.
7 Oman, p. 469.
8 Garros, p. 501; Martineau, *Napoleon's Last Journey*, pp. 135–48.
9 Pescatori, p. 53; Farinelli, pp. 186–7.
10 Palmer, *Metternich*, p. 299; Srbik, vol. 2, pp. 129–30. In Parma: Pescatori, pp. 87–8.
11 Solmi, pp. 404–5; Bourgoing, pp. 602–4.
12 Pescatori, p. 89. For the Beccherie, Farinelli, pp. 176–7.
13 Schiel, p. 188; Bourgoing, p. 605.

Epilogue: 12 December 1940, (pp. 235–8)

1 T. Aronson, *The Golden Bees*, pp. 391–2; R. Aron, *The Vichy Regime*, pp. 237–8.
2 A. Hitler, *Mein Kampf*, pp. 17–18.
3 G. Warner, *Pierre Laval and the Eclipse of France*, p. 254.
4 Pétain's message: Castelot, p. 365.
5 Eye-witness: Castelot, p. 366; General Laure's detailed account in H. Cotou-Bégarie and C. Huan, *Darlan*, pp. 350–1. Laure mentions a second Requiem at midday at which the Military Governor of Paris, General Otto von Stülpnagel, was also present.
6 A. Werth, *France, 1940–1955*, p. 12.
7 Schiel, p. 390.

Select Bibliography

Books

Abrantès, Laure, Duchesse d', *Mémoires de Madame la Duchesse d'Abrantès, ou Souvenirs Historiques* (Paris, 1835).

Andolenko, S., *Histoire de l'Armée Russe* (Paris, 1967).

Arneth, A. von (ed.), *Joseph II und Leopold von Toscana ... Briefwechsel* (Vienna, 1872).

R. Aron, *The Vichy Regime* (London, 1958).

Aronson, Theo, *The Golden Bees* (London, 1964).

Barnett, Corelli, *Bonaparte* (London, 1978).

Bausset, L-F-J, Baron de, *Mémoires anecdotiques ... de l'Empire* 4 vols. (Paris, 1827).

Beer, A., *Zehn Jahre Österreichischer Politik* (Leipzig, 1877).

Bergeron, Louis, *France under Napoleon* (Princeton, NJ, 1981).

Bernard, J., *Talleyrand* (London, 1968).

Bidou, H., *Paris* (London, 1939).

Botzenhart, Manfred, *Metternichs Pariser Botschafterzeit* (Münster, 1967).

Bourgoing, Jean de, *Le Fils de Napoléon* (Paris, 1950).

—— *Marie Louise von Österreich, Kaiserin der Franzisen – Herzegovin von Parma* (Vienna, 1953). Also published in French.

Bourrienne, L., *Mémoires de Napoléon Bonaparte* (Paris, n.d.).

Brett-James, Antony (ed.), *Europe against Napoleon: the Leipzig Campaign 1813* (London, 1970).

Bruce, Evangeline, *Napoleon and Josephine: an Improbable Marriage* (London, 1991).

Bryant, Sir Arthur, *The Years of Endurance* (London, 1942).

Carrington, Dorothy, *Napoleon's Parents* (London, 1988).

Castellane, Boniface de, *Journal du Maréchal de Castellane*, 2 vols. (Paris, 1895).

Castelot, André, *Napoleon's Son* (London, 1960).

Caulaincourt, Armand de, *Mémoires*, 3 vols. (Paris, 1935).

Chambonas, A. de la Garde, *Anecdotal Recollections of the Congress of Vienna* (London, 1902).

Chandler, D. G., *The Campaigns of Napoleon* (London, 1967).

—— (ed.) *Napoleon's Marshals* (London, 1987).

Christie's catalogue, *Napoleon, Nelson and their time: The Calvin Bullock Collection* (London, 1985).

Chuquet, A., *La Jeunesse de Napoléon*, 3 vols. (Paris, 1897–9).

Consalvi, Cardinal, *Mémoires*, 2 vols. (Paris, 1864).
Cooper, A. Duff, *Talleyrand* (London, 1932).
Corti, E. C., *Metternich und die Frauen*, 2 vols. (Vienna and Zurich, 1949).
Coutou-Bégarie, H. and Huan C., *Darlan* (Paris, 1989).
Crankshaw, Edward, *The Fall of the House of Habsburg* (London, 1963).
Criste, O., *Erzherzog Carl von Österreich*, 3 vols. (Vienna, 1912).
Cronin, Vincent, *Napoleon* (London, 1971).
Duffy, Christopher, *Borodino, Napoleon Against Russia* (London, 1972).
—— *Austerlitz, 1805* (London, 1977).
Esposito, V. and Elting, J., *Military History and Atlas of the Napolenoic Wars* (London, 1964).
Fain, P., *Manuscrit de mil huit cent douze* (Paris, 1827).
—— *Manuscrit de mil huit cent treize* (Paris, 1827).
Farinelli, Leonardo, *Maria Luigia, duchessa di Parma* (Parma, 1983).
Fenzensac, M. le Duc de, *Souvenirs militaires de 1804 à 1814* (Paris, 1863).
Fournier, A., *Der Congress von Chatillon* (Vienna and Leipzig, 1900).
Fraser, Flora, *Beloved Emma* (London, 1986).
—— *The Unruly Queen* (London, 1996).
Gachot, E., *Marie-Louise intime*, 2 vols. (Paris, 1911).
Garros, L., *Quel Roman que ma Vie: Itinéraire de Napoléon Bonaparte* (Paris, 1947).
Gaubert, H., *Le Sacre de Napoléon I* (Paris, 1964).
Gourgaud, G., *St Helena; Journal Intime*, 2 vols. (Paris, 1899).
Gregoire, L. de, *Le 'Divorce' de Napoléon et de l'Impératrice Joséphine* (Paris, 1957).
Grunwald, C. de, *Vie de Metternich* (Paris, 1938).
—— *Alexandre I* (Paris, 1955)
Guedalla, Philip, *The Duke* (London, 1931).
—— *The Hundred Days* (London, 1934).
Haas, Arthur G., *Metternich, Reorganization and Nationality, 1813–1818* (Wiesbaden, 1963).
Hales, E. E. Y., *Revolution and the Papacy, 1769–1846* (London, 1960).
—— *Napoleon and the Pope* (London, 1962).
Harewood, Earl of (ed.), *Kobbé's Complete Opera Book* (London, 1954 edition).
Heer, F., *The Holy Roman Empire* (London, 1968).
Helfert, A. von, *Maria Louise* (Vienna, 1873).
Horne, Alistair, *How Far From Austerlitz? Napoleon 1805–1815* (London, 1996).
Hurst, M. (ed.), *Key Treaties for the Great Powers, 1814–1914*, vol. 1 (Newton Abbot, 1972).
Kraehe, Enno E., *Metternich's German Policy, The Contest with Napoleon 1799–1814* (Princeton, 1963).
Langsam, W. C., *Francis the Good: the Education of an Emperor* (New York, 1949).
Las Cases M. J. D. de, *Mémorial de St Hélène* (Paris, 1823).
Lavalette, A. D. Chamas de, *Mémoires et Souvenirs*, 2 vols. (London, 1831).
Lecestre, L., *Lettres inédites de Napoléon I* (London, 1831).
Lefebvre, Georges, *The French Revolution* 2 vols. (London, 1964).
—— *Napoleon*, 2 vols. (London, 1969).

Lehmann, J. and Bassett, R. (eds), *Vienna, a Traveller's Companion* (London, 1988).
Longford, Elizabeth, *Wellington: The Years of the Sword* (London, 1969).
—— *Wellington: Pillar of State* (London, 1972).
Macartney, C. A., *The Habsburg Empire, 1790–1918* (London, 1968).
Mahan, A., *Marie-Louise* (Paris, 1938).
Mallet du Pan, J., *Mémoires et Correspondance* 2 vols. (Paris, 1851).
Mann, Golo, *Secretary of Europe* (Newhaven, rev. ed. 1957).
Marie Louise, *Correspondance, 1799–1847* (Vienna, 1887).
Markham, F., *Napoleon* (London, 1968).
Martineau, Gilbert, *Napoleon's St Helena* (London, 1968).
—— *Napoleon's Last Journey* (London, 1976).
—— *Marie-Louise, Impératrice des Français* (Paris, 1985).
Masson, F. C., *L'Impératrice Marie-Louise* (Paris, 1902).
—— *Napoléon Inconnu* (Paris, 1895).
—— *Napoleon and his Coronation* (London, 1911).
—— (ed.) *Private Diaries of the Empress Marie Louise* (London, 1922).
Mathy, Helmut, *Franz Georg von Metternich* (Meisenheim, 1969).
Mayr, J. K. (ed.) *Abhandlungen zur Geschichte und Quellenkunde der Stadt Wien* (Vienna, 1940).
Mazade, C. de (ed.), *Mémoires du prince Adam Czartoryski*, 2 vols. (Paris, 1887).
McClynn, Frank, *Napoleon* (London, 1997).
McKay, J. (ed.), *Essays in the History of Modern Europe* (New York and London, 1950).
Méneval, C. F. de, *Mémoires pour servis à l'Histoire de Napoléon I* (Paris, 1894).
—— (Méneval II) *Marie Louise et la cour d'Autriche* (Paris, 1909).
Metternich, Richard (ed.), *Mémoires, Documents et Ècrits laissés par le Prince de Metternich* 8 vols. (Paris, 1880–4).
Montesquiou, A. de, *Souvenirs sur la Révolution, l'Empire, la Restauration et le règne de Louis-Philippe* (Paris, 1961).
Napoleon I, Emperor, *Correspondance de Napoléon I*, 28 vols. (Paris, 1863–8).
—— *The Letters of Napoleon to Marie Louise* (London, 1935).
Napoleon, Prince, *The Memoirs of Queen Hortense* (London, 1928).
Narichkine, Natalie, *1812, Le Comte Rostopchine et son Temps* (St Petersburg, 1912).
Nesselrode, A., *Lettres et Papiers du Chancelier Comte de Nesselrode* (Paris, 1904–7).
Nicholas, Mikhailovich, Grand Duke, *Correspondance de l'Empereur Alexandre 1 er avec sa Soeur la Grande Duchesse Catherine* (St Petersburg, 1910).
Nicolson, Harold, *The Congress of Vienna* (London, 1945).
Olivier, Daria, *L'Incendie de Moscou* (Paris, 1964).
Oman, Carola, *Napoleon's Viceroy* (London, 1966).
Paget, A. and Green, J. R., *The Paget Papers* (London, 1896).
Palmer, Alan, *Napoleon in Russia* (London, 1967).
—— *Metternich* (London, 1972).
—— *Alexander I* (London, 1974).
—— *Bernadotte* (London, 1990).
—— *Twilight of the Habsburgs* (London, 1994).
Palmstierna, C. F. (ed.), *Marie-Louise et Napoléon 1813–1814, Lettres inédites* (Paris, 1965).

Pasqeuier, E-D de, *Mémoires*, 2 vols. (Paris, 1894).
Pedroti, P., *La Mission del Barone Marschall nei ducati di Modena e di Parma* (Modena, 1933).
Pescatori, A., *Il Declino di Una Ducato, 1831–59* (Parma, 1976).
Philips, C. S., *The Church in France, 1789–1848* (London, 1929).
Phipps, R. W., *The Armies of the First French Republic and the Rise of the Marshals of Napoleon*, 5 vols. (Oxford, 1926–39).
Rapp, J., *Mémoires du Général Rapp* (Paris, 1823).
Robbins Landon, H. C., *1791, Mozart's Last Year* (London, 1988).
—— *Haydn, Chronicle and Works, The Year of the Creation* (London, 1990).
Roider, K. A. Jnr., *Baron Thugut and Austria's Response to the French Revolution* (Princeton, NJ, 1987).
Ronciere, C. de la (ed) *Letters of Napoleon to Marie Louise* (London n.d.).
Rossler, H., *Oesterreichs Kampl und Deutschlands Befreiung* (Hamburg, 1940).
Rothenberg, G. E., *Napoleon's Great Adversaries: the Archduke Charles and the Austrian Army, 1792–1814* (Bloomington, Ind., 1982).
Sadie, S. (ed.), *New Grove Dictionary of Music and Musicians*, vols. 14, 19 (London, 1980).
Savary, General, *Mémoires du duc de Rovigo*, 8 vols. (Paris, 1828).
Schiel, Irmgard, *Marie Louise* (Stuttgart, 1983).
Schroeder, P. W., *Metternich's Diplomacy at its Zenith, 1820–23* (Austin, Texas, 1962).
—— *The Transformation of European Politics, 1763–1848* (Oxford, 1994).
Scott, S. F., *The Response of the Royal Army to the French Revolution* (Oxford, 1978).
Ségur, Philip de, *History of the Expedition to Russia* (London, 1825).
Shilder, N. K., *Imperator Aleksandr I* (St Petersburg, 1897).
Sipe, T., *Beethoven's Eroica Symphony* (Cambridge, 1998).
Solmi, Angelo, *Maria Luigia, Duchessa di Parma* (Milan, 1985).
Sorel, A., *L'Europe et la Révolution Française*, 8 vols. (Paris, 1904).
Soult, Marshal, *Mémoires du Maréchal-General Soult*, 3 vols. (Paris, 1854–55).
Srbik, Heinrich von, *Metternich, der Staatsmann und der Mensch*, 3 vols. (Munich, 1925–54).
Stürmfeder, M., *Die Kindheit unseres Kaisers* (Vienna, 1910).
Sutherland, Christine, *Marie Walewska, Napoleon's Great Love* (London, 1979).
Tarlé, E., *Nashestvie Napoleona na Rossiya – 1812 god* (Moscow, 1938).
Thiard, A. M. T. de, *Souvenirs diplomatiques et militaires de 1804 à 1806* (Paris 1901).
Thompson, J. M., *Lectures on Foreign History* (Oxford, 1925).
—— *Napoleon's Letters* (London, 1934).
—— *The French Revolution* (Oxford, 1943).
—— *Napoleon Bonaparte, His Rise and Fall* (Oxford, 1951).
Tulard, J., *Napoléon, 12 Octobre 1809* (Paris, 1994).
Tulard, J., Fayard J-F and Fierro, *A Histoire et dictionnaire de la Révolution française, 1789–1799* (Paris, 1987).
Turnbull, P., *Napoleon's Second Empress* (London, 1971).
Ullrichova, Maria, *Clemens Metternich, Wilhelmine von Sagan – Ein Briefwechsel* (Graz and Cologne, 1956).

Vandal, Albert, *Napoléon et Alexandre I*, 3 vols. (Paris, 1897).
Villefosse, L. de and Bouissounouse, J., *L'Opposition à Napoléon* (Paris, 1969).
Waissenberger, R. (ed.), *Vienna in the Biedermeier Era* (London, 1986).
Wangermann, E., *From Joseph II to the Jacobin Trials* (Oxford, 1959).
Warner, G., *Pierre Laval and the Eclipse of France* (London, 1956).
Webster, C. K., *The Foreign Policy of Castlereagh*, 2 vols. (London, 1925–31).
Weil, M. H., *Les Dessous de Congrès de Vienne*, 2 vols. (Paris, 1917).
Werth, Alexander, *France, 1940–1955* (London, 1956).
Wheatcroft, Andrew, *The Habsburgs* (London, 1995).
Wright, Constance, *Louise, Queen of Prussia* (London, 1970).

Articles in Periodicals

Casse, Baron de: 'La reine Catherine de Westphalie au Congrès du Dresde', *Revue Historique*, (Paris), vol. 36 (1888), pp. 328–35.

Grunwald, C. de: 'Les débuts de Metternich', *Revue de Paris*, August 1936, pp. 492–537.

—— 'Le Marriage de Napoleon et de Marie-Louise, Documents inédits', *Revue des Deux Mondes*, (Paris), vol. 38 (1937), pp. 320–52.

Hanoteau J. (ed.): 'Une nouvelle relation de l'Entrevue de Napoléon et de Metternich à Dresde', *Revue d'Histoire Diplomatique*, (Paris), vol. 47 (1933), pp. 421–40.

Hanoteau, J. and Bourgoing, J. de (eds.): 'Les papiers intimes de Marie Louise', *Revue des deux mondes*, (Paris), vol. 39 (1938), pp. 773–85.

Langsam, W. C.: 'An Imperial Understatement', *American Historical Review*, (Washington, D.C.), vol. 44 (1939), pp. 851–3.

Index

References to Napoleon and Marie Louise are represented by the letters N and ML respectively.